Maritime Men of the Asia-Pacific

True-Blue Internationals
Navigating Labour Rights, 1906–2006

STUDIES IN LABOUR HISTORY 18

Studies in Labour History

'...a series which will undoubtedly become an important force in re-invigorating the study of Labour History.' *English Historical Review*

The Studies in Labour History book series offers the reader the most recent and high quality research in the field. Labour history is defined in the widest sense to embrace not only labour and related social movements, but also workers in general and their relations with other groups in society. As such the series covers aspects of race, gender, ethnicity and culture as well as the more familiar topics of class, trade unionism and politics. While the key geographical focus rests upon the UK, the series is keen to publish research in the fields of transnational, global and comparative labour history. The current editor welcomes submissions from academics and others working in the area, including new researchers who are keen to publish their first monographs.

Maritime Men of the Asia-Pacific

True-Blue Internationals Navigating Labour Rights, 1906–2006

Diane Kirkby
with
Lee-Ann Monk and Dmytro Ostapenko

LIVERPOOL UNIVERSITY PRESS

First published 2022 by
Liverpool University Press
4 Cambridge Street
Liverpool
L69 7ZU

British Library Cataloguing-in-Publication data
A British Library CIP record is available

ISBN 978-1-80207-719-3 cased
ISBN 978-1-80207-751-3 limp

Typeset by Carnegie Book Production, Lancaster
Printed and bound by CPI Group (UK) Ltd, Croydon CR0 4YY

Contents

Figures

Acknowledgements

This project has been a collective effort. It grew out of an earlier history of Australian seafarers undertaken by Diane Kirkby, which prompted a conversation with Paddy Crumlin of the Maritime Union of Australia (MUA) for a further study. The result was a funding application to the Australian Research Council (ARC) for a Linkage Project between La Trobe University and the MUA. The grant (ARC LP140100546). was critical in enabling La Trobe to employ two postdoctoral researchers, Dr Lee-Ann Monk and Dr Dmytro Ostapenko, funding travel to vital international and interstate archives, and providing translation services for research in non-English-language materials.

We are indebted to Paddy Crumlin, the MUA, the International Transport Workers' Federation) and their several affiliates for their generous assistance. The MUA's Dr Penny Howard helped shape the project in its early days, facilitating our access to people, resources and attendance at meetings and conferences. These contacts sparked enquiries and offered insights. Willie Adams from the International Longshore and Warehouse Union (ILWU) sowed the idea of knowing more about Harry Bridges; the National Union of Seafarers of India's (NUSI) Abdulgani Serang shared his files of India at the International Labour Organization (ILO) and helped with material on NUSI activism. The daughters of Leo Barnes shared valuable and otherwise unavailable resources. Mac Urata in the ITF Tokyo office willingly answered our questions.

We have been fortunate in having the Noel Butlin Archives at the Australian National University as the repository of MUA records. The team of archivists there were an enormous help under trying circumstances. The ILWU archives in San Francisco have been a treasure trove and we thank archivist Robin Walker for her willing help and professionalism. We also received valuable assistance from the Modern Records Centre, University of Warwick, where the ITF records are held, the Institute for Social History archives in Amsterdam and the ILO archives in Geneva. The ILO Director, Guy Ryder, and former Deputy Director, Kari Tapiola, were welcoming and ensured assistance was available.

We owe thanks to the staff of various state and several university libraries and the National Library of Australia, all of whom have had a difficult time during the pandemic lockdowns. In addition we have received valuable help from Makiko Nishitani and Adam Zulawnik in translating Japanese-language books and materials; Nadia Rhook who helped with research in interstate archives; Sophie Couchman shared her expertise on Chinese material; and Kate Laing who was resourceful in finding obscure material. Caroline Jordan was a constant source of humour, generosity and invaluable editorial skills. The University of Technology Sydney provided a stimulating collegial research environment and wonderful colleagues of legal historians.

Lee-Ann Monk and Dmytro Ostapenko, whose excellence at research is unmatched, also proffered ideas and urged directions that shaped the final outcome. I am deeply indebted to them and their expertise. We have co-authored articles and they have written sections of this book. Ultimately, however, the concept of the project and the interpretation of the material (and any mistakes) are mine. The authorship is attributed to reflect the shared contribution and distribution of responsibilities among this team. We thank commissioning editor Alison Welsby for her great patience and advice; Leon Fink for insightful feedback on the manuscript; Ann Curthoys, Stuart Macintyre, Sean Scalmer and other colleagues in the Australian Society for the Study of Labour History who were always encouraging about the importance of this research. Special thanks go to Shaunnagh Dorsett and Amanda Nettelback for their inspiration and friendship; to Alec, Michael and Zoe for their loving forbearance, and to Ian and Yana for their strong support of Lee-Ann and Dmytro, over the years we have worked on this project. We hope the final work is informative and enlightening, does justice to those whose story we tell and encourages future engagement with these important questions.

A Note on Sources, Spelling and Terminology

Biographical information on key individuals may be found in the *Australian Dictionary of Biography*. Entries from the ADB have not been cited specifically in the footnotes. Biographical information taken from other sources, especially from overseas, has been cited.

In the decades spanning the turn of the twentieth century a spelling reform movement influenced some progressives to adopt a simplified form, usually dropping the 'u' from words like 'labour'. In 1912 the Australian Labor Party officially took this form of spelling for its title. We have not changed the spelling within our sources when quoting them although we conform to current Australian and English usage consistent with the Style Guide. We recognise that this may be confusing to readers who are therefore seeing variants of spelling, even, on occasion, in the same sentence.

Similarly, the terms used in our original sources are quoted to convey an accuracy of meaning consistent with the historical period we are writing about and the categories of labour that were then in place. Confronting as some of that language may now be, the usage of some terms and the struggle to replace them is the substance of the story we tell. Our purpose has been to convey something of the complexity of that endeavour and to illuminate the processes of interaction between groups and communities, organisations and sometimes individuals. At all times we have endeavoured to remember it is people who make this history and to write about them with respect and compassion for their lived experience.

Abbreviations

ACTU – Australian Council of Trade Unions
AISF – All-India Seamen's Federation
AIME – Australian Institute of Marine Engineers
ALP – Australian Labor Party
AMSA – Australian Maritime Safety Authority
ANL – Australian National Line
ASIA – Australian Stevedoring Industry Authority
ASOF – Australasian Steamship Owners' Federation
AWU – Australian Workers' Union
BSU – Bombay Seamen's Union
CCP – Chinese Communist Party
CIO – Congress of Industrial Organizations
CPA – Communist Party of Australia
CPGB – Communist Party Great Britain
CPUSA – Communist Party United States of America
CSU – Chinese Seamen's Union
DCC – Dockworkers Corresponding Committee
FOC – flag of convenience
FPC – Fair Practices Committee [ITF]
FSUA – Federated Seamen's Union of Australasia
ICFTU – International Confederation of Free Trade Unions
IFSDRW – International Federation of the Ship Dock and River Workers
ILO – International Labour Organization
ILWU – International Longshore and Warehouse Union
ISU – International Seamen's Union (USA)
ISU-B – Indian Seamen's Union-Bombay
ISU-C – Indian Seamen's Union-Calcutta
ITF – International Transport Workers Federation
IWW – Industrial Workers of the World

JDU – Japan Dockers['] Union
JMC – Joint Maritime Commission (of ILO)
JSU – Japan Seamen's Union
MLC – Maritime Labour Convention
MRC – Modern Records Centre, University of Warwick
MUA – Maritime Union of Australia
NBAC – Noel Butlin Archives Centre
MRC – Modern Records Centre
NAA – National Archives of Australia
NLA – National Library of Australia
NSUI – National Seamen's Union of India
NSW – New South Wales
NUS – National Union of Seamen (Britain)
NUSI – National Union of Seamen India
NZSU – Seamen's Union of New Zealand
P&O – Peninsula and Oriental
RILU – Red International of Labour Unions
SLNSW – State Library of New South Wales
SLV – State Library of Victoria
SLWA – State Library of Western Australia
SUA – Seamen's Union of Australia
TCC – total crew cost
TWF – Transport Workers' Federation of Australia
TUC – Trade Union Congress [UK]
UN – United Nations
WA – Western Australia
WFTU – World Federation of Trade Unions
WWF – Waterside Workers Federation of Australia

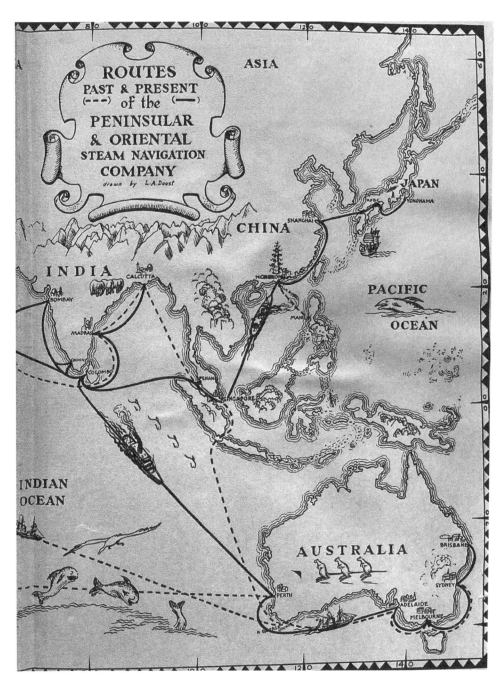

Shipping routes of the P&O Company in the Indo-Pacific, positioning Australia in Asia, from Boyd Cable, *A Hundred Year History of the P&O Peninsular and Oriental Steam Navigation Company 1837–1937* (London: Ivor Nicholson and Watson, 1937)

1

'By the Nature of Their Calling'
Themes of Region, Race and Militancy

Seafarers have a powerful story to tell. During the global pandemic, ships' crews were trapped at sea, unable to come ashore or be returned to their home ports. Their situation exposed inhumane treatment and the problem of enforcing their rights. One hundred years ago, US economists declared the world's seamen to be 'for the most part ... unfree,' that without legal protections they 'had the status of slaves.'[1] This was 'the peculiar status of the sailor,' to be bound by law to his ship, under penalty of imprisonment, in 'economic helplessness' and denied the rights of personal freedom open to shore workers.[2] Seafaring's differences from shore-based work has been a continuing theme of seafarers' history. They historically had been excluded from labour law as it had developed because seafarers were regarded as a special case: most of the regulations had evolved on the ships, as custom, not legislation.[3] More recent international investigations have found similarly: that life at sea for thousands of seafarers is modern slavery and that the serious legal handicaps and problems seafarers face is 'the dark side' of the global shipping industry.[4] The risk of being abandoned in a foreign port without money or means to return to their own country – a fact of life for

---

[1] 'Cargo-Ship Crews Are Stuck at Sea,' *The Economist*, 20 June 2020; Paul Taylor, *The Sailors' Union of the Pacific* (New York: Ronald Press, 1923), iii; Arthur Albrecht, 'International Seamen's Union of America: A Study of its History and Problems,' *Bulletin of the United States Bureau of Labor Statistics* no. 342 (Washington DC, US Bureau of Labor, 1923), 29.

[2] Taylor, *Sailors' Union of the Pacific*, iii.

[3] D. Fitzpatrick and M. Anderson, *Seafarers' Rights* (Oxford: Oxford University Press, 2005), 8–9.

[4] *Ships, Slaves and Competition: Inquiry into Ship Safety* (Charlestown, NSW: International Commission on Shipping, 2000), 3, quoted in Fitzpatrick and Anderson, *Seafarers' Rights*, v, ix; Jon Whitlow, 'Maritime Concerns of the International Transport Workers' Federation,' in *Current Maritime Issues and the International Maritime Organization*, ed. Myron H. Norquist and John Norton Moore (The Hague: Martinus Nijhoff, 1999), 177–89.

modern seafarers – exemplifies the peculiar status of the sailor compared with land-based workers.[5]

In 1917, a young Australian – 16 years old and in his first year of seafaring – found himself in that predicament, suddenly abandoned in the port of Bombay. The world was at war and merchant shipping was particularly targeted for attack, often by other, armed, merchant vessels known as raiders. When a raider appeared at the entrance to Bombay harbour, the ships' masters immediately headed their vessels out to sea, leaving behind crew who had gone ashore.[6] To an extent this was a usual seafarer story. Merchant shipping was always dangerous, even more so during a time of war. Sometimes an unscrupulous master would leave men behind to keep their wages; at other times they were gaoled for complaining about their conditions, and the ship sailed with a replacement crew.[7] Seafarers' rights, including the right to be repatriated home, were not universally guaranteed, and were hard to enforce without assistance from powerful organisations. International instruments, a seafarers' charter or, better still, an international labour convention did not yet exist.

This young seafarer's Bombay episode, however, was not a usual story. The youthful crewman was Alfred Renton (aka Harry) Bridges, the man who would go on to help found and lead the International Longshore and Warehouse Union (developing out of the International Longshoremen's Association) on the US Pacific west coast and become one of the outstanding labour leaders of the twentieth century. His experiences at sea and the injustices he observed fuelled his militancy. Being stranded in an Indian port left a lasting impression that he later recalled as influential in his growing political awareness. By the 1930s, 'this militant young Australian' was 'the most conspicuous maritime labor leader in the U.S. today' and he remained so for more than four decades (Figure 1.1).[8] Those decades saw a transformation in the conditions of seafarers and waterside workers struggling to achieve protections and enforceable rights. Union organisation empowered them and gave them valuable leadership. From the United States, Bridges maintained his connections to Australian unionists (as demonstrated by the photograph on the cover of this book) in a trans-Pacific activism which is reconstructed here, bringing new insights to the internationalism of twentieth-century maritime labour.

[5] Jonathan Hyslop, 'British Steamship Workers, c.1875–1945: Precarious before Precarity,' *Labour History* 116 (2019): 5–28.

[6] Robert Cherny, 'The Making of a Labor Radical: Harry Bridges, 1901–1934,' *Pacific Historical Review* 64, no. 3 (1995): 363–88, quoting his interview with Harry Bridges in 1986.

[7] See, e.g., 'No Help from Frisco: The Stranded American Sailors,' *Australian Star* (Sydney), 8 March 1907, 6.

[8] 'C.I.O. to Sea,' *Time* 30, no. 3 (19 July 1937): 12–14.

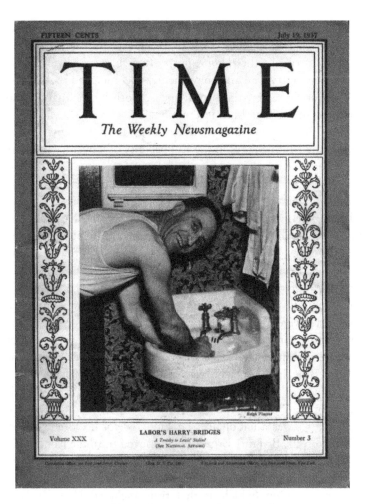

1.1 The 'militant young Australian.'
Harry Bridges,
Time, 19 July 1937

Harry Bridges is not the central subject of this book, but in key ways he distils its essential themes. The first of these is the internationalism which infused the labour movement from the outset and thrived as nationally based trade unions were established. He was 'the sailor ... [who] sees dimly the vision of a higher life,' readily recruited to the international socialist movement.[9] Seafarers were, 'by the nature of the[ir] calling,' prime candidates to become 'true-blue working-class Internationals,' according

[9] Benjamin T. Hall, *Socialism and Sailors*, Fabian Society Tract 46 (London: Fabian Society, 1893), 14.

to a contemporary US journal: their lived experience and workplace was international, 'their shipmates come from all nations. They know no color bar and no country. … [Their] home ports often change.'[10] Bridges' life fitted this description pretty well and conveniently encompassed the key countries of the Asia-Pacific region that is our focus. Both by inclination and lived experience, he was a 'true-blue' internationalist.

'True-blue' is an expression of authenticity, derived from the blue cloth produced in the Middle Ages in the English city of Coventry that remained fast and never faded with washing: 'as true as Coventry blue' has come to mean 'loyal and unwavering in one's opinions or support for a cause.'[11] In Australia it has taken on nationalist connotations. Australians have even adopted a popular song of that title, released in 1982, as an unofficial anthem for the national cricket and rugby teams, to be performed regularly at sporting events. While this might seem very apt given that Harry Bridges was originally an Australian, to be 'true-blue' is not a national identity; it is an aspiration to practice.

In the twentieth century, many seafarers and waterside workers, among other unionists, were or aspired to be internationalists and were unwavering in their support for the ideal. Their leaders who rose to prominence in national governments included Australia's Prime Minister during the First World War, Billy Hughes, who was head of the wharf labourers' union. He won a place for Australia at the 1919 Peace Talks, which established the League of Nations and the International Labour Organization (ILO), although Hughes was a nationalist, remembered for his potent advocacy of Australia's interests. Britain's Ernest Bevin moved from the London docks to parliament, serving in Churchill's 1940s wartime Cabinet and after the war as Minister of Labour. Australia's Robert Storrie Guthrie was the president of the seamen's union (which at that time included New Zealand) and simultaneously a Senator in the Australian parliament. Seamen's unionist Havelock Wilson and dockworker Ben Tillett were British Members of Parliament. The tradition continued later in the century. New Zealand's Waterside Workers' president Eddie Isbey served as a MP, a cabinet minister in the Labour Government and a shadow minister when it was in opposition. Bengali seafarer and founder of the All India Seamen's Union, Aftab Ali, returned to become Minister for Labour in post-independence Pakistan. Greg Combet was an organiser for the wharfies' union before he entered

---

[10] From the *Industrial Unionist*, official organ of the Industrial Union League, New York, republished as 'The Internationality of the Seamen,' in *Australasian Seamen's Journal* 8, no. 18 (1 September 1922): [7–10].

[11] See 'true blue,' q.v. www.phrases.org.uk/index.html. Cites John Ray, *A Compleat Collection of English Proverbs* (London: John Hayes, 1670).

the Australian parliament in 2007 and became a Minister in the Labor government.

Many, like New Zealand's William Belcher and later Toby Hill, Britain's Tom Mann, Australia's Jim Healy and Tom Walsh, moved from Britain to its former colonies and became prominent within the national labour movements there, joining each other in transnational organising for solidarity actions. In the middle and later decades, regional trade union leaders from the Asia-Pacific like India's Leo Barnes, Japan's Tomitaro Kaneda, California's Harry Bridges, and Australia's Jim Healy, Eliot Elliott, Paddy Troy and Tas Bull linked the region more closely with practical international activism. Some, like Leo Barnes, Pat Geraghty and James Tudehope represented maritime unions in the International Labour Organization, or, like Charlie Fitzgibbon, Tas Bull and most recently, Paddy Crumlin, on the International Transport Workers Federation (ITF). Many other lesser-known rank and file maritime unionists too numerous to mention made their way into parliament, facilitated by the existence of labour parties in Britain, Australia and New Zealand.

The collective activism of these men is the story of this book. The argument is centred on the Australian unions whose struggle for legal labour protections began within the framework of the British Empire when British shipping dominated the world's fleet, and they adopted a regional identification with the Asia-Pacific. That grew stronger over time. By the first decade of the twenty-first century, the Asia-Pacific region was a major supplier of the world's shipping fleet, at over 40 per cent of flag-state vessels, and the biggest supplier, at over 60 per cent, of the world's seafarers.[12]

'We in Australia are … part of Asia'

With a focus on Australian unionists' connections with New Zealand, Indian, Chinese and Japanese unions, as well as the Pacific coast of the United States, this book draws a new circle of connectedness between Australia and Asia, and around geopolitical realities, in a story that also decentres Europe. In doing so it brings a regional approach to the work of the ITF, European in origin and London-based for most of the twentieth century, and today a huge organisation of millions of workers worldwide.

Centring the study on Australia enables a much-needed regional (Asia-Indo-Pacific) perspective to be brought to the existing history of international maritime organisations, the ITF, and the ILO's Joint Maritime Commission

[12] ILO, 'Asia-Pacific towards Ratification of the MLC, 2006,' MLC Asia-Pacific Meeting in Cairns, Australia (3–6 May 2011), www.ilo.org/global/standards/maritime-labour-convention/WCMS_155179/lang--en/index.htm.

(JMC).[13] Australia's regional positioning and perspective made Australia's port workers particularly attractive to the European-based ITF whose efforts to recruit member unions from the region were frustrated for many years. When this finally changed, in the 1970s, it also transformed the ITF. How the ITF sought to expand its coverage to non-European parts of the world is told here, showing Australia (and New Zealand) playing a prominent part.[14] The book adds to and sometimes challenges the existing literature as it looks at the ITF from this regional perspective, its first moves towards organising in India and Japan (1930s), the opposition the ITF encountered from British and other European imperial powers and the disruption to progressive initiatives by the coming of war in the Pacific (1941–45). Decolonisation and the dismantling of old empires stimulated union growth after 1945, and the ITF, 'which had a long history of opposition to colonialism,' built on its base in India and Japan to spread its influence in Asia and into new regions – Africa, Latin America and the Pacific.[15] By the end of the century, Australia was playing a leading role in the region.

One of the obstacles to 'true-blue' internationalism was regional divisions, creating differences of experience and outlook among workers that shaped the identity and loyalty of their national organisations and their members. Australia's unique geographical location in both the Indian and Pacific oceans, and its imperial ties to Britain, created a regional and racialised identity that was self-consciously present for Australians. The proximity to countries of Asia has been a continuous shaping force in its history, a 'presence both within and outside Australia, shaping who Australians are, as well as the country's engagement with the wider world.'[16] As ties strengthened in the second half of the twentieth century, unionists accepted 'more and more we in Australia are becoming part of Asia.'[17] Its regional location also shaped northern hemisphere perceptions of Australia's value and place in international organisations.

Bridges' story helps position this study geographically, in the Indian ocean, where merchant seafarers from Britain and its colonies, as well as

---

[13] Leon Fink, *Sweatshops at Sea: Merchant Seamen in the World's First Globalized Industry* (Chapel Hill: University of North Carolina Press, 2011).

[14] K. Laffer, 'Australian Maritime Unions and the International Transport Workers Federation,' *Journal of Industrial Relations* 19 (1977): 113–32.

[15] ITF, *Solidarity: The First 100 Years of the International Transport Workers' Federation* (London: Pluto Press, 1996), 146.

[16] The scholar who has written most about this is David Walker. See David Walker and Agnieszkia Sobocinska, eds, *Australia's Asia: From Yellow Peril to Asian Century* (Perth: UWA Press, 2012), 20.

[17] 'From Federal Secretary Elliott … En route to Korea for May 1 Celebrations,' *Seamen's Journal* 22, no. 5 (1967): 110.

Europe, encountered each other in a potentially shared experience. The tensions between being both British yet colonial, both (white) Europeans and yet part of ('coloured') Asia, were exposed for Bridges when he was stranded in Bombay and can be seen playing out in the earliest struggles for labour standards by Australian seafarers and their dockside comrades. His standard public education and a middle-class family had emphasised the virtues of belonging to the British Empire. In India, though, he was exposed to other realities, and participated in the raw exercise of imperial power. Having to fend for himself until he could get another ship, he heard there was a demand for white men willing to be employed by the local police force. Consequently, uniformed in white linen to represent Britishness, he accompanied local patrols maintaining order. Bridges thereby saw a level of poverty, a squalor, he had never before encountered and which the uncritical pro-British sentiments of his early education had not led him to expect were a consequence of empire.

Bridges' career had started when his father 'hatched a plot' with an old Norwegian ship's master he knew who sailed small locally built packets on short trips off the Australian coast. He 'made it a speciality of shipping young boys to sea "in sail,"' Harry recalled.[18] Bridges Snr hoped it would cure his son of his dreams of going to sea. Instead, the boy was hooked, and later had rosy memories of good crews and plenty of food. He soon sailed on New Zealand ships and deep-sea routes to England, which went via Asian ports, and then later to the United States.

Being part of Asia was always an element of Australian seafarers' experience. As crew crossing the Indian Ocean, Australian seafarers observed the crowded, unsafe accommodation and harshness of discipline for indentured labourers sailing from Calcutta and Bombay. They also saw the cruelty of apartheid for 'coloured' and Indigenous African labour when they called in to the port of Durban. Facing and sailing the Pacific Ocean they observed Chinese crews working for 'coolie' wages. Their reactions to these experiences influenced their determination to fight for labour standards that were superior to those offered in Britain and which differentiated Australia from Britain's other Asian colonies. The presence of many African Americans who sailed into Australian ports did not feature when Australian unionists were protesting against 'coloured labour.' Their concern with 'colour' was equated with Asian labour, paid by 'coolie' standards under colonial systems of labour supply.

As an Australian in India, in 1917, Bridges confronted this relationship between race and labour. How Australian and other European trade unionists

---

[18] 'Harry Bridges' Return,' *Seamen's Journal* 22, no. 9 (1967): 222; 'The Life of Harry Bridges,' *Maritime Worker* (1 June 1938): 2–5.

engaged with Asia's, especially India's, colonised labour is a major theme of this book. What was also seared into Bridges' memory by the time he was interviewed in the 1980s was the act of taking upon himself the symbol of Britishness and the exercise of the power of white privilege. Bridges has been recognised for being committed to racial equality of African Americans within the ILWU.[19] His marriage in 1958 to Noriko (Nikki) Sawada took place in Nevada, which challenged and subsequently overturned Nevada's long-standing miscegenation laws. His active collaboration with the Japan Dockworkers' Union is an important story.

In the early years, when ships first began arriving in Australian colonial ports carrying Chinese indentured labourers to work as shepherds in place of convicts, the labour press condemned 'the pastoralist squattocracy' for turning to 'slave' labour.[20] As free, waged workers organised into trade unions, this opposition to coerced labour spread and became more vocal. The embryonic union movement from the 1830s sought to halt convict transportation, and then to defeat measures facilitating the importation of indentured labour. As the colonies moved to self-government and later federation, indentured and unfree labour was 'seen as degrading and inimical to the goal of a self-governing society based on citizenship and the dignity of labour.'[21] Australia's distance from European, and yet proximity to Asian, sources of labour supply were economic grounds for fearing lowered standards that increasingly fused with arguments against racialised categories. Hostility spiked when the economy was in a downturn. Opposition was always highest amongst unionists most likely to face competition and needing to combat capital's power to drive down local labour costs by recruiting in the cheapest overseas market. Among these were seagoing, and to a lesser extent wharf, labourers. Struggling against capitalism's imperative was to be a continuing thread in maritime labour history.

Small associations of seafarers began forming in 1864 but the first formal seamen's organisation in the Australian colonies followed within a year of Britain passing the Trade Union Act of 1871, removing the 'restraint on trade' doctrine that prevented workers combining. The seamen's union

[19] Bruce Nelson, 'The "Lords of the Docks" Reconsidered: Race Relations among West Coast Longshoremen, 1933–1961,' in *Waterfront Workers: New Perspectives on Race and Class*, ed. Calvin Winslow (Urbana: University of Illinois Press, 1998), 155–92.

[20] Maxine Darnell, 'Responses and Reactions to the Importation of Indentured Chinese Labourers,' University of New England, School of Economic Studies, Working Paper Series in Economic History no. 99-2 (November 1999), www.une.edu.au/__data/assets/pdf_file/0011/13340/ehwp99-2.pdf.

[21] Michael Quinlan and Constance Lever-Tracy, 'From Labour Market Exclusion to Industrial Solidarity: Australian Trade Union Responses to Asian Workers, 1830–1988,' *Cambridge Journal of Economics* 14, no. 2 (1990): 159–81.

quickly became an intercolonial body, and by 1880 had expanded to include New Zealand's union, which was founded in 1879, as the Federated Seamen's Union of Australasia.[22] The majority of Australian and New Zealand seafarers worked on locally owned, interstate or inter-island vessels.[23] They worked within a single labour market, the same shipping company hiring crew in either country and replicating the wages and conditions in each. While they functioned autonomously, and eventually separated, the Australian and New Zealand bodies cited each other's experience to bargain improvement in their own conditions.[24] The organisation of wharf labourers began in 1885, and soon all ports in Australia were quickly unionised.[25] With nationhood, these colony-based organisations later became federated, as the Seamen's Union of Australia (SUA) and the Waterside Workers' Federation (WWF). These two unions historically covered a majority of the maritime industry workforce, absorbing other maritime industry organisations until their eventual amalgamation into the Maritime Union of Australia in 1993. New Zealand followed a similar trajectory, with the wharf labourers and seafarers amalgamating in 2003.

This book brings their history of activism together in a single story in the century before those amalgamations. It necessarily locates the origins of that activism in the closing decades of the nineteenth century as steamships began to replace sail, and laws began to alter labour's bargaining power. The Australasian colonies' location in the Asia-Pacific waters was a critical dynamic in how that story unfolded.

When in 1878 the first steps were taken by Australian shipowners to replace local seafarers on the Australian coast with imported Chinese seamen, there was both union and wider public opposition. At that time actions focused on the Chinese themselves, initiating immigration laws in several colonies that in the following decade laid the foundations of national immigration restriction. Alternative actions were not considered or were

[22] Brian Fitzpatrick and Rowan Cahill, *A History of the Seamen's Union of Australia* (Sydney: Seamen's Union of Australia, 1981), 3–9; Conrad Bollinger, *Against the Wind: The Story of the New Zealand Seamen's Union* (Wellington: New Zealand Seamen's Union, 1968); David Grant, *Jagged Seas: The New Zealand Seamen's Union, 1879–2003* (Christchurch: Canterbury University Press, 2012), 9–18, 58–9.

[23] Fitzpatrick and Cahill, *History of the Seamen's Union of Australia*, 34, give a figure of 98 per cent of the SUA membership in 1909 working on coastal ships.

[24] Grant, *Jagged Seas*, 58.

[25] Margo Beasley, *Wharfies: A History of the Waterside Workers Federation of Australia* (Rushcutters Bay, NSW: Halstead Press, 1996); Phyllis N. Pettit, *The Wellington Watersiders: The Story of Their Industrial Organisation* (Wellington: New Zealand Waterside Workers' Union, 1948), 12–13; see also Anna Green, *British Capital, Antipodean Labour: Working the New Zealand Waterfront, 1915–1951* (Dunedin: University of Otago Press, 2001).

'howled down.'[26] In the 25 years following that strike, maritime unionists' strategic thinking shifted in the direction of promoting minimum labour standards for Australian workers, to implementing protections of those working and not just the exclusions of others.

Competition from foreign-owned (and subsidised) ocean steamers operating much more cheaply while extending their trade along the Australian coast and adjacent islands caused a major downturn in the industry in the 1880s. Australian-owned shipping companies in the Australasian Steamship Owners' Federation (ASOF) responded by claiming their ships were overmanned and crews were overpaid because their hours of work were too short. They proposed to reduce wages, especially overtime payments. The ASOF invited the unions to a major conference in Sydney Town Hall 'to endeavour by reason and discussion ... to arrive at what was fair and just between the representatives of the steamshipping companies and their employees.'[27] The ASOF emphasised the high costs of Australian labour, the lack of subsidies from colonial governments and the increased traffic of foreign shipping making competition difficult for them. The Seamen's Union, supported by the Wharf Labourers and Lumpers' Union, had threatened to strike, or maybe even to start a new company.[28] At the end of the conference they instead proposed that a Navigation Act should be passed, that the matter of their wages and overtime should be referred to arbitration and that regular conciliation should be instituted. To top it off, they added that a dinner, co-funded by the ASOF and the unions, should be organised.

This first proposal for an Australian Navigation Act coming from the Seamen's Union signalled a turn to legislation and parliament as another strategy to combat employers' organisational power. They also urged establishment of a court of conciliation that would meet monthly and make binding agreements between shipowners and unions.[29] These proposals were enacted by the colonial governments who established industrial tribunals and passed labour laws. Fifteen years after that Sydney shipping conference, immigration restriction, conciliation and arbitration procedures and regulation of the shipping trade were foundational measures of the new Australian Commonwealth. New Zealand had already established both compulsory arbitration and passed a Navigation Act. It is here that our story begins.

---

[26] Ann Curthoys, 'Conflict and Consensus: The Seamen's Strike of 1878,' in *Who Are Our Enemies? Racism and the Australian Working Class*, ed. Ann Curthoys and Andrew Markus (Sydney: Hale & Iremonger, 1978), 48–65.

[27] 'Maritime Conference,' *Sydney Morning Herald*, 22 September 1886, 6–7.

[28] 'The Seamen's Wages Question,' *Sydney Morning Herald*, 7 August 1886, 12.

[29] 'Maritime Conference,' *Sydney Morning Herald*, 30 September 1886, 6.

At the beginning of the twentieth century, the several colonial Australian unions of wharf labourers united to form the WWF, with William Morris (Billy) Hughes as the founding president. The Welsh-born Hughes (1862–1952) had become secretary of the Sydney Wharf Labourers' Union in 1899 and was the driving force behind the formation of the national WWF in 1902. He held the position of president until 1916. Yet Hughes was not principally a unionist. He was first and foremost a politician, a Labor Party organiser and a theorist, whose 'contacts with the industrial movement were incidental to his political career.'[30] Hughes had been a member of the New South Wales (NSW) parliament since 1894, lived in the Sydney waterfront suburb of Balmain, and then represented the Darling Harbour area as his electorate of Western Sydney as Australian Labor Party (ALP) member in the new federal parliament. Although he had never gone to sea or worked on the docks himself, wharf labourers were a significant proportion of his parliamentary constituency. 'He had come to know the wharves and the men who worked on them' and was keen to organise and represent them both industrially and politically.[31] He knew well their tough working conditions, the irregular, casual 'backbreaking toil' of shifting heavy bags, of its uncertainty and potential victimisation. Hughes knew too the strength and the power of 'the closely organised and united' shipowners and stevedoring companies who employed them.[32] WWF members and seafarers faced the same shipowners, in their growing organisational combinations, notably the ASOF. In parliament, Hughes used this knowledge and his position to establish new improved labour standards for maritime workers. This was official ALP policy. Though he had a very troubled relationship with organised labour and would later split the Labor Party during the divisive war years, for a time he was their staunch defender.

Once the colonies federated in 1901, the national government sought to pass its own maritime law, to protect standards for 'a class of worker whose labours went largely unobserved and unreported.'[33] In 1902, the ALP federal conference passed a resolution urging the passage of a law – a navigation act – to protect Australian shipping and its workforce, ensure adequate safety standards of equipment and manning, the regulation of accommodation for

[30] L.F. Fitzhardinge, *William Morris Hughes: A Political Biography*, vol. 1 (Sydney: Angus & Robertson, 1964), 169, 170.

[31] L.F. Fitzhardinge, 'W.M. Hughes and the Waterside Workers,' *Australian Journal of Political History* 2, no. 2 (1957): 169–80.

[32] Fitzhardinge, 'Hughes and the Waterside Workers.'

[33] Conrad Dixon, 'Seamen and the Law: An Examination of the Impact of Legislation on the British Merchant Seamen's Lot, 1588–1918' (PhD thesis, University College London, 1981), 298.

both passengers and crew and minimum safe working conditions.[34] Yet this was a measure grounded in what historian Ann Curthoys identified as the 'racism/defence of jobs and wages relationship' erupting in the 1878 seamen's strike.[35] Beliefs about white racial superiority dominated public policy at the turn of the twentieth century and inflected many policy measures.

Race and unionism: 'Relations of cooperation and rivalry'

This book contributes to a scholarship that confronts the problematic of racism within the labour movement, especially among socialists and maritime unions.[36] By exploring the contradictions and fluidity of positions it differs from studies which have seen only white labourism in the principles of early unionists, or seek to shift attention to non-British ports.[37] The book takes a long time frame to trace changes in worker activism and workers' ideas as these evolved in a context of challenges to their workplace.

Race, as Laura Tabili has said, is a relationship and not of itself an issue until it is made into one.[38] Indeed, it doesn't exist until someone makes it so. When and why, and by whom, are the questions that historians ask. How the ideas of racial difference shaped the maritime labour market from the mid-nineteenth century and framed the choice of strategies pursued by maritime unions in the twentieth century, is a large part of the story of the international maritime labour movement. Racial identity and anti-racism were debated by Australian and British socialists in the first decades of the twentieth century. Internationalist struggle against capitalism crossed racial lines and state borders and was intertwined with class struggle well before

---

[34] Ann Shorten, 'Imperial Validity and Maritime Education in Australia, 1869–1923' (PhD thesis, Monash University, Melbourne, 1976), 306.

[35] Curthoys, 'Conflict and Consensus,' 64.

[36] Neville Kirk, *Transnational Radicalism and the Connected Lives of Tom Mann and Robert Samuel Ross* (Liverpool: Liverpool University Press, 2017); Eric Arnesen, *Waterfront Workers of New Orleans: Race, Class and Politics, 1863–1923* (New York: Oxford University Press, 1991); Eric Arnesen, 'Biracial Waterfront Unionism in the Age of Segregation,' in Winslow, *Waterfront Workers*, 19–61; Curthoys and Markus, *Who Are Our Enemies?*

[37] Jonathan Hyslop, 'The Imperial Working Class Makes Itself "White": White Labourism in Britain, Australia, and South Africa before the First World War,' *Journal of Historical Sociology* 12 (1999): 398–421; Jonathan Hyslop, 'Steamship Empire: Asian, African and British Sailors in the Merchant Marine c.1880–1945,' *Journal of Asian and African Studies* 44, no. 1 (2009): 49–67.

[38] Laura Tabili, 'Race is a Relationship, and Not a Thing,' *Journal of Social History* 37, no. 1 (special issue, 2003): 125–30; see also Laura Tabili, 'The Construction of Racial Difference in Twentieth-Century Britain: The Special Restriction (Coloured Alien Seamen) Order, 1925,' *Journal of British Studies* 33, no. 1 (1994): 54–98.

1.2 'Asian Seamen,' *ITF Journal*, 1972, NBAC

1920 when the foundation of the Communist Party in different nations made anti-racism official policy.

The problem was that 'On the sea, competition is free, economic contacts are close, and coolie labor can be used in modern ships.'[39] Chinese and Indian seafarers were made the targets of this conversation in Australia and New Zealand but were themselves active in opposing indenture or 'coolie' labour by joining unions, local communist parties or international organisations. The Indian Legislative Council suspended the indentured labour system with regulations passed in 1917, which were followed by the Emigration Act of 1922 abolishing it.[40] India ensured its concerns were

[39] A.C. Garnett, 'China and Seamen's Strike,' *News* (Adelaide), 21 November 1925, 6.

[40] Frank Broeze, 'The Muscles of Empire: Indian Seamen and the Raj, 1919–1939,' *The Indian Economic and Social History Review* 18 (1981): 43–67; A.T. Yarwood, *Asian Migration to Australia: The Background to Exclusion, 1896–1923* (Melbourne: Melbourne University Press, 1964), 154.

heard at the International Labour Organization, and India's delegates were visible activists in the ILO's and ITF's work to establish a seafarers' charter. Chinese seafarers and Japanese dockworkers at key moments reached across the Pacific Ocean to involve Western (Australasian and US) unionists in their political and labour struggles. These overtures offer an alternative account of regional organising to the dominant narrative of exclusion along a 'colour line' that has prevailed to date.

Quite coincidently, the timespan of Bridges' life (1901–90) matches well, if not perfectly, the timespan of this study. The year of his birth coincided with Australia's officially becoming a nation, when the new federal parliament enacted immigration exclusion in an act which established what was known from then on as the 'White Australia policy,' whose object was preserving the nation as 'a white men's country.'[41] Driven by the imperative of reconciling its 'geographical circumstance' with its British–European political heritage, a long-lasting and 'passionate adherence to racial homogeneity' became settled national policy only slowly overturned.[42] This history is not just reduced to arguments and measures for exclusion, but also explores workers' efforts to reach beyond them. Maritime labourers were activists both in formulating opposition to the use of 'coloured' and indentured labour, and also in seeking connections across those racial divides in opposition to such policies. Both views were at times present simultaneously as unionists battled to empower themselves and find strategies of resistance to capitalist exploitation. In doing so they sought allies within an international brotherhood and engaged in actions of solidarity. They were not always successful in their aspirations or reflective on the assumptions of hierarchy in white identity positioning. International maritime union efforts to combat racism and xenophobia were at the end of the twentieth century still a work in progress.[43] Defining their struggle as the pursuit of change is the important story we tell.

As an Australian, Bridges' response to the racialised power structure of colonial India may have reflected events which occurred during his first decade when Asian seafarers were subjected to harsh, new, often contro- versial, restrictions on their mobility. It was not possible to be unaware when as a child he hung around the Melbourne docks, enthralled by the seagoing

[41] Myra Willard, *History of the White Australia Policy to 1920*, 2nd ed. (Melbourne: Melbourne University Press, 1967), 114; Marilyn Lake and Henry Reynolds, *Drawing the Global Colour Line: White Men's Countries and the International Challenge of Racial Equality* (New York: Cambridge University Press, 2008).

[42] Yarwood, *Asian Migration*, 2.

[43] ITF, 'Transport Workers: Beyond 2000,' Progress Report. Paper presented to 38th (Centenary) Congress, 1996, 26, para. 108, ITF Archives, Modern Records Centre, University of Warwick (hereafter MRC).

life. He would have known of the employment of South Asians among the crews, seen them in port, and heard the debates over the 'coolie standards' of their cheaper labour as 'Lascars' as he began his career. An acknowledgement of race was present in his recollection of wartime Bombay, the orchestrated politics of whiteness in pre-independence India that he recounted. It may have reflected the changes the Australasian Seamen's Union was undergoing during those early years of his career when he was at sea.

India has a central place in this book's narrative. India exported millions of indentured workers during the period of the Raj. South Asian seafarers were a large and growing proportion of the British shipping workforce over the course of the nineteenth century in the 'world of circulating labour' that had developed with the emergence of a globalising economy. By the early twentieth century, more Indian seafarers were staying ashore in Britain to take advantage of higher-waged work available in industries on land, while their employment and conditions at sea sparked concern among legislators and authorities as well as trade unions. In the cosmopolitan neighbourhoods of the ports, locals engaged with these newcomers in ways that were complex, not always as rivals but not entirely as equals, in 'relations of cooperation and rivalry that implied mutual recognition as a measure of practical equivalence if not strict equality.'[44]

Our research has shown how, as fellow-members of the British Empire, working for British shipowners, Indian and Australasian maritime workers also experienced these complex relations. They shared some common experiences as well as the fear of competing for jobs and lowering wages. Australian seamen's and waterside workers' opposition to the employment of cheap labour meant they also supported the formation of Indian trade unions, assisted striking Indian crews who demanded their rights and refused to sail and supported India's struggle for independence from British rule. Australia's ALP Prime Minister in the post-war years, former railways unionist Ben Chifley, had enormous admiration for, and developed a genuine friendship with, the newly independent India's Prime Minister Jawaharlal Nehru.[45] Nehru had inspired the head of the ITF Edo Fimmen as that organisation sought to reach into Asian countries in the 1920s and 1930s. Australian unions' relationship with Indian maritime labour is a complex, textured, interlocking story that can't just be reduced to immigration exclusion.

---

[44] G. Balachandran, 'Circulation through Seafaring: Indian Seamen, 1890–1945,' in *Society and Circulation: Mobile People and Itinerant Cultures in South Asia, 1750–1950*, ed. Claude Markovits, Jacques Pouchepadass and Sanjay Subrahmanyam (Delhi: Permanent Black, 2003), 89–130.

[45] Julie Suares, *JB Chifley: An Ardent Internationalist* (Melbourne: Melbourne University Publishing, 2019).

India was not the only Asian country circulating labour. Indentured labour also and initially came principally from China, and the first Australian opposition to 'coloured labour' was against the Chinese. This book shows how connection with workers in China and Japan changed when they began to unionise in the twentieth century. Indentured labour, bound up with the complex issue of race, however, continued to be resisted by maritime unionists trying to protect local labour. Conflict could undermine their efforts at transnational solidarity with Asian unionists, as a dispute we explore in the 1960s over Japanese contract workers, revealed.

Efforts at cooperation and solidarity between unionists across the Asia–Indo–Pacific region were identified in earlier studies of the 1920s by Julia Martínez and Sophie Loy-Wilson, and of the 1940s by Heather Goodall.[46] This book builds on these works and extends them back to the earliest years of the twentieth century, when both Australia and India were trying to establish their own merchant marines against the opposition of British shipowners. It continues that story of a confluence of interests into the second half of the century, extending coverage to Japan in the dockworkers' initiative to set up an Asia-Pacific alternative to the ITF in the period before the ITF established its own Asia-Pacific regional department. An Asia-Pacific identity fostered links through the World Federation of Trade Unions (WFTU) with the All-India Trade Union Congress and Asia-Pacific transport unions' solidarity actions, such as that 'against US armed interventions in Asian affairs' in Vietnam and Korea.[47] Much of this was shaped by the context of cold war alignments. There is a small literature on how regional workers' organisations have attempted to collaborate with each other under the conditions of a rapidly globalising economy.[48] Our study adds to this work with the story of earlier trade union efforts to build connections across the region.

---

[46] Julia Martínez, '"Coolies" to Comrades: Internationalism between Australian and Asian Seamen,' in *Labour and Community: Historical Essays*, ed. Ray Markey (Wollongong: University of Wollongong Press, 2001), 295–312; Julia Martínez, 'Questioning "White Australia": Unionism and "Coloured" Labour, 1911–37,' *Labour History* 76 (1999): 1–19; Sophie Loy-Wilson, '"Liberating" Asia: Strikes and Protest in Sydney and Shanghai, 1920–39,' *History Workshop Journal* 72 (2011): 74–102; Heather Goodall, 'Port Politics: Indian Seamen, Australian Unions and Indonesian Independence, 1945–47,' *Labour History* 94 (2008): 43–68.

[47] 'Asian Trade Union Seminar New Delhi, April 8–27,' *Seamen's Journal* 23, no. 2 (1968): 48; R.M. Wilson, 'Asian Trade Union Seminar,' *Seamen's Journal* 23, no. 5 (1968): 108–9; 'Asia-Pacific Solidarity with the Vietnamese People,' *Seamen's Journal* 23 (special supplement, 1968): 183–6.

[48] E.g., George Myconos, *The Globalizations of Organized Labour, 1945–2004* (Basingstoke: Palgrave Macmillan, 2005); Chris Rowley and John Benson, eds, *Globalization and Labour in the Asia Pacific Region* (London: Frank Cass, 2000).

A 'militant program of action for better living and rights of workers'[49]

Many historians have seen the principal shaping factor in maritime unions' militancy as 'deeply-rooted in a long-standing way of life and work on the waterfront.'[50] They have seen 'a remarkable rank and file militancy' (evident in Figure 1.3) as 'inherently anchored' in maritime labour, working under harsh conditions and tight controls, and in the relationships seafarers formed living in close proximity with others from around the globe.[51] Seafarers faced intermittent employment and low wages coupled with no apprenticeship training and frequent accidents or the risk of drowning, summarised as 'a loveless life, eternal monotony, and the daily recurring hazard of a violent death.'[52] On board they had cramped accommodation, were under 'a tightly organised system of command,' and, unlike shore workers, no ability to walk off the job even when the ship reached port. Put together, that was a recipe for fostering a workplace-based militancy.[53]

Several investigations in Britain, such as the Royal Commission on Unseaworthy Ships 1873, revealed the hazards for merchant seafarers who were sailing to the Australian colonies. The mortality rate of seamen exceeded all other occupations, even miners.[54] Undermanning, using aged ships, overloading them with cargo and cost-cutting on construction were common practices shipowners used in looking to maximise their profits. Shipwrecks were frequent around the Australian coast (close to 2,000 in a 20-year period), or vessels just disappeared en route across the Pacific.[55] Bridges was

[49] Tomitaro Kaneda, chairman of JDU, to Triennial All Ports Conference, Waterside Workers' Federation, September 1967, Minutes, 7. Waterfront Workers Federation Archives, Z432/Box 19, Noel Butlin Archives Centre, Canberra (hereafter NBAC).

[50] Bruce Nelson, *Workers on the Waterfront: Seamen, Longshoremen, and Unionism in the 1930s* (Urbana: University of Illinois Press, 1988), 4.

[51] Frank Broeze, 'Militancy and Pragmatism: An International Perspective on Maritime Labour, 1870–1914,' *International Review of Social History* 36, no. 2 (1991): 165–200; Erik Olssen, 'The Seamen's Union and Industrial Militancy, 1908–13,' *New Zealand Journal of History* 19, no. 1 (1985): 15.

[52] Hall, *Socialism and Sailors*, 13–14; Fink, *Sweatshops at Sea*.

[53] Olssen, 'The Seamen's Union,' 15. See also James Bennett, 'The New Zealand Labour Movement and International Communism, 1921–38,' in *Lenin's Legacy Down Under: New Zealand's Cold War*, ed. Alexander Trapeznik and Aaron Fox (Dunedin: University of Otago Press, 2004), 73–93 (86).

[54] Michael Quinlan, 'Precarious and Hazardous Work: The Health and Safety of Merchant Seamen, 1815–1935,' *Social History* 38, no. 3 (2013): 281–307 (288). See also Nicolette Jones, *The Plimsoll Sensation: The Great Campaign to Save Lives at Sea* (London: Abacus, 2007).

[55] Michael Quinlan, 'The Low Rumble of Informal Dissent: Shipboard Protests over Health and Safety in Australian Waters, 1790–1900,' *Labour History* 102 (2012): 131–55; Michael

1.3 MUA dockworkers, waterfront dispute, April 1998
Photographer Jessie Marlow. H99.23/11 SLV

himself shipwrecked twice in his very short seagoing career on the Australian
coast. The statistics on the current dangers at sea are disturbingly similar.[56]

Signing on for a single voyage, then being discharged at its end, meant a
mobile and constantly changing workforce. In ports there could be seafarers
from anywhere in the world who had left their ship and were available
for a new one. Many waterside workers were, like Bridges, seafarers who
had come ashore. Multicultural and cosmopolitan spaces, enabling the
fomentation and transmission of political ideas and information, could lead
to what some scholars call 'proletarian internationalism.' All worked in an
industry 'where dangers are always present and basic conditions uniquely
harsh.'[57] Ernest Bevin once eloquently said: 'no voice is capable, no pen
can write, no artist can paint, the real human tragedy' that was behind the

---

Quinlan, 'Industrial Relations before Unions: New South Wales Seamen, 1810–1852,'
Journal of Industrial Relations 38, no. 2 (1996): 269–93.

[56] Whitlow, *Current Concerns*.

[57] Bollinger, *Against the Wind*, 244; Tony Alderton, *The Global Seafarer: Living and Working
Conditions in a Globalized Industry* (Geneva: International Labour Office, 2004); Nathan
Lillie, *A Global Union for Global Workers: Collective Bargaining and Regulatory Politics in
Maritime Shipping* (New York: Routledge, 2006).

dockworkers' wage claims. He was putting their case at Britain's Court of Inquiry into the Wage Conditions of Dock Labour in 1919 and his powerful rhetoric was 'an indictment of the industrial system which allowed such conditions to continue.'[58]

Maritime workplace militancy and community political activism have been a powerful shaping force in Australia's labour history. From the pre-federation decade of the 1890s, when a major maritime strike influenced the kind of industrial relations' system the new nation would subsequently establish, maritime unions have been at the forefront of industrial campaigns and progressive politics. The waterfront has been the flashpoint for confrontations as seafarers and dockworkers took the lead in pursuing workers' rights. At the end of the century, former WWF official Greg Combet said it was 'a tough environment' in which 'everything was a fight to hold on to hard-won conditions.'[59]

Feminist historians have explored this militancy as masculinist activism, an expression or performance of gendered power. The overwhelming maleness of the seafaring workforce, and the fact that 'images and narratives of sea-going have afforded powerful ways of representing maleness' have generated an association between masculinity and seafaring 'that should make masculinity the key reference' point for maritime labour historians.[60] Twenty years ago, a US historian identified masculinity in the rituals of seafaring life.[61] More recently, Australian wharf labourers' collectivism and modes of resistance have been shown to be critical to their gender identity.[62] Historians have described the masculinity of dock workers as being tough, prone to violence and lacking discipline, while deeply bonded to each other and their union in a masculinity of solidarity that contrasted with the 'rogue masculinity' that sometimes took hold in wildcat rank

---

[58] Quoted by Robert Pearce, in 'Ernest Bevin: Robert Pearce Examines the Career of the Man Who Was Successively Trade Union Leader, Minister of Labour and Foreign Secretary,' *History Review* (December 2002): 19; Alan Bullock, *The Life and Times of Ernest Bevin*, vol. 1, *Trade Union Leader, 1881–1940* (London: Heinemann, 1960), 122, 130.

[59] Greg Combet, *The Fights of My Life* (Melbourne: Melbourne University Press, 2014), 53–4.

[60] Valerie Burton, '"Whoring Drinking Sailors": Reflections on Masculinity from the Labour History of Nineteenth-Century British Shipping,' in *Working Out Gender: Perspectives from Labour History*, ed. Margaret Walsh (Aldershot: Ashgate, 1999), 84–101.

[61] See M. Creighton, 'Fraternity in the American Forecastle, 1830–1870,' *New England Quarterly* 63, no. 4 (1990): 531–57.

[62] Laila Ellmoos, 'The Deep Sea and the Shallow Water: Masculinity, Mateship and Work Practices on Sydney's Waterfront in the 1950s,' in *Playing the Man: New Approaches to Masculinity*, ed. Katherine Biber, Tom Sear and Dave Trudinger (Annandale: Pluto Press, 1999), 186–99.

and file actions.[63] These scholars have shown the links between class and gender politics that underscored the story of militant maritime unionism that former SUA official Mick Doleman has acknowledged 'was a blokey culture.' But by century's end women were demanding changes. At the ITF Congress held in Delhi, in 1998, Kalpana Desai and Vijaya Kilkarni, from the Transport & Dock Workers' Union, India, called on more action to give women a place in the organisation.[64] Gender dynamics shadow this history; illuminating them is a work in progress.

In the twentieth century, maritime unionists' militancy was also directed towards international political causes. Their activism in solidarity actions for the cause of social justice for others is legendary.[65] In her history of the WWF, Margo Beasley pointed to the 'extraordinary moral leadership to the community at large' of a union that asserted 'unions not only have a right but an obligation to take stands on issues and events of importance to the entire Australian public.'[66] The Australian maritime unions are well known for their support of Aboriginal rights and as leaders on behalf of Aboriginal strikers.[67] They are also well known for their activism in relation to other colonised labourers. They refused to serve ships loaded with scrap iron for a militarising Japan in 1930s, detained Dutch vessels during the Indonesian struggle for independence in the 1940s, ensured the success of the oil embargo to fight apartheid in South Africa, opposed the Korean war in the 1950s and refused to transport military cargo to Vietnam in the 1960s. This activism focused on but was not limited to Asia and the Indo-Pacific. They were not usually impromptu campaigns and they involved international solidarity actions. Australian and New Zealand maritime unions officials were exposed to ideas and policies when they attended conferences organised by the United Nations, international bodies like the World Federation of Trade Unions, the International Confederation of Free Trade Unions, the International Labour Organization and the World Peace Council, all of which had policies encouraging activism.

Less well known is how their militant internationalism was taken on behalf of labour protections for all workers who share the seas. Being an

---

[63] Kathie Muir, '"Thugs and Bullies": The Deployment of Rogue Masculinity in the Campaign for Workers' Rights on Site,' *Australian Feminist Studies* 28, no. 75 (2013): 30–49.

[64] ITF, 39th Congress, New Delhi, 1998; see also Diane Kirkby, *Voices from the Ships: Australian Seafarers and their Union* (Sydney: UNSW Press, 2008), 201–3.

[65] John S. Ahlquist and Margaret Levi, *In the Interest of Others: Organisations and Social Activism* (Princeton, NJ: Princeton University Press, 2013).

[66] Beasley, *Wharfies*, ix; Diane Kirkby, 'Maritime Labour, Men of Power and the Dynamics of Activism,' Keynote Address to Labour History Conference, Perth, 2019.

[67] Alexis Vassiley, '"There's No Flies at Noonkanbah but the Scabs Are on the Way": Trade Union Support for Aboriginal Rights during the Noonkanbah Dispute, 1979–80,' *Labour History* 110 (2016): 77–95.

internationalist arose from the international nature of shipping – 'the mobile nature of its capital' – in the world's first (and most) globalised industry.[68] Once described as 'very good fighters' and tenacious in their political affili- ations, Australian maritime workers demonstrated the quality of being 'true-blue' when they turned to the pursuit of international labour rights.[69] This book is about actions to establish and maintain fair labour standards, driven by that sense of connection with workers across the world, and their belief that 'capital knows no country.' It argues that internationalism was an orientation, both personal (experiential) and collective (political), which was adopted union policy and was pushed by the leadership. An interna- tional socialist movement in the nineteenth century was attractive to a workforce that was already internationalised and for whom the prospect of revolution seemed necessary to remove their harsh working conditions. In the pre-existing internationalism of the maritime workforce, socialism found a ready acceptance and co-existence in the 'rootless and transient workers ... who lived and worked [under] oppressive conditions' where it 'grew like a hothouse flower' among waterfront workers 'peculiarly receptive to a radical critique of capitalism,' in their ranks and not just among their leaders.[70] There it survived as an organised force because it was rooted in reality, and nourished by contact with outside workers, sometimes communist party directives. The empirical evidence suggests a messy picture.

Internationalism was not always or only a commitment to a socialist politics. In the United States, the east coast dockers and seafaring unions were not radical or responsive to the political influence of the Industrial Workers of the World (IWW) as were those of the west coast and southern ports like New Orleans. The International Seamen's Union (ISU) in 1921 expelled the editor of its *Seamen's Journal* for his affiliation with the IWW, claiming that its 'revolutionary politics' that he was publishing were 'principles wholly contrary to [the] policy of the union.'[71] Consequently, the ISU halved its membership within just two years. Yet, given the nature of their industry and the size and power of the ISU – 19 unions representing all branches of seamen across the United States – it was a major influence in the ITF in the decades before 1920 when its membership was its largest ever.[72]

Being a member of the IWW was grounds for deportation when Australia and the United States enacted special legislation during the First World

---

68 Fink, *Sweatshops at Sea.*

69 Jaap Oldenbroek to Vincent Tewson, TUC, 25 March 1952, MS 292/993/5, MRC.

70 Nelson, *Workers on the Waterfront.* See also Bruce Nelson, *Divided We Stand: American Workers and the Struggle for Black Equality* (Princeton, NJ: Princeton University Press, 2001).

71 Albrecht, 'International Seamen's Union of America,' 26–7.

72 Albrecht, 'International Seamen's Union of America,' 23.

War and busily deported each other's IWW members. Bridges readily acknowledged his Marxism and earlier membership of the IWW from his days working in the port of New Orleans. He spent years battling deportation from the United States because of his alleged Communist Party membership.[73] Australia's maritime union leaders were often openly Communist Party of Australia (CPA) members, and there were times when Australian unionists too (notably Tom Walsh and Jacob Johnson in 1925) faced deportation by an anti-labour federal government. There were other times when ideological factionalism nearly destroyed their unions. ITF founder Tom Mann had been a major influence on socialists when he lived in Australia at the turn of the century but was refused entry by the Hughes' Nationalist government in 1918 and again in 1922 once he became a leading communist in Britain.[74] His fellow dockworkers, Ben Tillett and Ernest Bevin, always a staunch opponent of communism, remained among the strongest advocates of internationalism and socialism.

Decades later, Australia's Charlie Fitzgibbon likewise rejected communism when he took up a 'pragmatic internationalism' in leadership of the WWF. His internationalism was continued by his successor Tas Bull, who joined, then left, the CPA before he took on a leadership role. Meanwhile, Eliot Elliott and subsequently Pat Geraghty, among other members of the Seamen's Union, remained Soviet-aligned even when they were expelled from the CPA at the time of the Sino-Soviet split. What they all shared, over and above their differing ideological alignments, was a commitment to internationalised organisation, which they turned to practical action. Ideologues from the other side of politics were also always present, in shipowning companies and organisations, in exporters and users of ports and ships, and as free traders in parliament developing government policies opposing labour rights and protections.

By the middle decades of the twentieth century, the unions' militancy in an improved labour market had won concessions – higher wages for waterside workers as well as better on-board living conditions for Australian and New Zealand seafarers. But the economic centre of shipping had shifted, and subsequent decades brought global upheavals and new challenges. The waterfront has been the site of militant activism many times, and in all the countries discussed here. Some moments – like the British dockworkers' strike of 1889, the Australian and New Zealand maritime strikes of 1890, the Californian waterfront strike of 1934 and the Indian 'Lascars' strike of

[73] Alan Benjamin, 'Harry Bridges Again in American News: Some Would Deport Him,' *Mercury* (Hobart), 9 September 1938, 6.

[74] Frank Farrell, *International Socialism and Australian Labour: The Left in Australia, 1919–1939* (Sydney: Hale & Iremonger, 1981).

1939 – were turning points in international maritime organisational history. The Australian waterfront dispute of April 1998 was another moment of note in this long maritime labour history.

The largest of its kind in many years, the significance of the 1998 clash went beyond its local workplace issues. At its core was the employer's move (in a conspiracy with the government) to replace the unionised workforce with individually contracted workers, brought in for the single purpose of breaking the union. Demonstrating the power imbalance that existed between an individualised, unorganised workforce and a highly organised employer group acting with the unlimited support of state power, the MUA mobilised public support. Battling to enable and preserve workers' rights to organise was an international issue that had been more than a century-long struggle.[75]

This book places the significance of that dispute and its outcome in the long history of militant activism for fair labour standards that maritime unionists had fought nationally and in international forums. It reveals internationalism in action, in a story that traces the forging of strong links with other organisations and the long campaign for legally enforceable instruments protecting seafarers' rights. Several specific histories of these unions exist and earlier histories of the Australian left have touched on some of the events and people here.[76] This book brings these earlier studies together in a new international context, one which puts a regional perspective in the foreground. It is an extended study of how this particular workforce grappled with the changing meanings of internationalism, struggled to resolve the conflicts of racial difference, combated class power and built resistance to injustices. An international union journal once asked its readers to 'consider the wrongs perpetrated against the toilers of the sea ...'[77] Our task is also to consider how those toilers took action to defend themselves against those wrongs, and in doing so aspired to assist other workers to assert their rights.

[75] C. Smith, 'Internationalising Industrial Disputes: The Case of the Maritime Union of Australia,' *Employee Relations* 32, no. 6 (2010): 557–73.

[76] Robin Gollan, *Revolutionaries and Reformists: Communism and the Australian Labour Movement, 1920–1955* (Canberra: ANU Press, 1975); Farrell, *International Socialism*.

[77] *Industrial Unionist* (New York), in 'The Internationality of the Seamen.'

2

'Navigation as It Affects the Empire'
Australasian Labour Standards and British Merchant Shipping

In 1907, William Morris (Billy) Hughes, founding president of the WWF, travelled to London to put the case for Australian maritime labour standards. The instrument was to be the Navigation Act, which had to be passed by the Australian parliament and receive Royal Assent from the British. Hughes was part of the delegation to attend the Imperial Merchant Shipping Legislation conference, bringing together representatives of the Australian, New Zealand and United Kingdom governments. With the recently elected Prime Minister, Alfred Deakin, the principal Australian delegate was William Lyne, the Minister for Trade and Customs. He was accompanied by his departmental secretary, Harry Wollaston. Hughes was there as Minister for External Affairs. Accompanying him was Atlee Hunt, head of the External Affairs Department. Also among the delegates was Seamen's Union president and Senator, Robert Storrie Guthrie.[1] The New Zealand delegation consisted of the Prime Minister, Sir Joseph Ward, chairman of the Union Steam Ship Company, Sir James Mills, the [unnamed] secretary of the Marine Engineers Association and William Belcher, secretary of the New Zealand Federated Seamen's Union. The maritime unions of these former colonies had a vested interest in the outcome of this conference whose task was to discuss 'the whole question of navigation as it affects the Empire.'[2]

---

[1] 'The Navigation Conference,' *The Register* (Adelaide), 31 January 1907, 4; Fitzhardinge, *Hughes*, 185–6, also 184, 186–8, 306; Conference between representatives of the United Kingdom, the Commonwealth of Australia and New Zealand on the subject of merchant shipping legislation, Report, P.P. No. 15/1907, 2nd Session, Melbourne, 1907.

[2] Australia, Royal Commission on the Navigation Bill, 1906, *Report of the Royal Commission on the Navigation Bill of the Australian Commonwealth, 1904* (London: HMSO, 1906), https://parlinfo.aph.gov.au/parlInfo/download/publications/tabledpapers/HPP032016003242_1/upload_pdf/HPP032016003242_1.pdf.

Britain had recently passed a new statute, the Merchant Shipping Act 1906, as the latest in its long history of legislation regulating shipping and seamen. Australia and New Zealand were trying to pass their own laws in substitution for the previous UK Merchant Shipping Act of 1894. Since then, Britain had done little for merchant seamen and its legislation now penalised them relative to shore workers. New Zealand's Act, passed in 1903, was taken as a useful model by Australia, but misgivings expressed by British shipowners meant the Royal Assent was withheld from New Zealand until early 1905. Australia's Navigation Act, to apply only on the Australian coast, was introduced but had yet to pass through parliament.

The Imperial Conference was initially called in March 1905 by a Conservative British government that was largely opposed to what Australia was trying to do, but the Conservatives lost power to the Liberals at the end of that year. The incoming President of the Board of Trade, Lloyd George, chaired the conference which was also attended by other members of the Board of Trade and the Colonial Office, a prominent legal authority on Empire constitutional law, five shipowners and the national secretary of the National Union of Seamen (NUS), Havelock Wilson. Australia had taken the unusual step of sending members of the government as well as the Labor Party opposition to a conference of experts on what was effectively a labour matter. While the major Sydney newspaper thought the choice of delegates was 'scandalous,' Lloyd George was impressed: Hughes' mastery of the issues demonstrated the value of sending along both Government and Opposition representatives to Imperial Conferences.[3]

The history of this maritime legislation demonstrates the entwining of domestic labour regulation with empire. Australia's and New Zealand's efforts to establish their own labour standards had to be conducted in an imperial frame and were dominated by vested shipping interests protected by UK law. That legal, maritime and imperial history shaped the experience of maritime labour standards.

Imperial merchant shipping and the colonies

At the time of the Imperial Conference, the British Empire was reaching its peak. In 1914, the British shipping industry owned more than one-third of the world's shipping and British-owned shipyards built half of all new tonnage.[4] The previous 50 years had seen an enormous expansion in sea-borne trade

[3] Fitzhardinge, *Hughes*, 185, 188.

[4] Ralph Davis, 'Introductory Note to 1970 Edition' of Adam Kirkaldy, *British Shipping: Its History, Organisation and Importance* (Newton Abbot: David & Charles, 1970; first pub. London: Kegan Paul, 1914), v, vii.

and international commerce. Shipping was transformed with the move from sail to steam power, when the tonnage of goods carried by sea multiplied fivefold. From 1880, tramp steamers came to dominate the industry as a vast intercontinental bulk trade in grain, coal, timber and raw materials from the colonies for metropolitan manufacturing developed. Steamships required a network of coaling stations and repair facilities throughout the world. Greatly enlarged vessels carrying much heavier cargoes required expensive dock and harbour facilities and sophisticated equipment for handling. The steamship depended on a whole support structure of specialists – repairers, stevedoring agents, dock companies, insurers and a host of others – providing work for thousands and populating ports across the world. Little wonder merchant shipping was once described as 'the Imperial subject *par excellence*.'[5]

Technology is often seen as the cause of the transformation in shipping as the age of sail gave way to steam. Yet this began slowly. On the long run to Australia, steam, which required constant refuelling, was at a disadvantage relative to the speed of sail. The 'average length of a voyage scarcely improved before the 1880s' despite big changes: the size of ships increased with the use of iron, sailings could now be to regular schedules once the wind could be ignored, and shipping companies introduced the business model of the liner.[6] In the second half of the nineteenth century, a revolution occurred in the passage of emigrants: cargo liner traffic increased and passenger liners expanded to carry the rise in emigrant traffic.

Nevertheless, according to one shipping historian, 'The commercial development of steam had yet to come' and it was changes to the law 'more than any other single factor' that created Britain's 'imposing maritime industry.'[7] Britain's shipping dominance was originally achieved and maintained by its Navigation Acts passed in the seventeenth century to develop national shipping by restricting the carriage of foreign trade to ships built, owned and crewed by UK subjects. Reserving Britain's coastal traffic to British shipping and tying commerce/trade and national defence together – that is, the foundation of the merchant marine – was central to Britain's rise to world-wide supremacy as a maritime power.[8] Navigation Acts effectively 'made it illegal for foreign goods to reach [Britain] in any but British ships.'[9]

[5] Basil A. Helmore, 'Validity of State Navigation Acts,' *Australian Law Journal* 27 (21 May 1953): 16.

[6] R.H. Thornton, *British Shipping* (Cambridge: Cambridge University Press, 1939), 59–60; 72–80.

[7] Thornton, *British Shipping*, 43.

[8] Ernest Fayle, 'The Navigation Acts,' *Edinburgh Review* 228, no. 465 (1918): 22–42.

[9] Thornton, *British Shipping*, 4.

Only when these Navigation Acts were repealed did steam power accelerate. The government elected in 1848 with a mandate for Free Trade meant the navigation laws were attacked and quickly repealed and shipping was opened to commercial operators. Carrying mails by private companies was a new principle, it had until then been controlled by a government department and the change was profound in its consequences. It occurred first in 1837, to a company subsequently known as the Peninsular and Oriental Company (P&O), which was agitating for a mail service with the Australian colonies when the Navigation Acts were repealed. A Bombay–Suez service was run by the East India Company, under sail, and P&O were keen to undertake both the Australian and Bombay services for no additional cost. In 1852, P&O won the contract, which included a new service between Singapore and Australia as well as services to China, Ceylon and India. This complete break with tradition caused, within just 20 years, 'an astonishing change.'[10] British shipping's dominance by the second decade of the twentieth century was, in short, a consequence of its lead in free trade. To the British shipowner, free trade 'was not just a dogmatic political principle. It was his bread and butter,' and a deliberate policy pursued against protectionist labour policies.[11] Economic as well as political reasons tying merchant shipping closely to Britain's imperial rise also dictated the imperial relationship between Britain and its colonies.[12]

In the Australasian colonies, locally owned shipping was confined to running the intercolonial coastal trade around Australia and between Australia, New Zealand and Fiji. Colonial shipping companies also owned the port facilities for loading and unloading cargo. Long-haul voyages to more distant ports were undertaken by British or other foreign-owned European or American lines. Shipping companies operating in Australian waters fell into one of three categories – localised, coastal (between colonies), or overseas 'deep sea' shipping engaged in international trading. Most of the coastal companies were Australian owned, some with British investment. As shipping changed in the last three decades, the cost of shipping became more capital intensive, rising from hundreds to tens of thousands of pounds. Competition became acute, based on freight rates and passenger prices rather than the economic performance of labour, which remained dependent on customary organisation and rules.[13]

---

[10] Thornton, *British Shipping*, 22, 105–7, 25. See also Boyd Cable, *A Hundred Year History of the P&O Peninsular and Oriental Steam Navigation Company, 1837–1937* (London: Ivor Nicholson & Watson, 1937).

[11] Thornton, *British Shipping*, 94.

[12] Helmore, 'Validity of State Navigation Acts,' 16.

[13] David E. Morgan, 'Labour and Industrial Authority: Social and Industrial Relations in the Australian Stevedoring Industry, 1800–1935' (PhD thesis, University of Queensland, 1997), 183–5, 188–9.

Britain legally 'exercised a significant coverage of maritime activities within the colonies,' including the labour of merchant seafarers.[14] Over the nineteenth century, Britain controlled and closely monitored attempts by the colonies to introduce their own maritime labour laws. Imperial statutes dealing with merchant seamen became increasingly comprehensive as Britain intervened repeatedly, disallowing a series of colonial laws. While this intervention was extensive and 'to a degree not matched by any other British laws regulating labour,' the colonies still 'developed laws that deviated significantly from their British counterparts.'[15]

The dominance of British shipping and its imperial power created problems for the colonies. 'Colonial legislatures had to deal with British authorities that were less willing to permit variations from imperial maritime law than was the case with colonial master and servant statutes.'[16] British companies had privileges against colonial competition. The Australian colonies were empowered under British legislation to regulate their coastal trade but were subject to restrictions under the UK Merchant Shipping Act, which controlled British possessions.[17]

The UK Merchant Shipping Act 1869 (and later 1894), administered under the Board of Trade, set the boundaries of the colonies' powers of lawmaking by allowing colonial parliaments to regulate their coastal trade on condition the legislation was reserved and confirmed by the UK, treated all British ships in like manner and preserved the treaty rights of foreign states. Under the terms of the Act, colonial legislatures could pass legislation for vessels registered in the colony, provided such legislation was 'not repugnant to the [imperial] Merchant Shipping Act.'[18] 'Coasting vessels' were those which traded along the coast and sometimes of necessity voyaged beyond three miles from the coastline, so colonial statutes were still binding on the masters, crew and passengers of those vessels. The colonial acts passed by the various Australian colonial legislatures were not overturned by the later enactment of federal legislation, but they were narrowed in their application to ships trading between ports within the one particular state.[19]

Similarly, in India, British shipping monopolised the trade both internally and in international waters. India's shipping industry was eliminated and

---

[14] Michael Quinlan 'Regulating Labour in a Colonial Context: Maritime Labour Legislation in the Australian Colonies, 1788–1850,' *Australian Historical Studies* 29, no. 111 (1998): 303–24, at 305. For an account of British maritime labour law, see J.G. Kitchen, *The Employment of Merchant Seamen* (London: Croom Helm, 1980).

[15] Quinlan, 'Regulating Labour,' 305.

[16] Quinlan, 'Regulating Labour,' 324.

[17] Details in Kirkaldy, *British Shipping*, 258–9.

[18] Helmore, 'Validity of State Navigation Acts,' 16; Kirkaldy, *British Shipping*, 258–9.

[19] Helmore, 'Validity of State Navigation Acts,' 17.

was not revived until after India gained independence in the late 1940s. Consequently, with 'not a single vessel carrying an Indian flag,' all seafarers seeking employment had to do so on foreign, usually British, ships, which, in the view of an Indian trade union leader, 'resulted in the worst form of exploitation of seamen.'[20] This brought the maritime labour of Australia and India into conflict, but also gave them a mutual interest in their relationship to negotiations with Britain.

Accordingly, merchant shipping law generated intercolonial relationships that were in fact complex within the framework of empire. As one colonial newspaper pointed out, 'The introduction of fast steamers, has brought various parts of the Empire into closer relationship, and has multiplied the complications wrought by keen foreign competition. All this has completely changed the scope of navigation laws during recent years.' The editorial concluded, 'it is not surprising to learn that all sorts of anomalies have crept into the legislation affecting British and colonial owned vessels.'[21]

'Australianising the merchant service'

While Britain was internationalising its seagoing labour force, Australia and New Zealand were nationalising theirs. The very high mobility of the maritime workforce combined with the national economic importance of merchant shipping and commerce, overlapped with national defence. Australia was required, under terms considered at the Imperial Conference in 1902, 'to fund ships and supply naval reserve personnel for the protection of the Empire.'[22] The new national government then set about developing its own navy and merchant fleet for the defence of Australia.[23] In 1906, when the new UK Merchant Shipping Act was passed, Australia's leaders were coming to terms with 'a seismic shock to the balance of world power': Japan's victory over Russia in the war of 1904–5, making it the dominant naval power in the Pacific.[24] This 'rising Asian empire,' so near to Australia, posed a threat to Australia's security. New naval powers Japan, Germany and the United States now challenged Britain's sea power in a way that made concerns about the responsibility for Australia's defence

---

[20] Leo Barnes, *Evolution and Scope of Mercantile Marine Laws Relating to Seamen in India* (Bombay: Maritime Law Association of India, 1983), 315, 18–19.

[21] 'The Navigation Conference,' 4.

[22] Rosemary Broomham, *Steady Revolutions: The Australian Institute of Marine and Power Engineers, 1881–1990* (Sydney: UNSW Press, 1991), 79.

[23] 'An Australian Navy,' *Spectator*, 30 November 1901, 830.

[24] Judith Brett, *The Enigmatic Mr. Deakin* (Melbourne: Australia Text Publishing Co., 2017), 331.

2.1 Delegates at labour conference. Billy Hughes (centre front), Sydney, 1900
Photographer H. Linsell. NLA

imperative. In parliament, 'a new conversation began' about Australia's place in this world and its need to develop effective defences.[25]

The establishment of a merchant marine was part of this conversation, the spur for Australia to pass its own Navigation Act, 'actuat[ing] the Parliament [and] lift[ing] the subject to a plane of great importance above the ordinary considerations of party politics.'[26] The future Australian coastal trade was to be reserved for Australian-owned ships which would in a time of war become a source of supplying trained and skilled Australian seamen, on the model of Britain's merchant navy. To the parliament, which considered this goal to be of great national importance, higher freight costs might have to be the price paid for national security. In short, they sought to 'Australianise the merchant service.'[27]

The *Sydney Morning Herald* made the case that Australia needed to be manning ships of war necessary for the protection of the Common-

[25] Brett, *Enigmatic Mr. Deakin*, 331, quoting interview with Alfred Deakin in the *Herald* (Melbourne), 12 June 1905. See also Neville Meaney, *The Search for Security in the Pacific, 1901–14* (Sydney: Sydney University Press, 1976).

[26] Royal Commission on the Navigation Act 1924, *Report* (Melbourne: Government Printer, 1924), 2.

[27] This is Ann Shorten's phrase. See Shorten, 'Imperial Validity and Maritime Education.'

wealth and crewing ships for the mercantile purpose of giving 'our island continent' access to the markets of the world. 'A free nation [depends] on the efficacy and patriotism of its sailors,' according to the paper, and it was important to have 'British crews for British vessels,' particularly for war ships. The paper imagined there could come a time when the crew of a British or Australian ship whose crew was mainly foreign could be asked to fight against the country the foreign crew had come from. Consequently, it made sense to ensure crews were nationals. The 'unpopularity of the sea as a profession,' however, made this problematic. While '[f]or various reasons the calling of the sea is not so popular with Australian boys as it might be,' it was not just Australians. German boys 'looked no more kindly on the sea' than Australian or British boys, or those from the United States, France and Italy. Therefore, 'anything which would increase its popularity is desirable' and institutions that might prepare boys for the sea should be encouraged.[28] The *Sydney Morning Herald* advocated 'school ships,' and training for apprentices afterwards, first in the Royal Navy and later in the merchant marine.

Hughes was a strong advocate of such an Australian merchant navy. When he became Prime Minister during the First World War, he used the government's wartime powers to acquire its own ships and to turn captured German ships into merchant shipping vessels of the newly established Commonwealth Line.[29] In the decade before that, he was active in promoting Australian legislation that could achieve the same outcome to improve local labour standards, which meant overcoming British opposition. He was not an internationalist by inclination. Together with his close ally Bob Guthrie, he worked to transform the conditions of Australian maritime labour, advocating for a national merchant service based on superior labour standards.

In 1903, a Seamen's Union delegate to the NSW Labor Council announced that 'Ships in the Australian trade were now being manned with colored labor,' and he suggested 'the only way to protect the local seamen was to adopt a federal act compelling the observance of the Australian conditions of labor while trading on the coast.'[30] This strategy had grown in strength since it was first mooted in the 1880s. It called for enforcing wages and standards, not deporting or restricting the movement of people, as Australian seafarers faced competition which would drive down their wages. 'The only really effective fight that can be put up is by legislative action; make ourselves a

[28] 'White Sailors for Australian Ships,' *Sydney Morning Herald*, 31 August 1901, 8.

[29] Fitzhardinge, 'Hughes and the Waterside Workers,' 169, 170; also, Beasley, *Wharfies*, 17.

[30] 'Seamen's Union and Colored Labor,' *Sydney Morning Herald*, 3 July 1903, 6.

power to be reckoned with in the political arena,' the *Seamen's Journal* was arguing a decade later, 'and we can get laws that will allow us to live and earn our bread and butter ... without having to enter into competition with the Asiatic.'[31]

New Zealand unionists too fought hard to keep the employment of cheaper labour out of their local shipping industry. The most notable opponent of the use of Asian labour was William Belcher (1859–1926), who was part of the New Zealand delegation to the Imperial Conference in 1907 and one of the earliest officials of the Seamen's Union of New Zealand (NZSU). He had emigrated from Britain in 1879 and was working on the inter-island trade when he joined the union in 1882 and came to the leadership five years later. Known as 'a forthright and pugnacious union leader,' he dominated the NZSU for two decades.[32] Belcher saw the employment of cheap labour, especially from India, as a strategy shipping companies were using to undermine New Zealand wages and conditions, and he waged a public campaign 'to keep Lascars out of New Zealand ports and off all visiting ships.'[33] Once neutral, 'Lascar' became a racialised term. Historian Ravi Ahuja argues that the term 'Lascar,' which until 'the early nineteenth century had been a general designation for seafarers from the whole Indian Ocean region, was slowly transformed into a legal category to distinguish Lascars from "seamen" – the legal status of the former being different and markedly lower.'[34] By 1913, Belcher spoke 'as one who has had experience as a representative of the Empire in conferences,' saying he knew 'that there is a decided objection on the part of the Imperial authorities to grant the overseas dominions local autonomy so far as shipping law is concerned.' Belcher went on to say:

> But unless our colonial Governments have the right to enact the necessary shipping legislation to protect our colonial interests – the interests of both the owner and the seaman – we shall soon find ourselves in a fix. Our local mercantile marine will be a thing of the past, killed off by the cheap foreigner stepping in and gobbling up the lot.[35]

[31] 'Newcastle Report,' *Australasian Seamen's Journal* 2, no. 3 (1 July 1914).

[32] Grant, *Jagged Seas*, 32.

[33] Erik Olssen, 'William Belcher (1859/60–1926),' *Dictionary of New Zealand Biography*.

[34] Ravi Ahuja, 'Mobility and Containment: The Voyages of South Asian Seamen, *c*.1900–1960,' *International Review of Social History* 51 (2006): 117; Ravi Ahuja, 'Networks of Subordination – Networks of the Subordinated: The Ordered Spaces of South Asian Maritime Labour in the Age of Imperialism (*c*.1890–1947),' in *The Limits of British Control in South Asia: Spaces of Disorder in the Indian Ocean Region*, ed. Ashwini Tambe and Harald Fisher (London: Routledge, 2009), 14.

[35] 'Unfair Competition with the Australian Ship-Owner,' *Australasian Seamen's Journal* 1 (1 May 1913).

It wasn't only unions who were acting to protect their economic self-interests. Competition was also faced by shipowners. When international ships called at capital city ports in search of cargo, they often took on cargo between capital cities to maximise the use of hold space.[36] Australian and New Zealand shipowners facing competition from overseas shipping lines exploiting Asian labourers also had a vested interest in 'the question of the employment of white British seamen.'[37] Extending the protective policy of Australia to its merchant shipping was 'to protect the Australian ship-owner from unfair competition from subsidised foreign ships or poorly paid crews.'[38] As Australian seafarers had formed into unions and Labor Party members began to win elections and even government, they were joining with other liberals and protectionists who wanted limitations placed on free trade, and labour began receiving some supportive measures from government. As the doctrine of free trade drove the content of UK merchant shipping laws, the Australian colonies were moving towards protectionism.

Shipping was an industry where employers were able to avoid introducing the improvements in conditions provided by new labour laws that were being introduced for shore-based workers. The 1894 UK Merchant Shipping Act tied seamen into 'a number of consolidated and fossilized requirements' of labour relationship, just as other workers were receiving the benefits of a more liberal interpretation that was being applied to the employment relationship.[39] Maritime labourers were not covered by immigration or domestic factory laws and sought protection by other means. Their conditions were behind their fellows on land in Britain as well as the Australasian colonies. One of the goals of seafarers was to receive the same level of protections being afforded workers in manufacturing industries. They had the support of the *Sydney Morning Herald*, which argued 'the material advantages offered to seamen must be at least equal to those offered to men who follow other walks of life. In simple justice they ought to be greater, for there is the element of risk to be considered.'[40]

As the *Sydney Morning Herald* said, the safety of ships depended on the men crewing them. 'We want a good class of men to fill positions as officers and A.B.'s [able seamen] on board our ships; yet we offer no inducements. ... boys and men of the class we require find ... their services are more highly appreciated' in the wages and treatment they

---

[36] Morgan, 'Labour and Industrial Authority,' 185.

[37] Shorten, 'Imperial Validity and Maritime Education,' 305.

[38] Royal Commission on the Navigation Act 1924, 2.

[39] Dixon, 'Seamen and the Law,' 300.

[40] 'White Sailors for Australian Ships,' 8.

could receive on land. This affected the quality of officers also: 'you will never get a good class of man, or a good supply, unless you improve his food, his pay, and his living and sleeping accommodation.' An Admiralty committee had also recommended increasing the number of meals on board ship.[41]

That shipping was particular and distinct as an industry was partially a consequence of the long history of UK merchant shipping laws attempting to deal with the anomaly of seamen's legal position. They were civil workers employed under a state-supervised contract with many penal clauses. The system of articles, that is the specific form of agreement under which seamen were employed, originated in legislation from 1729. Binding the system of wage payment together with several disciplinary provisions from then on 'always cast employment at sea into a category on its own.'[42] To prevent crews leaving their ship for another that was promising higher wages, the original disciplinary provisions were extended at the end of eighteenth century to include 'desertion' and limitations were imposed on the rate of wages a ship's master could pay. Provisions now also included a process of certification of discharge. This certificate prevented a seaman being charged with desertion and was to be produced when he signed on for a new voyage. In the mid-nineteenth century, the law enabled agreements to be for a period of time or a number of voyages rather than a single trip. Measures became increasingly sophisticated with the transition from sail to steam but the tradition of signing articles, in a prescribed form, continued in Britain with little alteration until the Merchant Shipping Act 1970. Even then, the substance remained essentially unchanged until its repeal in 1972.[43]

Britain's repeal in 1849 of its pre-industrial navigation laws enabled and permitted a limitless supply of cheap labour as it freed shipowners from the obligation to employ British-born seamen, and allowed the employment of Indian and other foreign nationals.[44] The consequent influx of foreign seamen was not matched by legislation protecting that labour, such as limiting hours, stipulating manning levels, or changing the contractual relationship between workers and shipowners, all measures that might

[41] 'White Sailors for Australian Ships,' 8.

[42] Kitchen, *Employment of Merchant Seamen*, 330.

[43] Kitchen, *Employment of Merchant Seamen*, 331, 332. See also Dixon, 'Seamen and the Law.'

[44] The literature on Indian seafarers is vast. For examples, see Laura Tabili, *'We Ask for British Justice': Workers and Racial Difference in Late Imperial Britain* (Ithaca, NY: Cornell University Press, 1994), 43–4; Conrad Dixon, 'Lascars: The Forgotten Seamen,' in *Working Men Who Got Wet*, ed. Rosemary Ommer and Gerald Panting (St. John's, Newfoundland: Memorial University of Newfoundland, 1980), 278.

have inhibited trade. The legal changes preceded but accelerated the shift from sail to steam, which deskilled seafaring work, and made it easier for shipowners to replace skilled seamen on higher wages with a new pool of underpaid workers.[45] Consequently, British shipping companies employed and circulated large numbers of seafarers across the empire.

The shipping laws allowed British shipowners to employ these crews of different nationalities under differentiated terms and conditions: Chinese, Arab, Malay or European articles of agreement each offered different employment terms. 'Indian articles of agreement offered the worst terms of engagement, whether in relation to wages, accommodation, or food rations.'[46] While the proportion of Indian seamen in the workforce increased significantly after 1849, their wages became the lowest in the industry.[47] In 1907, Indian seafarers were paid a quarter of the Australian rates of pay. Indian seamen's hours of work were unregulated, and under the watch system of 'all hands at all times' they were expected to be ready to work at any time. Restrictions on discharge outside India prevented Indian seamen from seeking higher pay and better conditions by signing on 'under regular articles' on arrival in Western ports.[48] Put simply, Indian seamen were not being recruited into the British maritime labour force as the equals of British seamen, but in a special category of labour, as 'Lascars,' the maritime equivalent of 'coolie' (Figure 2.2).[49] Maritime labour law was discriminatory and created a pool of exploitable colonial labour.

Cheapening the supply of shipping labour meant British seafarers also fell behind. Australian seafarers were classed as British in these racialised categories created by the British laws. Shipping was an industry in which Australian workers might well compete directly for employment with the poorer paid workers from India, China and other nearby countries. Wharf work – although not handled by the shipping lines themselves – was often performed by seafarers as part of their articles of employment, which meant there was also potential competition between cheap foreign labour and

---

[45] Hyslop, 'Steamship Empire,' 60.

[46] Balachandran, 'Circulation through Seafaring,' 103.

[47] G. Balachandran, 'Recruitment and Control of Indian Seamen, Calcutta, 1880–1935,' *International Journal of Maritime History* 9, no. 1 (1997): 1–2.

[48] Ahuja, 'Networks of Subordination,' 15–17.

[49] G. Balachandran, 'Making Coolies, (Un)making Workers: "Globalizing" Labour in the Late 19th and Early 20th Centuries,' *Journal of Historical Sociology* 24, no. 3 (2011): 266–96; Ahuja, 'Networks of Subordination,' 14–17; Ahuja, 'Mobility and Containment,' 111; G. Balachandran, *Globalizing Labour: Indian Seafarers and World Shipping, c.1870–1945* (New Delhi: Oxford University Press, 2012), 18; Broeze, 'Muscles of Empire: 45.

2.2 Group of Lascars who refused to sail, Sydney, 1939
SLNSW

Australian watersiders.[50] Many historians have seen the history only in those terms, but to do so is to obscure other factors that were in play as all seafarers struggled against their conditions as workers.

The concept of nineteenth-century British labour law did not allow for the massive migration within and between colonies and nation-states of labour under indenture, most notably from India, China and Melanesia. Models of coercion and forcible movement were developed within the empire according to the labour needs of local industries in the various colonies. Labour law covered only free and contractual labour and not workers whose experience did not fall into this narrow category. Indentured or cheap labour became synonymous with 'coloured' or 'Asiatic' labour, and terms like 'coolie' and 'Lascar.' The

---

[50] Morgan, 'Labour and Industrial Authority,' 184; Beasley, *Wharfies*, 31; A.E. Gay, *England's Duty to Her Merchant Seamen* (Adelaide: Sands & McDougall, 1906), 198, claimed foreign ships were cheaper partly because they used their own crews while British ships used local wharf labour.

decades spanning the end of the nineteenth century ended such bonded labour and gave contractual rights to some workers.[51] Seafarers were not immediately or fully included. Those with the organisational strength of unions or higher bargaining power were better placed to negotiate and campaign to their own advantage, against the idea that 'because men go to sea, apparently, they are not to be granted the support that would come unquestionably for other workers.'[52] The vast majority of workers in the British Empire who were not British and white were not so well positioned to gain protections.

Current research into the legacies of British slavery is showing there were connections between former slaveowners in other British colonies and those who became successful merchants and shipowners in the early Australian colonies. As maritime labourers were justifiably wary about the possibility of importing slavery and indentured labour systems, they sought to protect themselves through setting standards in the shipping industry. They too resorted to the language of race. The conditions on British ships employing underpaid labour from India and China were unacceptable by local Australian standards, regarded as 'the worst living ships afloat': Australian unionists wanted the standards of their working conditions to be legislated for 'in a manner befitting white men.'[53]

'[P]rotect[ing] the local seamen': Australia's Navigation Act

Drafting of the Australian Navigation Bill began in 1902, under the direction of South Australian MHR Charles Cameron Kingston, who held the portfolio of Trade and Customs in the first federal ministry. Kingston retired from parliament in 1903 and handed responsibility to a public servant, Harry Wollaston, comptroller-general of Customs and the first Secretary of the Commonwealth Department of Trade and Customs.[54] English Navigation Acts and Merchant Shipping Acts were always under the Board of Trade. Shipping was an industry where trade, labour and nation-building policies coalesced. The debate accordingly grew around the divisions over free trade versus protection that dominated Australian parliaments at the turn of the twentieth century. Shipping came under the

---

[51] Alessandro Stanziani, *Bondage: Labor and Rights in Eurasia from the Sixteenth to the Early Twentieth Century* (New York: Berghahn Books, 2014).

[52] 'Cheap Labour: Who Are the Anti-Australians? The Thin Edge of the Wedge,' *Australasian Seamen's Journal* 8, no. 46 (1 January 1925).

[53] Gay, *England's Duty*, 154; 'Newcastle Report' (1 July 1914).

[54] David Day, *Contraband and Controversy: The Customs History of Australia from 1901* (Canberra: AGPS Press, 1996), 4–9.

Department of Trade, and maritime labour standards were tied to freight rates, making worker protections hard to achieve.

The new Australian constitution continued the UK practice of locating merchant shipping within Trade and Customs, which made it, under section 51, a federal government power. The only authority to legislate on industrial matters was confined to the single power to make laws to settle industrial disputes crossing state borders. As is well known, the Commonwealth used this power to set up the Court of Conciliation and Arbitration, under legislation also drafted by Kingston in 1902. Giving the commonwealth parliament the power to regulate its overseas and interstate trade terms and conditions, the constitution empowered federal laws and regulations for workers employed in the coastal shipping trade, under the administration of the Minister for Trade and Customs. The two constitutional powers of arbitration and trade developed legislation simultaneously in a conjunction of federal workplace and employment regulation of the maritime workforce. At the beginning of the twentieth century, wages and standards of employment on coastal ships were being set by industrial tribunals under the arbitration power, while minimum standards were to be set for ships arriving and engaging in trade on the Australian coast under the Navigation Act.

The Navigation Bill was introduced into the Senate in 1904, the same year as the Conciliation and Arbitration Act was passed. The bill did not arouse debate as a public issue in the way that industrial arbitration did except in relation to the training of officers, which had been omitted.[55] Wollaston, who had carriage of the bill on the floor of parliament, explained that it was adapting British legislation to suit Australian conditions. This might have been a reference to the fact that most seafarers employed in Australia (as was also true in New Zealand) were not born in Australia, and the boys who were Australian born, as the *Sydney Morning Herald* noted, were not attracted to seafaring. Wollaston argued the bill was designed to improve the wellbeing of seamen, to raise standards and make seafaring attractive to Australian youth, 'to encourage our young people to go to sea ... to raise the status of officers and seamen' and to establish 'a mercantile marine of our own.'[56] This was consistent with the principle known as cabotage enshrined in the original UK navigation acts for nationals to be employed in national merchant marines. The press noted that now 'Britain alone' was employing foreigners rather than sailors of its own nationality. The purpose of the Australian bill was to improve the conditions, and thus increase the attractions of sea life to 'people,' meaning obliquely 'white British seamen.'

---

[55] Shorten, 'Imperial Validity and Maritime Education,' 307–11.
[56] Shorten, 'Imperial Validity and Maritime Education,' 311.

'Our young people' meant Australians, who were classified as 'British,' and from now on were to be white under the new immigration policies.

The colonists of Australia (now citizens of the Commonwealth) were identifying and distinguishing themselves as 'British Australian' rather than British, with a regional outlook that positioned them in a proximate relationship to Asia. With Asian countries an increasing source of seafaring labour employed by British shipping companies, Australian labour and its newly elected Labor Party parliamentarians were pitched into conflict with British origins and imperial shipping interests as they sought to defend the nation from the possibility of being overwhelmed or even invaded by powerful Asian neighbours. Press interest in the Australian Navigation Bill, otherwise minimal, was aroused only in its relation to the White Australia policy. The parliamentary debate, however, did not use the language of white sailors; that was left to the press.

In an expression of this national identity at the moment of Federation, the *Sydney Morning Herald*'s editorial called for 'white sailors for Australian ships,' thereby equating 'Australian' with whiteness as it simultaneously spoke of the necessary qualities of the 'British race' for a national merchant navy. 'We ... claim for men of British race [a] preeminence in nautical matters. Indeed, it has been proved on thousands of occasions that in the time of danger the seaman of this stock is the man who unobtrusively does heroic work and blushes to find it fame.'[57] The editorial avoided denigrating Asians, instead using language that emphasised the qualities of Britishness, only mentioning some other European nations, and asking, simply, 'How are we to preserve this breed of heroes in its natural element?'[58]

In keeping with its intention to limit the British use of colonial labour, the Australian Navigation Act specifically applied only to 'British' ships, stipulating the number and nature of crews. All such ships had to have a duly certificated master and officers of differing grades who had to be British subjects and English-speaking. It included provisions relating to the qualifications of officers, the supply, engagement and discharge of crews, the payment of their wages, health and accident benefits, discipline and accommodation, as well as provisions as to safety, equipment, unseaworthy ships and prevention of collisions.[59] The Seamen's Union urged the Labor caucus on behalf of deck crew to support the new bill.[60] The engineers' union, the Australian Institute of Marine Engineers (AIME), founded in 1881, also supported the measure. They saw the bill as the means to better

---

[57] 'White Sailors for Australian Ships,' 8.
[58] 'White Sailors for Australian Ships,' 8.
[59] Helmore, 'Validity of State Navigation Acts.'
[60] Shorten, 'Imperial Validity and Maritime Education.'

their conditions, achieve an eight-hour day and establish proper control over the selection and competency of officers. They opposed certification that allowed those with no workshop training to take charge of small vessels.[61]

In 1903, a deputation of SUA members of parliament called on then Attorney-General Alfred Deakin to urge an early passage of the bill. But when informed this was unlikely, they asked that the government would separate the general navigation bill from the clauses concerning the competition between foreign-owned vessels with low-waged crews and Australian-owned vessels for the strictly local trade between Commonwealth ports. They urged that these clauses should be put into a separate bill together with provisions relating to the efficiency of seamen and the administration of legislation concerning their safety and wellbeing.[62] Perhaps they thought this would assist in getting it passed more quickly.

The bill was not passed on that first attempt. It was withdrawn and referred to a Royal Commission because of the complex legal as well as economic issues it raised and the opposition coming from free traders. Principally, the bill raised legal questions about the new commonwealth's jurisdiction over control of manning levels, certification of officers and regulation of the coastal shipping trade within the imperial context. The law could not 'be repugnant' to British imperial legislation that was applicable to the Australian Commonwealth, and the Australian parliament could only repeal sections of the British Merchant Shipping Act of 1894 with approval of the King in Council.

Hughes chaired the Royal Commission and was joined by eight others, four of them from the ALP, among them Senator Robert Guthrie (1856–1921), at that time also Seamen's Union president. Guthrie, unlike Hughes, had been a working seafarer. Since arriving from Scotland in 1878, Guthrie had worked in the coastal trade and as secretary of the South Australian branch of the Seamen's Union. He had been elected Labor member first to the South Australian parliament coincidentally with the Liberal government of Charles Kingston (who had drafted the federal Arbitration Bill) and moved to represent South Australia in the Senate on federation. He was deeply committed to improving seafarers' lives although doing so risked him becoming identified with the reformist liberal middle class more than the union members who crewed the coastal ships. According to the press in his home state, 'Few men have been more closely identified with Australian navigation matters or more intimately associated with Australian seamen,' than Guthrie.[63]

---

[61] Broomham, *Steady Revolutions*, 76.

[62] 'Federal Navigation Law Will Not Pass This Session. Seamen Want an Early Instalment,' *Age* (Melbourne), 1 May 1903, 6.

[63] 'The Navigation Conference,' 4.

Guthrie has been held responsible for much of the Navigation Act and his knowledge of the maritime industry was considered vital to the work of the Royal Commission. He was assisted by Hughes and Samuel Mauger, an anti-sweating Protectionist MP, in the probing questioning of witnesses. They elicited information of poor wages and sometimes unpaid labour as men worked the cost of their passage in long hours under unhealthy, dangerous conditions. Witnesses told of a lack of protection against injury, and of being forced to desert by ships' masters trying to avoid paying their wages. An equal number of maritime workers were witnesses as were officers. Also called were shipowners, traders, state government officials and doctors. It was a comprehensive investigation of the shipping industry in Australia. At the time, there were no minimum manning levels. The Sea Carriage of Goods Act of 1904 stipulated that ships had to be seaworthy and properly manned at the start of a voyage, but without means of enforcement the shipowners retained the power to decide what that meant. Guthrie pressed continually and extracted evidence of ships that 'were overloaded, unseaworthy and dangerous.'[64] He helped expose the plight of crews who were thus undertaking dangerous work, in the absence of workers' compensation legislation.

While deck crew had inferior living conditions, and engineers worked long hours in high temperatures, officers worked excessive hours that were serious for safety. The AIME used the delay between the introduction of the legislation in 1904 and the Royal Commission's report to lobby parliamentary committees. Crew requirements and manning levels were not specified by the Merchant Shipping Act of 1894, so could not be checked during inspections for seaworthiness and shipping losses. The Royal Commission investigated the cause of shipping accidents and concluded that undermanning, the exhaustion of officers and the frequency of shipwrecks were interrelated and just as dangerous as weak construction and overloading of ships. A former seafarer urged reforms would be 'for the welfare of shipowners, sailors ... in fact *the whole Empire!*'[65]

'[T]o increase the attractions of sea life'

The Royal Commission documented the increasing use of foreign labour in the Australian and international sea trade. Guthrie's determination to improve seafarers' conditions was apparent in its recommendations: for further consideration of the preference for British shipowners and producers in Australian trade, the employment of British seamen, the extension of the

[64] Stephen Garton, 'Robert Guthrie,' in *The Biographical Dictionary of the Australian Senate*, vol. 1, *1901–1929*, ed. Ann Millar (Melbourne: Melbourne University Press, 2000), 168–71.

[65] Broomham, *Steady Revolutions*, 76; Gay, *England's Duty*, 178.

Workers' Compensation Act to cover seamen and light load lines for vessels. The Commissioners' report argued strongly for the necessity of improved shipboard conditions and the frequent, regular payment of wages. The Commissioners focused on the low standards of British ships in dining and sleeping accommodation, 'the wretched conditions more akin to the East End of London or the slums of New York.' While foreign ships provided hot and cold running water, British ships provided single buckets for washing. The Commissioners called for more space and better ventilation, enhanced lighting in the sleeping quarters, quality food, the provision of hot water and proper sanitation ('urinals and privies'). They wanted the punishments for desertion to be abandoned and drew comparisons with European- and American-owned ships whose crews were better provided for. They were emphatic in their argument that provisions should apply to all ships registered in Australia, licensed to trade on the Australian coast, or whose articles of employment were drawn up in Australia and whose crews were discharged in Australia.

Arguing for improvements might have been to attract Australian deck crews and officers to shipping, as the *Sydney Morning Herald* had long before called for, but all crews were to have these minimum Australian standards, whatever their national/racial origins. British seamen too would nearly double the rates of their wages while their ships were in Australasian territorial waters, automatically falling back to the normal British level once the ship left.[66] The Commission's view was more concerned with keeping maritime conditions up to speed with the improving conditions under factory awards: 'There does not seem to be any reason why seamen should not be treated as well as men on shore.'[67] Guthrie's policy was to declare repeatedly that there must be a minimum wage to ensure a decent standard of living and measures to ensure that employers could not subvert this standard by their preference for foreign labour. Employers would have to pay indentured labour the same wages. When asked if British shipping companies would now 'be compelled to substitute white seamen for her ordinary Lascar crew,' Minister Lyne replied, 'Not necessarily, but [they] would have to pay the lascars white men's wages while in Australia, and' he added, to emphasise the point, 'not English, but Australian white men's wages.'[68]

In 1906, both the Navigation Bill and the Royal Commission report were again presented to parliament but stalled when its advocates were called to attend the imperial Merchant Shipping Legislation conference in London. As chair of that conference, Lloyd George was open to the colonial initiatives. He had been

---

[66] 'The Navigation Conference,' 4.
[67] Royal Commission on the Navigation Bill, 1906, *Report*.
[68] 'The Navigation Conference,' 4.

influenced by the Australian Royal Commission's report and incorporated its principal recommendations into the Merchant Shipping Amendment Act the new government passed in 1906. By the time the Australian delegates arrived for the conference in early 1907, their most important suggestions had been accepted although there were still important differences to be ironed out, most notably 'hostility to the determination of the Colonies to regulate shipping on their own coasts.'[69] Legally, the Board of Trade questioned whether Australia and New Zealand had the power to vary the Imperial law.[70] The Imperial Conference was called 'to consider to what extent Australia may legislate as affecting British and foreign shipping ... and to decide what powers British colonies possess, to penalise oversea shipping in favour of colonially owned vessels.'[71] The proposed conference was to reach some uniformity and remove ambiguities that existed in the constitutional arrangement. British officials and shipowners were concerned the Dominions were requiring them to meet different standards depending on a ship's port of call, and that these standards were not enforceable on their foreign competitors.[72]

Hughes was the most knowledgeable of the Australians present and, along with Guthrie, an experienced union negotiator. He was able to persuade the bureaucrats and win the consent of the shipowners to the essentials by his willingness to compromise on some details. The Australian delegation thus secured a victory at the Imperial Conference. Not unlike the 1835 UK Act, which had distinguished between foreign-going and home-trade vessels, the conference recommended 'that the coastal trade of the [Australian] Common-wealth be reserved for ships ... conforming to Australian conditions and licensed to trade on the Australian coast.' One British shipowner who attended claimed, 'We have lost nearly everything that we contended for.'[73] Another (who didn't attend) complained, 'from the English point of view,' Australia 'has the most narrowly selfish and provincially exclusive shipping combine in any part of the world' because it included both employers and workers. 'The officers formed a union, the engineers formed a union, and firemen and seamen formed a union, all for the purpose of forcing up wages, shortening the hours, increasing the number of hands, liberalizing the diet, and extending the shipboard accommodation.' It didn't stop there. Australian shipowners had also organised to eliminate competition and increase the charges for freight and passengers. 'Then all these unions or "rings" co-operated to "freeze out" the ships of the British companies which were outside the combine.' Political

[69] Fitzhardinge, *Hughes*, 184, 187.
[70] Fitzhardinge, *Hughes*, 183.
[71] 'The Navigation Conference,' 4.
[72] Fitzhardinge, *Hughes*, 183, 187.
[73] 'The Navigation Conference,' 4.

lobbying of the Commonwealth Government, 'by the shipowners on the one hand and the Seamen's Union on the other,' led to the bill which now compelled British-owned ships trading on the Australian and New Zealand coasts to pay Australian and New Zealand rates of wages and conform to all other local shipping conditions.[74]

The challenge now was to get the legislation passed through the Australian parliament. The Navigation Bill was revised and reintroduced into the Australian Senate but still it struggled to pass in 1907, 1908 and 1910 until finally it succeeded late in 1912. Once passed, the Act was reserved for the Royal Assent as required, and for many months, in Britain and Australia, shipowners and free traders campaigned against its becoming law. Shipowners opposed its protective provisions for Australian seamen.[75] British shipowners maintained that 'colonial' legislation ought not to apply to British ships. Australian owners objected that the Navigation Act would enormously increase their costs, for each seaman's accommodation would have to be almost doubled and compensation would have to be paid for sick and injured crew. Various companies employing white labour explained their costs would nearly double. Companies like P&O, who employed Lascars, would automatically have to increase their wages fourfold; they 'would actually have to pay as much' in wages as the Orient and White Star Companies. Having twice the number of crew, they would also have to provide twice the living accommodation, which 'would practically leave no room for passengers.'[76]

The controversy within the British government and among British shipping interests meant the Act did not become operational until well after the end of the First World War. The Act was shelved until after the 1914 federal election, then the outbreak of war postponed it further as the British government requested its implementation be delayed.[77] Labor Party Prime Minister Andrew Fisher announced it would be proclaimed in 1916, but he left office before that could be achieved. Instead, that year the country was convulsed by the conscription plebiscite and the ALP lost government. It took until 1921 before the first sections, the Coasting Trade provisions, were proclaimed, and it was not until 1923 that most of the other provisions were operative and vessels had to comply with Australian standards – the highest wages, accommodation and manning scales in the world.[78] Protectionists

[74] 'The Navigation Conference,' 4.

[75] Correspondence between Imperial and Commonwealth governments, 24 April 1911 (Comm. P.P., 1911), vol. 2, 1045; Fitzpatrick and Cahill, *History of the Seamen's Union of Australia*, 47.

[76] 'The Navigation Conference,' 4.

[77] Royal Commission on the Navigation Act 1924, 2.

[78] Royal Commission on the Navigation Act 1924, 2; 'The Navigation Conference,' 4.

encountered similar trouble with the Seamen's Compensation Act that was first passed in 1909 to give seafarers more generous compensation for injuries received while working on board ship than did the UK law. A second Act had to be passed two years later to take account of the High Court's judgment that the Commonwealth had no constitutional power to pass laws for ships only moving around the ports of a single state. Again, the shipowners challenged, but this time the High Court declared the Act valid.[79]

The Navigation Act was an initiative for labour standards that grew out of the changing 'racism/defence of jobs and wages relationship' in the growing steamship trade.[80] The Navigation Bill and subsequent Royal Commission report were couched in the language of labour standards and the much older principle of cabotage while the emphasis was on the unacceptable conditions of British ships and on raising the standards for all. This language obscured the racial dimensions of legislation that was intended to ensure protections for the crews and was taken for granted as excluding Asian crews.[81]

These legislative foundations laid the basis for political positioning for decades and grounded the maritime unions' ensuing campaign to maintain Australian labour standards. Once ships arrived on the Australian coast and carried their passengers and goods from port to port, they had to abide by provisions determined in Australian legislation. According to Percy Clarey, president of the Australian Council of Trade Unions (ACTU) and Minister for Labour in the Chifley ALP government (1945–49), this was 'the best navigation act in the world.' As an MP in 1952, he said 'it was an earnest attempt on the part of the Australian parliament to give seamen reasonable and decent conditions of employment, and make the maritime industry as safe as possible.'[82] It recognised that the maritime workplace was 'a special category compared with all other locations of industry.'[83] That recognition was also incorporated in the maritime deliberations of the International Labour Organization when it was set up in 1919. Only then did the Australian Navigation Act become operational. In the meantime, Asian crews sailing into Australian ports were subjected to the new provisions of the White Australia policy.

---

[79] Fitzpatrick and Cahill, *History of the Seamen's Union of Australia*, 48.

[80] Curthoys, 'Conflict and Consensus,' 64.

[81] One who has investigated the issue in Australia is Martínez, '"Coolies" to Comrades.'

[82] Australia, Parliament, Hansard, 1952, 3690.

[83] Australia, Parliament, Hansard, 1952, 3664.

3

'The Commonwealth and the Lascars'

Protecting Maritime Workers in a 'White Australia,'
1901 to 1914

Maritime labourers from Asia faced new restrictions on their movements and harsh treatment by officials following the passage of the Australian Immigration Restriction Act (1901) and New Zealand's two measures (in 1908 and again in 1920) controlling entry and settlement on racial grounds.[1] There were also, however, moments of connection with Australian unions.

One unexpected encounter occurred in the port of Brisbane in the summer of 1912. Workers had called a general city-wide strike, and members of the WWF were consequently refusing to unload cargo. Non-unionists had been brought in and were waiting on the wharf to get started when a British-owned vessel, the *Ockenfels*, arrived at the wharf with its Indian crew. Although ordered to assist the non-strikers with unloading, the *Ockenfels* crew instead walked off the ship. According to the local strikers, the crew 'turned in disgust … and flatly refused to scab.'[2] The group of 15 then 'marched in a body to the Trades Hall where their arrival caused a great scene of enthusiasm, and from which they marched back to the ship proudly wearing the little red badge, the unionists' Victoria Cross.' To the WWF this was an undoubted and very welcome sign of solidarity, all the more important because this was a crew of South Asian seafarers, and they had been the ones to initiate the action. It came as a surprise. To have 'our black brothers refuse to scab,' was taken as a sign of 'Socialism break[ing] down the barriers of race,' the Strike Committee's Bulletin declared, 'the dawn of a brighter day' appearing.[3] The 'barriers of race' were inherent in

---

[1] 'The Commonwealth and the Lascars,' *The Argus* (Melbourne), 24 June 1904, 6; P.S. O'Connor, 'Keeping New Zealand White, 1908–1920,' *New Zealand Journal of History* 2, no. 1 (1968): 41–65.

[2] 'Lascar Unionists, Our Black Comrades Refuse to "Scab." And March to Trades Hall,' Official Bulletin no. 11, issued by the Strike Committee, Brisbane, 12 February 1912.

[3] 'Lascar Unionists, Our Black Comrades Refuse to "Scab."'

3.1 Bombay dock workers on strike, 23 April 1932
Smith Archive/Alamy. From Planet News/TopFoto, Kent

the policies implemented by the shipping companies, in the government's policy of immigration restriction and in elements of the Australian labour movement. The *Ockenfels* story reveals another possibility as a trade union movement emerged in India (Figure 3.1).

'Mak[ing] ... unjust discrimination between races'

The White Australia policy was introduced by liberal protectionists, the nation's first Prime Minister Edmund Barton and his Attorney-General Alfred Deakin.[4] Its opponents included free traders who believed in the freedom of labour to move, or be moved like goods, to where it was needed: and those who had commercial and cultural interests and thought excluding Asians would needlessly offend Australia's nearest regional neighbours.[5] The Labor Party was prominent among its many advocates but restricting immigration on racial criteria was widely supported across the political spectrum. Even notable progressives such as Arbitration court judge Henry Bournes Higgins and founder of the Victorian Socialist Party, journalist R.S. Ross, held views about racial hierarchies and expressed racist sentiments.[6] It is easy to point to racism and find what historian John Rickard has called 'the slimier excrescences'[7] of its expression in the Australian press (most notably the *Bulletin*) and public statements of the late nineteenth and early twentieth centuries. It requires more searching to find the views of those who had a more open and cosmopolitan vision. They also crossed the political spectrum. Some were liberal humanitarians and Christian believers in universal brotherhood of all people; others were socialists pursuing worker internationalism, activists in the labour movement or traders in commerce.

The most vocal union espousing anti-Asian immigration views was the Australian Workers' Union (AWU), a land-based shearers and agricultural labourers' organisation.[8] Immigration restriction was also a labour policy designed to prevent the use/introduction of/capacity for indentured or enslaved labour which was favoured for the workforce by pastoralists and agriculturalists, and those keen to develop the more remote tropical areas of the Australian continent. In the debate on the bill, the ALP position was 'almost as much concerned over the threat to wages offered by the entry

---

[4] Yarwood, *Asian Migration*, 22–32. See Brett, *Enigmatic Mr. Deakin*.

[5] Kane Collins, 'Early Critics of White Australia, 1870–1914' (PhD thesis, Deakin University, 2006).

[6] Kirk, *Transnational Radicalism*; John Rickard, *H.B. Higgins: The Rebel as Judge* (Sydney: Allen & Unwin, 1984).

[7] Rickard, *Higgins*, 131.

[8] John Merrett, *The Making of the AWU* (Melbourne: Oxford University Press, 1986).

of European workmen under contracts made in ignorance of Australian conditions as over coloured immigration': it was not always clear whether a contract of indenture existed or not.[9] The maritime unions' leaders – Billy Hughes of the WWF and Bob Guthrie of the Federated Seamen's Union of Australasia (FSUA) – were ALP members of parliament. Their support for the policy initially reflected a more nuanced position of protectionism for all workers, though for Hughes it became more racially motivated over time.

The maritime unions were not usually concerned with migration, assimilation and reproducing the racial characteristics of the population which drove the worst of the arguments for a White Australia. Their public concerns were with protecting and maintaining wage rates and labour standards, not with assimilating (or not) new arrivals. They were keen to see restrictions imposed on foreign workers and were willing to use the means to hand though there was some confusion about how that might be done. When immigration restriction legislation was enacted, some SUA officials mistakenly believed it was intended as a measure to forbid foreign crews participating in the Australian coastal shipping trade. They were quickly corrected of their misapprehension.[10] While in port, ships' crews were exempted from the provisions of the Immigration Act, under section 3(k), which required the master to hold a crew muster and account for all members before his ship could depart again.[11] In 1910, during a strike by local unions, the WWF wanted to prevent a Chinese crew unloading a ship's cargo, and called on the government to apply the immigration provisions. Hughes, at that time Attorney-General, informed them that the crew was exempted under section 3(k) and the provisions of the Immigration Act did not apply.[12]

The immigration law excluded Asian people in order to keep the population unmixed and monocultural. But it also excluded 'those who might be prepared to come under contract to work for wages which, in the Australian people's opinion, were insufficient … and which would react injuriously on Australian employment.'[13] These restrictions were not limited by ethnicity or race to non-Europeans, they applied to all would-be immigrants from any country, although officials administering the policy were told to concentrate their attention on non-Europeans. While this may have been a logical outcome of the movement of indentured labour from China and India, it made the policy racially based, indiscriminately applicable to all 'non-white' people. From

---

[9] Fitzhardinge, *Hughes*, 164.

[10] 'Federal Navigation Law Will Not Pass This Session.'

[11] Yarwood, *Asian Migration*, 158.

[12] Yarwood, *Asian Migration*, 119.

[13] Willard, *White Australia Policy*, 121–2.

the 1860s, employers in the Australian colonies had also imported bonded labour from the Pacific Islands to work on sugar plantations.[14] Legislation to deport many of these Pacific Islanders and to disallow the entry of more quickly followed the immigration restriction legislation, another racially discriminatory act with the damaging purpose of creating a homogeneous whiteness. Even some Europeans were unacceptable as labour migrants. A proposal to recruit Italians for the Queensland cane fields was rejected by Minister Hughes in 1904, who, while claiming 'we should certainly not make any unjust discrimination between races,' yet made it clear that Northern Europeans were preferred because of the belief they would more readily assimilate.[15] Flaws in this reasoning were rarely pointed out.

For maritime labourers, immigration exclusion was less relevant than their concerns about labour conditions. These were tied to allowances the British government gave to private companies for the carriage of mails to Australia, which had profound consequences for the colonial seagoing workforce. Mail contracts made by the UK government on behalf of its colonies contained no restrictions on the sourcing, employment and proportion of national or foreign, including 'coloured,' crews. That grew in significance as the service to Australia – which was only one of their routes – necessarily came via Asian ports. South Asians, employed as 'Lascars,' were employed on the Australia, China and India route. In 1895, there were two lines carrying the mails under contract from Britain via the Suez Canal. The first, the Orient Company, employed only white labour. The second, P&O, had 'colored crews, [for] the whole of the deck hands and firemen.'[16] P&O's head, Sir Thomas Sutherland, claimed the company was 'obliged to employ Lascars' on their routes in the Indian Ocean and China seas. Sydney's *Daily Telegraph* predicted 'the trend of public opinion' would force the company to stop employing Lascars on their Australian liners; that if they wanted to continue their mail contracts, 'even [Sutherland] can't justify the exclusion of European sailors from Australian liners.'[17]

It seems the maritime unions held a pragmatic approach towards race nationalism, supporting it when their commitment to fair labour standards was advantaged by endorsing these as being white. Early on, Guthrie formulated the SUA's view which never wavered: 'What we say is that conditions ought to be fair all round. If oversea vessels engage in the

[14] Tracey Banivanua-Mar, *Violence and Colonial Dialogue: The Australian-Pacific Indentured Labor Trade* (Honolulu: University of Hawaii Press, 2007).

[15] Fitzhardinge, *Hughes*, 164.

[16] *Sunday Times* (Sydney), 17 February 1895, 5.

[17] 'Lascars and the P. and O.,' *Daily Telegraph* (Sydney), 'From our Special Correspondent,' 26 May 1896, 2.

interstate trade they must pay Australian rates of wages.'[18] That was the intention of the Navigation Act.

Shipowners were among those employers who hired labour on conditions to drive down costs and which were often described as being akin to slavery, with coerced or bonded forms of labour. It wasn't only wages that were low. Standards on board ship were at the centre of union concerns. They called for changes in the living arrangements and complained of the poor food and crew accommodation as designed to accommodate only 'coloured' crews. In 1906, Guthrie called representatives of the different state branches of the FSUA to a meeting that discussed the evidence of the Royal Commission, including the unhealthy condition of forecastles on many of the steamers and the unnecessary hardships which seamen therefore had to endure, such as the lack of bathrooms when the men working in the stokehold 'require[d] a bath almost as much as they do food.' From this meeting came the newly named Seamen's Union of Australia, a more national organisation than the loose federation of different colonial bodies that had been functioning before. Binding together the several various branches of the union, Guthrie said, would enable the members to initiate reforms in their working conditions, 'without in any way clashing with the interests of the shipowners, with whom it is intended to work harmoniously.' The meeting went a step further and decided actually to 'assist the ship owners to fight the unfair trade' – i.e., the competition between ocean-going steamers and interstate vessels on the coast – 'by bringing pressure to bear on the authorities to pass legislation.' The Melbourne press described the meeting as the 'most important yet held.'[19]

The issue of White Australia came to the fore when existing mail contracts were replaced when the colonies federated, and the new Commonwealth parliament passed the Post and Telegraph Act (No. 12) of 1901. The new Act stipulated that for future government mail contracts (from 1905), the companies could not employ 'coloured labour' on ships carrying Australian mail. The *Australasian* reported that 'It appears to be assumed that the new terms finally agreed to [were to be] the exclusion of lascars and Chinese from the stokehold, the forecastle, and the pantry.' While this solution 'may prove embarrassing to the Imperial authorities,' who refused to ban British subjects from employment 'simply on the basis they were of Asiatic race,' the *Australasian* suggested they could limit themselves to carrying the mails between London and Colombo, thus leaving Australians responsible for arrangements only 'for the section of the service which specially concerns Australia.'[20]

---

[18] 'Seamen's Conference. What the Men Seek,' *Argus* (Melbourne), 15 May 1906, 7.

[19] 'Seamen's Conference,' *Age*, 14 May 1906, 6.

[20] *Australasian*, 7 September 1901, 35.

Therefore, the Post and Telegraph Act (No. 12 of 1901) prevented the Commonwealth from making contracts for the shipping of the mail 'with any line of steamships that employed other than "white labour."'[21] It meant that the colonial arrangement between the federal government and the P&O shipping company to carry the mail from Britain to Australia for a subsidy could not continue unless the British company ceased the employment of Lascars. As the Lascars were from India, and therefore also part of the Empire, British authorities reportedly could not agree to exclusion 'solely on the ground of colour' and they ended the mail contract with Australia.[22] The Colonial Secretary had made it clear during the discussions on the immigration act that overt racial discrimination was to be avoided, especially naming the countries whose populations were to be excluded as this would offend fellow-Empire member India, and Japan, with which Britain had hopes for an alliance.[23]

The British could, however, and did, still allow the shipowners, notably the P&O company, to differentiate their labour force on the grounds of colour, and pay wages and conditions according to hierarchies of racial difference, so that South Asian crews or 'Lascars' remained – and became even more so – the most underpaid crews in British shipping. British authorities' disagreement with Australia seemed to be less about its policy on race per se than it was a conflict over the newly emergent nationalist protective labour policies, known as 'New Protection.' These required employers to pay minimum wages (i.e., now 'white men's wages') and remove the class of cheapened colonial (i.e., 'coloured') labour moving 'unfreely' around the Empire. Free traders dominated the House of Commons and principles for regulating labour in the interests of the shipping companies continued to be the mainstay of British merchant shipping legislation. Australia meanwhile sought to ensure labour standards by adopting a policy of protection by legislation (the Navigation Act) that was openly positioned in an avowedly racialised frame. In the new Commonwealth, economic and racial protectionism fused and became mutually reinforcing.

Amendments to the immigration law subsequently made the criteria more rigorous and narrow. Special treaties were entered into with the governments of Japan, India and China to ameliorate offence and allow special conditions of entry to merchants, students and family members of current residents.[24] The procedural provisions obscured explicit reference to race by establishing a language dictation ('education') test and allowed bureaucrats a huge

[21] Willard, *White Australia Policy*, 128.

[22] Willard, *White Australia Policy*, 128.

[23] Yarwood, *Asian Migration*, 26.

[24] A.C. Palfreeman, *The Administration of the White Australia Policy* (Melbourne: Melbourne University Press, 1967), 7–9.

breadth of discretion.[25] It was not only employment on subsidised mail ships that was now an issue in Australian waters. In the first decade of the twentieth century, with the formal institution of the new policy, Asian crews came under more surveillance and were vulnerable to new legal sanctions. The largest group to be affected were South Asian crews, the Lascars who had been sailing on British ships for virtually a century.

'Lascar seamen are often cruelly treated'

Concern about the employment of Lascars by British shipowners dated back to the period of the Napoleonic wars.[26] The first UK parliamentary investigation of Lascars on British ships was held in 1814 when the colonial settlement in New South Wales was less than 30 years old.[27] Reports of Lascars in Australian colonial ports, coming ashore for religious celebrations,[28] or in actions to protest at their conditions or circumstances,[29] appeared regularly in the press as the colony grew. By century's end, the residents of Sydney had 'become tolerably familiar with the appearance of the lascars employed on these boats.'[30] Circular Quay, where the ships docked in Sydney Harbour, was just at the end of the main business streets of the city. There people could see the Lascar crews 'squatting upon the wharf or the adjacent ground, preparing or eating their meals, washing their clothing, or simply [talking] amongst themselves, [in] their garments, of many hues.'[31] While the vessel was lying at the wharf, they could be seen on board busy at the various occupations, scouring and painting the decks and doing small repairs necessary during the stay in port.

There were some colonists, this reporter inferred, who might delight in the visual spectacle, the quaintness and diversity Indian crews brought to the townscape. Occasionally they ventured beyond the immediate area of the Quay, to sell 'birds, walking sticks, and other Eastern curiosities,' or set up a stand in some city nook. On Sundays they favoured the Botanic Gardens,

---

[25] Yarwood, *Asian Migration*; Palfreeman, *White Australia Policy*, 3.

[26] 'Lascar Seamen Are Often Cruelly Treated,' *Sydney Monitor*, 19 January 1833, 2.

[27] Report from the Committee on Lascars and other Asiatic Seamen, 1814–15 (No. 471), vol. 3, 217, cited in Quinlan, 'Regulating Labour.' See also Dixon, 'Seamen and the Law.'

[28] Ian Simpson, 'Cultural Encounters in a Colonial Port: The 1806 Sydney Muharram,' *Australian Historical Studies* 43, no. 3 (2012): 381–95, based on George Howe in *Sydney Gazette*, 24 July 1808.

[29] 'Lascars Protesting Their Conditions,' *Australian*, 17 February 1825, 2; 'Mutiny ...,' *Australian* (1831).

[30] 'Among the Lascars. How They Live, Dress, and Work,' *Sunday Times* (Sydney), 17 February 1895, 5.

[31] 'Among the Lascars.'

especially in the quiet hours before noon, wandering in groups 'seemingly much interested in the flora of the gardens.' Their presence lent 'a decidedly picturesque aspect' to the ships, 'and imparts color and character to the [city] scene.' There was an exotic oriental flair to these young men 'coming out in snow white trousers, colored tunics, and fez caps, with all sorts of gorgeous embroideries and bright colored turbans'; they almost resembled 'exotic plants.'[32] There was an attractiveness about their youthfulness, physical attributes and bearing: 'chatting and laughing in an animated fashion ... in their scarlet turbans and blue tunics ... [with] particularly regular features and bright black eyes' and carriage 'with an air of no little importance.' These were 'fellow subjects of our own,' to be welcomed as 'natives of the great Indian Empire over which the Sovereign of Great Britain reigns as titular Empress.'[33]

As workers, however, their quaintness and status as 'fellow subjects' disappeared: they were preferred by the shipping masters because they were thought to be sober, exploitable and docile, to be employed cheaply. Yet there were numerous instances of Lascars – 'rebellious,' 'troublesome,' 'aggrieved' – standing up for the rights that were given to them within the legislation, of 'refusing to sail,'[34] and sometimes consequently appearing in the local courts.[35] These were 'efforts to improvise opportunities for potential resistance within the elaborate regulations governing their employment' that Gopalan Balachandran argues were carefully chosen, deliberate actions that were only taken when in port, not while at sea where the power of the master was greatest. We can see further evidence of this kind of collective resistance by ships' crews in other reports, of them rioting[36] or of 'mutinies' sparked by ill treatment inflicted by their masters.[37] Balachandran's observation that resistance might have been simmering for weeks while ships were at sea, and erupted when they arrived in port, or at other moments of activity, is a pattern evident in incidents found in colonial reporting.[38]

[32] 'Among the Lascars.'

[33] 'Among the Lascars.'

[34] 'Rebellious Lascars – Refusing to Sail,' *Evening News* (Sydney), 8 January 1900, 6; 'Troublesome Lascars,' *South Australian Register*, 15 February 1900, 6.

[35] As in *Adelaide Observer*, 17 May 1851, 8; *Sydney Morning Herald*, 26 May 1864, 4; 'Mutinous Lascars,' *Daily Telegraph* (Sydney), 28 November 1890, 5; 'Strike of Lascars,' *Evening News* (Sydney), 29 November 1888, 5.

[36] As on the SS *Mongolia*. See *Sydney Morning Herald*, 16 December 1908, 6; 17 December 1908, 7; 18 December 1908, 4; 19 December 1908, 6.

[37] *Brisbane Courier*, 7 February 1852, 4; 'Murder on the High Seas,' *Geelong Advertiser & Squatters Advocate*, 17 December 1845, 1; 'Lascar Seamen Are Often Cruelly Treated,' *Sydney Monitor*, 19 January 1833, 2; *Empire* (Sydney), 7 February 1862, 5.

[38] Balachandran, 'Cultures of Protest.'

New legal provisions under the Immigration Restriction Act 1901 imposed restrictions on their movement and gave new meaning to the issue of 'desertion,' which was already a punishable offence for seafaring crews. On completing the period of employment for which they had signed articles, South Asian crews became 'prohibited immigrants' in Australia under the 1901 legislation and could not wander freely. It was always their right to be (and the shipowners' responsibility to ensure they were) repatriated to their home port. Ensuring this was done was one of the challenges faced by crews with unscrupulous masters. The immigration law provided for new penalties and held the master, agents and owners of vessels responsible for preventing their crews leaving. A clause was inserted to ensure shipowners adhered to their obligations. Section 9 stipulated: 'The master, owners and charterers of any vessel from which any prohibited immigrant enters the Commonwealth contrary to this Act shall be jointly and severally liable to a penalty, not exceeding £100 for each prohibited immigrant so entering the Commonwealth.'

Within months of the new immigration law coming into effect, six crew members of the P&O ship RMS *India* went missing just days before the ship left Sydney for London. Immediately warrants were issued for their arrest, but the authorities also acted to enforce the law by serving a summons on the ship's captain. He was fined five pounds for each of the absconded men in what was the first prosecution under section 9, and a term of imprisonment of six weeks each was imposed on the men.[39]

Seafarers everywhere had little recourse against the power of the shipowners or ships' masters, Lascars even less so. At sea it was physically impossible for them to maintain contact with their unions. So even though seamen's unions may have been influential and active in their home ports, while at work on board, Indian seafarers had to do their own negotiations without much guidance from their unions.[40] They were given some rights under their articles, but the practical application of shipping legislation was left to local magistrates. Offences under the Merchant Shipping Acts were heard in magistrates' courts, and in the nineteenth century in port towns and colonies these local magistrates were often merchants or shipowners who were themselves frequently ex-masters. In city courts in the early twentieth century, it was still very difficult for Lascar crews to get their complaints against harsh or violent (always white, British) officers heard, or even to have the assertion of their right to be provided with adequate food treated as legitimate.

---

[39] 'Lascars at Large. First Prosecution,' *Sydney Morning Herald*, 11 March 1902, 4; 'Absconding Lascars,' *Leader* (Orange), 12 April 1902, 2.

[40] Balachandran, 'Cultures of Protest.'

When a large group of 20 walked off their ship – called the *Argus* – early in 1904, refusing to return because the captain had been physically violent, the Melbourne court gaoled 'the three ringleaders' for a week and ordered the others back to their ship with a threat that they too might be sent to gaol. Testimony presented by the captain and ship's officers about the men's characters, their stubbornness and slowness to obey orders, while denying all knowledge of any cause they might have for complaint, was accepted with little attempt made by the court to match it with evidence from the sailors. The serang was questioned and admitted they were deserting. No translator was provided to enable the others to be questioned. The *Age* recorded each of their names and called it a 'strike,' although this was technically illegal and not the substance of the charge against them.[41] The *Geelong Advertiser* also called it a strike. This report said 'it was difficult to get at their grievance' because of the sailors' poor English, but that eight of them had complained of being struck by the captain. Their complaint went unheeded. All had refused to go back on board until there was a new captain, preferring 'to go to gaol or cut their throats.' They were consequently arrested for desertion and placed in the city watchhouse.[42]

The imprisonment of another group of Indian seamen by order of the South Melbourne Court later that same year was another case of questionable justice. The issues this time were more straightforward. The labour press came to their defence and demanded an inquiry. These men had walked off the *Obra* to complain about the food and were then charged with desertion or being absent without leave. The incident exposed the plight of Lascars – 'our poor black brothers' – who, 'exasperated with their treatment on board of a wealthy British-India steamship, with the grand old British flag flying from the top-mast,' were unable to achieve 'redress at the British Shrine of Justice.'[43]

Absent from these press reports were references to the colourful turbans and tunics of earlier reports. 'Their very appearance, which is described as "ragged, barefooted, and dirty," while the spokesman "was attired in a manner that scarcely satisfies the requirements of decency," was,' according to the labour paper *Tocsin*, 'almost sufficient to disprove any charge of desertion.' Police Inspector Milne said that so far as he could gather 'it was not desertion or anything of the sort.' The men had come ashore carrying a portion of their food, and made a 'complaint to the sergeant on duty.' That officer referred them to the Customs authorities. 'That,' said the inspector,

---

[41] 'Strike of Lascars,' *Age* (Melbourne), 24 February 1904, 6. Note Dixon's description of how dangerous and easy it was to be called mutiny under the legislation. Dixon, 'Seamen and the Law.'

[42] *Geelong Advertiser*, 23 February 1904, 1.

[43] Letter to the Editor, *Tocsin*, 3 November 1904, 3.

'comprises their offence.'[44] It was within the terms of their articles. The captain of the ship reportedly admitted that the men had complained about the food they were supplied with. Four of them had said they were prepared to go back if proper food would be provided in future, although the fifth had refused because the captain was 'no good.' The magistrate, however, brushed aside their views, responded impatiently, and gaoled them for four days, for desertion. 'Every seaman has a right to come ashore to make a complaint to a magistrate,' *Tocsin* pointed out. 'The Master cannot legally refuse permission, and these men, after landing acted solely as directed by the police.' *Tocsin* promised action. 'Unless all sense of justice is dead in Victoria, the circumstances of the case will be brought before Parliament. [Magistrate] Mr. M'Arthur's conduct especially demands investigation.'[45] The matter was indeed subsequently raised in parliament, by MP George Prendergast, leader of the Victorian Labor Party, but too late to overturn the injustice and without any effect on the magistrate.

Five years later, another incident – the affair of the ship *Kaliba* – brought a stronger response in a demand for investigation from John Haynes, a Member of the New South Wales parliament, publisher of *The Newsletter*, and formerly business manager among the founders of *The Bulletin*. 'We hear that … the whole crew of lascars have been arrested,' his newspaper report declared, 'that the men struck because of ill-treatment and their leader went with them to gaol as a protest.'[46] That in itself was not remarkable. Balachandran has pointed out that Lascar protests were always made in groups, not by individuals.[47] What was more unusual is the paper's exposure of the inequality in proceedings – 'At present only one side of the affair has been reported … However, we like to hear both sides' – and the expectation that the treatment of the men 'being kept in gaol till the ship sails' meant an enquiry was warranted.[48]

While the reporting of these incidents possibly indicates a new awareness of the presence and unjust treatment of South Asian crews was growing in certain liberal circles, it might also indicate they were being used by opponents of White Australia to discredit the policy. Maritime unions were not evidently present. Their energies were focused on weakening capitalists' interest in cheaper labour. This was not opposition to, or a critique of, White Australia. Nevertheless, as the lens through which the White Australia

---

[44] *Tocsin*, 10 November 1904, 5.

[45] *Tocsin*, 10 November 1904, 5.

[46] 'Lascars Arrested. A Whole Crew in Gaol,' *The Newsletter: An Australian Paper for Australian People*, 30 April 1910, 4.

[47] Balachandran, 'Cultures of Protest.'

[48] 'Lascars Arrested. A Whole Crew in Gaol.'

policy was interpreted and mobilised to advantage, it was more than simple, uncritical support. 'It goes well to show what the capitalists think of our "White Australia" policy, when they are prepared to take any despicable means in their power to introduce cheap foreign labor,' one SUA member argued. 'These are the people that would call on the men of the Australian mercantile marine, in the name of patriotism, to defend their trade, their ships, and their property, if threatened with an armed invasion,' which most Australians feared would come from China or Japan. Yet now these same people 'are prepared, by hook or by crook, to deprive the Australian ships and the Australian seamen of their trade and livelihood, that they … may possibly gain a few pounds, by under-cutting the Australian-manned vessel.'[49]

Another time, the seamen's union pointed to the irony of government policy 'spending thousands of pounds in furtherance … of retaining the Northern Territory for the white race' yet still allowing 'coloured' crews on ships in the coastal trade, which made the White Australia policy 'a mockery and a farce.' If the question of race was 'such a vital question that the Asiatic shall not gain a footing in the Australian continent, how much more vital is it that he shall not usurp a footing in our White Australian Merchant Service.' Without that, 'a White Australia is a chimera, an utter impossibility.'[50]

The SUA opposition to the threat that 'coloured labour' posed to their own wages and conditions was solid, but we can also detect evidence of ambivalence towards the ideal and a changing idea of how this category of labour was to be approached by the maritime unions.[51] With the attainment of nationhood, they had developed strategies and institutions that diverged from those of the UK. Sailing the shipping routes around the Pacific, Australian seafarers and waterside workers encountered and were influenced by ideas coming from the United States. The American Federation of Labor moved towards exclusion of cheap labour and the promotion of legislative protections, as did the ALP and sections of the maritime unions.[52] Others tended to be politically influenced by ideas of the IWW, which from the outset had adopted a position of anti-racism.[53]

Made up largely of migratory, unskilled labourers, the IWW was committed to the ideal of 'One Big Union,' incorporating all nationalities

---

[49] 'Newcastle Report,' *Australasian Seamen's Journal* 10 (2 February 1914).

[50] 'Newcastle Report' (2 February 1914).

[51] Martínez, 'Questioning "White Australia."'

[52] Albrecht, 'International Seamen's Union of America,' 4, 6, 17.

[53] Verity Burgmann, *Revolutionary Industrial Unionism: The IWW in Australia* (Cambridge: Cambridge University Press, 1995).

and races, and breaking down all divisions between workers. The Australian IWW inherited the anti-racism that was foundational to the American IWW as it 'adhered firmly to internationalism in theory and practice.' The IWW was the first to confront 'in any concerted way' racism in the Australian labour movement such as the maintenance of White Australia adopted by the Federal Labour conference of 1905.[54] Historian Verity Burgmann has argued that 'the ideas of the IWW prompted Australian socialists to reconsider their attitude to working-class racism, encouraging for the first time the development within the labour movement of a coherent anti-racist viewpoint.' Merchant seafarers and wharf labourers were a sizeable proportion of those who formed the first Australian locals of the IWW, which acknowledged 'no distinction of race, creed, or colour. Its policy is one of international working-class solidarity.'[55] There is, however, little or no extant evidence of maritime union activism in support of Asian seafarers who were targeted by government officials in these first two decades.

'[R]igid[ly] reading ... [the] Immigration Restriction Act'

The new provisions for White Australia not only limited the mobility of Asian seafarers, they also enabled/empowered overzealous officials to impose new indignities and cruelties on them. This was illuminated by the experiences of shipwrecked sailors, who, despite long-standing humanitarian protections guaranteed by law, were now treated as a threatening or even dangerous presence. Doing so raised the ire of sections of the public, especially amongst political opponents of the ALP and the liberal protectionist Alfred Deakin, notably those who did not agree with the White Australia policy.

When five Norwegian crew from a small steamer became stranded in Sydney, Hughes, as the responsible Minister, refused to allow them to be deported. The SS *Inger* was chartered to carry phosphate on the Australian coast and the SUA persuaded its crew to go on strike for the Australian wage rate. They were replaced by the master and left on shore. Technically now illegal immigrants, they were gaoled, but Hughes argued 'they were not the type of men likely to become a charge on the country.'[56] In contrast with the *Inger*, in November 1903 and June 1904, two British steamships manned by Asian crews were wrecked off the Victorian coast. The first, the *Petriana*, was carrying oil from Borneo, with a crew of 16 Chinese and 11 Malays

---

[54] Burgmann, *Revolutionary Industrial Unionism*, 80, 79.

[55] Burgmann, *Revolutionary Industrial Unionism*, 68, 80–1.

[56] Quoted in Fitzhardinge, *Hughes*, 165. See also 'Crew of S.S. Inger,' *Sydney Morning Herald*, 13 June 1904, 6.

under the command of five British officers, when it hit rocks and got stuck on a reef.[57] The officers – including the captain's wife and daughter – were taken off the doomed ship and accommodated in the nearest coastal town. The Asian crew members, however, had to stay on board because Customs officers 'flatly refused' to let them come ashore. They were moved from the stricken ship to the one that came to its aid, until they could be taken up to Melbourne, be transferred to a Japanese ship, and returned to their embarkation port of Singapore. Furore broke out in the press about their unheard-of harsh treatment, 'where a shipwrecked mariner was not allowed to put his foot on dry land.'[58]

This was different from the experience a group of Japanese seafarers had in January 1904 when the German-owned steamer *Elba* was wrecked on coral reefs during a storm off the Gilbert Islands in the Pacific. Several weeks later, the officers and crew arrived in Sydney. The 15 Japanese firemen, unlike the Chinese and Malay crew of the *Petriana*, were allowed ashore, albeit temporarily, until they could get a passage back to Japan, because Federal Customs authorities negotiated an arrangement with the Japanese Consul General. Consequently, on his assurance, they were allowed to land in Sydney on condition the captain of the *Elba* undertook – as was his obligation – to meet the costs of their repatriation to Japan and their keep while in Sydney.[59] Perhaps on this occasion the Customs officials had learnt from the public outburst their handling of the crew of the *Petriana* had sparked, but the Japanese also enjoyed a 'most-favoured nation' status in regard to the White Australia policy.[60]

The *Elba* incident brought comparisons between the Japanese and Germans that revealed how the new nation could also offend the old imperial European powers. When immigration officials sought to deport a German crewman who had been convicted and imprisoned for smuggling, they administered the usual dictation test (in Greek) and received assurance from the German Consul General that the sailor would leave the Commonwealth on completion of his sentence. As he didn't, Prime Minister Alfred Deakin then charged the Consul with breach of faith undermining trust, the context of the *Elba* incident making it clear that this 'extraordinary behaviour' was not true of the Japanese Consul's undertaking. Feeling insulted, the German

---

[57] Leonie Foster, 'Shipwrecks and the White Australia Policy,' *Great Circle* 36, no. 2 (2014): 68–84.

[58] 'The Shipwrecked Sailors,' *Argus* (Melbourne), 8 December 1903, 5.

[59] 'Wreck of the Elba. Japanese Allowed to Land,' *Sydney Morning Herald*, 8 March 1904, 6.

[60] Yarwood, *Asian Migration*, 2–3.

Consul consequently lodged a complaint against Australia with the Imperial authorities in London.[61]

A few months later, in June 1904, the P&O Royal Mail Steamer *Australia* hit the same reef off Point Nepean Victoria as had the *Petriana*, and joined 'the long list of ships lost in these waters' – another example 'of invested capital swallowed by the sea.'[62] This time there were passengers, approximately 60 white crew, including women working as stewards, and more than 160 Lascar and Goanese seamen involved. This meant differential treatment was accorded to those who were rescued. The passengers and white crew who were rescued from the stricken ship breakfasted in comfort on shore, but the Asian seamen, like the *Petriana* crew, were required to remain on board the rescue ship until they could be rehoused.[63]

Most of the crew were taken safely from the ship, but one of the unnamed Lascars was killed while unloading salvaged cargo at the pier when he slipped and was crushed between the wharf and the boat.[64] The Indian and Goanese could not enter Australia freely and had to be repatriated. Their upkeep and voyage home were P&O's responsibility under the Merchant Shipping Act. P&O had also to ensure none would abscond and escape the restrictions under the Immigration Restriction Act. Speaking in parliament, Billy Hughes, as the Minister for External Affairs, made it clear that the company would be held responsible 'for seeing that the terms of the Immigration Restriction Act are adhered to.'[65] Thus police were used to keep them under watch for the company, which Hughes claimed to be 'mystified' by, denying it was sanctioned by his Department.

Initial ideas of housing the rescued 'coloured' seamen at the nearby quarantine station were rejected in favour of taking them to the city and accommodating them all at the Sailors Home, where the white crew were taken. Consequently, they were escorted to Melbourne under police guard, wearing just light cotton garments in the middle of winter, and carrying 'ragged bundles swung across their shoulders' as they 'shuffled along.'[66] While the white crew were housed indoors, tents were erected in the yard, one for Lascars, one for the Goanese, straw was laid on the dirt floor, and iron beds and mattresses were provided. Heavy rain made the tent 'particularly uncomfortable' and turned the floor to mud. The next day they had to be moved into more substantial quarters in a shed. The police continued to guard the door and curious onlookers could only

---

61 'A German Complaint,' *Argus* (Melbourne), 27 April 1904, 5.
62 'Wreck of the *Australia*,' *Sydney Morning Herald*, 21 June 1904, 6.
63 Foster, 'Shipwrecks.'
64 'A Lascar Seamen Killed,' *Age* (Melbourne), 22 June 1904, 8.
65 Quoted in Foster, 'Shipwrecks.'
66 'Housing the Lascars,' *Age* (Melbourne), 21 June 1904, 6.

peer through the tiny windows at the men huddling in their blankets.[67] The public's curiosity was more excited than the press's response. Few objections were raised to the official indifference to the men's comfort as authorities prioritised adherence to the rules of immigration restriction over the equality of humane treatment.

Five years later, when the *Clan Ranald*, taking a load of wheat to London, sank within hours of departing from South Australia with a large loss of life, in 'one of the saddest [events] that has ever taken place in Australian waters,' people hoped some better treatment would be extended to the survivors. Immediately Senator Edward Pulsford from New South Wales wired then Minister for External Affairs and South Australian Labor MP Egerton Batchelor, sincerely hoping he would 'prevent any rigid reading of Immigration Restriction Act which would lessen hospitality for survivors, or reverence for dead,' in this new disaster.[68]

Pulsford published his letter in the press, which as the financial editor of Sydney's *Daily Telegraph* he knew well. He incorporated the correspondence he had written previously to Alfred Deakin about the wreck of the SS *Australian* in the Torres Straits in 1900 when Customs authorities at Thursday Island refused to allow the shipwrecked Chinese to land. He was a free trader who had long opposed the White Australia policy. In 1904, he sought to introduce amendments to the Immigration Restriction Act and the Postal Act that would make certain clauses less offensive to Asians and had published a book demonstrating his belief in the British Empire as a great Asiatic power.[69] He wanted officers of the Commonwealth to prioritise the safety and care of the victims, and he urged Deakin, now Prime Minister of the Commonwealth, to require officials to disregard nationality and facilitate the landing of all shipwrecked persons. No action was taken, and the next incident was even worse.

When the steamer *Aeon* was wrecked in the Pacific, in 1908, the passengers and crew, which included 33 Chinese, were cast away on an island for some weeks before being brought to Brisbane. This time, not only were the Chinese refused permission to land, 'but, much to their indignation, handprints of the whole 33 were taken.' Pulsford was worried the same thing was happening now with the *Clan Ranald* crew, that they too were being subjected to what he called 'the handprint indignity.' While 40 of the Lascars had drowned, the survivors 'were at once pounced upon by officials, and compelled to give their handprints.' Although indignity and humiliation

---

[67] 'Care of the Crew,' *Age* (Melbourne), 23 June 1904, 6.

[68] 'Shipwrecked Asiatics,' *Sydney Morning Herald*, 6 February 1909, 14.

[69] Mark McKenna, 'Pulsford, Edward (1844–1919),' *Biographical Dictionary of the Australian Senate*, 1:31–4.

'had already been imposed,' he still hoped that Customs officers might be instructed to carry out their duties differently.[70]

Atlee Hunt was the permanent Head of the Department of External Affairs and he administered the immigration law under the Minister and also controlled the officers employed by the Department of Trade and Customs for immigration matters. Hunt had influenced the drafting of the immigration restriction bill and the subsequent systems introduced to ameliorate strained relations with Asian nations. He also influenced the provisions of The Pacific Islands Labourers' Act (1902), and after 1906 responded to appeals from a newly formed Pacific Islanders' Association to allow some exemptions to their deportation.[71] It seems he may have exercised similar influence in the improved treatment of Lascar survivors of the *Clan Ranald*, although Egerton Batchelor, the South Australian Labor MP, was given the credit by the free trade press, led by the Melbourne *Argus*, which had stirred up trouble for Deakin at the time of the *Petriana* sinking.

Though the Immigration Restriction Act had not expressly exempted shipwrecked sailors from its 'severe provisions,' to the *Argus* it was appropriate that Batchelor had shown discretion for the 'special circumstances' of Lascars seeking shelter. His intervention to constrain the overzealous officials who would harass them 'as though they were undesirable immigrants seeking to slip into the country' by registering their fingerprints and taking sureties before they could even come ashore, was an 'absurd' use of the Immigration Act against men who 'could not possibly be a source of danger to Australia.' That they were not white was of no matter to the *Argus*. By adopting 'a kindly, humane consideration for distressed sailors' Batchelor was 'fulfilling the wishes of the people.' This the *Argus* applauded as 'not merely ... "correct," but magnanimous.'[72] The year before, Hunt had increased vigilance through a system of informants to solve another problem that had emerged: the large numbers of Chinese stowaways coming into the country (Figure 3.2). He recommended, and succeeded in having adopted, a new amendment to the Immigration Restriction Act to impose huge fines on shipowners. The consequent indignities and annoyances inflicted on Chinese passengers and crew were carried out by Customs officers in every port the ships passed through.[73]

---

[70] 'Shipwrecked Asiatics,' *Sydney Morning Herald*, 6 February 1909, 14; '40 Lascars Drowned,' *Daily Telegraph* (Sydney), 3 February 1909, 10.

[71] Helen Davies, 'The Administrative Career of Atlee Hunt, 1901–1910' (MA thesis, University of Melbourne, 1969).

[72] *The Argus* (Melbourne), 4 February 1909, 6; 'White Men Who Were Saved,' named by *Evening News* (Sydney), 1 February 1909, 5.

[73] Davies, 'Hunt.' See Day, *Contraband and Controversy*, 69–73.

3.2 Chinese seafarer wanted by immigration officials, 1914 National Archives of Australia. NAA: A2455, 1

At that time (1909), the SUA journal said nothing about the shipwrecked crews but did note the total number of Lascars employed on British ships was 43,960 and increasing. Two years later, the union observed Lascars were 'nearly 12 per cent. of the total mercantile marine!' which presented difficulties for recruiting British nationals for the navy in times of war that would become even more accentuated should numbers continue to increase. The SUA was hanging its hopes on the Navigation Act, which, 'thanks to the nationalism and patriotism of our legislators,' would protect the Australian trade and shipowners from the unfair competition P&O ships presented 'manned by lascars and subsidised by the British government.' The union suggested that the Imperial Government should take some similar protectionist action against 'the employment of colored labor in British ships.'[74]

The campaign the SUA waged against British shipowners' practices of forcing wages down was not limited to protecting Australian workers. The strategy they pursued – to raise the labour standards on British ships for all, regardless of race or origin – empowered Asian crews also, at least while they were working in Australian waters. In one example from the port of

---

[74] 'The Lascar Question' [editorial], *Australasian Seamen's Journal* 3 (1 July 1913).

Newcastle, the SUA could demonstrate how their strategy worked. A crew of 25 Chinese sailors and firemen arrived from Singapore to displace the white crew on a British-registered ship. But when the master started to sign on the Chinese, 'to his shock,' they 'demanded white men's money, and absolutely refused to sign on unless they got £5 and £6 a month,' which was almost double their Singapore agreement. The Chinese sailors were under a bond to be repatriated out of New South Wales: the captain needed a crew to replace those he had already paid off. Thus, caught in a quandary, he had no choice but to sign on the Chinese crew at the rates they demanded.[75]

This was the context for the *Ockenfels* episode involving Brisbane wharfies. The anti-labour press presented the story of the 1912 *Ockenfels* walk-off differently from the Strike Committee, contemptuously playing up the WWF enthusiasm as 'ecstatic delight' and reporting that 'the blacks were acclaimed heroes for the cause,' one speaker urging 'the strikers to have some of the spirit which had prompted the action of the coloured men.'[76] In contrast to the WWF, this report cast the *Ockenfels* crew's actions in an unheroic, less-radical, more-acceptable light, and charged the MP Harry Coyne, who reported it at the Trades Hall meeting, with lying:

> [Fifteen] lascars left the vessel and proceeded to the heart of the city. The lascars maintained that as their articles [had] expired, in two days they should not have to work and it was because of that only that they ceased work. Moreover, they demanded to be sent back to India in another vessel. Shortly after 13 o'clock they returned to the wharf.

This account made their action consistent with their articles of employment, and with previous walk-offs through city streets to find the appropriate authorities. It was in fact the serang's version of events, not the crewmen's. The next day, the *Telegraph* acknowledged it was 'the serang who related the men's grievance about their agreement' that they had published. Still, 'Nothing whatever was said about "blacklegs."' The WWF strikers were quick to reject this version. Labor politician Joe Collings asked, '[I]s it possible that a number of coloured men leave a ship and come up to the Trades Hall to get something fixed up in connection with domestic troubles?' He spoke from first-hand knowledge of the men coming to the Trades Hall, and said: '[T]he first man to whom they stated their grievance was … a member of the strike committee. They told [him] they "would not work with blacklegs." That is the actual truth, and the statement made in the "Telegraph" to-night is positively untrue.'

The incident of the *Ockenfels* walk-off illustrated the difficulty maritime workers faced in developing strategies of protest. The men had risked going

---

[75] 'Newcastle Report' (2 February 1914).

[76] 'Another Lie Nailed,' *Telegraph* (Brisbane), 13 February 1912, 4.

3.3 Seamen's Union Executive in 1916.
Robert Guthrie (centre front), Alistair Cooper (centre left), Charles Burke
(first on left, back row) and Percy Coleman (third from right, back row),
Australasian Seamen's Journal (1916), SLV

to gaol, the serang's story protected them from disciplinary action. Getting access to the crew to mobilise them or hear their side of the story was not feasible. Another reporter told how they had been unable to verify the statement made at Trades Hall about the 'black crew' coming out. The report described how the work of unloading the cargo had proceeded 'without any interference. Mounted, special constables and regular police, were stationed about the precincts of the wharf, in case disorder occurred. Pickets were posted about the various approaches to the wharf.'[77]

The action of the *Ockenfels* crew offers us only a glimpse into the intentions and consciousness of Indian seafarers and their willingness to engage in protest. It was a fleeting moment of encounter within the framework of White Australia. It seems improbable they had walked to Trades Hall mistaking it for a police station. We can be reasonably sure they were aware

[77] 'Unloading Steamer Ockenfels,' *The Week* (Brisbane), 16 February 1912, 15.

of the big strike across England and in northern European ports in 1911 and perhaps the cooperation between seafarers and dockworkers during it. Indian seafarers were part of the growing labour movement forming their own unions, and they would soon take militant action themselves. The first documented seafarers strike within India came just two years later, in Bombay in 1914, when, under the leadership of Mohammed Ebrahim Serang, deck and engine crew detained two P&O mail ships.[78]

The first recorded moves to form a seafarers' union in India were made at the end of the nineteenth century, when a very short-lived Calcutta branch of the Amalgamated Sailors and Firemen's Union, headed by Havelock Wilson, was founded in 1889, with an Anglican clergyman as the secretary. He later became an official of the UK union and the ITF.[79] Organisation in India was complicated. An organisation of Goans and Christians, the Goa Portuguese Seamen's Club, founded in 1896 in Bombay for the saloon crew of P&O, acting as a 'semiquasi union,' and later renamed as the Portuguese Seafarers Union, is taken as the foundation of the current National Union of Seamen of India, which celebrated their centenary in 1996. In Calcutta, Goans and Portuguese organised a separate seamen's club. Three years later (1899), Mohammed Serang arrived in Bombay and started organising seamen there, including deck and engine crew and P&O saloon crew – in short, all categories. Even when in 1919 the several unions amalgamated into the Indian Seamen's Union they continued to act with separate identities.[80]

When the Indian crew of the *Ockenfels* demonstrated solidarity with white Australians and acted on their acceptance of union principles, they gave a glimpse of their activism outside India. Yet racial categorisation of crews existed in the articles they had to sign. These constrained the actions available and made organised collective protests almost impossible – undoubtedly rare. The issue of race became particularly acute in Britain where seafarers increasingly had their wages reduced by competition with lower-waged foreign crews employed by the same British shipowners. Racial antagonism from the National Union of Seamen under the leadership of Havelock Wilson grew more intense in the first three decades of the new century, culminating in the Coloured Alien Seamen's Order of 1925.[81] Events in Australia unfolded differently. It was an international context framed within this British world.

[78] A.K. Arora, *Voyage: Chronology of Seafarers Movement in India* (Mumbai: National Union of Seafarers of India, 1996), 2.

[79] According to Arora, *Voyage*, 1.

[80] Arora, *Voyage*, 3; Broeze, 'Muscles of Empire'.

[81] Tabili, 'The Construction of Racial Difference.'

4

'To Break Down the Barriers Which Separate Races and Countries'

Socialists, Maritime Unionists and Organising Internationally before 1920

Maritime unionism in the UK was boosted by the transition from sail to steam. In 1887, Havelock Wilson founded the National Amalgamated Sailors' and Firemen's Union which later became the British National Union of Seamen (NUS), with himself as its president. Immediately the NUS began organising internationally to prevent the laying off of British crew members abroad and to adapt to an increasing proportion of foreign-born crew in the national seagoing labour force. Soon the NUS had opened branches in Hamburg, Antwerp, Rotterdam and Copenhagen.[1] In 1889, what became known as the Great Dock Strike in London catapulted its leaders, Ben Tillett and Tom Mann, to national prominence. Their success in forcing employers to give in to the dockworkers' demands strengthened the potential for further collective action. Tillett and Mann then joined with Wilson to found in 1896 the International Federation of the Ship, Dock and River Workers.[2] Within a year they were joined by Scandinavian and German unions and had organised the first formal conference in London, with several European maritime unions agreeing to coordinate their efforts in securing improved conditions, higher wages and fewer hours of labour.[3]

---

[1] Fink, *Sweatshops at Sea*, 122. See also Arthur Marsh and Victoria Ryan, *The Seamen: A History of the National Union of Seamen, 1887–1987* (Oxford: Malthouse Press, 1989).

[2] The International Federation of the Ship, Dock, and River Workers (IFSDRW), 'What We Want, Why We Want It, and How We Mean to Get It,' leaflet, October 1896, http://library.fes.de/itf/pdf/akp3796/akp3796_what-we-want.pdf; N.B. Nathane, *The International Transport Workers Federation: Its Character, Its Aims, Its Aspirations* (Amsterdam: ITF, 1922), MS 159/4/439, MRC. This story is told in Bob Reinalda, 'Edo Fimmen, ITF 1896–1945,' in *The International Transportworkers Federation, 1914–1945: The Edo Fimmen Era*, ed. Bob Reinalda (Amsterdam: Stichting beheer IISG, 1997), 39. See also Tom Mann, 'The Position of Dockers and Sailors in 1897 and the International Federation of Ship, Dock, and River Workers' (London: Clarion Newspaper Company, 1897).

[3] International Conference of Ship, Dock and River Workers, held in London, February

A third conference in 1898 broadened the organisation to include railways, and changed the new organisation's name to the International Transport Workers Federation.[4]

This was continuation of a 'firm and generous internationalism' which had emerged in the early decades of the nineteenth century amid the class divisions of industrialisation, with radicals and socialists organising a worldwide movement of contacts and solidarity.[5] Working through national trade unions and forming new international bodies to build the movement, socialists saw potential in the maritime workforce for recruitment to the cause. Australia and New Zealand, with their own burgeoning and active labour movements, also had huge maritime strikes in 1890. Their unions were included as part of the ITF founders' vision for international organisation, essentially as an extension of British shipping and given the mobility of labour between Britain and the colonies. Nevertheless, the Pacific colonies were in the Antipodes, geographically distant from Europe, and facing their own regional issues. Tracing the connections forged between British and Australasian maritime unionists as they sought a united workers' movement illuminates the strengths – and tensions – between geography and political economy that was shaping their experience.

'Champions of the men': The ITF founders and Australasia

Success of the 1889 London dockworkers' strike was vested on crucial financial support from Australian maritime workers. The Brisbane Seamen's and Wharf Labourers' Union made the very first instalment of £250 to the strike fund. This was immediately followed by £500 from the Sydney wharf unionists.[6] Overall, Australian labour and the public donated as much as £30,000 out of £48,700 raised in total for the strike fund.[7] The following year, during the 1890 Australian maritime strike, British dockers returned the favour to their Australian comrades. In August they voted for the initial donation of £1,000, published a manifesto of solidarity and agreed to impose a specific levy of a shilling per member. Mann, the dockers' union president, and Tillett, their secretary, took the lead in summoning public meetings,

---

1897, Minutes of Proceedings, http://library.fes.de/itf/pdf/akp3796/akp3796_1897_river.pdf (pages 1–3, 10).

    [4] Reinalda, *International Transportworkers Federation, 1914–1945*, 38–43.

    [5] John Saville, 'Britain, Internationalism and the Labour Movement between the Wars,' in *Internationalism in the Labour Movement, 1830–1940*, ed. Frits van Holthoon and Marcel ven der Linden (Leiden: Brill, 1988), 565–82, at 565.

    [6] P.F. Donovan, 'Australia and the Great London Dock Strike: 1889,' *Labour History* 23 (1972): 17.

    [7] Donovan, 'Australia and the Great London Dock Strike,' 18.

4.1 Tom Mann speaking at unveiling of 8 Hours Day Monument, Melbourne, 1906, SLV

holding rallies and prompting other trade unions to provide support. In September, when an Australian Strike Fund Council was formed, Tillett became its chairman and Mann was appointed as secretary. The Council subsequently raised £3,500 in total, which was in addition to £3,400 donated by the Port of London United Labour Council.[8]

Establishing and maintaining these connections with Australian unions was, in the beginning, built on personal foundations. Almost immediately after the ITF was formed, Tillett undertook an Australian lecture tour, commencing in August 1897 and finishing in July 1898.[9] Tillett travelled extensively around the country, visiting not only large Australian coastal capital cities but also smaller hinterland destinations such as Ballarat in Victoria and Gympie in Queensland, spreading the word of socialism and attracting large audiences.[10] The tour received great publicity in the local press and Tillett himself gained the title 'Napoleon of Labour.'[11] Audiences were broad, including maritime unionists, but consisting of intellectuals and professionals as well as workers. Samuel Smith, the Seamen's Union secretary, presided at the large gathering organised for Tillett at the Sydney Trades Hall, which 'was packed with representatives of the Unions and all of the reform bodies of the city.'[12] Subsequently, Smith accompanied Tillett on local trips, formally reporting his activities to union members.[13]

Tillett also spoke at other meetings of maritime unionists. In Hobart, after he 'spoke very straight,' local wharf workers 'unanimously decided to re-organise the old Wharf Labourers' Union and establish a federation with existing organisations in other parts of the world.'[14] Likewise, in Sydney, he addressed the meeting of the Sydney Wharf Labourers' Union. He 'spoke at great length' of cooperation, the need for solidarity, the problems of workers in Britain, Europe and the colonies. In Melbourne, Tillett addressed a crowded meeting at the Port Melbourne Town Hall. The meeting was

    [8] R.B. Walker, 'Media and Money: The London Dock Strike of 1889 and the Australian Maritime Strike of 1890,' *Labour History* 41 (1981): 49–50.

    [9] K.J. Ryan, 'Beatrice Webb, Sydney Webb, Ben Tillett and the Australian Socialist League's Rivalry with the New South Wales Labor Party,' *Journal of Australian Studies* 16, no. 33 (1992): 63–75.

    [10] 'Mr Tillett at Ballarat,' *Age* (Melbourne), 10 September 1897, 5; 'Visit of Mr Ben Tillett,' *Gympie Times and Mary River Mining Gazette*, 21 August 1897, 5. 'As many as a thousand attended his farewell meeting' ('Tillett Farewells'), *Clipper* (Hobart), 5 March 1898, 3.

    [11] 'The Forge,' *Tocsin* (Melbourne), 16 October 1897, 4.

    [12] 'Reception at the Trades' Hall,' *Worker* (Wagga), 7 August 1897, 2.

    [13] Visit of Mr Ben Tillett; 'Federated Seamen's Union,' *Australian Workman* (Sydney), 4 September 1897, 3.

    [14] 'Tillett Farewells.'

announced as one for 'all water side and other workers,' and J.B. Tucker, secretary of the Wharf Labourers' Union, also spoke briefly.[15]

Thus, the goals embedded in the establishment of the ITF proceeded in colonial ports of British imperial shipping. Just after the 1897 conference, Melbourne and Brisbane Trades' Councils wrote to the Federation's Central Office to express their sympathy and to promise cooperation once they had gained organisational strength in their own country. The Seamen's Union of New Zealand also extended their appreciation of 'the indefatigable efforts' of the new Federation.[16]

The third conference in 1898, which changed the organisation's name to ITF, also formalised the rules and principles of the new organisation as it extended membership. Railways and other transport workers (54 per cent) soon outnumbered dockers and seafarers (46 per cent). What had begun as 'this British organisation with continental members' had also changed: by 1902, when the east coast US longshore workers also joined, only 20 per cent of the membership was British.[17] The adopted constitution accentuated the position of the Federation as a global labour body by breaking down the membership into two categories – 'Extra European' and 'Inter European' unions. Affiliates of both types obtained similar benefits and responsibilities. They all received the Federation's organisational assistance, printed materials and possible 'financial support by means of a levy in cases of disputes,' at the cost of paying an annual subscription fee of fourpence per union member.[18]

When the ITF conference delegates were designing the concept of non-European member unions, they had in mind a prospective association with Australasian national labour organisations.[19] Australia and New Zealand shared the experience of the rapid growth of trade unionism. While Australian and New Zealand merchant sailors had earlier united into a single body, the FSUA, dock workers formed separate Australian and New Zealand Waterside Workers' Federations, in 1902 and 1906, respec-

---

[15] W.J. Mitchell, 'Wharf Labourers, Their Unionism and Leadership, 1872–1916' (PhD thesis, University of New South Wales, 1973) 81–2; Ben Tillett's movements, *Australian Workman* (Sydney), 14 August 1897, 3; 'Mr. Tillett at Port Melbourne,' *Age* (Melbourne), 7 April 1898, 6.

[16] Report Sheet from Central Office of the International Federation of Ship, Dock, and River Workers, leaflet, April 1897, http://library.fes.de/itf/pdf/akp3796/akp3796_1897_river.pdf (page 13); May 1897, http://library.fes.de/itf/pdf/akp3796/akp3796_1897_river.pdf (pages 14–17).

[17] Reinalda, *International Transportworkers Federation, 1914–1945*, 40, 41.

[18] IFSDRW, 'Agenda and Report for Conference to be Held at the Club and Institute Union, Clerkenwell Road, London, E.C., June 1898,' http://library.fes.de/itf/pdf/akp3796/akp3796_1897_agenda.pdf (pages 3, 13–14).

[19] IFSDRW, 'Agenda and Report, 1898.'

tively.[20] Perhaps British leaders of the ITF wanted to increase the 'British' proportion of their membership. Australian and New Zealand members were, as discussed in the previous chapters, British – often by birth and also by designation of national identity. Perhaps it was expected they would strengthen the ITF's opposition to 'coloured labour.' Havelock Wilson was familiar with the position the colonial unions were taking. As a young man in the 1870s, Wilson had served on Australian coasting vessels. For a few years he sailed to and from Sydney and Newcastle making occasional calls to other smaller New South Wales ports.[21]

In the light of such close ties between British and Australian maritime labour movements, it is not surprising that in 1898 – and after Tillett's lecture tour – the ITF promptly sent a formal invitation to the antipodean seamen's union to affiliate. Unexpectedly, perhaps, the union secretary's response was not very positive. He stated that after discussing the matter, branch representatives had decided first to form a broad and strong labour alliance on a national level before proceeding to forging formal international connections.[22] Their preference was conditioned by the FSUA's objectives for the union. Most of its members crewed Australian-flagged coastal vessels, which, as the Royal Commission of 1906 later pointed out, faced competition from foreign carriers using cheaper labour.[23] To secure employment for local seafarers, the FSUA actively campaigned for the monopoly of national ships in the coastal trade. This goal involved pursuit (only achieved in 1912) of the adoption of the Australian Navigation Act and required more domestic political and social support rather than external ITF assistance. Nonetheless, sporadic correspondence on contemporary changes in national maritime labour standards between Australian and New Zealand seafarers' union officials, on the one side, and ITF leaders, on the other, continued, until the start of the First World War.[24]

The British leaders continued to foster close personal connections with the local Australian and New Zealand labour movements. Tom Mann, who was to become the first ITF president, lived for several years (1902–9) in Australia (Figure 4.1). While there, in 1906, he co-founded the Victorian Socialist Party and became its secretary. Mann was an active advocate for internationalism, urging labour linkages across the oceans as an antidote

---

[20] Grant, *Jagged Seas*, 58; David McLaren, Secretary, New Zealand WWF, to Hermann Jochade, ITF Secretary, 26 February 1907, MS 159/3/B/2, MRC.

[21] Havelock Wilson, 'Arrival in Adelaide,' *Daily Herald* (Adelaide), 18 December 1911.

[22] IFSDRW, 'Agenda and Report 1898,' 8.

[23] Grant, *Jagged Seas*, 58–9; Samuel Smith, SUA Secretary, to Barton, 24 March 1902, and to Tom Chambers, ITF, 6 September 1902, MS 159/3/B/1, MRC.

[24] Correspondence from FSUA officials to Jochade, from 1906 to 1909, is in ITF Papers, MS 159/3/B/1, MRC; and between 1912 and 1913, in MS 159/3/B/3, MRC.

4.2 Tom Mann (right), first ITF president, in Australia, 1909,
with J.H. Ivy who paid his bail
SLV

to parochialism, advancing the idea through personal communication with union officials and through participation in various meetings of rank and file sailors and dockworkers.[25]

From the outset, racial categories dividing workers was a contentious issue, particularly for seafarers.[26] By 1914, there were as many as 50,000 South Asians working on British merchant ships in and around the British Empire under employment conditions that were often appalling, characterised by abuse and discrimination.[27] Havelock Wilson sought to recruit British seamen to work on British ships and opposed the employment of 'foreigners'

[25] Tom Mann to Jochade, 30 June 1909, MS 159/3/B/13, MRC; Tom Mann, 'The Industrial and Social Outlook in Australia,' *The Social-Democrat* 13, no. 8 (1909): 337–43; Tom Mann, 'Conditions of Labour in New Zealand,' *The Nineteenth Century and After: A Monthly Review* 52, no. 307 (1902): 393–9; Tom Mann, 'The Political and Industrial Situation in Australia,' *The Nineteenth Century and After: A Monthly Review* 56, no. 331 (1904): 475. See also Thomas Mann, *Tom Mann's Memoirs* (London: Labour Publishing Co., 1923), 202–3; Chushichi Tsuzuki, *Tom Mann, 1856–1941: The Challenges of Labour* (Oxford: Clarendon Press, 1991), 124–33; Joseph White, *Tom Mann* (Manchester: Manchester University Press, 1991), 124–33; also Kirk, *Transnational Radicalism*; C.G.W. Osborne, 'Tom Mann: His Australasian Experience, 1902–1910' (PhD thesis, Australian National University, 1972).

[26] See Reinalda, *International Transportworkers Federation, 1914–1945*, 39, 41.

[27] Dinkar D. Desai, *Maritime Labour in India* (Bombay: Servants of India Society, 1940), 183–200.

willing to sail for lower wages. The union he led organised foreign workers in order to prevent shipowners using them to drive down British seafarers' wages. He carried these ideas into the ITF. On the docks, the issue was not as sharp. 'Foreigners' were fewer in number, but as they were often used as strike-breakers, they encountered hostility from local dockworkers. The early dockers' unions, however, took a position of unity in brotherhood. Union membership was open to all and substantial fines were imposed on members for casting aspersions on other members, 'using unbecoming words' to refer to 'their religious opinions, nationality or antecedents.'[28]

When, in 1902, the ITF expanded to include US workers, the issue of race took on an added dimension. The New York longshore union under Edward McHugh had adopted a policy of non-racism, but the International Seafarers' Union, also an ITF affiliate, accepted only the inclusion of African Americans sailing on American ships and opposed the employment of Asians as crew. Discussion at the 1908 Vienna Congress erupted in 'a heated exchange' of anti-Chinese and anti-Japanese views led by Andrew Furuseth, the Norwegian-born leader of the ISU. Although he found support among some of the delegates, the majority view was to reaffirm opposition to strike-breakers and undercutters but not to object to seafarers of any nationality who were 'willing to work for European or American wages,' which would in fact maintain minimum labour standards for themselves.[29]

Ben Tillett, as the British dockers' leader and now ITF secretary, returned to Australia for another lecture tour in 1907 to promote direct contacts with domestic unionists.[30] A month in advance of the trip he sought help from Mann to organise a series of meetings throughout Australia.[31] The tour was extensive, again included visits to small places, and was publicised in the local press.[32] Tillett spoke about the evils of capitalism and promoted social democracy along the line of his speeches during his first visit to Australia.

In 1907, both Tillett and Mann were involved in the strike on the Sydney waterfront by the coal lumpers, who manually loaded coal in the fuel bunkers of steamships. Tillett and Mann headed to Sydney to lend their authority and support the cause as 'champions of the men on strike.'[33] They

---

[28] Reinalda, *International Transportworkers Federation, 1914–1945*, 39.

[29] Reinalda, *International Transportworkers Federation, 1914–1945*, 41; ITF, *Solidarity*, 40–1.

[30] Morris to Jochade, 7 March 1908, MS 159/3/B/2, MRC.

[31] 'Ben Tillett's Visit,' *Socialist* (Melbourne), 13 April 1907, 3.

[32] 'Ben Tillett in Tasmania,' *Crookwell Gazette*, 29 November 1907, 4; 'Mr Ben Tillett,' *Express and Telegraph* (Adelaide), 23 March 1908, 1; 'Ben Tillett in Prahran,' *Prahran Telegraph*, 6 July 1907, 5.

[33] 'Sydney Coal Lumpers' Strike. Messers Tillett and Mann Enter the Arena,' *West Australian* (Perth), 15 July 1907, 4.

4.3 Ben Tillett speaking at UK dockers' strike, 1911
ITF records, MRC

spoke to packed halls held across the city over the following days, including 'a march of 2,500 unionists through the streets, in defiance of a mayoral ban, and a rally of 10,000 in the Domain. After a three-month lockout, the lumpers returned to work with a better pay and better working conditions.

Havelock Wilson too returned to Australia. Following the big European seafarers' strike of 1911, which Australians did not join, in late 1911 to early 1912 Wilson made a trip to New Zealand for health reasons, to visit local hot springs and get treatment for his rheumatic gout (Figure 4.4). On the inbound leg of this journey, he briefly visited Adelaide, Melbourne and Sydney, meeting local unionists in each place. When making a first stop in Adelaide, he was met and welcomed by representatives of the South Australian branch of the Seamen's Union.[34] He mentioned his intention to conduct a more extensive lecture tour in Australia on his way back to Britain, yet this does not seem to have materialised. He was keen to recruit Australians to the NUS and to prevent British seamen jumping ship in

[34] 'Seamen's Friend. Mr. Havelock Wilson,' *Register* (Adelaide), 18 December 1911, 8; 'Mr. J. Havelock Wilson,' *Daily Telegraph* (Sydney), 19 December 1911, 14.

Australian ports. The rate of desertion was very high. His own comment on his purpose in visiting Australia was his 'endeavour to bring closer union, if it is possible, between the Australian seamen and ourselves.' He said: 'We have had for years an understanding that members of the British union with clear union books shall be recognised by the Australian Federated Union.'[35] This meant that if members of the British union got taken on by a ship on the Australian coast, their membership could be transferred to the Australian union, and the reverse would also be possible.

The question of free transfer was not, however, so easy to implement. The relationship between the Australian and the British unions did not improve with time. In 1920, Charles Burke, the secretary of the Queensland branch of the SUA (see Figure 3.3), after representing Australian seamen at the ILO Maritime conference in Genoa, went on to Britain. There he met with NUS officials to discuss, again, union membership transfer and reciprocal treatment. Despite mutual understanding being reached, the agreement was not fully honoured by the NUS while 'many Australian seamen refused to transfer to the union in Britain.'[36] Political differences with Wilson no doubt contributed to unionists' attitudes towards both the NUS and the ITF.

Waterside unionists developed a somewhat closer early relationship with the ITF. In April 1903, Joe Morris, secretary of the WWF, acknowledging receipt of some printed materials, wrote to Tom Chambers, ITF secretary, an account of recent local industrial disputes and a meeting with Tom Mann. The following year, Billy Hughes, as WWF president, wrote to Chambers asking for more specific information about ITF activities and functions. The Australian union even made preliminary plans to send a representative to the 1904 ITF Congress to be held in Amsterdam. These intentions did not materialise. Communication was interrupted by internal friction in the ITF after the relocation of the ITF headquarters from London to Hamburg, in 1904.[37] So serious were those conflicts and disagreements that British unions even temporarily withdrew from the ITF in protest at growing pro-German influences.[38] When Billy Hughes went to London for the Imperial Conference, in 1907, he met Wilson and re-established connection with Tillett, whom he had known in Australia. Hughes' old union, the Sydney Wharf Labourers, 'had recently light-heartedly joined' the ITF but Hughes distrusted the German connections

---

[35] 'The Federation of Seamen,' *Advertiser* (Adelaide), 18 December 1911, 10.

[36] 'Manning Ships. Transfer of Seamen,' *Daily Standard* (Brisbane), 16 March 1922, 6.

[37] Joe Morris, WWF Secretary to T. Chambers, ITF Secretary, 18 April 1903; William Hughes, MP, letter to T. Chambers, 10 September 1903; Ben Tillett, ITF Secretary to Hughes, 11 April 1904; Hughes to Ben Tillett, 31 May 1904, MS 159/3/B/2, MRC.

[38] Willy Buschak, *The International Transport Workers' Federation* (London: HMSO, 1981).

of the ITF, suspecting the German government of using an ITF-organised strike that year for its own purposes.[39]

It took some time for the new ITF secretary – Hermann Jochade, a German railway unionist – to re-establish regular contacts with the watersiders' unions in Australia and New Zealand. While informing Australians and New Zealanders about the development of European unionism, several times he raised the question of their possible affiliation with the ITF. Both unions were cautious in this respect, indicating two types of problems. While accentuating the general willingness of the leadership to seek a formal international partnership, they claimed that a majority of rank and file members had yet to be educated to accept the idea. They also raised concerns over the limitation of their financial resources to meet the cost of association.[40]

In stark contrast to a relatively intense ITF–Australasian communication, there were virtually no contacts made between the European-based ITF and Asian labour organisations in the pre-1914 period. To some extent this stemmed from the absence of representative Asian unions, which rendered it difficult for the ITF to build regional connections. More importantly, though, a part of the ITF membership strongly resented the possibility of unity with Asian workers. At the 1908 Vienna Congress, an attempt to adopt a resolution in support of recruiting 'foreign-tongued and coloured seamen' sparked scathing anti-Chinese and anti-Japanese (but not anti-Indian) comments from delegates concerned at losing the jobs of their union members due to competition from cheap, non-white maritime labour.[41] A compromise resolution was adopted, accepting them 'as members of the seafaring community' and 'welcoming' them as union members, provided, in an echo of the Australian maritime unions' position, they worked for European standards of pay and conditions.[42] The realisation of the importance of ITF alliances with Asian maritime labour on an equal footing was yet to come.

Once war broke out, in 1914, the severity of organisational and political problems brought on by the war made the ITF abandon its Asia-Pacific agenda altogether. The German location of the Federation's headquarters disrupted any direct contacts between the unionists of belligerent countries. Partially to rectify the problem, a small sub-secretariat was established at the Dutch Federation of Trade Unions. Yet, as the war progressed, political strains between unionists of the opposing military camps intensified dramat-

---

[39] Fitzhardinge, *Hughes*, 192.

[40] Correspondence from 1905 to 1913 in MS 159/3/B/2, MRC.

[41] ITF, *Solidarity*, 40–1.

[42] Reinalda, *International Transportworkers Federation, 1914–1945*, 41.

ically. As a result, after 1916, there was no trace of ITF activities until the end of the war.[43]

The concepts, social analysis, tactics and strategies which socialists advocated in that initial period were challenged and severely tested by the coming of war.[44] An example of this appeared in the Australian seamen's union journal in a letter written by three (and signed by 58) representatives of the British labour movement. They described themselves as pacifists, working in all countries for their ideals. They expressed their sorrow at the devastation. They felt 'not the slightest animosity' towards those 'officially described as our enemies,' which they described as 'dear and personal friends.' They appealed to Australian unionists to 'be with us in the general effort to break down the barriers which separate races and countries,' and they hoped for a future when 'we shall again be together in the attempt to destroy the prejudices which blind us to each other's good qualities.'[45] Australia's experience demonstrated just how difficult that was for idealists.

Australian Labor's war

Australia joined the war in Europe as a member of the Empire. The declaration of war came as Australia was in the throes of a federal election campaign. The leadership of the Seamen's Union – Bob Guthrie, the president, and Arthur Cooper, the general secretary (Figure 3.3) – urged members to support the ALP '… to protect Australian seamen against cheap European and Asiatic' labour.[46] The union's Federal Executive had apportioned funds to the purpose of assisting Labor's campaign. The sitting government had been 'callous' in its handling of the Navigation Act and maritime matters. Foreign vessels were being allowed to engage in Australian trade, and the union leadership was agitating for the purely Australian coastal trade to be restricted to Australian-registered vessels. A vote for Labor, the SUA leaders held, 'will be a vote for a White Australian Merchant Service, and humane and just shipping laws.'[47]

The ALP won the election, making Australia the only one 'of all the nations and empires which went to war in 1914' to have 'a workers'

---

[43] ITF *Solidarity*, 39.

[44] Jay Winter, *Socialism and the Challenge of War: Ideas and Politics in Britain, 1911–18* (Abingdon: Routledge, 1974), 1.

[45] 'The British Labor Movement and the War: To the Editor Australasian Seamen's Union Journal from Arthur Henderson, W.A. Appleton, C.W. Bowerman,' *Australasian Seamen's Journal* 3, no. 2 (1 June 1915): unpag.

[46] 'Federal Elections. An Open Letter to All Members of the Federated Seamen's Union of Australasia,' signed by Guthrie as President and Arthur Cooper General Secretary, 9 June 1914, *Australasian Seamen's Journal* 2, no. 5 (1 September 1914).

[47] 'Newcastle Report' (2 February 1914).

government.'[48] Prime Minister Andrew Fisher was a former miner, the Minister for Defence George Pearce was a carpenter, and Billy Hughes, president of the WWF, was Attorney-General. A little over a year later, by the end of 1915, Hughes was Prime Minister. The strain of waging war given the fierce opposition it generated on the political left and among sections of the working class proved too much for the ALP. Conscription, with Prime Minister Hughes leading the campaign, was opposed by large sections of the labour movement and acrimoniously divided the nation. Hughes' pursuit and prosecution under wartime regulations of the opponents of the war, conscription and militarism has been well documented as singular and unprecedented.[49] Consequently, Hughes lost the support and the presidency of the WWF. He was expelled from the ALP and formed a coalition of pro-conscriptionist, pro-war MPs, the Nationalist Party. With him from the ALP went his great ally, SUA president, Senator Bob Guthrie, who, like Hughes, also forfeited his union position. The Australian Labor Party – which had appeared 'as an irresistible force for economic and social reform'[50] – had split apart and lost government as Hughes continued to govern with the new coalition. 'Thus the impact of world war ... served to wreck a great party and transform a government.'[51] Hopes for enactment of the Navigation Act were once again dashed as enactment was deferred.

Discussion of excluding foreign-owned ships from the Australian coastal trade continued and sentiments against foreign labour were openly expressed in union publications during the war. Some anti-conscriptionists within the WWF argued that if Australian-born men were forced to fight overseas, their recently hard-won gains of pay and conditions would be threatened by employers importing cheaper immigrant 'coloured labour' to take their place.[52] Similar views were expressed by seafarers: 'that in the event of conscription being adopted, seamen should come under the exemption clause, as otherwise a large proportion of Australian seamen will be withdrawn from the coastal shipping, and their places will be filled by foreigners, which is an undesirable event at any time, but specially so at present when the country is at war.'[53]

---

[48] John Hirst, 'Labor and the Great War,' in *The Australian Century: Political Struggle in the Building of a Nation*, ed. Robert Manne (Melbourne: Australia Text Publishing Co., 1999), 47–65, at 47.

[49] Frank Cain, *The Origins of Political Surveillance in Australia* (Sydney: Angus & Robertson, 1983).

[50] Hirst, 'Labor and the Great War,' 49.

[51] F.B. Barrie, *The Conscription Plebiscites in Australia, 1916–1917* (North Melbourne: Historical Association, 1974), 14.

[52] Beasley, *Wharfies*, 41.

[53] *Australasian Seamen's Journal* 5, no. 9 (1 January 1918).

To the SUA, 'foreign crews' did not just mean 'coloured labour.' European – German and Scandinavian – crews were also unacceptable on the Australian coast and not just because of war enmities. When a Swedish vessel arrived in port the *Seamen's Journal* said: 'We do not profess to understand Swedish mercantile marine laws, or the Swedish language well enough to interfere with whatever articles are signed on board Swedish vessels.' Therefore, they went on, they had to rely on the ship's master, 'mustering his crew and informing them in Swedish (which he interpreted for our benefit) that he agreed to observe and adhere to the Commonwealth Award while engaged in the Interstate trade,' and gave a guarantee in writing that the increased wages would be paid when they arrived at their destination port, Port Pirie, in South Australia.[54] This theme is referred to again in the next issue because another Swedish ship had docked to load coal, also to take to Port Pirie. It was undoubtedly engaging in the purely coastal Australian trade, action that was blamed on the delay in the proclamation of the Navigation Act.[55] Even New Zealanders could be caught in the net of unwanted labour, as men were paid less under New Zealand articles than Australian. Signing them on to sail the Australia–New Zealand trade route could be seen as an attempt to introduce cheap labour.[56] Excluding foreign-owned ships was a way of equalising wages: foreign labour should be paid the same wages as white Australians. But it also meant that white labour could do the work 'coloured' or foreign labourers were doing. Reports on the experiment to use white divers in pearling in Broome appeared in an article that rejected the proposition that doing so had been a failure.[57]

The coming of war brought another dimension to 'foreign labour,' as enemy aliens were subjected to actions and ugly expressions from union members; patriotism became loyalty to Britain's empire and nationalism became focused on anti-German feeling. Exclusion was not confined to Asiatic or 'coloured labour.' In one instance, Sydney wharf labourers resolved 'not to work with Germans … or Turks,' whether naturalised as Australians, 'or not.' One wharfie, a naturalised German, took the matter to court and got an injunction granted against the Sydney Wharf Labourers Union to restrain any action from them interfering with or hindering him in gaining employment. Despite the union executive's advice to reconsider their decision, given the injunction, the membership upheld their resolution at a subsequent mass meeting.[58]

[54] 'Newcastle Report' (2 February 1914).

[55] *Australasian Seamen's Journal* 2, no. 6 (1 October 1914).

[56] *Australasian Seamen's Journal* 8, no. 32 (1 November 1923). In this and several issues there is discussion of signing on of men on New Zealand articles.

[57] 'White Divers: Pearlers' Experiments,' *Australasian Seamen's Journal* 2 (2 June 1913).

[58] 'Naturalised German Workers. Injunction against Wharf Labourers (From the

Seafarers sometimes would not want to sail with enemy aliens. When a white crew refused to sail with Chinese seafarers who had been substituted into the ship's crew after arrival in Australia they were prosecuted for refusal.[59] One discussion about the employment of foreigners seems to have been precipitated in part by men in Melbourne refusing to sail with foreigners, identified as Greeks, despite the men being fellow union members. Finally, this meant they were replaced by men who were not members. There was supposedly considerable debate, but only the final resolution, which was carried unanimously, was reported: 'That the relationship that exists between members of the Union should in no way be disturbed, but that officials in enrolling new members, should take every precaution to establish the fact that applicants are not enemy subjects.'[60]

Maritime unions were on occasion caught up in a more generalised xenophobia or ardent patriotism. In New Zealand, a captain was found responsible for the wreck of a scow (a particular kind of New Zealand vessel) and fined. While the court pointed out that the evidence did not show that the loss of the vessel was attributable to the fact 'that the master, both mates, and also four members of the crew were foreign born; and the second mate, who was at the helm when the vessel struck, was unnaturalised,' it directed this to the attention of the Minister responsible. In imposing the fine on the captain, the court expressed the view 'that no British ships should be allowed to be so officered and manned.'[61] That year too, the New South Wales Premier reportedly said 'that the Federal Government has directed that particular care shall be taken in future to prevent men of alien and neutral origin working on any ships or wharfs.' This meant more careful scrutiny and the introduction of a registration system so that employers would have a record of the origin and nationality of men they hired.[62] Maritime labourers were among those being caught in the government's zealous monitoring of loyalty and dissent under new national security laws.

Socialists, internationalists and anti-imperialists were subjected to harassment and prosecution by federal authorities to an unprecedented degree. Some persons were prosecuted for 'being on a wharf or dock or on board a ship without permission.'[63] The newspapers that were prosecuted

"Worker")',* Australasian Seamen's Journal* 2, no. 11 (1 March 1915): unpag.

[59] 'Newcastle Report' (2 February 1914).

[60] 'Supplement' to *Australasian Seamen's Journal* (1 April 1916), Annual Report of the Executive Council of the Federated Seamen's Union of Australasia, Report of Proceedings of the Seventeenth Session Assembled at Melbourne, 1 March 1916.

[61] 'Foreign Seamen,' *Australasian Seamen's Journal* 5, no. 7 (1 November 1917).

[62] 'Foreign Seamen.'

[63] 'Return of Prosecutions under the War Precautions Act and Regulations, including the Aliens Restriction Order' (typescript), House of Representatives, Canberra [1919].

were nearly all labour or left-wing periodicals as laws passed to control enemy agents turned into actions against activists critical of the government's policy on the war. This intensified once Hughes tried to introduce conscription, in 1916 – and, when that failed, tried again in 1917. Those maritime workers who were members of the IWW were liable to be caught under the Unlawful Associations Act 1916. Specifically targeted by this law, the IWW did not survive the war intact as an organisation, although the IWW did re-emerge in the mid-1920s as many who might have joined the IWW became foundation members of the Communist Party of Australia in 1920.[64] One of those was Tom Walsh, who in 1917 succeeded Arthur Cooper as SUA general secretary and soon replaced Guthrie as its president.

Australianising the merchant marine: The Commonwealth fleet of ships

Meanwhile the coming of war brought an opportunity for Hughes to realise his long-standing ambition for an Australian merchant marine. The federal government purchased or commandeered captured enemy ships to transport troops and foodstuffs and a number of steamers from the Strath line, prompting 'shipping and waterside circles in Melbourne' to speculate about the likelihood of commercial success.[65] In a long editorial about the purchase, the *Seamen's Journal* objected to an apparent proposal that these ships would be chartered to 'the shipping magnates.' It alleged this would result in the shipowners 'with their accustomed perfection,' screwing wages down to their lowest level, so that, 'before long, we will have the same condition of affairs which exist in South Africa.' There the government was proposing to man ships with 'coloured labour,' due supposedly to the shortage of white crews. There was a possibility that local shipowners, who 'have not been too favourable to Union labor of any description' may do the same, 'employing coloured crews under the same pretext.'[66]

The purchase of this Commonwealth fleet threatened competition for the shipping companies, and this had implications for conditions of the crews. If the ships were to remain on the British register, the press was speculating this would mean the employment of 'coloured' crews, 'unless the Government was prepared to spend enormous amounts of money in altering the vessels, so as to allow them to comply with Australian navigation laws.'[67] The SUA leadership (Guthrie and Cooper) immediately called in person upon the Minister for Customs. Response came later, when the Minister of

[64] Cain, *Political Surveillance*, 198.

[65] Victorian Branch Report, *Australasian Seamen's Journal* [no volume] (1 September 1916).

[66] 'The Shipping Muddle,' *Australasian Seamen's Journal* [no volume] (1 September 1916).

[67] *Australasian Seamen's Journal* [no volume] (1 August 1916).

the Navy clarified 'that all the vessels of the Commonwealth fleet would be manned by white crews, who would be paid Australian rates; and, should any of the vessels reach the Commonwealth with colored crews on board, they would be discharged, and sent back to their own country.'[68]

The SUA ensured Hughes would enforce the policy. When one of the ships arrived in the port of Newcastle with its mostly Indian crew, the SUA general secretary contacted Hughes, and 'the colored men were replaced with a crew of our [SUA] members.' A ship bringing sugar from Queensland to Sydney under contract with the federal government was similarly manned by 'black labor' (which usually meant from India). The SUA general secretary again lodged a protest but this time had to wait for Hughes to return to the office before receiving the reply that 'he was issuing instructions to prevent a recurrence.'[69] When a boatload of Maltese immigrants arrived in Sydney, in December 1916, closely followed by a second ship that was turned back at Fremantle, the union was alarmed that they had been brought in by shipowners to work on the Australian coast, perhaps on the new government-owned shipping line. They feared the motivation was to take the place of Australians who had enlisted, and 'to once again introduce the system of slavery and starvation that obtained only a few short years ago.'[70]

One editorial warned that the men sailing in the government fleet, which would be transporting the wheat harvest, were 'taking all the risks of war; in fact, even bigger risks than are the soldiers who are fighting our battles at the front.' These were the usual safety issues of stability, bad loading, storms and 'the grasping shipowner, who cares more for the fat dividends than he does for the safety of his crew' but also included the risk of submarines. The editorial ended on the hope that the men employed by the government would receive better treatment 'as a striking contrast to that meted out ... by the shipping sharks.'[71]

The SUA executive reported their anxiety 'that Commonwealth conditions should prevail' when ships were being manned by cheap labour, whether that was European or Asian. They had sought and received ministerial assurance that in future the Commonwealth ships would 'be manned by white labor ... Union labor; the ships to sign articles in Australia, and adhere to the principles laid down' in the Arbitration Court Award of 1911, and subsequently. Union officers had taken responsibility to ensure that

---

[68] 'The Shipping Muddle: Victorian Branch Report,' *Australasian Seamen's Journal* [no volume] (1 September 1916).

[69] 'The Shipping Muddle: Report from New South Wales,' *Australasian Seamen's Journal* [no volume] (1 September 1916).

[70] 'Coolie Seamen,' *Australasian Seamen's Journal* [no volume] (1 December 1916).

[71] *Australasian Seamen's Journal* [no volume] (1 November 1916).

conditions on all ships were similar to those in the coastal trade between the Australian states, and agreements would not become less favourable to the SUA members. Included among these efforts was having the 'disgraceful' accommodation on the ships improved. 'Many of those ships were conceived and constructed to carry black crews, under squalid conditions in which no self-respecting white man could live.'[72] The union urged considerable alterations and confidently believed the relevant department would carry them out given how well government and union policy coalesced.

'Honor the men of the mercantile marine!'

The war took a huge toll of merchant seafarers. If seafarers survived attacks from submarine torpedoes or exploding mines, they often then died from exposure and starvation in open boats that were not provided with wireless facilities. The initial optimism of international maritime union organising came to an end. The NUS held a conference to protest against the actions of German U-boat commanders and crews shooting defenceless seamen waiting for rescue. The SUA hoped an Australian seafarer might attend to represent Australian seamen. General secretary Cooper cabled Havelock Wilson nominating their Newcastle agent, Quartermaster-Sergeant Alex Campbell, then at the front in France. In the spirit of their shared contribution to the war, and the interchangeability of British and Australian unionists, Cooper suggested that if Campbell could not get leave, perhaps Wilson could 'represent Australia himself'.[73] Despite their very high mortality rates during the war, the death rate at sea was high even before hostilities broke out. To put this in perspective, the *Seamen's Journal* pointed out that 'more seamen in British ships were drowned in two years before the year 1914, than all Australian and New Zealand soldiers killed on the Gallipoli Peninsula, from the time of their memorable landing to the day of their splendidly conducted evacuation.'[74]

Australian seafarers received some heightened respect for the contribution they were making to the war effort. A 'celebrated naval writer' in one news outlet wrote glowingly of Britain's merchant navy, which the Australian union said 'of course, includes the Australians crewing transports in both the Mediterranean and in home waters.'[75] Shipowners too expressed the new

---

[72] Executive Council's Report, 'Commonwealth Ships,' *Australasian Seamen's Journal* [no volume] (1 November 1916).

[73] [No title], *Australasian Seamen's Journal* 5 (1 August 1917).

[74] D.R., SS *Carawa*, 'Our Brave Seamen,' *Australasian Seamen's Journal* [no volume] (1 August 1916).

[75] Australia's shipping representative, H.B.G. Larkin, in the High Commissioner's

4.4 Havelock Wilson
in India, 1910
ITF records, MRC

appreciation of merchant seafarers. The SUA was bemused at 'the wonderful change that has come over owners lately.' Seamen, previously denounced as 'brutes of men,' were now praised for 'their courage, daring, and determination to let no risk or hardship deter them from their duty,' in line with the sacrifices servicemen were making, one shipping company executive told an audience of shareholders.[76]

The praise was hollow. Wharf labourers were able to take advantage of the increased shipping and demand for speedy turnarounds that were a consequence of wartime conditions, and they made some gains in their pay and conditions.[77] Australian shipping crews, however, lost ground. They were not paid a war bonus and their wages and conditions deteriorated in comparison with British and US merchant navy crews whose pre-war wage rates more than doubled by 1918. That Australia's seafarers who could sign

---

Report, 1914–15, reported in *Australasian Seamen's Journal* [no volume] (1 July 1916).

[76] 'Mercantile Marine Praised: Aid Given to Fighters,' *Australasian Seamen's Journal* 4, no. 11 (2 April 1917).

[77] Beasley, *Wharfies*, 41.

on to British ships received the war bonus left a sense of grievance with those rank and file who could not, especially when the Australian government, asked to do the same as 'all the Allied nations' had refused 'absolutely.'[78] By the time they relented, in October 1918, the war was virtually over. A new, more militant leadership was in charge of the SUA and 'a state of justifiable discontent [wa]s smouldering in their ranks.'[79] Seafarers were asking again when the Navigation Act, which had been 'passed by the people's representatives' more than six years previously, was to be put in force.[80]

This was the period when Harry Bridges went to sea. Bridges' career as a seaman was brief (1917–22), but it began in an eventful year and covered a crucial period in the history of international labour militancy. He later attributed his political views and success as a labour leader to things he learned in his Australian youth which coincided with the turbulent events of the war and immediate post-war period. As a schoolboy he lived through the divisiveness of the First World War, hearing heated family discussions, or observing the protests and speechmaking in the city streets and on the banks of the Yarra river. As support of his case that it was Australia not Moscow that had shaped his politics, Bridges told one US government deportation hearing that Australia was able to elect (and had elected) a waterfront worker and unionist (Hughes) as its prime minister. He would also have known that Prime Minister Hughes had been expelled from the WWF when he called the 1916 conscription plebiscite, which split the ALP, and that he had broken with his former party charging it with disloyalty for supporting a Great Strike in 1917.[81]

That year Bridges was abandoned in Bombay was a tumultuous year for worker protests. Bridges was subsequently able to say Australia was the only country where a Great Strike had occurred, and ahead of the Bolshevik revolution in Russia. In Bridges' home port of Melbourne, seamen had walked off their ships as soon as scabs started unloading cargo, and they stayed out although the SUA was not officially on strike. Bridges, who was on shore leave, joined with other seamen marching to an army camp to prevent soldiers becoming strike-breakers. That year he also met Adela Pankhurst when she was imprisoned for destroying property during a protest

---

[78] Fitzpatrick and Cahill, *History of the Seamen's Union of Australia*, 48, 46; Victorian Branch Report, *Australasian Seamen's Journal* 7, no. 3 (1 July 1919).

[79] *Australasian Seamen's Journal* 6, no. 5 (1 September 1918).

[80] *Australasian Seamen's Journal* [no volume] (February 1919).

[81] Dolores Janiewski, 'Forging an Australian Working-Class Identity through Myth, Story-Telling and Maritime Mateship: Becoming Harry Bridges,' *Labour History* 116 (2019), quoting 'Mr. Hughes' Appeals to Loyal Unionists,' *Geelong Advertiser*, 15 August 1917, 3; Robert Bollard, *In the Shadow of Gallipoli: The Hidden History of Australia in World War I* (Sydney: NewSouth Publishing, 2013), 112–56.

against the rising cost of living. Pankhurst had recently married Tom Walsh, SUA national secretary, and Bridges' aunt who worked at the prison was able to arrange for young SUA member Harry to visit her.[82]

Tom Walsh soon received national notoriety as the leader responsible for organising a successful seamen's strike, in 1919.[83] When the longshoremen of the US west coast also went on strike that year, their Australian counterparts refused to handle the cargo of American vessels in a sympathy protest. That boycott of non-union ships lasted until 1934 and was one reason, Bridges claimed, the Port of San Francisco formed a company union. Shipowners could then claim that ships sailing to Australia were technically 'union ships' so they would be handled by the WWF. They even allowed ISU delegates to visit the ships so they would appear more truly union to the Australian watersiders.[84] Given this mutual support, Bridges thought that his being Australian got him on to the 1934 strike committee, which we now know changed the course of US waterfront labour history.

'[O]f seamen, by seamen, for seamen': A new internationalism emerges

The experience of the First World War had brought unionists to a new realisation of the necessity for international organising. Historian Bruno Cabanes has written: 'In reality the Great War was also a social laboratory for workers' rights.'[85] It aroused 'deep feelings against injustice' and unions engaged in the struggle for labour rights realised the need for legal protections. The war was, he argues, 'a decisive turning point in the redefinition of humanitarianism' and gave rise to 'a new international politics of rights.'[86] At the war's end, the 1917 Bolshevik revolution in Russia energised a more radical internationalism.

The Australian union welcomed the formation of the International Seafarers' Federation (ISF), which met in London, in 1919, attended by representatives from the United States, United Kingdom, Norway, Sweden, Denmark, the Netherlands, Belgium, France, Spain and Italy. Reportedly Greece, Australia, New Zealand, Japan and Argentina were also possible

---

[82] Janiewski, 'Forging an Australian Working-Class Identity.' See also 'Pankhurst,' *Socialist*, 14 September 1917, 4.

[83] Richard Morris, 'Mr. Justice Higgins Scuppered: The 1919 Seamen's Strike,' *Labour History* 37 (1979): 52–62.

[84] Harry Bridges, 'Relating History as I Personally Know It,' ILWU, Proceedings of the Fifteenth Biennial Convention of the International Longshoremen's and Warehousemen's Union, 1963, 181–2.

[85] Bruno Cabanes, *The Great War and the Origins of Humanitarianism, 1918–1924* (Cambridge: Cambridge University Press, 2014), 85, 3.

[86] Cabanes, *Origins of Humanitarianism*, 17, 79, 8.

attendees. On the agenda was consideration of ways to recognise union cards in any part of the world and the payment of contributions and benefits to members of affiliated organisations.[87] This organisation was a breakaway from the ITF, which the British NUS and the American ISU had left in 1917 for being 'too sympathetic to socialism.'[88] The departure of the seamen's unions left the ITF even more a railways' and dockworkers' organisation: 'the organised seamen have been in the minority, both as regards delegates present and numbers represented,' reinforcing, to the SUA, the need for seafarers to organise themselves.[89] Thus the SUA described the initiative as being 'of momentous importance to the future welfare of seamen everywhere. Never before in history has there been a gathering of this kind. ... The conference is therefore truly the first real international conclave "of seamen, by seamen, for seamen."' The ISF, formed in 1918, was led – as secretary – by Chris Damm of the Belgium union. In June 1920, the ISF met at an International Conference of Seafarers in Genoa, and it lasted until the 1930s when the ISU also ceased to exist.

The separation of seafaring unions from land-based shore workers was a recognition of the different nature of their working experience that surfaced frequently in international organisation. The SUA, however, far from seeing the ITF as too sympathetic to socialism, was itself even more so under its post-war leadership.

---

[87] 'Seamen of the World Unite,' *Australasian Seamen's Journal* 7, no. 11 (April [*sic*] 1919).

[88] A short account of the split is provided by Hartmut Rubner, 'The International Seamen's Organisations after the First World War: Professional and National Interests in Conflict,' in Reinalda, *International Transportworkers Federation, 1914–1945*, 77–80.

[89] Apparent in the agenda of their meetings. See ITF, Report of Proceedings of International Conference of Transport Worker Organisations, Amsterdam, 1919; ITF, Report of Proceedings of International Transport Workers Congress, Christiana, 1920.

5

'Our Duty Is to Foster a Spirit of Internationality'

Maritime Unions and International Labour Organising in the Aftermath of War

In the resurgent burst of internationalism that flourished in the aftermath of the First World War, the SUA leadership decided the time had come for the world's seamen to 'formulate an International policy to guide them in future.'[1] Emboldened by the Soviet revolution and the spread of European communism, their ambition had expanded from concentrating on their own local issues to an international orientation. They called on the seamen of the world to organise a conference – somewhere in Europe – where seafarers could meet, 'without regard to country, race, or creed.' Their discussion would go beyond questions of hours, wages and working conditions generally, to no less than 'the welfare of mankind' which 'depends so much on us and our labor.'[2]

Seafarers liked to emphasise internationalism as deeply embedded in the mobile nature of their work. They were not limited by territory and roamed regardless of their nationality across the seaports of the world wherever their jobs were located, which meant 'the seaman is an international worker in the full sense of the word.'[3] Identifying as internationalists and organising across national boundaries was also a defensive measure against the international power of shipowners, who in their 'vast shipping combines' were accumulating great fortunes.[4] Working conditions of 'low wages with little or no protection from disease and accidents' were imposed by shipowners' greed,

---

[1] H.J. Murray, General President, and Thomas Walsh, General Secretary, 'To the Seamen of the World,' *Australasian Seamen's Journal* 7, no. 11 (1 April 1920). See also letter signed H.J. Murray and Thomas Walsh to Fellow Seamen and Comrades, 14 May 1920, MS 159/3/C/61, MRC.

[2] Murray and Walsh, 'To the Seamen of the World.'

[3] 'The Internationality of the Seamen.'

[4] Matthew Hayes, 'Newcastle Branch Report,' *Australasian Seamen's Journal* 8, no. 34 (1 January 1924).

and 'sanctioned by the laws of every country.'[5] Shipowners could simply use the ships from other nations when any one group of seamen went on strike. The unions' call for international organisation was a strategy to match that power with workers' resistance. The SUA's urge to bring the world's seafarers together was based in the reality of these conditions but was energised by a new revolutionary politics and commitment.

'The internationality of the seamen'

Other internationalist moves by seafarers were already under way in Europe. Soon after the Armistice, in November 1918, the transport unionists of neutral Sweden and the Netherlands initiated rebuilding the ITF. Their efforts led to the first post-war ITF conference, which was organised in Amsterdam, in 1919. Apart from reuniting German and British labour organisations and moving the ITF headquarters to Amsterdam, the conference laid down the foundations of new internationalist policies and principles of the ITF.

Simultaneously, a new group, The International Congress of Seamen's Organisations, met in February 1919 and urged the establishment of a permanent governing body, with a general conference and a supervisory office, for the international regulation of maritime labour.[6] The Paris Peace Conference a few months later set up the International Labour Organization, which was to be based, and meet regularly, in Geneva. The establishment of the ILO was partly to give expression to humanitarian concerns and to empower and bolster worker resistance to the exploitation that one Australian seafaring unionist called 'the foul conditions … [of being] worked almost to death … and then cast aside like old scrap iron.'[7] The ILO was also a response to the more ambitious goals expressed in the SUA's call to use their strength in the cause of politics 'for the welfare of mankind.' ILO measures might defuse and manage the more militant politics that maritime working conditions could provoke.

The International Congress of Seamen's Organisations held to the principle that maritime questions and maritime labour required special consideration and special machinery. They wanted a dedicated body as they sought 'a speedy improvement' in their conditions of work, arguing that it was 'as necessary … as in the conditions of work of shore workers.' They did

---

[5] Murray and Walsh, 'To the Seamen of the World.' See also Joseph P. Goldberg, 'Seamen and the International Labor Organization,' *Monthly Labor Review* 81, no. 9 (1958): 974–81.

[6] 'The Joint Maritime Commission and the Maritime Work of the ILO,' *International Labor Review*, 62, no. 5 (1950): 337–63.

[7] Hayes, 'Newcastle Branch Report.'

not succeed. The Commission on International Labour Legislation decided against the creation of two permanent labour organisations, one dealing exclusively with the conditions of land-based workers and the other with the work of seamen. Instead, it resolved that there would be a special meeting of the ILO's International Labour conference devoted exclusively to the affairs and 'very special questions' concerning seamen.[8] The first session of the International Labour conference was held in Washington, DC, later that year. The Hours of Work (Industry) Convention, which the conference adopted, also included transport by sea and inland waterways within its scope. The second International Labour conference, held in Genoa, in 1920, was devoted solely to maritime issues. Australia had SUA official Charles Burke as their seafarers' union representative and as the shipowners' delegate, Captain Thomas Free of the Royal Naval Reserve. New Zealand was not represented. The two Australian government representatives were William Leslie and the former SUA president, now Senator, Robert Storrie Guthrie, architect of the Navigation Act and key player in the Hughes Royal Commission of 1906.[9] Thus a direct line was established between Australia's early legislative efforts for seafarers' protection, its well-established labour unions and the new international standards being formulated.

Under the guidance of Albert Thomas, the first Director of the ILO, the seamen's organisations agreed not to pursue their request for a separate maritime labour organisation on condition that a maritime section of the ILO, and a joint commission made up equally of shipowners and seamen, was set up. The Congress proposed that the representatives of the employers would be shipowners and 'heads of shipping undertakings and fishing concerns,' and that workers' representatives would be seamen, of different grades, and including fishermen.[10] Thus the ILO Governing Body established a Joint Maritime Commission (JMC) to be consulted on questions of maritime labour and advise on maritime questions. The chair of the Governing Body called and presided over JMC meetings whose deliberations were to assist the technical maritime service of the Labour Office. By the Third Session of the ILO's Governing Body, in March 1920, the JMC had grown to be 12 members: five shipowners and five seamen chosen by the conference in Genoa, and two additional members chosen by the ILO Governing Body.

In 1922, the British dockers' union joined with 13 others to form the very large Transport and General Workers' Union while the British seafarers

---

[8] 'The Joint Maritime Commission and the Maritime Work of the ILO.'

[9] See League of Nations, International Labour Conference, Second Session, Genoa, July 1920, Proceedings, xxii.

[10] 'The Joint Maritime Commission and the Maritime Work of the ILO.'

remained in their own organisation, the National Union of Seamen, which had been formed in 1887. That demarcation was replicated in these early years of the ILO, which formally established the principle of a distinction between maritime and shore-based industries even when they were on the waterfront. The International Congress belief – that maritime matters were in need of special handling – was built into the processes that were to be followed in the ILO. The International Labour conference, at its Third Session, adopted a resolution that no conventions or recommendations passed by the ILO Conference would 'apply to those employed in the mercantile marine unless they have been passed as a special maritime question on the agenda.'[11]

Furthermore, questions about maritime matters that were put forward to the ILO Conferences for consideration were first to be considered by the JMC, as the preamble said, 'seeing that misunderstanding may arise as to the position of those employed in the mercantile marine.' This resolution meant that separate maritime sessions considered the conventions and recommendations applying to seafarers. Only rarely and only after they had been discussed at the JMC were maritime matters submitted to general sessions of the conference. Thus, the JMC was intended and set up only to advise and make recommendations for the Governing Body and the conference to take action, as they saw fit. As a result, in its first 30 years, the JMC met in 15 sessions and the International Labour conference adopted 25 conventions and 12 recommendations for the regulation of maritime employment. However, there were hitches. Originally set up as a bipartite body of just shipowners and seafarers, it was hard for the members of the JMC to reach agreement. The seafarers pushed the Governing Body to have government representatives included which would break the impasse and also make the JMC a tripartite section, in line with other ILO sections. The shipowners, however, consistently resisted. In an effort to conciliate their differences over the inclusion of government members, a compromise was found by adding a new provision to the standing orders, namely that 'the Commission may also recommend ... that tripartite subcommittees be convened to discuss any matter appropriate.'[12]

The SUA was at first unimpressed by the ILO and its Congresses: 'in no sense can that Congress be considered as representing organised Labor.' The SUA was also very suspicious about this 'New Charter for Seamen' when it was initiated by officials and government delegates in 1920 and said it 'must be watched carefully by those who go to sea.' The SUA had not been consulted or notified, yet Britain was 'the first of the countries' who would be participating in the International Labour conference to be held in

---

[11] 'The Joint Maritime Commission and the Maritime Work of the ILO.'
[12] 'The Joint Maritime Commission and the Maritime Work of the ILO.'

Washington 'to prepare a programme of demands on behalf of seamen.'[13] In announcing the new charter, in January 1920, the *Australasian Seamen's Journal* quoted a report from the British press that an international minimum wage and uniform standard hours for seamen would revolutionise their conditions of service. Havelock Wilson had presented a set of demands to be taken by the British Government delegate (J.G. Barnes). These included protective standards – of accommodation and provision of food, manning scales, life-saving appliances and limitation on deck loads. In addition, there were rights – to minimum wages and standardised hours, to receiving a portion of the wages they had earned when coming ashore in a foreign port; for their wages to be paid from the date they signed their articles to the day crew were paid off, and if shipwrecked, to continue until they reached home; for compensation for loss of life, accidents and loss of effects. Other demands related to the pilotage of ships, which should be: (a) compulsory, (b) restricted as to nationality, (c) not undertaken by ships' officers. The final demands were for the reconstruction of wireless maritime telegraph services and the establishment of National Joint Maritime Councils as well as an International Joint Maritime Industrial Council.

The SUA, however, did not trust Wilson and thought that Barnes too was 'wholly on the side of the capitalists.'[14] They suspected collusion to keep wages low and hours high, reporting that 'the representatives of the British seamen had already agreed with the representatives of the British Government as to the policy to be adopted' even before the conference assembled in Genoa, in 1920. Shortening the hours of seamen's labour had been one of the most important matters the Genoa conference had been called to consider. 'Most of the seamen of Great Britain were under the impression that as a result of that conference their hours of labor would be reduced, and they had everything to hope for in view of the fact that the hours of labour in all other countries were being reduced for seamen. The men in British ships had every reason to expect a change.' But Wilson had already reached agreement with the British Government: a sailor's week was to be 56 hours, the firemen's was 48 hours and the stewards, 70 hours. The SUA felt strongly 'the conditions agreed to by the representative of the seamen ... leave everything to be desired.'[15]

The SUA further criticised the proposed charter for being too moderate. Some of the proposals were not worth wasting time over, except possibly to remove them from their articles. Seamen should not be satisfied with

---

[13] 'New Charter for Seamen: Demand for International Minimum Wage and Standard Hours,' *Australasian Seamen's Journal* 7, no. 9 (15 January 1920).

[14] 'New Charter for Seamen.'

[15] 'Secret Diplomacy,' by Mercator, *Australasian Seamen's Journal* 8, no. 14 (1 May 1922).

5.1 Australian delegates to Joint Maritime Commission of ILO, SUA Assistant
Secretary Patrick Geraghty (far right) 1972, NBAC N38

receiving a 'portion of wages earned' to spend when they were in a foreign
port. The provision did not change the power relationship: 'those wages ...
are ours; then let us ... collect them, and not allow the capitalist to withhold
any part of them until it suits him.'[16] It was to be some years before the SUA
attitude towards the ILO shifted.

The constitution of the JMC was heavily oriented towards northern
European membership. The shipowners' members at the First Session were
from Belgium, Canada, Japan, Sweden and the United Kingdom. The
seafarers' members came from France, Germany, Italy, Norway and the
United Kingdom. The only Asian representative (Japan) was there as a party
to the Peace Treaty, but the *Seamen's Journal* noted it had been criticised for
violating the provisions of the Peace Treaty, notably 'providing the right of
association.' At the General conference, the representative from Belgium
reproached Japan for the government's refusal to allow the workers to form
unions, and for its methods of selecting its labour representatives.[17]

[16] 'New Charter for Seamen.'
[17] Peggy, 'The Black Pan: Our Glorious Ally,' *Australasian Seamen's Journal* 7, no. 8
(15 December 1919).

Over time, other countries were included in the JMC, but it was not until the 1930s that the standing orders allowed membership to be extended to include eastern Europe, the Americas and some Asian countries (including Australia) by permitting a larger number of regular members and doubling the number of deputy members. The change was approved by the Governing Body, in 1937, when Australia together with Denmark, Greece, India and the United States were added to the countries represented by shipowners' members and deputy members. Australia was also among the countries added to the seafarers' list, the others being Argentina, China, Denmark, India, Norway and the United States. The inclusion in the JMC of these non-European countries expanded (a little) the racial diversity of membership, while Fascist governments in other countries – Germany and Spain – meant they were dropped from the list of shipowners' representatives and Germany was also dropped from the list of countries having seafarers' members and deputies.[18] Soon Japan too was expelled from the ILO.

'The International Brotherhood of Seamen'

Combating the power of shipowners who relied on racialised categories of workers to keep wage rates low and accommodation provisions minimal, meant strategies for dealing with these racialised differences was an ongoing challenge for maritime organisations. At the ITF's meeting in 1919, in Amsterdam, there was no disagreement amongst the delegates considering Japanese and Indian labour organisations: they voted unanimously to adopt a resolution declaring they had to become members of the ITF. It was not for any high-minded principles but 'lest the Asians became a danger to the European workers.'[19] What also made that conference important, however, was the appointment of Edo Fimmen, a Dutch trade unionist, as the new federation secretary. Holding the position for around two decades and having a great influence amongst European labour activists meant Fimmen was able to take the revitalised ITF into new regions.[20]

Fimmen was a committed internationalist and anti-racist. He had regular correspondence with a number of emerging independence leaders in the colonies of European powers, including Jawaharlal Nehru of India. He actively promoted – through ITF forums and periodicals – an idea of interconnectedness, that the support of 'the social struggle of the workers

[18] 'The Joint Maritime Commission and the Maritime Work of the ILO.'

[19] Report of Proceedings of the International Conference of Transport Workers' Organisations, Amsterdam, 1919, 28.

[20] ITF Solidarity, 86; Bob Reinalda, 'The ITF and Non-European World,' in Reinalda, International Transportworkers Federation, 1914–1945, 119–21.

in China, Japan, India, etc.' was essential to maintain and extend labour rights in 'the old industrialised countries.'[21] Two new favourable factors – the growth of unionism in Japan and India, and the founding in 1919 of the ILO as an agency of the League of Nations – helped the ITF to commence forging regional relations in Asia.

International European developments were followed and noted in Australia.[22] There, unions adopted an outward-looking approach that went beyond the nation and could 'save the world from war, and insure that, for the future, the ships, the seamen, and their labor shall be used in the interests of the working class ... Comrades, as men, we cannot evade our responsibilities toward the world and toward humanity.'[23] They held that 'a far greater sense of comradeship and brotherhood prevails among the toilers of the sea than anywhere else,' and this was solidifying and becoming 'more intense' as 'the seaman is groping his way into the path of solidarity,' leading to better conditions.[24]

They were indeed groping their way. In this spirit of a path to solidarity, Australian seafaring unions took an interest in the activities of, and were reaching out to, Asian workers. Australia was positioned awkwardly in the ITF division of the world, with a cultural and institutional inheritance from Britain and a geographical location in the Asia-Pacific region. This ultimately affected the perspective of the largely British or European-born unionists. At war's end they argued that seamen will have to be prepared to take their stand for humanity against capitalism in various ways when the desire for profits once again 'forces war ... on the world': for they assumed that next war would be in and for control of the Pacific and the Far East.[25] Asian countries were not 'the Far East' but Australia's near neighbours. They shared the seas, had traded for centuries with the Indigenous population, and their people (especially from China) started settling in the colonies once these were established. European Australians long feared a threat of invasion from China and in the decades after the First World War this was being expressed in new geopolitical terms as a threat from Japan.

With India, however, Australia shared membership of the British Empire, which added complexity to the matters of racial dynamics and maritime unionism that both national and international labour organisations were grappling with. During the war, Indians who had entered Australia started

---

21 ITF *Solidarity*, 42–3.

22 Peggy, 'The Black Pan,' *Australasian Seamen's Journal* 7, no. 8 (15 December 1919).

23 Murray and Walsh, 'To the Seamen of the World.'

24 'The Internationality of the Seamen.'

25 P.E. Coleman, 'The World War: Australia and Problems of the Future,' *Australasian Seamen's Journal* 7 no. 2 (2 November 1914).

asking could Australians 'honourably continue to treat them as we do, whilst they are shedding their blood in our cause.'[26] The experience of war, especially India's contribution alongside Australians in the Dardanelles, changed Australia's perception of and relationship with Indians resident in Australia, and helped recalibrate dynamics within the Empire.[27] Indentured labour was abolished in the Empire, which reduced the danger of cheap Indian labour being imported.[28] Yet Indian seafarers continued to be employed in large and increasing numbers by British shipping companies, as the legal category of 'Lascar' remained untouched until 1958.[29]

Japan was the country that loomed largest after the war, not only as a major shipping nation but in posing a threat because of the White Australia policy. An article in the *Seamen's Journal* predicted that as Japan was now an ally, after the war Japan would 'demand that its people not be discriminated against by Australia or other British dominions.' Japan could not be expected 'to endure such shame' for long and England was unlikely to support the national racial immigration policy: 'Our future is fogged by this great color problem.'[30]

The author of this piece, Percy Edmund Coleman (1892–1934), had started as a seafarer at the age of 13, but only three years later he had come ashore to work in the office of the Sydney branch of the Seamen's Union (see Figure 3.3). From there he was subsequently appointed general secretary of the United Clerks Union of New South Wales, before he enlisted and served overseas during the war, spending some time afterwards touring the United States. He was elected as ALP candidate to the Federal parliament in 1922, became Australia's representative at the ILO in 1930 and subsequently at the British Commonwealth Labour conference in London. In writing this article for the union journal, he seemed to be condemning the White Australia policy for the enormous insult it gave to Asian nations, grouping them with incurables, lunatics and criminals of the worst type by demanding the fingerprints even of those who have a legal right to enter. 'Not one of us, if of another color, would be prepared to endure this treatment without resentment.'[31] So he argued the immigration policy could not be defended on any grounds, ethical, moral or religious. Yet he presented a confused position, reflecting several sides simultaneously, conceding the standard

[26] Coleman, 'The World War: Australia and Problems of the Future.'

[27] Kama McLean, *British India, White Australia: Overseas Indians, Intercolonial Relations and the Empire* (Sydney: NewSouth Publishing, 2020), 103, 129, 17.

[28] McLean, *British India, White Australia*, 12.

[29] Barnes, *Evolution and Scope of Mercantile Marine Laws*, 38.

[30] Coleman, 'The World War: Australia and Problems of the Future.'

[31] Coleman, 'The World War: Australia and Problems of the Future.'

'opening the floodgates to the great wave ... [that] would overwhelm our insignificant[-sized] population ... economic system ... and ... commerce,' making 'national unity ... an impossibility.' Having adopted the policy, discussion of how the policy might be maintained included becoming an ally of the United States, which was the power in the Pacific, encouraging white migration from Europe or creating a strong navy and army because Australia risked 'an inevitable attack by Japan.' Australia must either prepare for war to defend its policy or drop 'the vaunted racial superiority' and allow 'the oil to mix with the water.'[32] The SUA chose to navigate a path of reducing 'the vaunted racial superiority' by encouraging organisation regardless of racial identity. While not always successful at avoiding the assumption of superiority or of being patronising, the union endeavoured to be inclusive rather than building membership based on race. Whiteness was not a criterion for union membership.

'There is no color bar in the Seamen's Union,' the journal was announcing in the 1920s, 'to adopt one would be fatal to the future of seamanship.'[33] Like the US union, the Australians took the pragmatic view that shipowners would too easily find crew to man their ships among non-unionised, 'coloured' seamen. Equally importantly, to organise those who were employed in all the world's shipping meant more would be carrying the gospel of unionism, having themselves experienced the benefits. The principle of excluding only Asian seafarers (which the United States had chosen to do) was unacceptable, 'not likely to create a friendly atmosphere' between Australia and other nations in Australia's region of the world. It was better to promote labour's international message of solidarity. In a complete reversal of earlier policies, the SUA now argued 'How utterly ridiculous it is to suppose that by excluding Asiatics, either from the unions or from "OUR COUNTRY", we can rid ourselves of their competition.' Preferred strategies were uniting the working class in one industrial union, compelling Labor to have an international policy, and to do only those things which can pass the scrutiny of the international working class. Their position was clear and unchanged in one key feature: 'Any scheme of indenture or slavery ought to be resisted most vigorously,' but otherwise 'all colored men, whatever their nationality, who work in Australian industries, ought to be organized' for cooperation and comradeship and because unorganised workers 'constitutes a menace to us all.'[34]

There was new leadership of the SUA and a new era of militancy developed

---

[32] Coleman, 'The World War: Australia and Problems of the Future.'

[33] John Observa, 'The White Australia Policy and the OBU,' *Australasian Seamen's Journal* 8, no. 36 (1 March 1924): 7.

[34] Observa, 'The White Australia Policy.'

5.2 Tom Walsh [1925]
Photograph Carlos
Federico (Cantarito)
Bunge Molina y Vedia

in the post-war years as internationalism took on a more ideological slant. Like many seafarers, Thomas Walsh (1871–1943) was an internationalist by experience and ideological commitment. For eight years he was at the helm of the SUA, elected as general secretary in 1917, then as president from 1922 to 1925. These were critical years in the history of the SUA and the Australian labour movement, with a general strike in 1917 and the formation of the Communist Party of Australia in 1920. Walsh had left his native Ireland and had been working on the Australian coast since 1893, in the difficult days of depression and the aftermath of defeat of the great maritime strike of 1890, which had prompted the formation of a Labor Party in several states and a turn towards political rather than direct industrial action. He became active in the union as the SUA's Newcastle agent from 1908. Within a year he was on the SUA Federal Executive, and then was elected as New South Wales branch secretary, in 1912.

The years of Walsh's leadership were some of the most turbulent yet also successful in the union's history. As general secretary of the Seamen's Union, Walsh clashed with Hughes when in 1919 he organised the biggest strike in the SUA's history and was consequently imprisoned for three months.[35] 'The Australian seaman of 1919,' especially after his treatment over the war bonus, was ready to throw down the gauntlet. He 'will not therefore be satisfied by the proclamation of the Navigation Act' and had taken the action of 'tying up ships and refusing to go into the Federal Arbitration Court.'[36] The system of arbitration had been rejected early on by the UK labour movement but was a constant source of discussion and interest within socialist circles once it had been established in Australia and New Zealand. The Arbitration court protected seamen's employment in comparison with their contemporaries overseas. It required the formation of unions to represent workers wanting to have their disputes settled and this fostered union membership. This system differentiated Australia (and New Zealand) from the United States, where judge-made law was 'persistently – and grossly – hostile to trade unions' and anti-union doctrines were much more powerful.[37] The proportion of the workforce that was unionised was much higher in Australia. The virtue of the awards system was their legally enforceable industry-wide application once decided by the court or commission.

When he married Adela Pankhurst, in 1917, Walsh brought another unexpected dimension of militancy to the SUA. Adela Pankhurst was well known in socialist circles in Victoria, and well connected via her prominent family to political activism in the UK. She was a founding member of the Women's Peace Army, formed to oppose the war and conscription. A noted public speaker, she had been gaoled and was on bail, with Prime Minister Hughes threatening to deport her, when she met and married Walsh. Marriage gave a new direction to her radical activism and to the SUA, as her feminism added to his socialism. Together they made a formidable couple. With Walsh's election to the position of SUA general secretary, Pankhurst took on the work of editing the union's journal. She often wrote articles under the pseudonym of her initials, A.C.M.P.W.; sometimes, as one contemporary recalled, while breastfeeding her newest infant. Life was a financial struggle for the growing family and many of her articles detailed the domestic drudgery of working-class women's lives, where the 'pregnant wife works ceaselessly in a hot kitchen, washing, ironing, mending, cooking,

---

[35] Morris, 'Mr. Justice Higgins Scuppered,' 52. Arthur Cooper, the former General Secretary, and now member of the Board of Trade, and Guthrie, still a Senator, were called on as 'moderates' to help broker an end to the strike. See 'The Maritime Strike,' *The Capricornia* (Rockhampton), 26 July 1919, 16.

[36] 'Seamen's Demands,' *Australasian Seamen's Journal* 6, no. 3 (1 September 1918) and *Australasian Seamen's Journal* 7, no. 3 (1 July 1919).

[37] David Brody, 'American Labour Law as a Model for Australia? Or, Can You Get Here From There?' *Labour History* 97 (2009): 189–98.

caring for a sickly, crying baby.'[38] There was also a discernible change in the tone and content of articles appearing under Tom Walsh's name: perhaps her words were slipped in, bringing a perspective that was often missing from union deliberations.

> Deprived of the pleasures of home and family life by the conditions of our calling, we seamen are almost complete strangers to our children, mere callers at our homes, and our wives must suffer the intolerable strain of separation from husband and breadwinner. Is it not time that we seamen made an effort to secure for ourselves and our families a fitting share of the vast wealth we create?[39]

The couple were founding members of the Communist Party of Australia, which met in Sydney in October 1920. Adela left after a year. Tom lasted one year more. But neither was prepared to remain as the CPA took a doctrinaire direction, although they continued to share internationalist ideals and campaign against racism. Tom Walsh as the SUA general secretary refused to countenance racist policies or language. He moved the union away from Guthrie's policy of working harmoniously with the shipowners and supporting the reformism that underlay the White Australia policy platform upheld by the previous leadership. Under Walsh's leadership, the SUA's earlier position of internationalism and inclusion strengthened. On one occasion he refuted a demand that SUA officials 'must, or should' change the Union rules to declare that:

> no more aliens, with the exception of those already in the Union, shall be admitted to membership ... [and that] Our ships must be manned and officered by men of Australian birth – men with Australian aspirations and ideals; men in whom is implanted love for and pride in the land of their birth. ... These are the men we want. There can be, there must be, no place in the Australian mercantile marine for the foreigner.[40]

In reply, Walsh, himself Irish-born, wrote that 'The foreign seaman ... is no foreigner – he is a brother worker.' He argued that where someone was born was outside the individual's control and should never prevent anyone's membership of the union. He spoke of 'The International Brotherhood of Seamen' and deplored sentiments that 'tend only to race hatred and national prejudice,' fomenting bitterness between unionists instead of cultivating international comradeship. To achieve working-class unity, they needed

---

[38] Verna Coleman, *Adela Pankhurst: The Wayward Suffragette, 1885–1961* (Melbourne: Melbourne University Press, 1996), 89.

[39] Murray and Walsh, 'To the Seamen of the World.'

[40] 'Australian Sailors for Australian Ships,' *Australasian Seamen's Journal* 5, no. 12 [sic] (1 April 1918).

to 'recognise the class interests of all workers, irrespective of nationality,' which was 'the greatest menace to working-class unity.' The SUA was to be inclusive and open to new members. 'Our duty is to foster a spirit of internationality.' While he condemned 'bitterness founded on racial animosities,' Walsh spoke of seafarers' rights, as he said nationality should never jeopardise any seamen's 'right as a unionist to sail in any ship.' He also pointed out that most Australian seamen had come from another country. That had been important in building up the union. It should not now be grounds to deny a man 'the right to participate in the conditions [that] some of his fellow countrymen helped to establish, and he, himself, is willing to uphold and extend.'[41]

A similar argument for internationalism was presented by Indian trade union leader W.P. Wadra, president of the Madras Labor Union, speaking to the [British] Trade Union Congress in Glasgow, in 1918. His speech spoke of the sufferings of the Indian labourer, of underpaid Bengal miners and impoverished textile workers. It was reported in the *Seamen's Journal* because it explained how interconnected workers were: 'When the Indian textile workers struck, they were told that their wages could not be increased because the Lancashire workers were standing in their way, and when the Lancashire textile workers wanted their wages increased they were told that the Indian textile workers were in the road of any increase. So it goes on.' When he said: 'workers everywhere must join hands in the fight against capitalism, whether the capitalists be white, brown or black,' the delegates as a body 'rose … and enthusiastically applauded the Indian comrade. A resolution was passed pledging financial assistance to the Indian Trade Union Movement. The Unity of labor is the hope of the World. Speed the day!'[42] That year, race riots by maritime workers broke out in Liverpool and Glasgow.[43] No riots or similar events occurred in Australia.

This period saw the strengthening of organised seafarers' trade unions in India and members of the SUA becoming active in assisting Indian seafarers in their disputes with ships' masters. When a group were stranded in Australia because the master of their ship, the SS *Batavia*, had led them to believe they were engaged to sail to India, and then changed the itinerary, the SUA helped them until they secured a passage home in another ship. They had signed on at Philadelphia, on condition that they would be

---

[41] Thomas Walsh to The Editor, *Australasian Seamen's Journal* 5, no. 12 [*sic*] (1 April 1918).

[42] Peggy, 'The Black Pan: Indian Labour Representatives,' *Australasian Seamen's Journal* 7, no. 8 (15 December 1919).

[43] Jacqueline Jenkinson, 'Black Sailors on Red Clydeside: Rioting, Reactionary Trade Unionism and Conflicting Notions of "Britishness" following the First World War,' *Twentieth Century British History* 19, no. 1 (2008): 29–60.

paid off at an Indian port within four months, in a clause inserted in the Articles of Agreement. When it became clear the ship was now going from Melbourne to South Africa instead, they refused to work given the distinct breach of their Agreement. Consequently, they were prosecuted and, even with assistance from a solicitor, were sentenced to seven days' imprisonment. After serving that sentence, and again refusing to work, they were prosecuted a second time and this time sentenced to six weeks' imprisonment. The ship sailed without them, and with a replacement non-union white crew, while they served out their sentences.[44]

The *Seamen's Journal* published the letter 'our Indian comrades' wrote to express their gratitude for the SUA's support during this difficult incident through their own words: 'The uncommon, unusual, and unexpected sympathy and love that was showered upon us … from the generous, genial, benevolent breast of your Organisation … is not only ever to be remembered, and never to be forgotten, but has bound us so much with the tie of brotherly love and gratitude.' They said: 'We do not know how we shall thank you for your spontaneous, disinterested kindness, irrespective of cast [*sic*], prejudice, and religious animosity. It has given us a chance to create a better fellow feeling and understanding for the defence of the people like us from the vile, iron grip of the so-called master.' They ended with a prayer that 'love and affection will run from heart to heart of the men in our condition in every corner of the world, for the peace of the world and the preservation of humanity.' It was signed by Bhupendra Nath Roy, Ahammad Adda, Buz Ruk Ali, Bin Mahammad, Abudl Hassin, John Ali and Mr Mahad Hafiz, of a Calcutta address.[45]

It is likely that the Melbourne branch had provided practical financial help to the crewmen for the legal assistance they had, and in finding them a ship for the voyage home. The men's letter suggests that the moral support and sense of connection from the union was particularly valued. For the SUA, the Indian crew's actions in standing firm against the master were an indication of changing power. Gone were the days 'when the Shipowner at his will could exploit the colored seamen without the risk of him adopting any retaliatory measures.' Another ship from the same company, the SS *Ooma*, 'manned by a colored crew' of all nationalities, among whom were a number from the United States, had also struck trouble. The 'coloured' Americans 'were evidently not servile enough for the Master.' They were put off the ship in Melbourne. Attempts to recruit a crew of Maltese at a

[44] John O'Neill, Branch Reports, Melbourne Branch Report, 'Indians Refusal to Work,' *Australasian Seamen's Journal* 8 [*sic*] (1 September 1923).

[45] 'Our Indian Comrades: To the President of the Seamen's Union of Australasia,' *Australasian Seamen's Journal* 8, no. 33 (December 1923).

lower wage failed when the Maltese refused to work for rates less than the Australian standard. The company eventually relented. The union welcomed the show of resistance as a sign that shipowners were losing the power to exploit them, and 'coloured' seamen were learning to insist on a fair and just wage instead of being 'starved and sweated and compelled to live under [degrading] conditions.'[46]

Another Australian seafarer wrote: 'I have no national feelings to pander to ... I have nothing against the Indian seamen on account of their color. They are the victims of the system the same as we are, and the only objection I have against them is on the ground that "master" uses them to reduce the living standard of the European seamen.'[47] During Walsh's time as leader, there were often articles on Asian countries and their workers' actions on their own behalf.[48] And the union's previous policy of not opposing the White Australia policy while promoting Australian labour standards for all races became more pointedly focused on the ironies of the governing class's position, and the principles that a White Australia was supposed to contain. The union pursued the inconsistencies in arguments by the policy's supporters. They noticed that the *Bulletin* made no adverse comment when the government granted permits to ships manned with cheap Asian labour to carry passengers between ports on the Australian coast, nor did it support the Seamen's Union when it objected to these violations of the official policy.[49] It reiterated the earlier argument about why capitalists supported White Australia, and that Australia would not develop through importing indentured labour, or sowing the evil seed of slavery, which was tantamount to degradation and cruelty.[50]

'The people of Australia must keep their land clean and free from slavery ... It degrades the slaves, it degrades every citizen of the nation which permits it,' as could be seen in the United States and South Africa, and 'the vast populations of Asia [were] set against being exploited by Western Capitalism.'[51] Lord Leverhulme had suggested that 'Australians admit colored labour to do the "donkey work" as he calls it, and to keep the colored laborers as "beasts of burden."' But the SUA argued 'men are men, not beasts – whether their skins are black or white – and all strive to be free ... to find happiness and self-expression.' Therefore, describing 'certain

---

[46] O'Neill, 'Indians Refusal to Work.'

[47] Hayes, 'Newcastle Branch Report.'

[48] 'News from Japan by "Tokyo,"' *Australasian Seamen's Journal* 7, no. 10 (1 March 1920).

[49] John Observa, 'The "Bulletin" and Immigration,' *Australasian Seamen's Journal* 8, no. 37 (1 April 1924).

[50] 'Beasts of Burden,' *Australasian Seamen's Journal* 8, no. 35 (1 February 1924): 10–12.

[51] 'Beasts of Burden.'

races and classes' as being beasts of burden, 'without rights, without feelings' enables atrocities towards them. 'A person who speaks of his fellow creatures as "beasts of burden" is hardly worthy of civic recognition in a country which prides itself on its advance[d] civilisation.'[52]

The SUA opposed the use of subsidies for trade by ships carrying cheap labour. 'Shipping profiteers' were trying to induce the Minister for Customs to grant them a subsidy for the trade between Australia, India and other Eastern ports. The Seamen's Union asked the Labor Party to ensure that those subsidised ships must 'pay Australian wages and institute all the conditions under which Australian seamen work.'[53] They believed this was responsible given that the money belonged to the Australian people. Turning a blind eye to or facilitating practices of using cheap labour that was tantamount to slavery meant principles went out of the window when profits were involved. Australian maritime unionists continually pointed out that it was 'shipping profiteers,' 'shipping capitalists,' who were the instigators and perpetrators of racial exploitation as a means to drive down labour costs. Cheapness also meant disempowered crews, poorly trained in matters of safety, and 'not ready to demand inspections when the ship is on the danger line' unlike 'those who have a knowledge of what is required' and, most importantly, 'will stand on their rights and demand a "fair run."'[54]

This point was demonstrated in an incident when a sailing ship manned with equal numbers of Indian and European seamen arrived in Newcastle. The Indian crew lodged a complaint against the captain and the mate, which was, as required, handed to the local police. The captain reportedly denied everything, and responded by turning on the Indian crewmen, arguing that they were inadequate for the job. He claimed that in bad weather the Indian crew were of 'little use,' and that he depended on 'white seamen [who] were his "fall-back" when things were rough.' The inference, according to the union, was that higher-paid European crew were preferred for their greater seamanship, which they saw as an admission that the drive for profits only pushed the hire of cheaper labour, placing everyone's lives at risk, especially when crews were unqualified or legally unable to complain. One occasion of such an unseaworthy ship being crewed by cheap labour resulted in the loss of 33 lives, yet 'The loss of life at sea does not concern the shipowner, nor can he be held responsible for it; God is usually blamed.'[55]

[52] 'Beasts of Burden.'

[53] Peggy, 'The Black Pan: Subsidies and Profits,' *Australasian Seamen's Journal* 8, no. 38 (1 May 1924).

[54] Hayes, 'Newcastle Branch Report.'

[55] Hayes, 'Newcastle Branch Report.'

The issue of cheap labour in this line of thinking that made it inseparable from safety was not solved by simply excluding 'coloured' crews from the competition for employment. Steps to establish minimum labour standards, and to empower the workforce to demand that safe practices were adhered to, needed unity of the international brotherhood of seafarers. So that unsafe ships, undermanned and overloaded with improperly stowed cargo, could not be sailed, the Australian union was pursuing strategies of organisation and reaching out to seafarers across racial divides. These steps were also being taken within the ITF.

'[S]triv[ing] to cultivate international comradeship'

At the time the ITF reunited in Amsterdam, in 1919, the Japanese maritime trade union movement comprised around 20 small associations that had emerged in response to poor employment conditions in the national shipping industry – the third largest in the world. The initial development of local maritime unionism progressed in isolation, with no contacts with foreign labour organisations. In 1920, however, the Japanese government appointed Kunitaro Hamada and Choyei Horiuchi – two maritime labour activists – as advisers to the workers' delegates at the ILO Maritime Labour conference at Genoa, in 1920. The experience gained in Europe and 'a full investigation of Western methods' led Hamada and Horiuchi to promote the idea of a single, industry-wide seafarers' organisation in their home country. This work resulted the following year in the establishment of the amalgamated Japan Seamen's Union (JSU), which very soon grew into a powerful organisation with a 90,000 strong membership.[56]

From the very outset, the JSU was willing to use international means to gain more strength in industrial relations on a national level. Two major issues of concern to the union were securing the right of collective bargaining agreements and participation in the labour recruitment process controlled by the government-supported Seamen's Relief Association. In this context, at the sixth ILO Conference, Mitsusuke Yonekubo, adviser to the Japanese Workers' delegate, made inquiries on the rights of the government and unions to control the hiring process of maritime labour. At the ninth ILO Conference, Itoshi Narasaki, JSU president, presented a memorandum against the unjust labour policies of the Japanese government. In the late 1920s, partially because of these international actions, the government

---

[56] G. Mogi, *Japanese Shipping Trade and the Seamen's Trade Union Movement* (Amsterdam: ITF, 1931).

5.3 English troops departing for the colony of Hong Kong to quell seamen's
strike, 1922
© Tallandier/Bridgeman Images

allowed the JSU to take part in the national Joint Maritime Board, which
obtained the right to manage seamen's labour exchanges.[57]

Unlike Japan, where the growth of the seafaring workforce was brought
about by the expansion of the national shipping industry, in India the growth
was from a larger number of Indians as well as residents of the neighbouring
countries traditionally manning foreign-flagged vessels. Similar to Japan,
Indian seamen were represented at the inaugural ILO Maritime conference
in Genoa, in 1920. The president of the Bombay Asiatic Seamen's Union,
A. Mazarello, and two more rank and file Indian seafarers, travelled to
Italy for the meeting. In the subsequent years, Indian unionists continued
attending ILO forums.[58] This involvement promoted public awareness of
their problems as 'Lascars' and raised 'the intelligent and active interest
of seamen's organisation in Europe to the conditions of their comrades in
India.'[59]

The participation of the ITF on the one side and Japanese and Indian
seamen's unions on the other in ILO maritime meetings and conferences
provided a continual meeting place for officials from both sides to seek

---

[57] Mogi, *Japanese Shipping Trade.*

[58] Desai, *Maritime Labour in India*, 183–200; Theodore G. Mazarello, Maritime Labour
in India (Bombay: Maritime Union of India, 1961), 67; Arora, *Voyage*, 3.

[59] Desai, *Maritime Labour in India*, 188.

more permanent direct forms of contact.[60] The global nature of the shipping enterprise and common industrial problems of the seafaring workforce explicitly encouraged this collaboration. In 1924, Mitsusuke Yonekubo, of the Japan Seamen's Union, attended the ITF Hamburg Congress on a non-official basis. A draft convention of the International Seamen's Code prepared by the maritime section of the congress for the ILO prompted Yonekubo to take part in the ITF congress.[61] That document was crucial for seafarers around the world by setting up international standards for many industrial issues, including recruitment, hours of work, manning requirements, training, shipowners' liabilities, and welfare in ports. At the thirteenth maritime ILO Conference, which took place in Geneva in October 1929, Edo Fimmen and Kunitaro Hamada, Japan union leader, finally considered in detail a question of formal partnership between the ITF and the JSU. As the parties reached the agreement, the Japan Dockers' Union officially joined the Federation in March 1930 and a union delegate participated in the ITF London Congress held in September the same year.[62]

There was also growing convergence in the positions of the ITF and Indian maritime unionists. The small relief organisations, which provided help to distressed Indian seafarers and which had appeared in Calcutta and Bombay in the early twentieth century, merged after the First World War into two separate unions in each of those cities. In the 1930s, the Calcutta-based Indian Seamen's Union (ISU-C) brought together around 23,000 members, and the union with the identical name in Bombay (ISU-B) united 12,000. In addition to these two major unions there were several minor ones affiliated to a national organisation – the All-India Seamen's Federation, headquartered in Calcutta.

The seamen's section of the ITF and the International Mercantile Marine Officers' Association arranged a joint conference in 1928 to initiate an inquiry into the working conditions of Asian seafarers on European ships. The relevant report published in 1930 supported equality of wages and treatment, as the work done by both classes of seamen was the same.[63] A few related publications then appeared in the ITF newsletter as well.[64] In January 1929, the ISU-B became an ITF affiliate and in September the following year a union delegation attended the ITF London Congress. Syed

---

[60] Bob Reinalda, 'Success and Failure: ITF's Sectional Activities in the Context of International Labour Organization,' in Reinalda, *International Transportworkers Federation, 1914–1945*, 137–41.

[61] ITF, Report of the International Congress, 1924, 134.

[62] Mogi, *Japanese Shipping Trade*, 21, 24–5.

[63] Desai, *Maritime Labour in India*, 62–3.

[64] Arora, *Voyage*, 5–6.

Munawar, the ISU leader, was then elected to the ITF General Council. The ISU also formed a branch in Britain in 1929 to represent the voices of Indian seaman engaged in the British shipping sector.[65]

The ITF leadership realised the difficulties they faced of building formal links with non-European unions. Fimmen believed that a personal visit by an ITF official would have a greater positive impact than constant appeals and letters. He urged the delegates of the 1922 ITF Congress to send a representative on a global tour to engage with non-European unionists personally, speak with them, attend their congresses, and thus prepare the way for their affiliation. The proposal failed because of a lack of finances. Their intensifying contacts with Japanese and Indian seamen's unions in the 1920s, however, enabled the ITF to draw on local support to organise a trip. This meant the 1928 Stockholm Congress could approve an official visit to the Asia-Pacific region to recruit new affiliates and establish the Far East secretariat of the Federation.[66]

While managing to enlist Japanese and Indian seamen's unions, the ITF failed to attain the same success with Australian maritime labour organisations. Just after the war, the call by the Federated Seamen's Union of Australasia suggesting the organisation of a large joint international conference in a European city was circulated as a pamphlet around overseas seafarers' organisations, including the ITF. The proposed forum would serve political rather than industrial ends. It was hoped that it would 'formulate a common policy which could be acted upon by seamen all over the world in the event of another war being forced on mankind in our own time.'[67] The FSUA's plan never materialised and after 1920 links between the Australian union and the ITF all but ceased.

Havelock Wilson's influence in the ITF and the JMC would not have encouraged contact.[68] The SUA leant away from the British–European connections and more towards the US unions across the Pacific, with which it shared the IWW philosophy of 'One Big Union' and anti-racism.[69] The SUA journal quoted at length the argument from the *International Unionist* that 'race prejudice' was the seafarer's chief enemy. They wanted to be, as that journal claimed, a union of seamen where 'national prejudice … does not exist … in the same sense as it does among other workers.' Given their conditions of work,

---

[65] Arora, *Voyage*, 6, 9.

[66] ITF *Solidarity*, 89; Reinalda, 'The ITF and Non-European World,' 121. The records of the 1928 Congress contain reports on Asian affiliates, http://mrc-catalogue.warwick.ac.uk/records/ITF/1/1/15.

[67] 'Fellow Seamen and Comrades,' MS 159/3/C/61, MRC.

[68] On Havelock Wilson, see *Australasian Seamen's Journal* 8, no. 18 (1 September 1922).

[69] Peggy, 'The Black Pan: Is the O.B.U in Japan,' *Australasian Seamen's Journal* 8, no. 5 (1 August 1921).

'where many nationalities are to be found on the same ship,' they sought to become immune to attempts by those – shipowners, ships' masters and even some union officials – seeking to instil prejudice amongst seamen against other seamen. Seamen were instead 'carrying the gospel of international solidarity and industrial unionism to the most remote corners of the world.'[70]

The post-war relations between the ITF and Australian dockworkers were somewhat more sustainable. In 1919, the WWF initiated the establishment of the Transport Workers' Federation of Australia (TWF) – a loose national association of transport trade unions.[71] The same year, the new organisation's secretary contacted the ITF through British unionists to obtain information on the new structure and working of the Federation with an ultimate aim to explore a possibility of affiliation. TWF members continued leisurely discussions of a prospective partnership with the ITF until 1926 when the WWF secretary finally informed the ITF that the idea could not be implemented due to opposition from small unions and the SUA's internal conflicts.[72]

Separately, an exchange of letters took place directly between the Waterside Workers and the ITF. A few times the Australian union was asked to send its representative to the ITF, but these invitations commonly produced polite declines on the basis of the high cost of overseas trips. In 1926, however, the WWF Committee of Management put on the official agenda the question of a formal alliance with the ITF. The vote on the resolution was negative, as was reported to Fimmen: that 'this Committee in view of the need of local organisation cannot see its way clear to agree to affiliation with the International Transport Workers' Federation.'[73] Such an unenthusiastic response stemmed from the contemporary problems experienced by Australian waterside unionists who were being confronted by the Nationalist Party government's determination to curb the union's industrial power. Indeed, over the following decade, the employment of non-unionised waterfront labour and the creation of the opposition Permanent & Casual Wharf Labourers Union nearly destroyed the WWF, which was able to revive only in the very late 1930s.[74]

Just after the First World War, correspondence also resumed between the ITF and New Zealand waterfront unionists, who were asked a few times to consider the issue of affiliation. Even though some union officials thought

---

[70] 'The Internationality of the Seamen.'

[71] Morgan, 'Labour and Industrial Authority,' 433.

[72] Correspondence, November 1919–May 1926, MS 159/3/C/55, MRC.

[73] Correspondence, January 1920–March 1926, MS 159/3/C/55, MRC; J. Morris to Fimmen, 20 October 1926, MS 159/3/C/55, MRC.

[74] Beasley, *Wharfies*, 76–103.

positively of the idea of Federation membership, the plan was not put into action in the 1920s due to the lack of support from other transport unions in the country. Things took a new turn in 1930 when the New Zealand union's James Robert travelled to Europe as a member of the national delegation to an ILO Conference. Robert simultaneously led the WWF organisation and the local peak labour body – the New Zealand Alliance of Labour. During the conference in Geneva and a separate visit to Stockholm he was able to meet Edo Fimmen to discuss 'the necessity of international cooperation.' These personal meetings resulted two years later in affiliation of the New Zealand waterside union to the ITF.[75]

This act was more of an exception in the history of the pre-1939 relations between the ITF and Australian and New Zealand maritime unions. Despite the continuity and relative ease of their informal interaction, it did not develop into a more formal long-lasting partnership. One explanation was the lack of practical necessity for them to seek support internationally to protect local labour standards. Even against British and American fellow seamen, let alone the ILO maritime labour recommendations, Australian merchant ship crew members enjoyed better employment conditions, with higher wages, an eight-hour working day and two weeks' annual leave.[76] Most of their contemporary problems had a localised regional character and origin, which in turn required local means of resolution. Given the financial obligations ITF membership imposed, the payoffs of membership were small. There were also internal frictions and a bitter contest for the SUA leadership between Tom Walsh and Jacob Johnson, Sydney branch secretary, tearing the union apart from the mid-1920s.[77] With the Great Depression soon driving down jobs, union membership and revenue, the SUA was not actively seeking contact with the remote European-based ITF.

[75] Correspondence, 1927–30, MS 159/3/C/55, MRC; Steve Hughes and Nigel Haworth, 'A Distant Detachment: New Zealand and the ILO, 1919–1945,' n.d., www.ilo.org/public/english/anniversary/90th/download/events/newzealand/hughes2.pdf.

[76] Fitzpatrick and Cahill, *History of the Seamen's Union of Australia*, 52, 56–7.

[77] J. Morris to Fimmen, 19 March 1926, MS 159/3/C/55, MRC.

6

'[T]o Ensure ... Fair Conditions of Labor'
Navigating Class, Nation and Empire in the 1920s

Tom Walsh once told a large gathering of seamen that if they weren't prepared to stand up and fight for their rights then they didn't deserve to have any. 'Everything we have won here we have won by fighting.'[1] These were militant words, but they carried harsh consequences. Two months later Tom was taken from his family home, rudely woken before dawn by a loud knocking on their door when police came to arrest him on behalf of the Deportation Board. A pregnant and upset Adela was left trying to soothe seven frightened crying children.[2]

The harrowing episode was the culmination of months of conflict and years of struggle. As Australia's maritime unions ramped up their militancy in the 1920s, they encountered a new, hard-line conservative government. Hughes had long since lost the support of the labour movement, especially his former union, the WWF. Following the 1922 election, when his party failed to win a majority, he also lost the Prime Ministership when the new Country Party refused to serve in a coalition he led. Under the new leadership of Stanley Melbourne Bruce, hostility towards the maritime labour unions rocketed to a whole new level.

Stanley Bruce (1883–1967) could not have had a more different background from the labourist Hughes and his waterfront constituents. The closest Bruce came to maritime labourers was in the view he had of ships sailing past the window of the family home overlooking Port Phillip Bay. Born into a prosperous family in a bayside Melbourne suburb, Bruce was a businessman, a graduate of Cambridge University, who had been called to the Bar in London.[3] He had been both wounded and decorated in the war, but served

---

[1] Reported in 'British Seamen's Trouble,' *Labor Call* (Melbourne), 27 August 1925, 7.

[2] Adela's recounting of the events is in Thomas Walsh and Adela Pankhurst Papers, MS 2123, NLA; Coleman, *Adela Pankhurst*.

[3] David Lee, *Stanley Melbourne Bruce: Australian Internationalist* (London: Continuum,

as a commissioned officer of the British not the Australian army. He too was an internationalist, according to his most recent biographer, because of his commitment 'to the ideal of peaceful collaboration among nations' to solve issues that one country on its own could not do. He was able to synchronise this with an Australian nationalism and a staunch defence of British imperialism because he saw them all as a single world.[4] To leaders of the labour movement, he lacked an Australian perspective.

His was the internationalism of capital. The family firm he inherited was an importing business originally established with partners in England. Bruce continued to have strong ties to financiers in England where he lived much of his life, even after 1918 while he was a backbencher in the Australian parliament. He became Prime Minister in 1923 when the newly formed Country Party members refused to form a coalition with Hughes to enable the minority Nationalist Party to govern. Forging and maintaining that coalition with the Country Party was a hallmark of success for Bruce's government that continues today in the Liberal–National (formerly Country) Party coalition. It was disastrous for the unions. Taking the interests of primary producers as being those of the nation shaped the government's approach to legislating on labour matters. The government could justify taking action against maritime unionists just by pointing to the economic losses incurred by waterfront and shipping disruptions.[5]

Bruce's term in government thus heightened the political power of primary producers in parliament and reinforced Australia's position as within the frame of empire. Australia's heavy dependence on shipping, and vulnerability in its reliance on British-owned shipping for the marketing overseas of its primary products, coalesced with Bruce's ties to Britain and business interests. As chair of his family's trading company, Bruce saw the achievement of cheap and efficient shipping through the lens of his own capitalist self-interest. In short, he was 'incapable of seeing his own class interests as part of the broad national picture.'[6] He was unfriendly to labour, and actively hostile to socialism. Bruce saw militancy by unionists 'as a perverse preference for conflict over cooperation and as a threat to the … domestic and international order' he favoured, and he consequently 'embark[ed] on inflexible and ruthless industrial policies.'[7]

2010).

    [4] Lee, *Bruce*, x, ix.

    [5] Heather Radi, '1920–29,' in *A New History of Australia*, ed. Frank Crowley (Melbourne: Heinemann, 1974), 397.

    [6] Lee, *Bruce*, 49; Judith Brett, 'Stanley Melbourne Bruce,' in *Australian Prime Ministers*, ed. Michelle Grattan (Sydney: New Holland Publishers, 2000), 126–38, at 138.

    [7] Lee, *Bruce*, 50.

According to an eminent contemporary Canberra journalist, Prime Minister Bruce saw Australia 'as a gigantic joint-stock company' in which good responsible citizens were people who accepted their allocated role 'silently and obediently.' Filtered through his 'inborn aristocracy,' a son loyal to a father who had helped found the very elitist Royal Melbourne Golf Club, he saw those who struggled against their conditions, resisted class power or went on strike as 'dangerous rebels who must be crushed.'[8]

Historians' judgement of Bruce and his ministers has not been favourable. The 1920s was a period of increased militancy across all industries, not just the maritime. Industrial disputation in Australia was not, however, as bad as in England and was no worse than in other industrialised nations. Governing according to 'strict business principles,' Bruce showed no understanding of or sympathy with those who did not share his 'extraordinarily narrow and privileged social world.'[9] His Attorney-General, Sir Lyttelton Groom, represented a prosperous rural electorate in Queensland, where constituents faced very few economic problems. Groom 'showed little awareness of the post-war problems of working people ... [nor] of the difficulties experienced in the large industrial cities.'[10] Yet he was charged with designing legislation that impacted directly on their lives. Groom was followed as Attorney-General by John Latham, who is better remembered today for his support of the Menzies' government's anti-communist legislation when sitting as Chief Justice on the High Court in the 1950s. Latham, a cold, stern man, as a government minister 'brought a formidable zeal' to the exercise of his duties, and he continued to give private political advice to anti-labour politicians throughout his long judicial career, despite his public claims to impartiality.[11]

The scene was set for a clash between the national government, tied more closely with the interests of imperial shipping reliant on colonised labour, and national maritime unions, more closely integrated with an international working-class movement. As Bruce set about protecting the economic interests of his class, the disempowered Hughes could only snipe from the sidelines. The maritime unions became the focus of government attention and a target for a Red Scare. In the background was the newly founded ILO with its dedicated maritime labour conference. International expectations

[8] Lee, *Bruce*, 2; Warren Denning, quoted in Lee, *Bruce*, 51.

[9] Brett, 'Stanley Melbourne Bruce,' 132, 135.

[10] David Carment, 'Sir Littleton Groom and the Deportation Crisis of 1925: A Study of Non-Labor Response to Trade Union Militancy,' *Labour History* 32 (1977): 46–54, 47.

[11] Stuart Macintyre, *The Reds* (Sydney: Allen & Unwin, 1998), 102–3; Fiona Wheeler, 'Sir John Latham's Extra-Judicial Advising,' *Melbourne University Law Review* 35, no. 2 (2011): 651–76.

of maritime labour rights being embodied in conventions prompted action at last on Australia's still-languishing Navigation Act. This was both a last hurrah for Hughes' Prime Ministership and the first of Hughes' protections for seafarers to be unwound.

'[N]o Act is of more importance'

On 1 July 1921, while Hughes was still Prime Minister, the Navigation Act 1912 finally became operational. Just two years later, when Bruce was now Prime Minister, the Tariff Board unexpectedly reported that the Act's protectionist policy had seriously affected Australian trade. While free traders might be expected to criticise 'such important legislation,' it was 'alarming' and unexpected for a protectionist body to do so and especially with such severity.[12] The report pointed to the cost of freight between Australian ports being equivalent to or even greater than freights between Britain to Australia.[13] Tasmania's smallness of trade meant it was no longer a regular port of call for overseas shipping. The federal government responded to this pressure by amending the legislation to introduce licences allowing overseas companies to carry cargo and passengers around the coast. In order to protect their interests, the shipowners' association (ASOF) monitored very effectively federal and state legislation which impacted on shipping and 'continually pressed for favourable conditions and emphatically rejected any claim of monopoly.'[14] The government was listening.

Primary producers and free traders in parliament jumped into action. 'Like a breath of old times,' as the Minister for Trade and Customs, Austin Chapman, said, once again the parliament had before it a discussion of the Navigation Act. Within days of the Tariff Board report, West Australian farmer and Country Party MP John Henry (Jack) Prowse was using its findings to move that parliament appoint a Committee of Inquiry. Prowse claimed that 'No Act upon the statute-book is of more importance than the Navigation Act' and 'nothing has a closer relation than sea-carriage to our future development.' His criticism was, he claimed, not on the labour foundations of the Act. Prowse acknowledged that the Navigation Act 'was brought into being providing conditions and pay in advance of any other country' and as a consequence it was indeed 'in advance of any similar Act in any part of the world, particularly in regard to the conditions provided for men working on board ship.' In this he was conceding what the liberal press had said of 'the need for legislation of this kind.' The *Age* had reported, 'This

---

[12] *Age* (Melbourne), 21 August 1924, 8.
[13] *Argus* (Melbourne), 17 July 1923.
[14] Morgan, 'Labour and Industrial Authority,' 270.

country ... was forced to protect its shipping trade; to encourage, for many reasons, the growth of a mercantile marine, and to ensure that seafaring workers are granted the fair conditions of labor conceded to those on shore.'[15]

Instead, Prowse centred attention on the impact on trade, 'its strangling effect' on 'every industry in Australia.' He spoke of Australian shipowners being given a monopoly, freights becoming prohibitive, irregular and inadequate services being provided, that trade with the Islands had been lost, and labourers were seeking higher wages in the Arbitration court to cover the artificial rise in costs. Prowse was open about his own interest in wanting an inquiry in order to secure a fair deal for his home state of Western Australia (WA) and that he was personally disadvantaged compared with farmers in the eastern states. He was joined by Nationalist Party Members who endorsed the claim that the Navigation Act had completely driven 'a good deal of shipping' out of Australian waters.

The proposal that the Act needed to be altered received speedy approval, perhaps a sign that amendments were already being planned. A committee was formed of state representatives with Prowse as chairman. The Select Committee subsequently became a Royal Commission, which sat in 1924, when 46 of the Navigation Act's 425 sections (most of them dealing with pilots and pilotage) still remained inoperative. Unlike 1906, this time the Commissioners could not agree, so their report contained three different positions, three different sets of recommendations. The first report, by Country Party MPs Prowse and Seabrook; the second by Labor parliamentarians Frank Anstey, G.E. Yates and Senator C.S. McHugh; the third by two Nationalist Party Senators, W.L. Duncan and H.E. Elliott. The liberal press was unimpressed. The Commission was a waste of money. These reports 'bear out almost precisely' the previously held opinions of the members at the time they were appointed. Although the Commissioners had all heard and seen exactly the same things, still they 'differ[ed] widely even on questions of fact. The separate findings destroy each other, and therefore can yield no result important enough to justify a fraction of the expense.'[16] The *Age* claimed that Prowse and Seabrook, 'the Free-trader and the Tasmanian,' had realised that 'the case against the Navigation Act is weak in comparison with that presented in favor.' So they had criticised instead the interstate shipping companies, and charged them with being a monopoly associated with British shipping companies. They were unequivocal that the Navigation Act had failed to develop an Australian merchant marine, but the *Age* was equally critical: 'Australia's mercantile marine may not be all

[15] 'Navigation Act, Effect on Australian Trade, Three Different Versions,' *Age* (Melbourne), 21 August 1924, 10.

[16] *Age* (Melbourne), 21 August 1924, 8.

that it ought to be, but not one of the three sections of the Commission has shown how it can be improved to the country's advantage.'[17]

Prowse and Seabrook's report was the least favourable. Anstey, Yates and McHugh were equally sure that the attack on the Navigation Act from the Tariff Board, alleging that the Act had caused Australian trade to suffer, was ill-founded; Duncan and Elliott argued that repeal of the Act would doubtless 'bring more foreign and non-British competition which would react very quickly against the wages and working conditions of our Australian seamen and against the best interests of Australia as a whole, unless some other form of protection be given.'[18]

The *Age* newspaper pushed for the government to negotiate new legislation with the British government, what they called 'an Empire navigation act,' which would preserve the coastal shipping of Australia to the merchant marine of the British Empire.[19] The two ALP members (Anstey and Yates) in their minority report recommended that official administration of the Act should be changed and the Director (who was thought to be too sympathetic to shipowners) made directly responsible to a Minister.[20] The permit system gave British companies some access to coastal shipping. After the Royal Commission 1924, more amendments were made to the Navigation Act, increasing access for British shipping companies and providing the WA government with exemption from the coasting provisions for the state-owned shipping company which plied between the North Coast WA, Singapore and the Dutch East Indies.[21]

British shipping companies wanted to expand their engagement in Australian trade as other countries passed laws restricting British shipping, so they invested in Australian companies.[22] In a supplementary memorandum to the Royal Commission report, Labor's Frank Anstey examined the structure and operations of Australian shipping to point out how the Navigation Act was not the cause of changes to coastal trading. He wrote that shipping on the Australian coast was 'one great corporation ... grafted into each other, not as Australian shipping companies, not as one great Australian Mercantile Marine Corporation' but grafted without their national identity 'to the mammoth combine of oversea shipowners, in which the "Inchcape Group" is the predominant partner' controlling 'the movement of Australian products, not only on oversea [*sic*] routes, but along thousands of miles of Australian

[17] *Age* (Melbourne), 21 August 1924, 8.
[18] Royal Commission on the Navigation Act 1924, 78.
[19] *Age* (Melbourne), 21 August 1924, 10.
[20] Royal Commission on the Navigation Act 1924.
[21] Reported in *Australian Seamen's Journal*.
[22] Morgan, 'Labour and Industrial Authority,' 269.

coast line.' Yet, he pointed out, this in itself was not the remarkable fact. Rather, it was that so many 'alleged Australian' companies were disguising their connection. 'Acting under Aliases as if they were criminals seeking to escape attention. They are not. They merely wish to hide from the public the extent, value, and power of their unified interests.'[23]

Anstey (1865–1940) had insight from having been a seafarer and an early member of the Seamen's Union, which he joined in 1883, 40 years previously. He had stowed away aged 11 on a passenger vessel bound for Australia. In Sydney he signed on as 'bosun's boy' and for ten years worked on ships in the Pacific Islands trade. He had experienced the brutality of a seafarer's life, and having sailed to Asia and seen the 'coolie' trade around the Pacific, subsequently carried 'a hatred of slave labour, a strong belief in White Australia, and a romantic interest in island life.' In his supplementary report, published in instalments in the labour press, Anstey pointed out that overseas shipping had for many years not carried interstate cargo on the Australian coast, except in isolated instances. 'The chartered oversea vessel for local trade was a thing of the past' and had been so 'many years prior to the Navigation Act.' Overseas liners found that carrying interstate cargo was not economically rational: it 'interfered too much with the loading or unloading of cargoes to or from oversea ports' and the legislation 'does not affect that fact.'

Anstey pondered the Australian Shipping Combine's support of the Navigation Act, and proposed that coastal shipping benefited from the Act's protection of passenger traffic. Boats of all nations carried passengers. The number carried between Australian ports by foreign vessels was steadily increasing prior to the outbreak of war. This 'was not only eating into the traffic of the local registered companies, but also into the local passenger traffic of British companies.' The benefit of having the Navigation Act was to reserve this passenger trade for registered companies locally. While that excluded both foreign and British competitors, the British Shipping Combine nevertheless supported the Act because 'a large section of the fleet operating on the Australian coast is P. and O. property, and these overseas property interests in coastal vessels are steadily increasing.' In this way 'the existence of the Navigation Act excludes the foreigner from local passenger trade, while the British ship-owners pick up their share per medium of their local registered vessels.'[24] Thus Anstey wrote of the Australian shipping business as 'one vast non-competitive combine. It is a monopoly.' Yet that was not

[23] Frank Anstey, 'Structure of the Australian Shipping Monopoly: Its Personnel and its International Links,' *Westralian Worker* (Perth), 28 August 1925, 10.

[24] Frank Anstey, 'Structure of the Australian Shipping Monopoly: The Mode of Operation,' *Westralian Worker* (Perth), 4 September 1925, 3.

created by the Navigation Act. 'Abundant evidence' from official documents, taken on oath, found in books and newspaper articles, showed that 'the shipping combine on the Australian coast existed long years before ... All the Navigation Act did was to cut foreigners out of the local passenger traffic and reserve such traffic for British and Australian interests.'[25]

The Navigation Act survived the Royal Commission, and its remaining provisions were operationalised, gradually, over the next three years.[26] Having the Navigation Act meant SUA activism was able to ensure that protective provisions of Australian standards – of safety, wages and on-board conditions – were applied on all ships trading on the Australian coast, especially 'that damaged or overloaded ships, with improperly stowed cargo, did not get clearances to sail from the Department of Navigation.'[27]

With the post-war recession passed, and a waterfront busy with trade, the WWF and SUA pressed to improve what were their continuing bad working conditions. The strategy of militancy and working within the arbitration system worked. Another seamen's strike and a new award in 1922 had gained them better conditions. When, in 1924, the shipping employers refused to renew the seamen's articles in the same terms as their existing arbitration court agreement, the union began tying up the ships, in a dispute that was settled relatively quickly when the shipowners capitulated. That's when Bruce, who was at that time also acting Attorney-General, rushed new legislation through the parliament amending the Navigation Act. Suspension of its provisions was now permitted for overseas shipping, thereby threatening Australian seafarers' jobs with competition on the coast from cheaper labour. Other measures were to follow.

The next pillar of Hughes' protections for Australian seafarers that came under the Bruce government's attention was the Commonwealth Line of ships that Hughes had established during the war years. This was disbanded, with the government once again blaming the unions' militancy and obscuring how the Commonwealth Line had brought unwelcome competition to private shipowners. The ASOF had since 1911 opposed the West Australian State Shipping Commission. Opposition to state ownership united the overseas and interstate companies.[28] In 1923, the Commonwealth Line was placed under a board to avoid competition with private enterprise.

---

[25] Frank Anstey, 'Structure of the Australian Shipping Monopoly: The Coastal Combine and the Local Trade,' *Westralian Worker* (Perth), 11 September 1925, 4.

[26] See *Official Year Book of the Commonwealth of Australia*, 17 (1924), 1054–5, www. ausstats.abs.gov.au/ausstats/free.nsf/0/5463CBDD5D8E55F5CA257AF00012EA23 /$File/13010_1924_bk17.pdf.

[27] Fitzpatrick and Cahill, *History of the Seamen's Union of Australia*, 57–8.

[28] Morgan, 'Labour and Industrial Authority.'

Two years later, the government started considering the terms of sale and by 1928 had sold it off cheaply. Critics of this decision alleged Bruce had colluded with the overseas shipping companies and had pressed them to delay any freight increases until after the federal election. He had written to shipping baron Lord Inchcape seeking a delay until a conference could be set up, an intervention that was successful in postponing a confrontation between Australian and overseas interests.[29] It was just one instance of his closeness to the shipowners.

As the Prime Minister, Bruce lacked a consistent industrial relations policy. The government's harsher approach and more power for the shipowners flowed from Bruce's desire to maximise market and investment opportunities. He wanted to attract British capital to Australia and to improve productivity, which made industrial peace a priority. He appealed for cooperation. He was impatient with employers who complained about arbitration and was dissatisfied with the efficiency of Australian industry. At the same time, he had no tolerance for unions resorting frequently to strikes and flouting arbitration awards.

In the first six months of 1925, industrial strife ballooned as the SUA was in dispute with the shipowners over where crews should be hired or 'picked up,' i.e., who had control of the hiring process. With the threat of deregistration hanging over them, and gaol terms and fines imposed on their leadership, the SUA persevered with their action, in a series of stoppages around the coast.[30] Deregistration from the arbitration system would mean the union no longer had an award setting their conditions, nor the legal power to enforce union rules or collect dues. They would have to depend on the Navigation Act to safeguard their conditions. Yet shipowners had previously refused to comply with the SUA demand that award conditions be incorporated into ships' articles of employment. The ASOF now pushed and succeeded in having the SUA deregistered. Country Party leader Earle Page said their strike was 'like a bolt from the blue,' against an award of the arbitration court, and 'the Seamen's Union deliberately had itself deregistered.'[31] Many non-Labor politicians blamed foreign influences, communists, for disrupting industries and communications across the country.

The strike was settled, however, by agreement between the unions and the shipping companies. That was in July 1925. A month earlier, Bruce had introduced a new bill into parliament amending the Immigration Act to curb the militancy of the SUA. This was not immigration exclusion but deportation. It was not based on race but on being 'Red' or engaging

[29] Lee, *Bruce*, 81.
[30] 'Seamen Again Defiant,' *Sydney Morning Herald*, 15 January 1925, 9.
[31] Debate on Maritime Industries Bill, 1929, Hansard.

in militant industrial protest. Attorney-General Groom, who had used deportation previously as a political control mechanism, drew up the provisions now introduced into parliament. The SUA found its leaders being subjected to additional punitive measures. Deportation was no longer just to be for seeking to overthrow the government or belonging to an outlawed political organisation such as the IWW, whose members were covered by the Unlawful Associations Act passed by Hughes' government in 1916. The new measures extended the category of persons for deportation to those who had offended against the industrial arbitration laws – which already carried a gaol term – or the commerce/trade laws. This created a new category of offenders, those who were seeking to 'disrupt the community's life.' The measures specifically threatened union officials. They were drafted hurriedly and rushed through parliament with such haste it was obvious that the government planned to make early use of them.[32] The response from the labour movement was equally strong. 'The Deportation penalty is a monstrous abuse of power,' declared the *Westralian Worker*.[33] 'No union can stand by and see such a gross travesty of justice enacted without a strong protest,' Trades Hall secretary, E.J. Holloway said, and any attempt to do so 'would be fraught with serious and far-reaching consequences.'[34]

'[A]lways an immigrant'?

Matters soon came to a head. The idea that SUA officials were anti-Australian (in not supporting the White Australia policy) re-emerged with vehemence when the union decided to give support to striking British seamen in August 1925. This was 'an English dispute between English workers and their English employers,' affecting Australia 'only because it involves transport to and from this country.'[35] It became a local crisis because of the government's response.

The cause of that strike was the agreement made by the leader of the NUS, Havelock Wilson, with British shipowners, that their wages, already much lower than during the war years, would be reduced further by one pound (10 per cent) a month. The British seamen's decision to strike 'came as a bombshell to the ship-owners' who had, apparently, been given no warning that there was dissension within the NUS. Soon ships were held up

---

[32] Carment, 'Sir Littleton Groom and the Deportation Crisis of 1925.'

[33] 'Overseas Ships and the Australian Standard. Wages Reductions Precipitate Strike,' *Westralian Worker* (Perth), 28 August 1925, 5.

[34] 'Federal Government's Drastic Action,' *Labor Call*, 27 August 1925, 7.

[35] Alfred Foster, 'Two Great Strike Issues,' *Australian Worker* (Sydney), 16 September 1925, 17.

at various ports around Australia as 4,000 British seamen defied their own union.[36] The seamen's grievance arose from the actual reduction, which was in spite of the huge profits the shipping companies had made during the First World War, and the fact that British shipping was 'the wealthiest combine in the world.'[37] It was a 'dramatic lowering of a standard of living that was already too low.'[38] They also resented the fact that it occurred without their consent or knowledge, after they had signed their articles and embarked on the voyage to Australia. Indeed, they only learned of it on coming ashore. So the NUS deal was in contravention of their articles. The action was made worse by the ships' masters seizing their clothes and possessions as soon as they left their ships, and the shipowners' subsequent decision not to pay the allotments from their pay that were due to their families back in the UK. Adela Pankhurst Walsh's sister, Christabel Pankhurst, spoke harshly at public gatherings in Liverpool of the shipowners' callous treatment of seafarers' families and the many wives and children dependent on their already dismal wages. An Australian minister of religion, the Revd F.J. Maynard of Brisbane, denounced the shipowners' withholding of the allotments: '[T]his is not clean fighting, it is hitting below the belt. It is unBritish[,] unChristian, and unmanly.'[39]

This was a strike with international implications. Led by the Soviet-inspired breakaway faction of the NUS, the Militant Minority Movement, who were not only opponents of Wilson's but had international ambitions, the strike was a potential threat also to imperial shipowners. The action spread to British crews in South African and New Zealand ports, leading some scholars to describe it as 'a strike across the empire.' But no strikes erupted in Asian ports; only in what were 'the white dominions.'[40] Not surprisingly, the strike was strongest and lasted longest in Australia, where it had wide support. Lowering wages, already 'the lowest of white men's wages,' was tantamount to imposing a 'coolie standard' that had long been opposed by Australian unions. The WWF supported the British seamen financially but decided not to impose a black ban on British ships as they were the only union whose entire membership would be affected. The

[36] 'The Shipping Strike in Australia: Summary of News from Australian Labour Papers, August 26th to October 2nd,' MS 993/1, MRC.

[37] 'Greatest Betrayal in History,' *Labor Call*, 3 September 1925, 1.

[38] 'A British Strike in Australia,' *Australian Worker* (Sydney), 26 August 1925, 3.

[39] *Australian Worker* (Sydney), 16 September 1925, 14; '"Immoral and Revolting": Action of British Shipowners. Brisbane Clergyman's Outspoken Criticism,' *Worker* (Brisbane), 17 September 1925, 14.

[40] Baruch Hirson and Lorraine Vivian, *Strike across the Empire: The Seamen's Strike of 1925 in Britain, South Africa and Australasia* (London: Clio Publications, 1992) does not recognise this aspect of the strike.

leadership decided the cost to their members would be too high. The SUA's leaders Tom Walsh and Jacob Johnson organised a meeting for the men in Sydney at which Walsh and Johnson, among others, urged them to fight back.[41] The SUA did not itself go on strike. Neither Walsh nor Johnson was a member of the Communist Party or aligned with the Minority Movement, yet they were officially blamed for the strike.

In one particularly partisan attack, ex-president of the Victorian Employers' Federation and a one-time seafarer, T.R. Ashworth, called Walsh 'a destructionist ... not a trade unionist,' who had 'done the men wrong in directing them ... to act as revolutionaries.'[42] It was his fault they – 'simple and ignorant men' – had been gaoled (Figure 6.1). Ashworth called on the government to put him 'in his proper place.'[43] The British Shipping Combine cabled Bruce urging him 'to take steps to enable the men to carry out their contract.' Havelock Wilson also wrote to the government condemning the SUA leadership and thereby adding to the pressure being applied by British shipping and employing interests.[44] This angered Australian labour even more. Wilson had not contacted any of the ALP leaders, the five state Labor Premiers, the trades hall councils or other union leaders.[45]

To Australian labour, the issues were clear. The cause was just. British seamen's wages were already too low, well below that of Australians, and Wilson was too close to the employers. He had just recently been banqueting and toasting in champagne with them, 'a reactionary of the worst type ... who delights in friendship with the bosses.'[46] The CPA press called Wilson 'that hoary troglodyte of trade unionism' and a 'class collaborator.'[47] Henry Boote in the Sydney *Worker* called him 'this monstrous Sea-Hawk,' and charged him and the British shipping combine with attempting 'to bring British seamen down to the degraded economic level of the coolies it employs whenever it can.'[48] The ALP press accused him of 'the greatest betrayal' and running an Employment Bureau rather than a union, as no

[41] 'British Seamen's Trouble,' 7; also reported in 'British Seamen on Strike,' *Australian Worker*, 26 August 1925, 15.

[42] T.R. Ashworth, 'The Story of the Unofficial Strike of Seamen in Australia: which was a Communist Plot to Destroy the National Union of Seamen' (pamphlet), 17, 19, 20, MS 159/5/3/44, MRC. This series of articles first appeared in the *Age*. See Will Ross, 'The Best and Worst Brains of Nationalism,' *Labor Call* (Melbourne), 12 November 1925, 11.

[43] Ashworth, 'The Story of the Unofficial Strike of Seamen in Australia,' 19, 20.

[44] 'British Seamen on Strike,' *Australian Worker* (Sydney), 26 August 1925, 15.

[45] 'Greatest Betrayal in History.'

[46] 'A British Strike in Australia,' *Australian Worker* (Sydney), 26 August 1925.

[47] 'Put Them in the Discard,' *Workers' Weekly* (Sydney), 28 August 1925, 3.

[48] 'A British Strike in Australia.'

6.1 Striking British seamen on their way to prison in Melbourne, 1925
Photograph K3215. Geoff McDonald Collection,
Noel Butlin Archives Centre, Canberra

one could be hired except through his agency.[49] Other, moderate members of
the labour movement came out in solidarity against the wealthy shipowners,
particularly the Inchcape group: 'the most notorious of the shipping
companies,' with large interests in Australian ships interlocked with overseas
shipping companies.[50] The ALP paper in WA said 'Australians believe in
humane and just treatment of those who "go down to the sea in ships."
If sacrifices have to be made, then let them be made by the shipowners
out of their own huge profits.'[51] This was a sentiment shared by leading
barrister and later arbitration court judge Alf Foster, who said the men's
'case was unanswerable' and its merits could not be doubted by fair-minded
Australians. From the women's pages in the newspapers there was sympathy

[49] 'Greatest Betrayal in History.'
[50] 'Overseas Ships and the Australian Standard,' 5.
[51] 'Starvation Wages: Policy of Overseas Shipowners,' *Westralian Worker* (Perth),
4 September 1925, 1–2.

for the strikers who couldn't keep decent homes on what they earned: 'hardly more than half' an Australian seamen's wage, 'and British shipowners ought to be ashamed of themselves' (Figure 6.2).[52]

The Australian government wasted no time in activating its new legislation. On the grounds that delaying Australia's export produce would be a great economic loss, the federal government issued a proclamation asserting that there was a state of serious industrial unrest prejudicial to the peace, order and good government of the Commonwealth. SUA leaders Walsh and Johnson were arrested and brought before a specially constituted board to show why they should not be deported. The board concluded they should be, on grounds they had 'hindered and obstructed the transport of goods ... in relation to trade or commerce with other countries,' and the Minister ordered their deportation:

> The Prime Minister has conceived the idea it is his business to act as proxy for the British Shipping Trust in its dispute with its employees. The Companies are not registered in Australia: the employees are not citizens of Australia. Yet Bruce puts himself into the quarrel on the side of the shippers. ... Low wages are the cause of this dispute; deportation will not cure it.[53]

The Labor Party argued this was a broader attack on unionism. In the absence of widespread support for the particular SUA officials, who were at ideological and personal odds with each other, it seemed more likely that the government's real target was unionists, especially those who subscribed to 'foreign doctrines.' In their belief that exceptional measures were justified against communist officials, 'the government had forged a sledgehammer to crack a nut,' methods that would neither prevent nor settle the current strike.[54] 'All the talk about communists ... was mere moonshine,' obscuring the government's intention 'to deal with the current maritime dispute.'[55]

With the two officials being held in detention, the SUA lawyers applied for a writ of habeas corpus, which took the matter to the High Court. The issue before the court was whether Walsh and Johnson, as long-term residents of Australia, still came under the provisions of the Commonwealth's immigration power, the only power under which the Commonwealth could deport them. Walsh had come to Australia before the colonies federated,

---

[52] Foster, 'Two Great Strike Issues'; 'Women's Sphere: Snapshots at the Passing Show,' *Westralian Worker* (Perth), 11 September 1925, 12.

[53] 'Overseas Ships and the Australian Standard,' 5.

[54] Radi, '1920–29,' 399; Carment, 'Sir Littleton Groom and the Deportation Crisis of 1925.'

[55] ALP MP, Edward Riley, quoted in Carment, 'Sir Littleton Groom and the Deportation Crisis of 1925.'

6.2 Cartoon. Organised labour opposing deportation, 1925,
Labor Call (Melbourne), 3 September 1925

so the court's opinion was unanimous: that he was not an immigrant. Johnson's case was a little different. He had arrived from the Netherlands after federation, in 1910, though he had never left and had been naturalised in 1913. The majority opinion was that he too was no longer an immigrant: '[T]hat there comes a point in time ... at which he could no longer be said to be an immigrant,' and that point had been reached; 'he had become a member of the Australian community.' This decision was not unanimous. Isaacs J dissented, on the principle that 'immigrants were always immigrants.'[56] There was no judgment made on the government's dealing with an industrial problem by deporting union leaders, only whether the power of deportation could reach those who had lived in Australia for so many years. The final judgment of the High Court was that the deportation was unconstitutional, and the unionists should be released. Groom's replacement (by Latham) as Attorney-General was announced that same day.

The crisis illustrated government attitudes towards union militancy and a ruthless official response to what they perceived as foreign trouble-makers. The Attorney-General's 'unrealistic and dangerous disregard for democratic liberties' in pursuit of labour movement radicals nevertheless did not lose them the subsequent election, suggesting most Australians supported this view.[57] The government, however, had presented a misleading picture, which made the 'Red' menace and industrial problems into an election issue. There was irony in the Bruce government's pursuit of high-profile non-communists as a means to pursue a more intense offensive against communists and foster 'a climate of repressive conservatism.'[58] The new Attorney-General Latham amended the Crimes Act, unprecedentedly broadening the definition of unlawful activity and hitting strikers with new penal sanctions. There was also a human cost. These were 'fatiguing and distressing' times for Tom Walsh and his family. Adela had the heavy physical work of juggling childcare with visits to Garden Island detention facility and worries about their financial resources. Perhaps it was exhaustion that contributed to her premature labour and the loss of their infant daughter. Tom found the months in detention with his 'rancorous opponent' Jacob Johnson strenuous. On release, he was 'ill and shaken,' and worried about a diminished income and depleted SUA funds.[59] The troubles with Johnson over leadership of the union escalated. The government had gone from measure to measure as it committed itself 'spectacularly and unreservedly to eliminating strikes.' It then turned to changing the Arbitration Act and seeking wider industrial powers.[60] (We can see similar procedures and policies followed by the Liberal–Country Party (L–CP) government in the 1950s.)

---

[56] Zelman Cowen, *Isaac Isaacs* (Melbourne: Oxford University Press, 1967), 171, is also the source for Johnson's birth in the Netherlands. Most sources describe him as Swedish-born. The press frequently called him Johanssen.

[57] Carment, 'Sir Littleton Groom and the Deportation Crisis of 1925'; Radi, '1920–29,' 400.

[58] Macintyre, *The Reds*, 102.

[59] Coleman, *Adela Pankhurst*, 102–3.

[60] Radi, '1920–29,' 400; Macintyre, *The Reds*, 103.

6.3 Tom Walsh
and Adela
Pankhurst
Walsh working
at home, *c.*1940,
NLA

'[I]n pursuit of harsh and inflexible industry policies'

In 1928, the government's next move was a major review of the Conciliation and Arbitration Act. Amendments included penalty clauses and compulsory court-supervised ballots, which unionists found objectionable. Then, as a federal election loomed, a waterside strike threatened over the WWF's latest industrial arbitration award. They had 'never won a reputation for sweet reasonableness.'[61] In a move designed to break the WWF, on advice from WA Senator George Foster Pearce, Bruce rushed through legislation to create a system of licensing waterfront labour which he presented to the

---

[61] W. Jethro Brown, 'The Strike of the Australian Waterside Worker: A Review,' *Economic Record* 5, no. 1 (May 1929): 22–33.

electorate as a stand against industrial mayhem.[62] Pearce was elected as a free trader, a former trade unionist and member of the ALP who had followed Hughes into the Nationalist Party. He was unsympathetic to socialism and critical of strikers and union leaders (which he had once been).[63]

The Transport Workers Act 1928 allowed only labourers who had acquired a licence to work on the wharves, replacing membership of the union as a qualification for wharf work.[64] The Bruce government's action in hurrying it through parliament meant 'autocratic rule under Parliamentary sanction was substituted for legislative process.' The strike, however, continued, as those non-unionists who had taken the available jobs were now given preference for the licences. Violence erupted on the waterfront, but the legislation remained in force as a coercive weapon to control waterside workers. All too soon, 'the strikers' simply became 'the unemployed' as the Depression hit hard.[65]

Prime Minister Bruce had become 'a polarizing and deeply unpopular figure.'[66] The judges who sat on the industrial arbitration tribunals and made the awards were not always, at least in their own view, unsympathetic to workers' claims about their conditions. Some saw that wharfies' employment conditions needed reform. While conditions 'may be alleviated by the humanity or vision of employers ... industry which rests on a basis of casual labour does not readily lend itself to those measures of reform.'[67] The arbitration court existed to ensure standards. Australia was 'a community almost unique' in having high real wages and in providing machinery in the institution of arbitration that promoted stability, peace and justice in trade and industry, as part of an inherited 'rich legacy of law, order and free political institutions.' But it required loyalty. This it was not getting in the 1920s, 'in the face of a new psychology' of resistance to the court's awards, demonstrated in the WWF's adoption of 'a policy of defiance.'[68] Compliance with arbitration was at odds with some unionists' preference for direct industrial action. But arbitration as an institution and its determinations on an Australian standard of living and fair labour standards for workers

[62] The 1928 legislation and WWF strike is well covered by Beasley, *Wharfies*, among others, and most recently by Phoebe Kelloway 'Queensland Workers in 1928 Waterside Strike,' *Labour History*, no. 16 (May 2019).

[63] John Merritt, 'Pearce, Sir George Foster (1870–1952),' *Biographical Dictionary of the Australian Senate*, online edition, https://biography.senate.gov.au/pearce-george-foster/.

[64] Brown, 'Strike of the Australian Waterside Worker,' 29.

[65] Richard Morris, 'Australian Stevedoring and Shipping Labour under the Transport Workers Act, 1928–47,' *Great Circle* 11, no. 2 (1989): 17–31.

[66] Lee, *Bruce*, 50.

[67] Brown, 'Strike of the Australian Waterside Worker,' 23.

[68] Brown, 'Strike of the Australian Waterside Worker,' 24.

was being demolished, not by labour militants, but by the conservative forces aligned against them, 'in a showdown partly engineered by the government.'[69] Bruce rewrote the Arbitration Act which he brought to parliament in 1928, after the SUA was already deregistered.

The culmination of this conflict between maritime unionists and the Nationalist government came in new arbitration legislation, the Maritime Industries Bill, introduced into parliament in August 1929. The immediate spur for the bill was Nationalist Party state premiers wanting the Commonwealth to leave arbitration matters to the states.[70] It was called the Maritime Industries Bill because it proposed to keep only the maritime industries within the control of the federal arbitration court by setting up industrial committees for the shipping and waterside industries.

In moving the second reading of the bill, Prime Minister Bruce blamed the militancy of the maritime unions as the cause for the measure. They had 'treated the arbitration court as they treated the Commonwealth Line of Steamers, which was sabotaged out of existence.' Having been warned that the government would dispose of the Line if they continued their strikes and obstructions, the unions had paid no heed, so the Line had ceased to exist. 'The time has now arrived for the Commonwealth arbitration court also to disappear.' But he also showed that it was the arbitration court itself that the government saw as unworkable. 'It has hampered industry, has been the means of closing avenues of employment, has restricted the development of our enterprises ... It is time that we threw this machinery on one side and took other steps to place ourselves on a more economic basis.'

Former WWF president and ex-Prime Minister Billy Hughes opposed the bill. He charged the Prime Minister with hypocrisy and alleged the few provisions relating to the maritime industries had been 'deliberately inserted for the purpose of misleading the people.' Hughes claimed the actual purpose of the bill was to destroy the federal system, 'the temple, so diligently built up by his predecessors, which made the basic wage possible' and created the Australian standard of living. Another Labor Party MP spoke similarly in defence of the arbitration court, 'which has set up fair standards of living, and prevented sweating.'[71] Other opponents saw the bill as penalising large sections of Australian industry, and hardly being conducive to industrial peace because it deprived both sides, employers as well as workers, of their industry awards. Arguments that others, not 'just

[69] 'Seamen Again Defiant,' 9.

[70] See also G.T. Powell, 'The Role of the Commonwealth Government in Industrial Relations, 1923–1929' (MA thesis, Australian National University, 1974).

[71] W.M. Hughes, on Maritime Industries Bill, Second Reading, 5 and 6 September 1929, Hansard.

those belonging to the employing class,' should be considered and that the nation's workers who were important in the country's industries also had the right to be protected were also contributed to the debate.[72]

Percy Coleman, the former seafarer and SUA office worker and now an MP, had 'no doubt whatever that the object of this ... bill is to smash the power of the maritime workers' organisations. There can be no other reason.' He also criticised the proposed administration – the industrial committees to be set up – describing them as 'semi-political in character' given that the powers were to be vested in the Minister, and the Attorney-General would have too much discretion. 'Under this measure, not even the basic wage will be safe.' Coleman argued 'that coolie competition and price-cutting in the maritime industry will determine the economic ability of the industry to pay a certain wage standard.' He was in no doubt of the effect: 'Coolie competition will be possible because of the suspension of certain sections of the Navigation Act. Absurd anomalies will be caused because ships trading between Australian and New Zealand ports, will not be subject to the control of the Commonwealth awards.' He noted 'how careful the Government has been to safeguard the interests of the employers. There will be no disclosure of the financial position of the shipowners, unless the court orders it.'[73] Another Labor Party MP, future Prime Minister John Curtin, argued:

> This bill does more than repeal one of the finest chapters in the industrial history of Australia – it opens up a black and dismal prospect. It makes the workers weak in the presence of the enemy, and the enemy strong to impose his own will ... striking a vital blow at the workers ... the very soul of the Australian nation.[74]

Within months, 'black and dismal' times for maritime workers did indeed follow the legislation. Bruce had ceased to be prime minister and had lost his own seat at the federal election, which the ALP won. But the WWF struggled against the licensing system. The Transport Workers Act 1928 placed fetters on WWF activism. For ten years, the SUA was racked by internal conflict between Johnson and Walsh, and seafarers' conditions deteriorated while the union had no status within the arbitration court. The sale of the last of the Commonwealth Line of ships to a British shipowner

---

[72] Mr Price, on Maritime Industries Bill, Second Reading, 5 and 6 September 1929, Hansard, 633–4; A. Green, on Maritime Industries Bill, Second Reading, 5 and 6 September 1929, Hansard, 639.

[73] Percy Coleman, on Maritime Industries Bill, Second Reading, 5 and 6 September 1929, Hansard, 653.

[74] John Curtin on Maritime Industries Bill, Second Reading, 5 and 6 September 1929, Hansard, 711.

deprived many Australian seafarers of jobs and halved the wages of those who were kept on. An unknown writer asked if a 'coolie' standard was inevitable, given the vast wealth concentrated in the few rather than being spread across the many.[75] The Depression – which came early to shipping – took more jobs from both the wharves and the crews. By 1935, membership of the SUA was under half (3,600) what it had been at its height in 1923 (7,500). A new Arbitration award imposed licences on seafarers and prompted a disastrous strike that year, pushed by the Militant Minority Movement faction which had now taken control of the leadership. At the end of it the union was even more disempowered.[76]

While the maritime unions entered the doldrums, Stanley Bruce renewed pursuit of his international career. From 1932, he was back in London where he still enjoyed respect for his business acumen. As Australia's High Commissioner, 1933–45, he performed a diplomatic role representing Australia at the League of Nations and advocating wholesale reform of the international economic system. He became a director of both the P&O and British India Steam Navigation shipping companies and sat in the House of Lords as Bruce, of Melbourne.[77]

'Training Indians for nautical careers'

Notably missing from those supporting the British seamen's strike in 1925 were the crews hired on Asiatic articles whose wages were even lower than 'the lowest white men's wages.' Indian crews conspicuously did not come ashore to join the strikers despite being urged by British officers. Four ships' crews refused to participate and a fifth set sail.[78] Indian seamen were fighting their own battles to raise their wages above 'the coolie standard' and being employed as 'coolie competition.' India was also struggling against imperial power and it looked to Australia's Navigation Act as a possible model for providing employment and career opportunities for its nationals. Almost simultaneously as Australia was having a Royal Commission on the Navigation Act in 1924, India set up a significant governmental enquiry to investigate the prospect of having a national merchant marine. It was a moment when 'Indian seamen briefly succeeded in unhinging some consti- tutive assumptions of their "coolie" status' and the Indian 'government

---

[75] 'Is a Coolie Standard Inevitable?' *Westralian Worker* (Perth), 18 September 1925, 3.

[76] L.J. Louis, 'Recovery from the Depression and the Seamen's Strike, 1935–6,' *Labour History* 41 (1981): 74–86. See also Fitzpatrick and Cahill, *History of the Seamen's Union of Australia*, 68–86.

[77] Lee, *Bruce*, 105–8.

[78] 'Colored Crews Refuse to Participate,' *The Age* (Melbourne), 24 August 1925, 9.

even pronounced "lascar" to be a degrading term whose use ought to be discontinued.'[79]

India's experience differed from Australia's because its seafarers struggled to overturn their colonial conditions of employment and deeply entrenched ideas about their racial inferiority. As British colonies, laws for merchant shipping both in Australia and India originated from the British Merchant Shipping Law and followed Acts passed in the British parliament. India shared the aspiration to have a merchant navy, to break the monopoly British control of shipping employment, to create opportunities and standards for its own national crews. Australia sought to enshrine the old imperial principle of cabotage, and to wed it to the new principle of protection of labour standards. India tried to follow Australia's example. 'Indian seamen were covered by both British and Indian Acts, with British acts prevailing over corresponding provisions in Indian Acts.' This was a pattern followed in India until the Indian Merchant Shipping Act 1923, which consolidated all previous acts and stayed in force until after independence.[80]

This Act, 'entirely one-sided and openly intended to invest shippers and shipping agencies with arbitrary powers while allowing no rights or protections of any sort to sailors,' created many handicaps for Indian seafarers. They had no choice of ship, could be dismissed without reason after only a few months despite signing on for 12, and payment of wages was not guaranteed.[81] Like Australia's Navigation Act, the Indian Merchant Shipping Act provided that officers had to be British and English-speaking. The Indian Mercantile Marine Committee of 1923 was charged with considering measures that could usefully be taken: 'for the liberal establishment of Indians as Deck executive Officers and Engineers in the Royal Indian Marine; for the establishment of a nautical college in Indian waters ... and for the creation of an adequate number of State scholarships for training boys in England.' Also included were the acquisition of training ships, the encouragement of shipbuilding and 'the construction of the necessary dockyards and engineering workshops in one or more ports.'[82]

The voices of Indian seafarers were heard through their Seamen's Union representatives in a written submission made to that Committee. They pointed out that 'prejudice against the Indian's aspirations' prevented Indian crew from 'becoming officers and engineers in the mercantile marine.' A proportion of seamen (at least 10 per cent) were literate, a smaller proportion (2 per cent) spoke English and were trained in English schools. Like the Australian labour unions, the Indian Union called for the coastal trade to be

---

[79] Balachandran, 'Making Coolies.'

[80] Barnes, *Evolution and Scope of Mercantile Marine Laws*, 317.

[81] A. Colaco, *A History of the Seamen's Union of Bombay* (Bombay: Pascoal Vaz, 1955), 58.

[82] Documents in David Erulkar Collection, Reid Library, University of Western Australia.

6.4 NUSI leader Mohammed Ebrahim Serang (undated)
Courtesy NUSI, Mumbai

reserved for Indian companies, to break 'the monopoly and domination of powerful non-Indian interests.' Also like the Australian Royal Commission Report of 1906, it called for the establishment of training for local crews. There were insufficient ships owned by Indians that could employ Indian apprentices and so no training could occur.

The unionists giving evidence were from the Indian Seamen's Union. The first organisation of seamen in Calcutta was reorganised and merged with the Asiatic Seamen's Union (for saloon crew) and the deck and engine crew organised by Mohammed Ebrahim Serang, to become the Indian Seamen's Union at the end of the First World War (Figure 6.4). The ISU called a strike in 1919 and got the wages of seamen increased.[83] Their evidence is in contrast to the testimony given by British administrators – a shipping executive and a Marine Surveyor who claimed he had never come across an Indian who would be 'eligible for the Bridge of a large Government vessel.' Even those he'd found to be 'good bright and worthy [junior] officers,' he said, were so only while under European supervision. It would, however, take many years to reach 'anything like the standard our own British Officers have.' He concluded with sympathy for the aspiration of Indians to have a merchant marine, 'but the habits and customs of centuries cannot be changed or altered within one generation.' '[Y]ou must have a British Officer as a superior always.'

The Committee reported in 1924 and argued confidently that 'We see no reason why the sons of these men should not be encouraged to aspire

---

[83] Letter from Ramen Guha, General Secretary, National Union of Indian Seamen to ITF, 25 September 1950, ITF Archives, MSS 159/3/0/73/A, MRC; Broeze, 'Muscles of Empire', 48–50.

to become officers ... especially as some of them are already educated to enter the learned professions [of law, medicine, etc.].' They rejected the idea that boys had to be sent to England for proper training and urged the establishment of a training ship in Indian waters. They added that guaranteed employment had also to be provided. In short, the Committee argued the case for the development of Indian shipping and that enough engineers and officers could be found from the Indian population 'if proper training facilities were made available.'[84] The provision of an Indian merchant navy was inseparable from the provision of training of Indians for nautical careers.

It took two years for the Committee's recommendations 'to recognize the need for the training of Indians for nautical careers' to be brought before the Legislative Assembly for debate, which it finally was in March 1926. Here we see in practice how the British colonial state represented itself as promoting sound economy. When Sir Charles Innes, who was Member for Commerce and a year later would become Governor of Burma, spoke for the government, he was, he said, anxious to replace the 'propaganda' promoting the views of the Committee with 'facts.' Innes separated the matter of establishing an Indian merchant marine (i.e., reserving the coastal trade to Indian ships) from the matter of providing training for Indians to become officers. To properly train boys to become officers they should be sent 'home' – to England – where they would also learn to mix with English boys, but he conceded that, despite the cost, a training ship in Indian waters would be agreed to.

Then he introduced the issue of cost, and insisted: 'we have to balance national sentiment on the one hand and economic considerations ... on the other.' The Indian Mercantile Marine Committee, he implied, had given up on or not understood, the 'very difficult subject' of shipping economics. But he and the Commerce Department had not: they 'had spent two years considering what would be the economic effect on India of instituting this policy.' He cited the experience of Australia, where freight rates had been increased as a consequence of protecting Australian labour. By this [mis] use of the Australian experience, Innes deflected the push for an Indian merchant navy, which had to wait until Independence was achieved. 'The efforts of India ... to have its own Merchant Shipping Act materialized [only] in 1958.'[85] At that time, the term 'Lascar' was replaced by 'Indian seaman.'

Indian seafarers' strategies to overcome their 'coolie' status and improve their wages and conditions included having the Merchant Shipping Act amended, organising more union members and engaging internationally.

---

[84] Barnes, *Evolution and Scope of Mercantile Marine Laws*, 20.
[85] Erulkar collection; Barnes, *Evolution and Scope of Mercantile Marine Laws*, 317.

In 1926, Aftab Ali became an organiser for the ISU, which launched a successful campaign against the Indian system of brokerage for recruitment, which was subsequently abolished.[86] He travelled to Europe to organise Indian sailors crewing German and English ships. He wrote to Edo Fimmen of the ITF identifying himself as representative of the Indian Seaman's Union, New York branch, when he was in Germany encouraging Indian crews to unionise and reporting his efforts to the Indian Seafarer Union in Calcutta. He sought help from the ITF 'to ensure that every attempt is made' to organise Indian seafarers into unions, including those on Dutch ships, so they might 'improve their wages and working conditions.'[87] Ali's work took him to the ILO ten years later as Indian unions ramped up their efforts for seafarers' rights.

[86] Letter from Guha to ITF, 25 September 1950, MRC.

[87] Letter Mohamed Ali to Edo Fimmen, 7 January 1926, MS 159/3/C/294, MRC. We have taken this to be Aftab Ali because of its date, his connection with both New York and Calcutta and his appeal to the ITF, all of which have been matched to Aftab Ali in other studies.

7

'Seamen of the Orient'

Globalising the ITF and Embracing Asia, c.1920s to the 1930s

When the ITF was reconstituted in 1919 it resolved to bring into membership 'the unions of the British colonies America, Australia, India and Java.'[1] Ernest Bevin of Britain's Transport Workers Union urged that 'also Japan' must be brought in.[2] All these countries were Britain's wartime allies. Bevin endorsed the need for European organisations struggling for their constituent members to embrace other countries and saw in Japan a rising industrial power, which, as always, was built on costs borne by the working class.[3] He argued this would provide protection for European labourers. In the difficult immediate post-war years, it also gave the European workers a way of unifying after their wartime enmities, which had caused huge casualties in the merchant navy.

While finding common ground enabled the European unions to move forward organisationally, they found it a challenge. Feelings against reunification were stronger amongst the seafarers than the dockers. The British NUS was strongly anti-German and the proposal to revive the ITF after the war 'aroused bitter opposition' from NUS president Havelock Wilson.[4] That year, Wilson set up a new, separate organisation solely of seafarers, the International Seafarers' Federation, with himself as president. Rather than reach out to the German Transport Workers Union as he tried to re-establish contact, Wilson instead asked Hugo Stinnes, 'the notorious Big Capitalist of Germany,' to act as conciliator.[5] In 1922, during the International Seamen's conference held at Hamburg, delegates passed a resolution

---

[1] A.K. Arora, *I.T.F. in Non-European World (1896–1953)* (Bombay: Maniben Kara Institute, Hind Mazdoor Sabha, [1994]), 12, MS 611/11/9, MRC.

[2] Reinalda, *International Transportworkers Federation, 1914–1945*, 117.

[3] Bullock, *Ernest Bevin*, 1:266.

[4] Bullock, *Ernest Bevin*, 1:113.

[5] 'Havelock Wilson and Hugo Stinnes,' by 'J.I.E.' 'Newsletter,' *Australasian Seamen's Journal* 8, no. 14 (1 May 1922): 12.

condemning Wilson's actions in approaching 'a capitalist enemy' to act as mediator rather than ask the ITF, or deal directly with the German union. Signatories to the resolution were seamen from the UK, Germany, Sweden, the Netherlands, Norway and Belgium. The International Seafarers' Federation was consequently 'fully decrepit.'[6] Belgian delegates to the initial post-war ITF meeting were similarly passionate about the German transport unions' silence on that nation's U-boat campaign, which had caused the loss of so many thousands of Allied seafarers' lives. They proposed a resolution of condemnation. Bevin, as leader of the dockers, supported the criticism but took a more moderate position towards the inaction of the German unions, and he drafted the constitution for a revived ITF.[7]

Bevin had come to trade unionism later than the other prominent British maritime unionists, the ITF's founders, Wilson, Tillett and Mann. He had been working as a drayman and joined the Dockers' Union during the strike in 1910 when he organised a carters' branch. A year later he became a paid official, three years later a national organiser, and in 1920 was assistant general secretary. Bevin was not entirely at ease with the direction the post-war ITF would now take. His appeal to humanitarianism, consistent with other initiatives on behalf of workers in this period, diverged from the stance of European members of the ITF, like the Dutch-born Edo Fimmen, who was inspired by events in Russia. Bevin was an internationalist, 'impressed by the need to overcome national frontiers in trade-union organization.'[8] Yet his was 'a belief in practical international action,' finding expression in the ITF. He 'never flirted with Communism and ... from first to last rejected Bolshevik methods as incompatible with the democratic traditions of the Labour movement.'[9] Fimmen, on the other hand, had a vision of internationalising the ITF, which included an anti-colonialist, anti-imperialist agenda akin to the Soviet vision. The critique of colonised labour within the empires was strengthened within the Comintern that was established soon after the Russian revolution of 1917. The initiative under Fimmen's leadership signalled that a new direction was under way for the Eurocentric ITF: a shift from the pre-war 'unspectacular and unpolitical' ITF able to do little more than gather statistical data to one with 'the potential to exert influence and effect structural change' in reaching beyond the North Sea and Atlantic Ocean.[10]

---

[6] 'Havelock Wilson and Hugo Stinnes.'

[7] Bullock, *Ernest Bevin*, 1:114, citing the ITF Minutes.

[8] Bullock, *Ernest Bevin*, 1:113.

[9] Bullock, *Ernest Bevin*, 1:232. For a fuller explanation of Bevin's opposition to communism, see Bullock, *The Life and Times of Ernest Bevin*, vol. 3, *Foreign Secretary, 1945–1951* (London: Heinemann, 1983), 105–7.

[10] Sigrid Koch-Baumgarten, 'Edo Fimmen: An Iron Fist in a Silken Glove: A Biographical Sketch,' in Reinalda, *International Transportworkers Federation, 1914–1945*, 52–68.

Of the British founders of the ITF, only Tom Mann was in line with Fimmen's views. Mann would go on to become a leader of the Communist Party in Great Britain; Ben Tillett worked alongside Bevin in the dockers' union and as a Labour MP. Havelock Wilson, a Liberal Party MP, went in another more conservative direction as he pursued seafarers' separate interests. His alternative organisation functioned for a few years alongside the ITF but did not survive. His union's (the NUS) opposition to the employment of 'coloured labour,' strengthened in the aftermath of war, placed it at odds with Fimmen's stance of inclusion and anti-racism. Fimmen saw internationalising as a counterforce to capitalism, a view shared by the British president of the ITF, Concemore Cramp. At the Paris Congress, in 1926, Cramp urged the ITF to continue strenuously increasing non-European affiliations. 'Capitalism is world-wide,' he said. 'It knows no distinction of race or colour.' The working class must do likewise and 'make it impossible for … capitalists to grind their millions from coolie labour and to play off Asiatic or African workers against the better organized workers in other lands.'[11]

Underlying these white European efforts to embrace non-Europeans and ensure fair standards for all was the thought that 'backward countries' would drag the economic standards of 'more progressive lands' down to their level of poverty. 'On the sea,' but not only on the sea, 'the workman with a high standard of living finds himself closely pressed by the cheaper labor of backward lands … British seamen … are in competition for the world's trade with European seamen, who are receiving little more than half the British rates, and with Asiatic seamen, who are more poorly paid still.'[12] The renewed effort to expand the ITF was part of a push, a practical – necessary – recognition of the interconnectedness of international shipping and its maritime workforce. A similar concern to reduce or eliminate substandard working conditions, which were 'the basis for international competitive advantage' among the shipowners, was motivating ILO activity at that same time.[13]

The emphasis on labour standards and uncontrolled competition made talk about 'coolie labour' less about race than economics, as organised labour tried to reach an international working class. On one occasion, the SUA journal's discussion of the exploitation of Chinese 'coolie' labour in the maritime industries included an attempt at humour:

'Coolie' is an expression which comes from two Chinese words – 'coo' (which means hard, dirty and unpleasant) and the word 'lie' (which means

---

[11] Quoted in ITF, *Solidarity*, 88.
[12] Garnett, 'China and Seamen's Strike.'
[13] Goldberg, 'Seamen and the International Labor Organization,' 975.

work). The fact that the Chinese worker is called by the name of coolie clearly indicates the unpleasant and hard nature of this work, and the miserable economic position which he occupies.[14]

The etymology of 'coolie' actually lies in South Asian history. To those on the receiving end, the tactic of racialising labour through humour, however well-intentioned the motivations, seemed only designed 'to secure the interests of white men.'[15]

One way of avoiding references to race was to speak of *countries* and their responsibility for setting standards, pointing to the 'limit to the differences which may exist between the labor standards of any two countries.'[16] Competition between countries depended on the closeness of their economic contact. Standards could be maintained by 'tariff walls and Navigation Acts and loyal preference for the goods and services of well-paid labor, together with the superiority of that well-paid labor,' but was not sustainable once 'backward countries' industrialised if they didn't also set similar labour standards to 'the progressive country.'[17]

The non-European countries that Bevin named and the ITF considered important to embrace were a mix of such 'progressive' and 'backward countries,' perhaps an unexpected grouping with the links between them not immediately apparent. America and Australia had active national labour movements and shared a Western perspective; India had only embryonic labour organisations but was a major supplier of seafaring labour within the British Empire and its shipping industry; Japan was primarily a shipowning country, where 'Capitalism begins to develop … and a start is being made with labour legislation.'[18] As a geographical grouping, they came within Asia and the Pacific as a region of interlocking shipping routes, although the United States also had a very large Atlantic seaboard. They brought a diverse mix and experience of geography and history.

Of those countries, only Japan was not a colony or former colony of Britain. Only Australia faced both the Pacific and Indian oceans, a vital linking to the subcontinent of India in what is now known as the Indo-Pacific region. Australian unions were thus seemingly well positioned to facilitate the ITF's endeavour. 'Here in Australia,' the SUA pointed out, 'we are isolated. We want news from other countries, [and want] every seaman … when he is returning to bring to us the doings and the papers of the working-class in

---

[14] 'China: Capitalism's United Front,' *Australasian Seamen's Journal* 8, no. 25 (2 April 1923).

[15] Arora, *I.T.F. in Non-European World*.

[16] Garnett, 'China and Seamen's Strike.'

[17] Garnett, 'China and Seamen's Strike.'

[18] Bevin, quoted in Reinalda, *International Transportworkers Federation, 1914–1945*, 117.

7.1 Crew of a Chinese ship, *c.*1930s
Photographer Michael Maslan. Getty Images

other countries.'[19] Yet Australia, like the United States, was not playing a willing cooperative role within the ITF. Not all transport unions had joined the ITF, among them the maritime unions. 'The white workers in Australia, South Africa, Americas show little or no inclination for affiliation with the International in Europe, due to remoteness, long distance, costlier travel … and little direct benefits.'[20] To get them to do so involved overcoming issues of regional identity, imperial connection and sometimes ideological commitment, in which race was deeply embedded.

Significantly absent from the list was China, which had been so significant in providing the labour force for the trans-Pacific trade. Chinese seafarers were employed on US ships and were also prominent in British shipping and ports (Figure 7.1). They had been sailing on European shipping lines since the mid-nineteenth century and made up the majority of the deck crew and engine room ratings on the direct steamship service running between Liverpool and China.[21] Yet it took initiatives from the Chinese themselves, calling on the ITF for help in their 1925 strike, before they found a place in the ITF.[22]

Australia's geography was a driving force in its own struggle for labour standards, making it strategically useful to European–British objectives.

[19] *Australasian Seamen's Journal* 8, no. 14 (1 May 1922): 15.

[20] Arora, *I.T.F. in Non-European World*, 21.

[21] Gregor Benton and Edmund Gomez, *The Chinese in Britain, 1800 to the Present: Economy, Transnationalism, Identity* (Basingstoke: Palgrave Macmillan, 2008), 80, 75.

[22] See Arora, *I.T.F. in Non-European World*.

Australia's maritime unions were keenly fostering awareness of industrial activism with regional seafarers – 'fellow-wage slaves' – in neighbouring countries in Asia and the Pacific: New Guinea, Fiji, Samoa, Tonga, the Solomon Islands and the Gilbert Islands. In 1922, a deputation from the Solomon Islands calling on the Seamen's Union leadership for assistance was taken as evidence that the SUA policy 'not to close the union's door to any man because of race or colour' was having effect.[23]

'Awakening of the East'

That SUA policy of reaching across the Pacific and being inclusive and open on questions of race meant the union journal noted 'two tremendous strikes' that had taken place in Japan and China, in 1922. The first was of Japanese seafarers who struck for an increase of 27 per cent in their wages. The second was of Chinese seafarers in Canton and Hong Kong who also sought increased wages, of 30 per cent, and better working conditions. These strikers – 'our fellow-seamen' – were victorious in both actions.[24]

The Chinese seamen's strike in Hong Kong was a turning moment in China's history, noted by the mainstream Australian press as 'the first of its kind in the East.'[25] A more extended report from the labour press, quoting from a former ship's captain, pointed to China becoming Westernised, as seen in the rapid growth of its trade unions. The strike was 'the most serious and extensive of its nature in the Orient.' The Chinese Seamen's Union was 'now a very powerful organization,' having grown in just seven years from being 'an organisation of no importance, whatsoever' to being in a position to 'dislocate the Chinese shipping trade, and even interrupt the Pacific mail services.' Over 100 steamers were laid up in Hong Kong Harbour as a result of the strike.[26]

The SUA emphasised the significance of this militancy in East Asia for shipping companies' ability to use Asian seamen as cheap labour. Consequently, the US union, the International Union of Seamen, now intended to 'throw the doors open to Asiatic seamen' and to open union branches in all ports of China and Japan which would benefit organised labour in both of their countries. Instead of being in competition, Asian seamen would become 'a valuable asset to the labour movement and to the seamen's organisations in

---

[23] 'Federated Seamen's Union of Australasia: Report of the General President and the General Secretary for the Year Ended 1922,' *Australasian Seamen's Journal* 8, no. 25 (2 April 1923): 2.

[24] 'The Strike of the Asiatic Seamen's Union Members: Startling Change in American Union's Attitude,' *Australasian Seamen's Journal* 8, no 15 (1 June 1922).

[25] 'Chinese Seamen's Strike,' *Argus* (Melbourne) 4 April 1922, 8.

[26] 'Chinese Seamen on Strike,' *Worker* (Brisbane), 9 February 1922, 17.

7.2 Chinese seamen outside Chinese hostel in Liverpool, 1942 Photographer Bert Hardy/ Picture Post/Hulton Archive via Getty Images

particular.' Once they were 'organised and working in harmony with other seamen's unions throughout the world,' shipowners would find it impossible to hire any but union seamen, and at union wages and conditions.[27] The rate of unionisation had to spread to other countries to avoid workers from one country being substituted for other – striking – seafarers. The Australian union acted similarly.

In its annual report, the SUA executive in 1922 also reported that Indian ports were now organising. This was welcomed as an overdue recognition that they were 'used by the master class in opposition to the European workers' and in hope that 'they will take an international view of matters and recognise capital knows no country.'[28] The SUA also acknowledged the need to overcome the middle class's support of foreign capitalists.

The 'foreign capitalists' in the British colonies were alarmed at the unrest in Asia, which was partly a protest against colonial domination –

[27] 'The Strike of the Asiatic Seamen's Union Members: Startling Change in American Union's Attitude,' *Australasian Seamen's Journal* 8, no. 15 (1 June 1922).

[28] 'Coolies Organising,' *Australasian Seamen's Journal* 8, no. 25 (2 April 1923): 3.

the beginning of independence movements. China was 'a colony of world imperialism,' dominated by 14 imperialist powers, including the United States, Japan, Italy, Russia and Britain.[29] In Hong Kong, the Governor, Sir Reginald Stubbs, insisted from the beginning of the seamen's strike that it was political in motivation, 'almost wilfully turning a blind eye to the real economic grievances of the Chinese seamen.'[30] Like other British officials and colonial authorities in South China, the Hong Kong Governor was convinced that the strike was a conspiracy, orchestrated by Sun Yat-sen's government in a province heavily under communist influence, whose purpose was to drive out the British from South China and Hong Kong. British official reporting of the strike therefore 'was unmistakeably shrouded in an intense anti-communist mentality and terminology.'[31] As the seamen's strike extended to a general strike, even impacting on the staff of Government House, the British Consul General changed his thinking from believing the strike had a genuine economic origin. The Chinese press, too, on behalf of the Chinese elite and merchants (and business interests located in London) became fully persuaded that the strike was due to Bolshevik influence.

Historians dispute the extent of Bolshevik motivation, arguing the communist role was minimal and unknown to the Chinese population, even the strikers.[32] Only some of the known leaders were aware of, and had some contact with, the communists in South China, and only after the strike had started. Indeed, one interpretation holds the seamen's strike responsible for being the catalyst for bringing Chinese workers together and forming a new collective relationship of solidarity.[33] Persecution of the Seamen's Union by the authorities prompted a wider strike in sympathy. Successful wage claims followed. Furthermore, the seamen's action broke open the relationship with the merchants, who now appeared as adversaries of impoverished workers, not community leaders.

The SUA journal was abreast of these events and the nuances of the anti-foreign agitation. A general article about labour organisation in China included references to the seamen, and emphasised the foreign shipowners' resistance to the strikers while Chinese shippers came quickly to an agreement. The result was that as the strike lengthened it assumed an

---

[29] Arora, *I.T.F. in Non-European World*, 15.

[30] Chan Lau Kit-ching, 'The Perception of Chinese Communism in Hong Kong 1921–1934,' *China Quarterly* 164 (December 2000): 1044–61.

[31] Kit-ching, 'Perception of Chinese Communism in Hong Kong.'

[32] Kit-ching, 'Perception of Chinese Communism in Hong Kong.'

[33] Chan Wai Kwan, *The Making of Hong Kong Society* (Oxford: Clarendon Press, 1991), 195.

increasingly anti-foreign character.[34] Later, another article, like subsequent Chinese Communist Party histories, gave more credit to the communists in organising the strike. This article argued that it was 'inevitable that such exploited workers will rise in revolt,' and that this was happening as a consequence of the influence of the Soviets, the Russian revolution having raised the consciousness of Chinese workers. Labour organisations had grown rapidly throughout China's industrial districts and there had been numerous strikes indicating prevailing industrial unrest. The article also pointed out that the most important of them was the dockers' strike in Canton and later in Hong Kong, which at the time was the largest port in the world. It had ended with international capitalism's surrender and 300,000 workers celebrating their success 'to the refrain of the Internationale.'[35]

Three years later, there were also several short articles concerned with striking mill workers in Shanghai, and an article written specially for the SUA by Sam Chin Ging, then secretary of the Chinese Seamen's Union.[36] It reported growing discontent and indignation among tens of thousands of Chinese seamen at the shipowners' non-observance of the agreement concluded between the Chinese Seamen's Union and the Shipowners' Committee, as a result of the seamen's victorious strike in 1922. The Agreement had been signed by the chairman of the Shipowners Committee, the British Consul General at Canton, a delegate of the Seamen's Union (Chak Hon Ke) and was further guaranteed by Hong Kong's most prominent businessman and philanthropist, Sir Robert Ho Tung. The article claimed the shipowners and the British Colonial Government at Hong Kong had violated every one of these three clauses in the Agreement, while the Chinese seamen, in the person of the Chinese Seamen's Union, had kept faithfully to the Agreement ever since its solemn conclusion. It then provided the Agreement in full, to show the flagrant violations deliberately committed by the shipowners in coalition with the British Colonial Government. Their campaign to have the Agreement adhered to was discussed in detail. It concluded with an appeal 'to our brother workers in China and all other countries, **but particularly to the seamen** [bold in original],' to assist them by declining to man ships for China. 'You will only be helping the enemies of the Chinese seamen,

[34] 'The Labor Problem in China,' *Australasian Seamen's Journal* 8, no. 21 (1 December 1922): 12.

[35] 'China: Capitalism's United Front,' *Australasian Seamen's Journal* 8, no. 25 (2 April 1923).

[36] Sam Chin Ging, 'The Seamen's Union in China,' *Australasian Seamen's Journal* 8, no. 51 (15 June 1925).

and we are not prepared to believe that Australian seamen will descend to such a dastardly action.'[37]

During this strike the Chinese Seamen's Union also appealed to the ITF for help. This (1925) was the first point of contact between Chinese workers and the ITF. The following year, the ITF explained in its newsletter that European unions had to recognise the struggles in China, India and Japan as their own, and take active steps to improve the standard of living in those countries, if they were to maintain and extend the gains they had made previously for themselves.[38] This was a recurring theme, an argument for pragmatism not ideology, that recognised but did not push the internationalism of working-class interests versus capital. That language was more likely to be found in the publications of the SUA, which through its connections with the Communist Party had some direct contact with other communist seafarers.

A union journal article on foreign competition began by arguing that capitalists argue a reduction in wages must occur if industry is to survive and that foreign competition is given as the (false) reason why this is necessary. The article set out a number of examples of attempts to reduce the wages of seamen in Britain and America and said governments were prepared to go a long way further than wage reduction; governments were 'prepared to lend all the forces of the State to the shipping interests whenever the Capitalists call them out for aid,' as Britain had illustrated against the Chinese seamen at Hong Kong and Canton. The journal pondered whose competition was feared by the British shipowners trading in Chinese waters. It said wage reduction was also being forced on workers in Japan, who had 'far more to fear from the competition of foreign workers than has hitherto been imagined.' While Japan's seamen had been able to retain what was won by them during the war years, and had also recently forced an increase in wages, workers in other industries in Japan were having their wages and conditions compared unfavourably with wages paid in other countries, to force them to agree to a cut.[39]

Chinese and Japanese seamen in this period understood their need for support from overseas unions who were better able to perform regionally and internationally. At great risk to themselves, given the severe repression they were under, they reached out for pan-Pacific ties of international solidarity, through both the medium of print and also personal contact.[40]

[37] Ging, 'The Seamen's Union in China,' 16.

[38] 'The Colonial Question,' *ITF Newsletter*, December 1926, quoted in Reinalda, *International Transportworkers Federation, 1914–1945*.

[39] By The Snipe, 'The Same Old Story: Foreign Competition,' *Australasian Seamen's Journal* 8, no. 21 (1 December 1922): 2.

[40] Josephine Fowler, 'From East to West and West to East: Ties of Solidarity in the

The Australian maritime unions were therefore a key connection. The SUA accordingly encouraged members to consider the conditions of the Japanese, pointing out that while Australian conditions and wages might now be a little better, there was no cause for concern about the Japanese lowering Australia's standard of living. Australian shipowners, 'despite all their boasting,' were not more generous than their Japanese counterparts, and 'we must remember what hard and continuous fighting has been needed to secure them,' which if they relaxed would quickly lose them all they had gained.[41]

A bill for the amendment of Japan's Seamen's Act was presented to the parliament in 1923. The changes fixing the minimum age of employees in Japanese ships were consistent with the ILO 1920 Genoa Convention, setting the age of 17 or 18 for trimmers or stokehold hands. Fifty per cent of trimmers on Japanese ships were under the age of 18. Japanese shipowners were protesting with the usual cry of 'legislating for a small section only.'[42]

There were others in Australia, non-unionists, who were also calling for greater attention to be paid to labour standards and events occurring in Asian countries. 'Australia needs to take more interest in the East, and realise how closely her progress is wrapped up with that of her colored neighbors,' wrote one.[43] An astute observer, a lecturer in philosophy at the University of Adelaide, Campbell Garnett pointed out the connections that were to be drawn between the Chinese anti-foreign strikes and those of British seamen on the Australian coast in 1925. The underlying causes of both disturbances were the similarity of conditions. Garnett conceded that comparing Australian rates of wages and working conditions with those of British seamen compelled sympathy with the British strikers but argued their strike was 'foolish and wasteful because it was a blind and hopeless rebellion against the logic of facts.'[44] In fact, the British seamen's strike was largely led by the UK Minority Movement, founded in 1923–24 as the British section of the Red International of Labor Unions (RLIU), closely following the policies of the Third Communist International to recruit

Pan-Pacific Revolutionary Trade Union Movement, 1923–1934,' *International Labor and Working-Class History* 66 (2004): 99–117; Josephine Fowler, *Japanese and Chinese Immigrant Activists: Organizing in American and International Communist Movements 1919–33* (New Brunswick, NJ: Rutgers University Press, 2007).

[41] Seamen's Union of Australasia, Annual Report, 1922.

[42] Peggy, 'The Black Pan: Japanese Seamen,' *Australasian Seamen's Journal* 8, no. 27 (1 June 1923): 3.

[43] Garnett, 'China and Seamen's Strike.' A. Campbell Garnett, MA, Litt.D., lecturer in philosophy, University of Adelaide, was the author of *Instinct and Personality* (London: George Allen & Unwin, 1928).

[44] Garnett, 'China and Seamen's Strike.'

members from trade unions. To Garnett, the unrest in China, by contrast, was logical – a consequence of the fact that China was 'in the throes of a rapid industrial revolution.' China also had a system of 'unequal treaties' whereby foreigners possessed portions of China in 'independent and wealthy colonies in China's greatest cities, hav[ing] secured for themselves immunity from Chinese law and taxation. And hav[ing] obtained control of the Chinese Customs Office.' This had created a situation of 'Chinese opinion which feels sufficiently bitter and is strong enough numerically to organise a formidable protest against these treaties.' Consequently, the strike was also a general anti-foreign demonstration.[45] Anti-foreign protests, however, were not only anti-British, they were also anti-Japanese, and the strike had started by the killing of a worker in a strike riot in a Japanese factory in Shanghai.

Meanwhile, the Seamen's Minority Movement, which worked within the NUS, was espousing policies that would be appealing to Asian and 'coloured' seamen in Britain, such as self-determination for colonial peoples, thus 'introducing them to a radical if not revolutionary political perspective' to forge a common trade union movement among diasporas of non-European seamen.[46]

Garnett's analysis repeated the interconnectedness of imperial and global investment and production and claimed that 'with the increasing industrialisation of the East the problem is becoming more and more pressing.' He then injected the element of fear that underwrote the White Australia policy: 'When the vast resources of coal, iron, and labor of China become organised and developed on modern lines,' which was rapidly proceeding, 'this industrial "yellow peril" will have become very real.' The reference to 'yellow peril' may have been ironic, but it may also have been intended as a straight comment. Australia's regional position and close proximity to Asia shaped much of the public discourse.[47] The maritime unions were pursuing their connections with Asian countries within and against the framework of this fear and the public endorsement of a racially based national identity, but also independently of the ITF, at least for a time.

---

[45] Garnett, 'China and Seamen's Strike.'

[46] G. Alonso Pirio, 'A Note: Minorities' Responses to Racism in the British Seamen's Union,' *Comparative Studies of South Asia, Africa and the Middle East* 4, no. 2 (1984): 56–8, 57.

[47] For a full elaboration, see David Walker, *Anxious Nation* (St Lucia: University of Queensland Press, 1999).

ITF moves into 'extra-European countries'

The ITF outreach to Asia unfolded slowly and with mixed success. In 1924, the ITF agreed to enlarge its General Council to include Asian delegates and unions from India and then China joined in 1926–28 and 1930. Thus, Asian representation on the ITF General Council was strengthened and the 1930 Congress included one delegate each from India and Japan.[48] In 1927, the ITF journal tried to explain that the question of expansion was not a racial one but a labour one. The fear of competition 'could be solved only if Asian labourers were to be employed on the same conditions as Europeans and if members would support the Chinese and try to recruit them as union members.'[49]

Bevin's role in the ITF as leader of the dockers continued to be influential and, according to his biographer, more constructive than that of Havelock Wilson. Wilson antagonised the Asian (Chinese and Indian) maritime labourers residing in British port cities and working for British companies with his overtly racist policies.[50] He also did not enjoy admiration or respect within the Australian unions. There were a number of references and articles condemning Wilson for collusion with the shipowners, along the lines that, 'Mr Havelock Wilson, MP, has gone over to the capitalists in Great Britain.' '[W]e do ask: What is to be said about a labor representative who agrees with the representatives of capitalism as to what the policy of labor is to be at a conference purposely called for the consideration of labor conditions?'[51]

Demonstrating the interconnectedness of maritime labour, Wilson had a vested interest in the fortunes of the SUA as he feared his members might desert ship in Australian ports and sign on for the higher wages paid on the Australian coast, consequently reducing the dues paid to the NUS. On a personal level, Wilson thus maintained a continuing engagement with the activities of the Australian seamen's union. Wilson was hostile to Walsh when the SUA supported the striking British seamen in 1925, and he wrote a critical letter to the government that MPs quoted in order to condemn Walsh in parliament. Yet for the few years after Walsh had been ignominiously removed from the leadership in 1926, Wilson kept him supported financially until Wilson's death ended the connection. Wilson harboured

---

[48] See Reinalda, *International Transportworkers Federation, 1914–1945*; Arora, *I.T.F. in Non-European World*, 26.

[49] Reinalda, *International Transportworkers Federation, 1914–1945*.

[50] Tabili, 'The Construction of Racial Difference.'

[51] 'Secret Diplomacy,' by Mercator, 7.

hopes of the NUS taking over the SUA.[52] Interpersonal connection did not translate into formal organisational association. Under the new leadership and subsequently that of the Militant Minority Movement (which was established in Australia in 1928 and gained control of the SUA in 1933) the SUA spiralled into factional chaos, losing its outward focus and its journal once Tom Walsh and Adela Pankhurst Walsh were no longer at the helm and editing.

It was only after Wilson's death, in 1929, that the ITF started taking more energetic steps towards Asian countries. At the ITF Stockholm conference, in 1928, Edo Fimmen spoke against racism and 'the contempt with which the white rulers treat the coloured races [which] is also found among the white workers, [although] milder in character, nevertheless ... [as] somewhat inferior.' He urged them to offer support to workers in colonial and semi-colonial countries, as a matter of solidarity as well as self-interest. He said that raising 'coloured' crews' wages was a strategy to prevent white wages going down: 'European exploiters were the common foes of white and coloured workers' because of the difficulty of preventing them 'using the coloured workers as permanent crew.' Fimmen also spoke of union racism: 'we must not only free ourselves from feelings of race superiority but must also remove the suspicions against the white race coloured workers [have] had for centuries.'[53]

The 1928 Stockholm conference began 'a new era' for the ITF's attempt to reach out to the 'extra-European' world, with Fimmen leading and extending it to become 'a true world-wide organization,' urgent 'in the struggle against militarism, the coming war peril and against the growth of imperialism.' Bevin wanted the references to races, war and imperialism deleted from the proposed Resolution, and questioned why 'Sovietism and US imperialism were not mentioned.' His proposal was defeated.[54] In 1926, a committee of the ITF had recommended equal wages to be paid to 'coloured' seamen and encouraged them to form strong trade unions and pay reasonable fees.[55] There were three Indian unions affiliated to the ITF, but their plight was poor. Among Bombay seafarers about half of union members were employed in the catering departments, with the other half in almost equal numbers divided between the deck and engine room. Those from Goa mostly were employed in the saloons of passenger vessels. The ITF had (since 1920) wanted to abolish the serang system of hiring and

---

[52] This is examined in detail in Donald Fraser, 'Articles of Agreement: The Seamen's Union of Australia, 1904–1943' (PhD thesis, University of Wollongong, 1998).

[53] Arora, *I.T.F. in Non-European World*, 20.

[54] Arora, *I.T.F. in Non-European World*, 22.

[55] Arora, *I.T.F. in Non-European World*, 25.

7.3 Striking Chinese crew of SS *Silksworth* leaving Newcastle NSW courthouse, October 1937, Newcastle Region Library

have Indian crews sign on as individuals. This request from the Bombay and Calcutta trade unions was rejected by the Indian government. The ITF urged the British and European unions to give them assistance.[56] The 'awakening of the East,' demonstrated by strike activity 'should spur the European movement materially and morally to help the Eastern workers in their struggle against capitalist exploitation.'[57]

Fimmen's deep commitment to anti-colonialism and internationalism thus led him to undertake personal visits. In June 1931, the ITF Council made a decision to delegate Fimmen to undertake a mission which involved attending Japan, China, India and Indonesia, then called the Dutch East Indies.[58] 'All organisations ... wrote back that they welcomed the sending of a delegation and were prepared to cooperate zealously to make the visit successful.' Japan and India were considered the most important countries for the ITF, so most time was allowed for them; China and Indonesia, being of secondary importance, were allocated a shorter time. In the mid-1920s, the ITF had condemned the Dutch colonial regime

[56] Arora, *I.T.F. in Non-European World*, 26.
[57] Arora, *I.T.F. in Non-European World*, 18.
[58] 'Preparation for the Visit of I.T.F. Delegation to the Far East,' undated MS, MRC.

in Indonesia for preventing the formation of unions or any attempts to raise the standard of living of the inhabitants by deporting Dutch union activists. They caused the matter to be raised in the Dutch parliament. In 1925, during an Indonesian dockworkers' strike, the ITF asked European workers to support the Indonesian dockers in their own economic interest, warning that capitalists would shift their enterprises to the colonies and cause unemployment in America and Europe. With rising industrialisation in India, China, Japan and other countries, where the conditions were terrible, Fimmen wondered why the unions of Britain should not organise the workers of Bombay, Calcutta and other parts.[59] 'Successes scored by nationalist revolutionary movements, [the] awakening of [the] Chinese proletariat, [a] powerful strike tide ... ha[d] stricken panic into the hearts of imperialists.'[60]

Thus, suspicious of Fimmen's agenda and political leanings, the British and Netherlands governments refused to grant him visas to enter their colonies. The Federation had to abandon the initial plans to arrange a large transport workers' conference in India.[61] Fimmen had struck up a friendship with the cosmopolitan, Cambridge-educated, Indian independence activist Jawaharlal Nehru (1889–1964). Nehru was an internationalist, seeking to reconcile his Fabian socialist views with a subcontinental critique of nationalism that, when he became India's first Prime Minister (in 1947), later became recognisable as a non-Western, decolonising push for economic and social rights.[62] He and Fimmen 'were in regular correspondence' as the Indian National Congress planned and organised civil disobedience actions against the British government, who, Nehru said, 'were not going to give in unless they absolutely have to.' As Nehru himself anticipated the possibility of being arrested, he wrote: 'the struggle in India has a tendency to become a racial one,' which many wished to avoid, and they relied on friends in Europe to help them in this goal.[63]

The ITF's campaign for India 'began' with ITF support for Indian seafarers' demands for an eight-hour day and the invitation to Indian delegates to come to London. The 1930 ITF Congress, held in London, was attended by 'Ben Tillett, champion of Indian workers' and Mohammed Daud, the first Indian representative elected to the General Council. Daud proposed that the ITF should press governments of the East, particularly the

[59] Arora, I.T.F. in Non-European World, 14.

[60] Arora, I.T.F. in Non-European World, 16.

[61] Reinalda, 'The ITF and Non-European World,' 121–2.

[62] Manu Bhagavan, India and the Cold War (Chapel Hill: University of North Carolina Press, 2019).

[63] Arora, I.T.F. in Non-European World, 30.

Indian legislature, to pass the eight-hour law for seafarers, as per the ILO Convention. The Congress accepted Daud's offer for India to host the first ITF regional conference in the Far East. However, British officials refused to issue a visa for Fimmen. On the grounds that a Royal Commission had already investigated workers' conditions in India, 'further enquiry by a foreigner [was] unnecessary and undesirable,' especially at a time coinciding with a big railway workers' strike.[64]

Fimmen, however, was able to travel to Japan and China in the second half of 1931. His visit to Japan was the more successful of the two. This was the first visit a European trade union official had made to Japan and he came away with a huge amount (100 kg) of information.[65] As guest of the JSU, and with the Japanese government's assistance of police protection, he spent around five weeks touring the country, meeting local unionists and speaking to various audiences. In Tokyo, Yokohama, Nagoya, Osaka, Kobe and other cities, he addressed thousands of seamen and visited factory sites.[66] His activities led to the opening of the ITF Tokyo office, which had to be managed by the JSU on behalf of the Federation.[67] Fimmen was impressed with the JSU, which had grown out of 49 seamen's unions and also included dockworkers. JSU was 'a great advocate of ITF,' with strong finances, its own building and a large number of dedicated officials.[68]

Was this a public relations triumph for the now-militarised and imperialist Japanese government that was beginning to wage war with China? Towards the end of the decade, former SUA federal secretary Tom Walsh and Adela Pankhurst Walsh also visited Japan and were impressed by the attention showered on them by the fascist government. By then war was brewing and the Walshs' visit was perceived as a security risk by the Australian security services, while their active support of Japan meant they were seen as turncoats by their former union allies on the Left.[69]

Fimmen's visit to China was the less productive partly due to political circumstances.[70] There were problems with the arrangements the ITF had made for

[64] Arora, *I.T.F. in Non-European World*, 27, 32–4.

[65] ITF, *Solidarity*, 92.

[66] Arora, *I.T.F. in Non-European World*, 34.

[67] Mogi, *Japanese Shipping Trade*, 21, 24–5; J.F. Soares, 'Japanese Seafarers and their Union,' *ITF Journal* 5/6 (1959): 56–62; Takao Matsumura, 'Anglo-Japanese Trade Union Relations between the Wars,' in *The History of Anglo-Japanese Relations 1600–2000*, vol. 5, *Social and Cultural Perspectives*, ed. Gordon Daniels and Chushichi Tsuzuki (London: Palgrave Macmillan, 2002), 265–7.

[68] Arora, *I.T.F. in Non-European World*, 34.

[69] Fraser, 'Articles of Agreement.'

[70] Matsumura, 'Anglo-Japanese Trade Union Relations between the Wars,' 238; Reinalda, 'The ITF and Non-European World,' 122–3.

contacts, difficulties in finding interpreters, but, more specifically, he found the public was preoccupied with the civil war between the Shanghai and Nanking governments and the Japanese occupation of Manchuria. 'What I have seen, and what I have heard and experienced ... has caused me great concern and anxiety,' Fimmen wrote. Trade unions were state controlled, 'there [was] no freedom of organization' and 'Chinese workers [had] no rights.' He appealed to Chiang Kai-Shek and his government: 'In the name of the brethren and comrades abroad of the Chinese workers and the Chinese people themselves ... to stop the terror ... and to repeal the so-called emergency laws.'[71]

Fimmen left China after a few weeks and travelled to the Philippines and then to Hong Kong and Singapore, which as British colonies allowed him to disembark but refused him permission to venture further. As part of this ITF Asian outreach, suggestions were also made to hold an Asian and Australasian Transport Workers' conference.[72] Australian trade unionists did try to organise a Pan-Pacific Congress in Sydney, built on close links between the NSW Labor Council, which had communist leadership, and Red International Labour Union sections in the Far East.[73] This, however, did not eventuate.

Overall, Fimmen's journey of 1931–32, while undoubtedly of historical significance, was not a huge success in achieving change for the ITF. The cancellation of the conference in India was a big blow and an alternative could not be found at short notice. There were only seven unions in the Far East that belonged to the ITF, five of them in India, one each in China and Japan. The ITF was rarely invited to attend non-European conferences.[74] In the following several years, the rise of militarism in Japan and the Sino-Japanese war made collaboration between Japanese unionists and the ITF difficult. Moreover, the Japanese government forced the seamen's union to withdraw from the ITF in 1939 before dissolving the union the following year.[75]

The coming of the Second World War put an end to ITF plans in the Asia-Pacific. In August 1939, the SUA was reporting positively of proposed plans for an ITF conference to be held in Wellington, New Zealand, in early 1940. The prospect had been discussed by the Maritime Transport Council (Sydney) at its last meeting, which resolved to put it before the membership of the unions. SUA members at their stop-work meeting had endorsed the ITF suggestion.[76] But the conference had to be called off –

---

[71] Arora, *I.T.F. in Non-European World*, 35–6, quoting Fimmen's letter to Chiang Kai-Shek, 8 December 1931.

[72] Asian Transport Workers' Conference, *ITF Journal* 11 (1960): 238–9.

[73] Farrell, *International Socialism*, 66, 65.

[74] Arora, *I.T.F. in Non-European World*, 37.

[75] Soares, 'Japanese Seafarers and their Union'; Reinalda, 'The ITF and Non-European World,' 123.

[76] Branch Reports [Sydney], *Seamen's Journal* 1, no. 1 (September 1939): 12.

until 'the downfall of Nazism has been accomplished.' The ITF expressed their wish 'to take up again our plans to strengthen our relations with the transport workers of Australasia,' and expressed their confidence 'that you will be prepared to attend our Conference, and perhaps take a more direct part in the international activities.'[77] In a subsequent communication, the ITF essentially argued that while 'the working class abhors war and violence; it hates imperialism.' Consequently, 'checking German imperialistic aims' was now the ITF's 'supreme object.' The ITF had long fought Nazism, even before the Nazi Party came to power and started destroying trade unions. Doing so now, 'if possible with greater intensity,' was 'to free the world from these last remnants of a dying imperialistic age.'[78]

The ITF's involvement in the resistance to the fascist governments in Germany, Italy and Spain was logical, critical and effective in sabotaging railway transport, derailing trains or secretly misdirecting freights and armaments. Seafarers were able to report as expert observers on marine installations and defences to help the Allies. Networks of contacts established in Germany before the war became the core of intelligence about movements once war was declared. The Nazis had to patrol railway stations and ports to prevent losses, and thus troops were kept from the front. The cost to workers of this wartime activism was enormous. Communist maritime workers were at risk of death from the Nazis but could also be interned – as five seafarers from Germany were in France, as enemy aliens, by the Allies. Several former leaders of the ITF, among them Hermann Jochade who had been ITF secretary 1904–16, were either shot by the Nazis or sent to concentration camps where they subsequently died.[79]

The ITF's success in reaching the 'extra-European world' between 1919 and 1945 was therefore thwarted by larger geopolitical realities and impediments. Fimmen's vision – of 'proletarians whether white or brown, yellow or black standing shoulder to shoulder in the fight against capitalism … paint[ing] the world Red' – was not realised.[80] Before 1939, the ITF did increase the number of unions (by 30) and countries (by 18) that were now affiliated, and these numbers increased again before 1945 (a further 32 unions from 15 non-European and 4 European countries),[81] but the achievements were less than Fimmen had hoped for. The ITF outreach into Asia nevertheless

---

[77] 'International Transport Workers Federation,' *Seamen's Journal* 1, no. 2 (November 1939): 8.

[78] 'International Transport Workers Federation,' *Seamen's Journal* 1, no. 5 (March 1940): 9.

[79] ITF, *Solidarity*, 96–8.

[80] Arora, *I.T.F. in Non-European World*, 22.

[81] ITF, *Solidarity*, 114.

seemed to have some impact. In 1938, Harold Butler delivered a report to the ILO in which he pointed out that India's enormous territory and nine major languages made union organisation difficult, but that railway workers, seamen and dockers at that time had 'fairly effective unions.'[82] ILO conventions were 'still in the process of being ratified' and hours of work and safety issues on the docks remained unregulated. But change depended more on the desire for it among the people themselves, not just by legislation: it required an 'educated public opinion,' and he saw that possibility in the 'ferment of new ideas' and demands for social reform.[83] Butler's report drew comparisons between India, China and Japan's adaptation to modern industry in order to estimate the consequences of ILO conventions for the standards of protection being applied. He observed that China had not reached the same level of industrialisation as the other two, while 'India, like Japan, ranks among the eight states of chief industrial importance, and as such is allocated a permanent seat on the Governing Body of the International Labour Office.'[84]

'No scrap iron'

As war developed between Japan and China, Chinese unions again called on their counterparts in the West for assistance. The Japanese assault on China which began in 1931 and was followed by invasion in 1935, was well publicised by expatriate Chinese as well as by the Communist Party. It led to cooperative actions between unions and the community such as when the SS *Silksworth* arrived on the Australian coast in 1937 carrying a Chinese crew complaining about mistreatment. They sought help and were given shelter by local communists while the maritime unions declared the ship black. Large protests in the port cities of Newcastle and Sydney highlighted the cargo (wheat) was being carried in a Japanese-chartered ship to Japanese-occupied China. This forced the government to withdraw the prosecutions the captain had initiated against the crew.

At first, Communist Party efforts to stop the transport of munitions to Japan failed to generate action by the British unions.[85] Two years later, full-scale undeclared war mobilised an anti-fascist wave of support for

---

[82] Harold Butler, 'Problems of Industry in the East with Special Reference to India, French India, Ceylon, Malaysia and the Netherlands Indies,' ILO Studies and Reports 29 (Geneva: International Labour Organization, 1938), 7, 19, 8.

[83] Butler, 'Problems of Industry in the East,' 14, 9.

[84] Butler, 'Problems of Industry in the East,' 5, 3.

[85] At the TUC Congress, 1932, such a motion could not even be put to a vote. See Bullock, *Ernest Bevin*, 1:511.

7.4 ILWU members loading ship, and Chinese community picketing against sending scrap iron to Japan, San Francisco 1938, photographer Glenn D. Lym, *Chinese Digest*, January 1939, 11

China.[86] The UK's China Campaign Committee's newsletter was reproducing items from Chinese newspapers and reporting that 'labour organisations throughout Australia are deciding for a boycott of Japanese goods,' including Fremantle's dockers, the Adelaide Trades and Labour Council and the Road Transport Workers Union in Victoria, in addition to boycotts in India being led by Nehru.[87] In New Zealand, in October 1937, Dunedin waterside workers declared they lacked sympathy with the bombing of defenceless towns, women and children and they decided not to load any more scrap iron for Japan.[88] Between December 1937, when missionaries in Shanghai

[86] For a detailed account, see Tom Buchanan, *East Wind: China and the British Left, 1925–1976* (Oxford: Oxford University Press, 2012), 61–73.

[87] *China Bulletin* 1 (16 November 1937): 8–9, Per 24633d.158 (no. 1–5, 1937–8), Bodleian Library, Oxford.

[88] 'Waterside Workers Boycott Japan,' *Worker* (Brisbane), 5 October 1937, 21.

called for a boycott, and February 1938, when the Scandinavian transport workers' unions decided to impose one, dockers in several UK ports took 'spontaneous action' in what was becoming an international movement that included Sydney.[89] In Australia, by 1937, peak labour bodies (the NSW Labor Council and the ACTU) were supporting union actions in support of Chinese crews or against Japanese aggression. The ACTU had imposed a consumer boycott on Japanese goods and the WWF was refusing to load scrap iron destined for Japan. Australia was represented among 19 countries at the International People's Assembly and World Boycott conference held in February and the United States also had a boycott movement. The China Campaign Committee called for an embargo on oil and war materials being sent to Japan.[90]

Then, a year later, Port Kembla waterside workers, under the leadership of the branch secretary Ted Roach, refused to load the SS *Dalfram* with its cargo of pig iron for Japan.[91] Similar action was under way on the San Francisco waterfront. There, however, it was the local Chinese community who organised a picket to prevent longshore workers loading a Greek ship with scrap iron for Japan, cargo they said would become bombs raining on Chinese civilians. They called on the longshoremen to join them. Although the Waterfront Employers' Association, fearing a coastwide shipping tie-up, insisted the picket be abandoned and that the workers observe their existing contracts, the longshore workers voted not to cross the picket line, although they did not refuse to work.[92] The ILWU and CIO called a coastwide conference to promote an embargo on all materials being shipped to Japan and the ILWU undertook to broaden public support. The 5,000 strong community protest then confronted the Employers' Association and marched through the city, singing and thanking the ILWU for their support.[93] They had achieved their aim of drawing attention to the Chinese cause. The next day, ILWU members were back at work loading the ship.

While the *Dalfram* was eventually loaded – after three months they were coerced back to work by government threat of using the Transport Workers Act 1928 – it was undoubtedly a political victory for the WWF, which had challenged the government's appeasement policy towards Japan. The union could claim its stand was vindicated when Australia and Japan were later

[89] *China Bulletin* 3 (15 December 1937); *China Bulletin* 4 (8 January 1938).

[90] *China Bulletin* 2 (30 November 1937).

[91] This has been covered by many historians. See especially Jon White, 'The Port Kembla Pig Iron Strike of 1938,' *Labour History* 37 (1979): 63–77.

[92] *San Francisco Call Bulletin*, 20 December 1938, 7; *San Francisco News*, 19 December 1938, 5.

[93] Lim P. Lee, 'Chinatown Goes Picketing,' *Chinese Digest*, January 1939, 10; copy held in ILWU archives, San Francisco. See also *San Francisco Chronicle*, 21 December 1938, 1, 4.

7.5 Crew who refused to take SS *Dalfram* with its cargo to Japan 1938, *Seamen's Voice*, December 1938, SLNSW

at war. British dockworkers were 'lionised' by the British Left for taking the lead and so too were Australia's wharfies hailed for taking this action. Even Billy Hughes, still a member of the government, later expressed his support, and Isaac Isaacs, the Supreme Court judge who alone had upheld the government's power to deport the SUA's officials in 1925, expressed 'unbounded admiration' for the union's 'noble stand' against Australia's trade in munitions materials.[94]

What is less remembered about that WWF action is the Indian seamen who were with the crew supporting the protest. One of them, Alaf Khan, was among those who ultimately refused to sail with the ship when it departed with its cargo for Japan.[95] Another, Mahomet Goula, the leader of

[94] Quoted in Len Richardson, 'Dole Queue Patriots,' in *Strikes: Studies in Twentieth Century Australian Social History*, ed. John Iremonger, John Merritt and Graeme Osborne (Sydney: A&R and ASSLH, 1973), 143–58.

[95] Rupert Lockwood, *War on the Waterfront: Menzies, Japan and the Pig-Iron Dispute*

the Indian crew in the stokehold, was taken from the ship at the company's request and placed in an institution for the mentally ill, supposedly on a charge of opium addiction. SUA secretary William Daley insisted he was 'entirely sane ... not distressed and ... in perfect health,' and that the move was intended to intimidate the crew, while the labour press called it 'a trumped-up charge' and the local Member (ALP) questioned the Minister for Health in parliament.[96] Daley promptly went to visit Goula, who was released, and Daley escorted him out of the institution the next day. Nine seamen were left stranded in Sydney, dependent on public donations to help them survive.[97]

At the time of Edo Fimmen's death, in 1942, Japan's militarisation and imperial ambitions had plunged most of the countries of the Asia-Pacific into war and Japan was bombing the northern Australian city of Darwin. Invasion threatened, just as many had feared. India had not achieved independence and was split between support for, and opposition to, imperialist Britain. Many were asking: 'Why after 180 years of British rule are the people so poor, illiterate and poorly nourished?' When the Viceroy of India declared India was a belligerent country participating in the war 'without even consulting' the people or Central Assembly of India, workers took action in protest. With their growing militancy, seamen were at the forefront.[98]

'No war for us'

By 1939, 'Lascars' were being described in the Australian press as 'good seamen, efficient, trustworthy, and courageous,' playing 'an important part in the Empire's shipping,' and 'ordinarily so familiar to Sydney people as they walk nonchalantly in the streets when on leave from their ships.'[99] Once war was officially declared, however, 'walking nonchalantly' rapidly gave way to protest marching. A group of 52 crew members from the British steamer *City of Canberra* marched in a body through the city centre, disrupting busy peak-hour traffic and drawing crowds of onlookers.[100] Their action was part

---

(Sydney: Hale & Iremonger, 1987), 33, 76; 'From Far Kashmir,' *Daily News* (Sydney), 23 February 1939, 5.

[96] 'Seized on *Dalfram*. Indian Put in Reception House,' *Daily News* (Sydney), 8 December 1938; 'Is "*Dalfram*" Seaman Framed? Union Secretary Thinks So,' *Workers' Weekly* (Sydney), 9 December 1938, 1; 'Allegation in Parliament,' *Sydney Morning Herald*, 9 December 1938, 13.

[97] 'Seamen's Plight, Stranded in Sydney,' *Daily News* (Sydney), 20 February 1939, 5.

[98] [Communist Party of Great Britain], *Colonial Information Bulletin*, India Special Number, vol. 3, no. 12 (30 November 1939), 2, 3, MRC.

[99] 'The Lascars,' *Daily Mercury* (Mackay, Queensland), 30 December 1939.

[100] 'Lascars March in Sydney,' *Argus* (Melbourne), 23 November 1939, 3; press coverage

of an international strike by rank and file Indian seamen employed on British ships that caused stoppages in the British ports of Glasgow and Liverpool, as well as South Africa, Mozambique, Burma and the West Indies – 'almost all the ports of the world except India.'[101] By December, hundreds were in prison and communists in Bombay had also held a big strike of 100,000 workers.[102]

In Australia, the strike began in September when the Indian crew of the SS *Speybank*, then in port in Wollongong, refused to sail unless the captain agreed to a 100 per cent increase in their wage, as compensation for the heightened risk created by the recent outbreak of war. Other crews followed their example, walking off their ships in ports on both the east and west coasts. By early November, shipping line operators were estimating 'at least six ships employing Lascar labour had been affected and hundreds of Lascars were involved.'[103] Owners, reportedly 'losing thousands of pounds through the delays,' were importing new crews of Chinese and Malays to replace striking Indian seamen being repatriated to India. Charged with absenting themselves without leave or cause, 118 soon landed in Sydney's Long Bay Gaol.[104]

Among the hundreds of strikers were the crew of the British freighter *Peshawur*, who refused an order 'to turn to' and left the ship. Determined not to return, 50 men subsequently spent a cold and hungry night camped on the wharf.[105] One of the crew, waiter R. Vaz, explained their reasons: 'Ship go to England. We want to go to Calcutta. Whole crew want to go home. No war for us.'[106] The crew of the *Elmbank* on strike in Fremantle and with only two months of their agreements remaining, also sought an assurance they would not be taken into the war zone and would be repatriated to Calcutta at the expiration of their agreements. Their (unnamed) spokesman indicated that they were prepared to undertake a voyage 'into the Atlantic Ocean if they were at the outset given the war bonus of £50 a head and received double

---

was extensive.

[101] Letter from Guha to ITF, 20 August 1950, 2, which also claims the strike was organised by the ISU, perhaps in Britain, as ISU involvement is not apparent in the spontaneous actions taken by ships' crews in Australia.

[102] [Communist Party of Great Britain], *Colonial Information Bulletin*, 3, MRC. See also Tony Lane, *The Merchant Seamen's War* (Manchester: Manchester University Press, 1990), 175.

[103] 'Lascars Win Double Rates,' *Tribune* (Sydney), 3 October 1939, 1; 'Lascars Sent to Prison,' *Sydney Morning Herald*, 2 November 1939, 5. Wartime censorship means it is not always possible to identify the ships involved, but see 'Seamen Strike at Fremantle,' *Workers Star* (Perth), 28 October 1939, 1; 'Lascars Desert,' *Canberra Times*, 9 November 1939, 5.

[104] 'Lascar Desertions,' *Townsville Daily Bulletin*, 9 November 1939, 1; 'Lascars Happy in Gaol,' *Sydney Morning Herald*, 13 November 1939, 12.

[105] 'Seamen Walk Off Ship,' *Tribune* (Sydney), 11 November 1939, 1; 'Lascars Camped on End of Wharf,' *Newcastle Sun*, 9 November 1939, 20; 'Striking Lascars Arrested,' *Daily News* (Sydney), 10 November 1939, 2.

[106] 'Lascars Won't Sail in Ship,' *Daily News* (Sydney), 8 November 1939, 1.

pay, double rations and warmer clothing. "We are poor people,"' he declared, "'and we must think of our families. What would they do if we were killed?'" With that in mind, 'they most desired … to be taken back to India.'[107]

Their refusal risked reigniting the old ideas that had circulated in the late nineteenth century when blaming the men for shipwrecks rather than the faultiness of ships had seen Indian seamen called cowardly and panic-stricken in emergencies. But the dangers to merchant seamen in time of war were now known to be undoubtedly real. Among the striking crews were men who had seen service in the previous war, when 3,500 Indian seamen serving on British ships died. A further 1,200 were interned as prisoners of war, at least 40 of whom also died. SUA secretary William Daley told a meeting of the Labor Council of NSW that some among the strikers 'had had experience of being submarined.'[108] In Sydney, where the Indian crews of two British wool freighters were also refusing to sail, their (again unnamed) spokesmen declared 'that they would rather go to gaol in India … than risk the U-boats.'[109] Indeed, several of the ships involved in the walk-offs in Australia were subsequently torpedoed.[110]

Indian crews may have been inclined not to risk their lives given the strengthening independence movement. Indian support for Britain's war was ambivalent and Britain was now hardening its own 'single-minded' focus on its fortunes in Europe. The threat of actual war or invasion was too distant for India's leaders to be concerned, and the public was pressing them to use the war to take advantage of Britain's vulnerability.[111] The sentiments of strikers in Australia reflected this reality according to the Communist Party paper. *Tribune* reported that they had declared their reluctance 'to risk their lives and leave their families in want, in a cause in which they are not particularly interested.'[112] In an earlier interview, their spokesman explained

---

[107] 'Lascars Hold Out,' *West Australian* (Perth), 27 October 1939, 11. See also 'Shipping Dispute,' *Westralian Worker* (Perth), 3 November 1939, 3; 'Lascar Seamen Demand War Risk Rates,' *Daily News* (Perth), 25 October 1939, 11.

[108] Lane, *Merchant Seamen's War*, 178; Balachandran, *Globalizing Labour*, 202; D.R.B. Mitchell, Inspector, Investigation Branch, Sydney, 20 November 1939, to the Director, Commonwealth Investigation Branch, 'Trouble with Lascar Crews at Sydney,' series A432, 1939/1101, National Archives of Australia (NAA); Labor Council of N.S.W., Authorised Report, *Australian Worker* (Sydney), 29 November 1939, 8.

[109] 'Afraid of U-Boats,' *Daily News* (Sydney), 28 October 1939, 2.

[110] The *Elmbank* was torpedoed and sunk by a German submarine in 1940 and the *Speybank* captured by the Germany auxiliary cruiser *Atlantis* in 1941. See *The Ships List* (last updated 3 January 2017), www.theshipslist.com/ships/lines/bank.shtml. The *Peshawur* was torpedoed and sunk near Madras in 1943. *The Ships List*, www.theshipslist.com/ships/lines/pando.shtml.

[111] Yasmin Khan, *India at War: The Subcontinent and the Second World War* (New York: Oxford University Press, 2015), 10–11.

[112] 'Lascars' Firm Demand,' *Tribune* (Sydney), 24 November 1939, 3.

that while the men had no desire to hinder the war effort, 'Indians could hardly be expected to show special enthusiasm for the war, until India had been granted a greater measure of self-government.'[113]

Overriding these other considerations was the more obvious fact that Indian seamen saw an unprecedented opportunity to press their demands for increased wages and more attention to their conditions. The men on strike in Australia in late 1939 were among some 30,000 to 40,000 Indian seamen employed on British ships on the eve of the war and represented a quarter of the British maritime labour force.[114] Their labour was indispensable to the industry and essential to Britain's prosecution of the war, providing an ideal moment to press for their rights as workers. Indian seamen had to that point received little real support from Western seafarers and the international organisations they had established. In the decades preceding the 1939 strike, the British union had demonstrated no inclination to stand with Indian seamen in their struggle to assert their rights. The NUS had long opposed the employment of Indian (and indeed other 'foreign') seamen in British shipping, an opposition which intensified in the 1920s and 1930s. The NUS rebuffed their overtures when Indian seamen's unions attempted to forge relationships with other seafarers' organisations in the mid-1920s. Again, in Britain, in 1939, the NUS provided 'little support' to the striking Indian crews.[115] Australian unions took an approach that was in sharp contrast to the NUS.

[113] 'Lascars on Strike,' *Tribune* (Sydney), 21 November 1939, 3.

[114] Lane, *Merchant Seamen's War*, 174, 157; Tabili, *'We Ask for British Justice,'* 162; Balachandran, 'Searching for the *Sardar*,' 209.

[115] Balachandran, 'South Asian Seafarers,' 193; Balachandran, 'Cultures of Protest,' 65. See also Marika Sherwood, 'The Comintern, the CPGB, Colonies and Black Britons, 1920–1938,' *Science & Society* 60, no. 2 (1996): 137–63.

8

'Lascar Seamen Stand up for Rights'

Asserting Independence, c.1930s to 1949

In 1936, Aftab Ali, president of the ISU and among the most important labour leaders of pre-Independence India, delivered a major speech to the International Labour conference in Geneva.[1] Calling on the ILO to make an immediate enquiry into the employment of Indian seamen, he condemned the Indian government's utter failure to improve their conditions, in particular to end the rampant corruption which existed in their system of recruitment.[2]

It was a significant gesture of standing up for Indian seamen's rights but only one moment in their prolonged struggle against being treated as 'coolie competition.' Their union organisation expanded after its origins at the turn of the century, encouraged by the foundation of the ILO and a growing nationalist movement, and there were several seamen's unions which made some important gains. In Calcutta, in 1919, and Bombay, in 1920, seamen's unions struck work, winning significant wage rises of between 35 per cent and 50 per cent.[3] Still they faced formidable opposition, from shipowners determined to keep their labour cheap and a colonial state unwilling to countenance reform.[4] They formed new organisations, recruited more members and reached out to international organisations, joining the ITF in 1924 and participating in international forums. The creation of the ILO in 1919 was an important opportunity in this widening strategy. Not

[1] He is listed in the ILO Conference proceedings as Member of the Working Committee and General Council of the National Trades Union Federation; President, Bengal Trades Union Federation; President, Indian Seamen's Union Calcutta; President, Bengal Mariner's Union (Calcutta List of Members of Delegations, etc., 7). See also Ahuja, 'Mobility and Containment,' 139; Balachandran, 'Circulation through Seafaring,' 126.

[2] 'Lascar Seamen Stand Up for Rights,' *Tribune* (Sydney), 14 November 1939, 1; International Labour Conference, Twenty-First and Twenty-Second Session, Geneva, 1936, Record of Proceedings (Geneva: International Labour Organization, 1937), 159–63.

[3] Broeze, 'Muscles of Empire,' 61, 50.

[4] Documented in Desai, *Maritime Labour in India*.

only was it an impetus to unionisation; over the next two decades its maritime sessions provided a forum that Indian seafarers could use to their advantage, to assert their goals independently of government, to help mobilise international support and to overturn their colonial status enshrined in law.

Ali attended the ILO as the official Indian workers' delegate (Figure 9.1). He spoke, as he told the conference, with the authority of first-hand knowledge. In 1922, 'in search of work, education and experience,' he had signed on as a coal trimmer on a ship sailing for America.[5] He jumped ship in New York, taking advantage of the effective legalisation of desertion by the Seamen's Act of 1915.[6] For several years he worked onshore in casual store jobs and barber shops, all the while educating himself through reading, mixing with trade unionists and exploring political ideas, 'training in syndicalism.'[7] Ali returned to India in 1925 well-informed and motivated. Manfur Khan had founded the Indian Seamen's Union in 1919 which a year later merged with the Indian Seamen's Benevolent Union to form the National Seamen's Union, which then changed its name to become the ISU in 1921.[8] At Manfur Khan's invitation, Ali became an organiser for the ISU in 1926, rising quickly to the position of general secretary.

As Ali's 1936 speech to the ILO indicates, reform of the system of recruitment was one of their main aims. The Indian government had not ratified the earlier ILO convention on the employment of seamen. Instead, it set up an investigation, the Seamen's Recruitment Committee (referred to as the Clow Committee after its chairman A.G. Clow). That committee revealed that the existing system, in which crews were engaged via a series

---

[5] International Labour Conference, 1936, Record of Proceedings, 160; Caroline Adams, *Across Seven Seas and Thirteen Rivers: Life Stories of Pioneer Sylheti Settlers in Britain* (London: THAP Books, 1987), 59; Gopalan Balachandran, 'South Asian Seafarers and their Worlds c.1870–1930s,' in *Seascapes: Maritime Histories, Local Cultures and Transoceanic Exchanges*, ed. Jerry Bentley, Renate Bridenthal and Kären Wigen (Honolulu: University of Hawaii Press, 2007), 197.

[6] Balachandran, *Globalizing Labour*, 160–1. On the Seamen's Act 1915, see Taylor, *Sailors' Union of the Pacific*, 110–35.

[7] Adams, *Across Seven Seas*, 60; Ashfaque Hossain, 'The World of the Sylheti Seamen in the Age of Empire, from the Late Eighteenth Century to 1947,' *Journal of Global History* 9, no. 3 (2014): 443.

[8] Adams, *Across Seven Seas*, 60; Gopalan Balachandran, 'Searching for the *Sardar*: The State, Pre-Capitalist Institutions and Human Agency in the Maritime Labour Market, Calcutta, 1850–1935,' in *Institutions and Economic Change in South Asia*, ed. Burton Stein and Sanjay Subrahmanyam (Delhi: Oxford University Press, 1996), 209, 221–2.

of intermediaries, resulted in the 'systematised extortion' of Indian seamen.[9] The UK (Whitly) Royal Commission on Labour reported in 1931 that seamen's main concern was the 'prevalence of bribery' and found that a high 'level of unemployment among seamen was among the main causes of corruption.'[10] Unions also conducted their own enquiries. A thorough investigation of unemployment among Bombay seamen, partly instigated and funded by the Servants of India Society, drew heavily on evidence from members of the ISU. Its report, published in 1928, found 'complaints about bribery and corruption are universal.' They were largely levelled at the engineers and officers, but also included a union president who was also an officer of a shipping company. The author of the report recommended that while it was nearly impossible for the union to implement actions like boycotting specific ships, it would be 'possible to mitigate some of the evils of unemployment by rationalising recruitment.'[11]

Condemning the system at the ILO in 1936, Ali recalled his own experience when he signed on 14 years earlier and 'never saw my first month's wages.' The persistence of the bribery which had existed at that time exposed government claims to the contrary. Nor was it confined to Indian brokers and ghat serangs. Ali told the conference British officers were also complicit in the system of extortion.[12] The system of debt and dependency that was created, and which had been described explicitly in the 1928 union study, limited the Indian seaman's 'freedom of contract,' ensuring their 'docility' and 'reliability' that shipowners and officers valued.[13] The Indian government representative, Sir Firoz Khan Noon, countered Ali's charge with reassurances of the government's 'wholehearted sympathy' and desire to remove the abuses, saying that it was putting the recommendations of the previous inquiries into effect, albeit so far without success.[14] He also cautioned Ali about the threat of criminal prosecutions hanging over the heads of union members, and urged Ali to withdrew his proposal for an enquiry as all the evidence was already available. Ali shrugged off the threat but did withdraw his call for an enquiry. He had made his point.

Reforming recruitment was necessary if Indian seamen were to overturn their colonial relations of employment. These were organised by language or dialect, sometimes from the same village, or based on religious groupings

[9] Balachandran, 'Searching for the *Sardar*,' 223–8. The quote from the Clow Committee is at 227. See also Balachandran, *Globalizing Labour*, 79–82.

[10] Butler, 'Problems of Industry in the East,' 14.

[11] 'Seamen in Bombay: Report of an Enquiry into the Conditions of Their Life and Work,' Bombay, 1928, 4, 10, 20, MS 159/5/7/587, MRC.

[12] International Labour Conference, 1936, Record of Proceedings, 160.

[13] Ahuja, 'Networks of Subordination,' 30.

[14] International Labour Conference, 1936, Record of Proceedings, 161.

8.1 Strikers inside their hostel, Sydney, 1939
SLNSW

in different areas of the ship: saloon crews were principally from Goa; in the engine room were largely 'Mohamaden [*sic*] seamen' and Punjabis; Hindus from Bombay tended to be deck crews.[15] They reportedly found unity living closely together while waiting for employment. The unions, however, challenged the stereotype promulgated by shipowners and state officials that 'Lascar' crews were bound together by pre-existing social relationships, which ensured their subservience to the serang. Unions argued to the Clow Committee that the serang did not have to be a 'relative, village strongman, or chief,' that Indian seamen were no different from other workers in their ability to come together and form an effective crew.[16] The 1928 union-sponsored report reiterated the government's Clow Committee's recommendation for the establishment of an employment bureau to place recruitment on a systematic basis, replacing 'the powerful and vested interests which cheat the seamen out of their due remunerations.'[17]

[15] 'Seamen in Bombay,' 5–15.
[16] Balachandran, *Globalizing Labour*, 88; Balachandran, 'Conflicts in the International Maritime Labour Market,' 95. On the role of the serang, see Balachandran, 'Searching for the *Sardar*,' 210.
[17] 'Seamen in Bombay,' 21.

Indian seamen's goals for themselves, their stand for their rights, was on show in Ali's speech at the ILO in 1936, with its forthright condemnation of the Indian government. Ali was accompanied by Mohamed Ibrahim Serang, secretary of the National Seamen's Union of India (NSUI), who was attending as a workers' adviser. Historians have noted a difference in the 1936 ILO Conference, with all the representatives for India for the first time being Indians, including Khan Noon, the government representative, who was the High Commissioner to Britain. An increasing assertiveness was consequently visible in comparison with their role in the ILO session of 1920.[18] The Indian delegates in 1936 were resolute in their support of the proposed Hours of Work convention, refusing any special treatment. Ali declared their 'gratification' that it contained 'no invidious exclusion' of them 'from the benefits ensured for seamen generally,' as earlier versions had done. He expressed surprise at the 'voices raised against' it, the regulation of working hours being 'a long-standing question,' and hoped that 'those who are now opposed to it will consider the wisdom of voting for it while they can and not wait until they are forced to accept it.'[19] Those opposed were the UK representatives. Their position reflected the NUS's accommodation with the shipowners, long criticised by the Australian union and described by rival union leader Emanuel Shinwell as a 'blunt bargain' in which 'the trade union keeps the men in order, the employer in return agrees to employ union men only.'[20] The NUS 'negotiated a longer … week for British seamen' and allowed 'an even longer working … week for Indian seamen.'[21]

As long ago as 1899, Indian seamen had voiced their protests against the NUS's strategy as they sought to protect themselves against efforts by the NUS to deprive them of their livelihoods. That year a group of 'lascars, serangs and other native seafaring men' from Bombay sent what one newspaper called 'an extraordinary petition' to the Secretary of State for India. They were protesting against moves that were then being debated in the House of Commons that required the accommodation provisions of the British Merchant Shipping Act to be applied also to Lascars. The men rejected the idea that the accommodation that was allotted to the Lascar crew should be the same as that allotted to British sailors. They

---

[18] Broeze, 'Muscles of Empire,' 61–2; Balachandran, 'South Asian Seafarers,' 194.

[19] International Labour Conference, 1936, Record of Proceedings, 126–7.

[20] Balachandran, 'Conflicts in the International Maritime Labour Market,' 73. The quote is from Shinwell, in Balachandran, 'Making Coolies,' 282. See also Marika Sherwood, 'Race, Nationality and Employment among Lascar Seamen, 1660–1945,' New Community 17, no. 2 (1991): 239.

[21] Balachandran, 'Making Coolies,' 285. See also Marsh and Ryan, The Seamen.

wanted jobs for the many not comforts for the few. 'The proportion of native Lascars to European seamen required for a vessel is nearly two to one,' they explained, and existing vessels were built in accordance with the requirements of the Indian legislation, with crew 'lying close by, and lik[ing] to huddle up together, after their beloved Indian fashion.' They pointed it would be 'impossible under existing circumstances' for the present shipping companies to comply with the new requirement, to 'provide the accommodation required for native seamen by the English Act on the English scale.' Consequently, they feared 'employers would have to dispense with the services of the natives.'[22]

This was the plan behind what seemed to be a benevolent move to improve their conditions, to bring them up to English or 'white men's' standards. Their petition claimed that the proposed change to the accommodation was 'not a blessing, but a curse in disguise'; that enforcing the clause for greater space in the forecastle would throw 30,000 Lascars out of work. While they would thus 'be deprived of a healthy and honest means of livelihood' there would be no gain for the British sailors. They appealed for consideration of their situation: 'Though poor and ignorant, we are human beings,' they said. Their petition called for the respect they deserved as workers, as they appealed for recognition. 'We have braved many a storm, and have been ready to give our lives in the performance of our duty, as our officers will testify. … we rendered exceptionally good service, as the records show.' They wanted to tell the NUS's president, MP Havelock Wilson, 'that his benevolence will prove our bane; that, as we have done him no wrong, and if he really wishes us well, he will … spare us the pursuit of his attentions.' They hoped parliament would 'refuse to listen to him' and 'would leave us alone,' that they 'may not be made the victims of a fatal philanthropy.'[23]

Assertiveness was not new to Indian seafarers, although the means and forums for it changed.[24] Forty years later, Ali ended his 1936 speech to the ILO Conference with a warning to his own government. The Indian government, he said, should remember that the 'question of the employment of Indian seamen will have to be settled,' and 'it will be better for all parties' if that was done by a Convention, as the conference was suggesting; 'if not, everyone will suffer.'[25] The Indian government's

---

[22] 'An Extraordinary Petition,' *North Western Advocate and the Emu Bay Times* (Tasmania), 28 September 1899, 2.

[23] 'A Petition from Lascar, Sailors,' *Adelaide Observer*, 23 September 1899, 29. *The Times* (London), 23 March 1901, reported: 'Courts Declared P&O Must Provide Same Accommodation as for Europeans.'

[24] Naina Manjrekar, '"Violent and Not Quite Modern"? Lascars and Everyday Resistance across the Sail–Steam Divide,' *Labour History* 116 (2019): 29–55.

[25] International Labour Conference, 1936, Record of Proceedings, 163.

subsequent failure (or possibly refusal) to ratify the 1936 ILO Convention prompted the formation of a new organisation, the All-India Seamen's Federation (AISF) in June 1937, which brought together some 40,000 seamen from six unions in a national organisation under Ali's presidency.[26] In 1937, the unions also began a campaign of industrial action to reform the system of recruitment. In December, the Bombay Seamen's Union (BSU) called a strike which lasted four months, demanding that 'seamen should be employed in rotation.' Unemployed seamen protested and picketed outside shipping company offices, disrupting crew recruitment.[27] Processions of seamen, intent on presenting their demands for reform to government, were confronted by heavily armed police. Seamen, including BSU officials, were arrested under the criminal law, as the government representative Khan Noon had warned Ali might happen if he persisted with his demands.[28] In October 1938, the AISF, 'frustrated in its attempts to make any significant headway' on its demands in India, served the Shipping Federation with a log of claims demanding a substantial increase in wages, reform of recruitment, and improvements in working hours, overtime and other conditions. Showing the continuing utter disregard with which shipowners treated Indian seamen's demands for improved conditions, the Federation, which had 'consistently refused to recognise the AISF,' failed even to acknowledge the letter.[29] Indian seafarers' wages had not increased since 1919. This prompted a more militant response, and their struggle entered a new phase on the eve of the Second World War.

In 1939, the AISF extended its reach to Britain and Ali appointed a relative, Surath Ali, already active, as the UK representative.[30] With war on the horizon, the government and shipowners had one more reason to refuse to improve seamen's conditions, but events took an unexpected turn. War provided another moment for Indian seamen to assert themselves and claim their rights – to repatriation, to payment of a war bonus as other seamen received, to recognition of their needs and circumstances. They lost no time in taking action. It seems it began as a spontaneous movement and rapidly spread.[31]

---

[26] Broeze calls it 'refusal.' 'Muscles of Empire,' 62.

[27] For example, 'Bombay Seamen's Demonstration,' *Times of India*, 8 December 1938, 14; 'Bombay Seamen's Demands,' *Times of India*, 17 January 1939, 18; 'Shipping Companies Harassed,' *Times of India*, 4 February 1939, 12.

[28] International Labour Conference, 1936, Record of Proceedings; Desai, *Maritime Labour in India*, 188 and 193–6; Colaco, *History of the Seamen's Union of Bombay*.

[29] Broeze, 'Muscles of Empire,' 63–4 and Desai, *Maritime Labour in India*, 191.

[30] Other historians name him as Surat Ali (this is quoting a letter from Guha to ITF, 20 August 1950, MRC).

[31] [Communist Party of Great Britain], *Colonial Information Bulletin*, 3, MRC.

'In accordance with the world-wide tradition of international solidarity'

Australian maritime unions immediately lent their support to the strikers. There had been interactions and several other instances of active cooperation between Indian (and other Asian) seamen and the Australian unions for decades. By the late 1930s, these were more conspicuously political. Through these encounters and other means the SUA were both aware of and sympathetic to the issues which concerned Indian seamen. In August 1939, for example, the *Seamen's Voice* set out in detail the corruption in recruitment of Indian seamen and expressed sympathy with the low wages and 'heavy and soul-destroying labour conditions' Indian seamen endured, 'especially on Indian articled vessels.'[32] They were 'different colors, but same class,' in the words of *Tribune*.[33]

Australian maritime unionists' support for the strikers was a combined effort by the WWF and SUA, and took several forms, beginning with the immediate need for food and accommodation. In Fremantle, the local secretary of the SUA, Joe Byrne, put the *Elmbank* strikers in touch with local Labor Party officials who provided meals and accommodation at the local Trades Hall.[34] In Sydney, wharf labourers expressed their solidarity by taking up a collection for the crew of the *Peshawur*, who had spent a night camped on the wharf. WWF officials paid for a meal at a local café for another 30 crew found walking about the streets 'hungry and penniless.' The following day, the SUA arranged accommodation for them at an Indian boarding house. A little over a week later, WWF members loading the *City of Canberra* contributed two shillings each to its striking crew in a 'tarpaulin muster.' The day after the crew demonstrated in the city, waterside workers contributed more money to their cause.[35]

Beyond this immediate practical assistance, Australian maritime unions also lent the strikers organisational support in their confrontation with their employers. Officials from Fremantle's port unions and Trades Hall negotiated an agreement on the *Speybank* crew's behalf, in which the master agreed not to take the crew out of the Indian Ocean and to discharge or repatriate them to Calcutta from its last 'port of call' in the Indian Ocean. The agreement also provided for payment of wages in full during the

---

[32] 'How Indian Seamen Get Jobs,' *Seamen's Voice* 2, no. 8 (1939): 2. This was the publication of the SUA Queensland Branch, September 1937–January 1939.

[33] 'Different Colors, but Same Class,' *Tribune* (Sydney), 14 November 1939, 1.

[34] 'ALP Helps Lascars,' *News* (Adelaide), 26 October 1939, 4.

[35] 'Arrest of 62 Lascars,' *Sydney Morning Herald*, 10 November 1939, 12; 'Seamen Walk off Ship,' *Tribune* (Sydney), 11 November 1939, 1.

crew's absence from the ship, entitled crew members 'or their dependants to compensation for death or injury received through enemy action' and included a clause prohibiting any subsequent victimisation by the ship's master or its owners for their stand at Fremantle. We know something of the Indian seafarers' view of this through press reports. Speaking with the press after its conclusion, unidentified spokesmen for the crew declared it 'more satisfactory to them than would have been the granting of their alternative demand ... for double pay and rations, £50 war bonus, etc.'[36] And in a gesture *Tribune* characterised as 'in accordance with the world-wide traditions of international solidarity,' the SUA paid for legal representation for the *Peshawur* crew.[37] Surviving sources make it impossible to know what conversations passed between the Indian strikers and the SUA and how this assistance was initiated.

By early November, the situation was sufficiently serious to precipitate a meeting between the shipowners' representatives and Australia's Attorney-General. This was Billy Hughes, the one-time president of the WWF, now pursuing a national security agenda which promised definite action. Government officials had already arranged to fly the Deputy Shipping Master at Calcutta, Khan Bahadur Fazlul Karim, to Australia in the hope that he might be able to persuade the striking men to continue serving while replacement crews were found. He was accompanied by the Marine Superintendent of the Ellerman Line, Captain T. Forsyth, whose ships were among those affected.[38] After discussion with the company, Hughes instructed his officers to assure the men that the Australian government 'would guarantee the terms upon which they could return to India' consisting of 'a 25 per cent increase in wages; compensation arrangements at present in force to be continued; sign off at Bombay and ... transport to Calcutta.' The men, however, were adamant that they would not return to the *Peshawur* after the ill-treatment they had received during the voyage. Warnings that deportation under the Immigration Act might mean a return as 'compulsory passengers,' running 'the same risk' as if they had worked the ship back to Bombay, did nothing to weaken their resolve to be repatriated. At the conclusion of their subsequent trial, the prosecution (appearing for the captain) pressed the court to impose 'a substantial penalty'

[36] 'Lascars Rejoin Ship,' *West Australian* (Perth), 28 October 1939, 13; 'Victory for Indian Seamen,' *Workers' Star* (Perth), 1 November 1939, 1.

[37] Seamen Walk off Ship; 'Three Weeks for Lascar Seamen,' *Tribune*, 21 November 1939, 4; The Seamen's Union of Australasia ... Dr. to and in a/c with – SULLIVAN BROS., Solicitors, 31 March 1943, Seamen's Union of Australia Federal Office and Sydney Branch, series MS E183/25/6, NBAC.

[38] J.F. Murray, Secretary, Marine Branch, Department of Commerce, 9 November 1939, to Secretary, Attorney-General's Department, 'Trouble with Lascar Crews at Sydney,' series A432, 1939/1101, NAA.

8.2 Strikers arrested and prosecuted being moved by police paddy-wagon,
Sydney, 1939
SLNSW

in order to deter other crews. 'In a time of national emergency,' the prosecutor said, 'it is important that ships should be kept to schedule. This vessel has been held up for nearly a fortnight.' After a four-day hearing, the court sentenced the men to three weeks' hard labour (Figure 8.2).[39]

The British press in India remarked on the confusion that had caused the strike. The Seamen's Federation had asked for a 50 per cent increase for crews, but as each ship was then treated separately some crews got 100 per cent, others only 25 per cent. 'Naturally there is discontent. ... They want a standard rate of pay.' Furthermore, variable punishments were being applied. 'It seems a pity that for other people's muddles seamen taking war risks should be sent to jail in some cases for two months, in other cases for one month in different ports of the empire,' while in England, in one case where the crew 'obviously had the sympathy of the court,' the magistrate fined them the minimum (5 shillings) and gave them 14 days to pay.[40]

[39] Mitchell, 'Trouble with Lascar Crews at Sydney,' NAA; 'Lascars Gaoled for 3 Weeks,' *Daily News* (Sydney), 18 November 1939, 2.
[40] 'Indian Seamen,' *Statesman* (Calcutta), 21 November 1939; *Statesman* (Calcutta), 23 November 1939.

Two days after the *Peshawur* verdict Karim and Forsyth arrived in Sydney, having successfully negotiated an end to a strike by the crew of a ship in Brisbane en route.[41] Over the following days they attempted to persuade the *City of Canberra* crew to return to the ship, with little success. Offered double wages and repatriation to Calcutta if they agreed to take the ship to Colombo, the men continued to refuse, reportedly disinclined to trust company assurances that they would not be taken into the war zone. In the meantime, Karim and Forsythe had persuaded 24 members of the crew of another ship, shortly due for release from gaol, to take the *City of Canberra* to sea. Its departure opened the way for prosecution of the original crew as prohibited immigrants under the Immigration Act.[42] Only hours after it sailed, the managing director of the shipping company asked Customs officials to take the men into custody. While the company hoped to have the men on a ship to Calcutta within the week, he argued that they should not be at liberty in the meantime. There were 'native crews' arriving in the port that week, he explained, that it was necessary to keep the *City of Canberra* crew from contacting, or else it 'will make the task of dealing with such crews all the more difficult and perhaps impossible.' Clearly, he feared the spread of rebellious ideas among them. 'The only way we can see to prevent the [striking] crew getting in touch with the [arriving] crews … is if the men are in gaol.'[43] The government eventually took action.

Even as the bureaucratic wheels were beginning to turn, the *City of Canberra* crew were on the march to protest against their treatment on the streets of Sydney. After their arrival at the Central Police Station, Forsyth attempted to persuade them to crew another ship, offering in addition to 'a 100 per cent. increase in wages … a guarantee of £50 that they would not be taken elsewhere than Colombo.' But the men again refused, reportedly repeating: 'We do not believe you.'[44] Nor could they be persuaded to return to their lodgings in Redfern. After a night accommodated (without charge)

[41] Undated memo [17 November 1939], and Mitchell, 'Trouble with Lascar Crews at Sydney,' NAA; 'Lascar Crew: Trouble Overcome,' *Sydney Morning Herald*, 20 November 1939, 9.

[42] Mitchell, 'Trouble with Lascar Crews at Sydney,' NAA; 'More Lascar Crews on Strike,' *Tribune* (Sydney), 21 November 1939, 1, 3; '55 Lascars Refuse to Board Ship,' *Daily News* (Sydney), 20 November 1939, 5; 'Lascars' Fears,' *Sydney Morning Herald*, 21 November 1939, 10; 'Lascar Seamen Demonstrate,' *Australian Worker* (Sydney), 29 November 1939, 7.

[43] Managing Director, W.G. Deucher Pty Ltd, 22 November 1939, to Collector of Customs, Sydney, desertion at Sydney of 43 Lascars and 9 Goanese crew, series SP42/1, C1940/2755, NAA.

[44] 'Lascars March in Sydney.'

in the Bourke Street Gaol,[45] the company proposed moving the men to a 'disued factory in Waterloo.' This proposal met with considerable resistance from the men who 'wanted to be paid off in Sydney, with passports and fares back to India.' Informed 'that under their articles they could be paid off only at Calcutta, also that they would be given letters to hand to the shipmaster there, instructing him to pay them in full,' the men continued to resist, with the 'argument' reportedly 'waged in the street.' Finally, they agreed to board the waiting bus and were taken to the factory.[46] *Tribune* reported that on arrival there the men 'refused point blank to get out of the bus. After further consultation between Forsyth and police the bus was taken to the Bourke Street Gaol and the men taken inside but not charged with any offence. The move isolated the strikers from their supporters: SUA secretary Daley later remarked that he 'had had considerable difficulty in arranging an interview with the men at Waterloo.'[47]

The Minister ordered Customs officials to initiate proceedings with a view to the crew's deportation on the first available steamer.[48] To minimise publicity and the possibility of further demonstrations, the arrest took place in the early hours of the following morning, when 'more than 100 police gathered outside the factory' in Waterloo. A struggle developed when one of the men attempted to resist arrest; another was reportedly 'disarmed by a constable with a drawn revolver' after allegedly drawing a knife. Once in custody, Customs officers administered to each man the required dictation test of the White Australia policy. With them inevitably failing this language test, as it was designed for them to do, they were declared 'prohibited immigrants.'[49]

In India, Aftab Ali did not support the strike. He was eager to express a willingness to settle by arbitration, to offer conciliation by postponing

---

[45] C.F. Marks, Acting Boarding Inspector, Customs and Excise, Sydney, desertion at Sydney of 43 Lascars and 9 Goanese crew, SS *City of Canberra*, 23 November 1939, ends his report of events on 22 November with the men taken by bus 'to premises occupied by the Fitzroy Stevedoring Co., Woolloomooloo, opposite No. 4 Wharf,' series SP42/1, C1940/2755, NAA.

[46] 'Knives Drawn by Lascars,' *Newcastle Morning Herald*, 24 November 1939, 13; 'Lascars to Go to New Lodgings,' *News* (Adelaide), 23 November 1939, 9.

[47] 'Lascars Stand Firm,' *Tribune* (Sydney), 24 November 1939, 3; 'Lascars Cause Excitement: Demonstration in Sydney,' *Age* (Melbourne), 23 November 1939; Department of Information, Censorship Breaches, Lascar Seamen Case, 1939, series SP109/3, 354/01, NAA, also reports refusal to leave the bus; Labor Council of N.S.W., Authorised Report, 8.

[48] Telegram, Interior to Collector of Customs, Sydney, 23 November 1939, desertion at Sydney of 43 Lascars and 9 Goanese crew, series SP42/1, C1940/2755, NAA.

[49] A.G. Bennett, Acting Deputy Crown Solicitor, to Crown Solicitor, 24 November 1939, Attorney-General's Department, 'Trouble with Lascar Crews at Sydney,' series A432, 1939/1101, NAA; 'Police Round Up Lascars,' *Sydney Morning Herald*, 24 November 1939, 11.

the AISF's log of claims, and most importantly to reaffirm their anti-Nazi position. 'We are as committed as the British.'[50] An allegation that subversive influences – 'Nazi agents in Australia' – were at work among the strikers, inciting them to 'desert' their ships, was circulating. Several press reports revealed that the source of the rumour was in fact the shipping company representatives, who had suggested it to Attorney-General Hughes (and apparently the press).[51] It seemed that officials found it hard to accept that Indian seamen's activism could be an industrial dispute simply against the exploitation they had experienced over many decades. British shipowners and the government viewed the 'rebellions' of Indian seamen 'as isolated and irrational,' rather than driven by the actuality of the 'discrimination and frequent brutality' that was their experience.[52] Striking crews in Australia, as Aftab Ali did, rejected the misrepresentation of their motives. The crew of the *Peshawur* were emphatic that they had not been acting under influence of any political activity, either Nazi or Indian nationalist. They were simply not prepared to risk sailing to England through a danger zone. They had been promised repatriation to India many times, 'and felt they could no longer believe any similar promises.'[53] The spokesman for the *City of Canberra* crew similarly asserted: 'We need no one to persuade us to save our own lives.'[54] While they were undoubtedly receiving assistance from members of the Communist Party, that too is not evidence they were under influence, as some would claim. Harold Butler's 1938 report to the ILO on South and East Asia had said strikes were frequently attributed to political or communist agitation, but the 1931 Whitly Commission had stated 'we believe that there has rarely been a strike of any importance that has not been due, entirely or largely to economic reasons.'[55] In this case, economics and safety coalesced.

Here too, and perhaps most importantly, Australia's maritime unions lent their support, challenging the interpretation of events advanced by the shipowners and the government. The SUA ridiculed the suggestion of Nazi

---

[50] 'Indian Seamen,' *Statesman* (Calcutta), 21 November 1939; *Statesman* (Calcutta), 23 November 1939.

[51] 'Lascars Desert'; 'Lascar Desertions,' *Townsville Daily Bulletin*, 9 November 1939, 10; 'Mr Hughes Tries to Fathom Problem of Lascar Seamen,' *Newcastle Morning Herald*, 9 November 1939, 9.

[52] [Communist Party of Great Britain], *Colonial Information Bulletin*, 3 ('Indian Seamen and the War'); Tabili, *We Ask for British Justice*, 164; Georgie Wemyss, 'Littoral Struggles, Liminal Lives: Indian Merchant Seafarers' Resistances,' in *South Asian Resistances in Britain, 1858–1947*, ed. Rehana Ahemed and Sumita Mukherjee (London: Continuum, 2012), 44–5.

[53] 'Mysterious Spell Makes Lascars Desert,' *Mercury* (Hobart), 14 November 1939, 2; 'Arrest of 62 Lascars,' *Sydney Morning Herald*, 10 November 1939, 12.

[54] 'More Lascar Crews on Strike,' *Tribune* (Sydney), 21 November 1939, 1.

[55] Butler, 'Problems of Industry in the East,' 16–17.

influence, publishing a letter which declared that there was not 'the remotest possibility' that the men were influenced by Nazism or any other 'ism.' According to its author, H.S. Singh, who acted as an interpreter for the SUA at the trial of the *Peshawur* crew, the truth was much simpler. 'These lascars,' he explained, 'are very poorly paid ... From their pitiful appearance it can be judged that they are extremely overworked and underfed and clothed.' Alarmed by news of torpedoed British ships, they preferred 'to remain in an Australian prison rather than endanger their lives for the sake of a few shillings a month.' Their 'scanty pay' did 'not allow them to insure their lives' and so provide 'for their families.' Would, he concluded, 'an increase even of one hundred per cent in their pay justify them to risk their valuable lives?'[56] The secretary of New South Wales Trades and Labor Council, a Mr. R. King, considered it 'only natural that they should resent returning to the ship' with the risks they were asked to take and the meagre pay they received.[57] They were, rather, he said, 'the victims of intense exploitation by the magnates of Britain. They had declined to take the ship through the war zone on a miserable pittance of 6/- per week.'[58]

Support from the labour unions was thus not only of practical assistance, it also gave political legitimacy to Indian seamen's claims for the labour rights enjoyed by Western seafarers. The unions had succeeded in getting the issue raised in parliament and continued in subsequent press reports. By contrast with the mainstream press, the labour press argued that the men were motivated by the exploitation they endured. There were reports of testimony being given in court in their defence although no evidence of that testimony survives. The *Australian Worker* reported that the men were protesting 'against the slave-like industrial conditions and war-time risks to which they were being subjected.' The hearings disclosed, the report said, 'that there was no restriction as regards their hours of labor, while their rates of pay averaged ... less than one shilling per day!' SUA Sydney branch secretary, Chris Herbert, also spoke of the 'deplorable' conditions the men endured. His remarks on their unrestricted hours of work and low pay rates echoed the reported court testimony.[59]

---

[56] 'Indian Seamen,' *Seamen's Journal* 1, no. 2 (1939): 7; Mitchell, Inspector to the Director, Commonwealth Investigation Branch, 17 November 1939, series C320, CIB771, NAA, identified Singh as the interpreter for the SUA during the *Peshawur* trial.

[57] 'Mr Hughes Tries to Fathom Problem of Lascar Seamen.'

[58] Labor Council of N.S.W., Authorised Report.

[59] 'Why the Lascar Seamen Left their Ships,' *Australian Worker* (Sydney), 22 November 1939, 11; 'Lascar Seamen on Strike,' *Australian Worker* (Sydney), 22 November 1939, 20; Labor Council of N.S.W., Authorised Report. The men's own testimony went unreported, and only received a brief mention in 'Lascar Crew Troubles,' *Sydney Morning Herald*, 14 November 1939, 11, 12.

Even Attorney-General Hughes conceded that 'the chief reason for the[ir] refusal was "the natural disinclination of any man to get 'blown up' – a disinclination not confined to Indians."' He attributed no credit to the labour movement, or indeed the strikers themselves, for this realisation. He had come 'to this conclusion,' he said, 'after a long conference' with Karim. He seemed anxious to reassure the public that the striking Indian seamen were being treated fairly, offering an 'assurance that the lascars would be repatriated to India.' Karim, also present, assured the press conference 'that everything possible had been done for them.'[60]

Karim's intervention – at the government's invitation and in company with the shipping company representative – was an example of the difficulties Indian crews had to overcome. While the *City of Canberra* and *Peshawur* crews stuck to their guns and refused to return to their ships, the crews of other (unnamed) ships did agree to sail when Karim 'met the men collectively and individually, reasoned with them and won their confidence.' The men, 'despite subversive Communist influence,' then rejoined their ships. Karim then led them in a congregational prayer, 'the men pledged their loyalty to the British Empire and prayed for the safety of the ships and crews.' On his return to India, Karim said: 'The Indian *lascars* are brave men. They kept the Empire trade route open during the last war, and, I am sure, they will act up to that tradition this time.'[61]

After a week in Long Bay Gaol, the men from the *City of Canberra* were taken by bus, under police escort, to the Walsh Bay wharf, where they boarded a steamer bound for Surabaya and Calcutta. Less than a week after their departure the crew of the *Peshawur*, by then at the end of their three-week prison sentence, were convicted of being prohibited immigrants and 'sentenced to four months' imprisonment with hard labour,' pending their deportation 'as soon as arrangements could be made for a ship to take them back to India.'[62] Their conviction marked the end of the strike in Australia. In India, the shipping companies agreed to an increase on their pre-war wages for all Lascars on 12-month foreign articles, to take effect retrospectively, and to last for the period of the war.[63] The strike, while not

[60] 'Lascars Fear May Be Blown Up,' *News* (Adelaide), 24 November 1939, 5; John Fisher, 'Hughes Praises Karim,' *Tribune* (Sydney), 28 November 1939, 1; 'Lascars' Demands are Conceded,' *Australian Worker* (Sydney), 29 November 1939, 11; 'Can See behind Lascars' Dispute,' *Daily News* (Sydney), 25 November 1939, 6.

[61] All these quotes are from '"Lascars Are Brave Men": Traditions Recalled,' *Statesman* (Calcutta), 14 December 1939, 7.

[62] Bennett to Crown Solicitor, series A432, 1939/1101, NAA; 'Lascars in Court,' *West Australian* (Perth), 7 December 1939, 15; 'Lascars Again in Court,' *Daily News* (Sydney), 7 December 1939, 8.

[63] 'In Brief,' *Manchester Guardian*, 9 December 1939, 10.

8.3 A striking crew taken to Philip Street Police Station, Sydney 1940,
NAA A11666

supported by Aftab Ali, who had been so active in getting international
recognition for Indian seamen's rights, was a pivotal moment in their long
struggle, the culmination of two decades of organisation and activism.
They were punished with gaol terms, but shipowners had to concede their
demands. Their activism continued (Figure 8.3). After the war, Australian
and Indian seafarers again worked together, this time in opposition to Dutch
shipping and for Indonesian independence.[64]

The ILO Seafarers Charter was achieved in 1946 but in India a period of
great disruption followed. On achieving independence in 1947, the country
was partitioned, which the ILO had to manage.[65] Immediately it became
apparent that the majority of engine room and deck crew ratings came
from eastern Pakistan; the majority of seamen in the port of Calcutta were

---

[64] Goodall, 'Port Politics.'

[65] James Mowat, *Seafarer Conditions in India and Pakistan* (Geneva: International Labour
Organization, 1949); Conditions of Employment of Seafarers of India and Pakistan in
London, 1959, MS 159/3/0/115 (file name: 1959, Employment of Indian and Pakistani
seamen), MRC.

Pakistani nationals. Divisiveness and factionalism ran deep. Aftab Ali and several other officials of the ISU went to Pakistan with a large amount of the union's money. They were charged with misappropriation and the union was deregistered but then was reregistered. 'Members of the ISU who did not go to Pakistan now claim[ed] themselves as the bona fide and representative body of the seamen in Calcutta port.'[66] The Calcutta Maritime Board was set up in 1947 and the rights of trade unions were seriously curtailed. Only a fraction of those seamen looking for work in Calcutta were finding it.

These divisions were compounded by the onset of the cold war and the spread of what one unionist called 'communalism.' Aftab Ali was described as 'a communalist' and ineligible to continue as a representative of the seamen of either Pakistan or India because of his 'black record' – of not holding ISU elections from 1937 to 1947 and for misappropriating the union's funds. 'He should be persuaded to withdraw as the self-appointed representative or expelled from the ITF and the ILO.' The writer pointed out the proportions of the crews. In the catering department, 90 per cent were Indian, engine room crew were 90 per cent Pakistani and deck crew were 60 per cent Pakistani and 40 per cent Indian. There were appeals to the ITF to be alert to these divisions. 'Our attitude may be belligerent, but if Mr. Aftab Ali is regarded as a leader or anyone else of ITF in India, our resentment will be natural.'[67] This letter concluded with plans to set up a joint Indo-Pakistan Maritime Board. A decade after independence, the term 'Lascar' was finally removed from legislation when the Indian Merchant Shipping Act 1923 was amended.

Chinese seamen's strike

Chinese seafarers also went on strike in Australia when war was declared in Europe. The first of these actions was recorded when a ship berthed at the New South Wales coastal town of Port Kembla, in October 1939. Nine Chinese seamen reportedly 'threw themselves on the ground near the wharf and refused to move,' claiming that the ship was 'sailing under sealed orders, and would go into a war zone.' The Chinese Consul General was called to intervene. Consequently, four members of the group then consented to returning to the ship, whose owners agreed to repatriate the others and pay full wages.[68] The pattern of strikes continued. There were

---

[66] Letter from Guha, to ITF, 20 August 1950, 5–6.

[67] Letter from Guha to ITF, 20 August 1950, 7 – a very different assessment it seems to Giasuddin Ahmed, *Aftab Ali: The Hero of Indian Seamen* (Bengal: Create Space, 2017) (in Bengali).

[68] 'Chinese Seamen's Lie-down Strike,' *Sun* (Sydney), 11 October 1939, 7.

8.4 Chinese Seamen's Union meeting, Trades Hall, Sydney, 1944
Photograph Hood Collection, SLNSW

some 20,000 Chinese seafarers employed by the British merchant marine and they called several strikes in Australian ports as well as in British ports, often involving violence and gaol.

The war brought Australia's regional location into sharp relief when Japan and the United States entered into hostilities in the Pacific in December 1941. As former European colonies in East and South-East Asia were rapidly occupied by the advancing Japanese army, hundreds of evacuees landed in Australia. Among them were at least 2,000 Chinese seamen. Some left their ships and found work, effectively deserting and entering the country as illegal immigrants. Others, like those in Fremantle in 1942, went on strike for higher rates of pay and improved conditions. Some 500 Chinese seamen were involved, soldiers were sent in, many seamen were wounded and two were killed. The government refused to charge the men responsible.[69] Payment of the war risk bonus created a massive sense of injustice

---

[69] E.M. Andrews, *Australia and China: The Ambiguous Relationship* (Melbourne: Melbourne University Press, 1985) 119. Official record of the strike is in NAA, A4144 8 pt. 1.

for Chinese crews, who were denied it, as it did for the Indians. But their wages were higher than those of Indian crews although still much less than what was paid to white Australian or British crews.

Both Indians and Chinese were at risk of contravening the Immigration Act if they jumped ship in port, despite the wartime conditions. In one standout case, two of the Chinese seafarers who arrived in Sydney in 1942 and left their ships were charged with being prohibited immigrants. An amendment made in 1932 to the original Act extended the time period for authorities to find immigrants and apply the dictation test. This enabled them to use it against seamen who were otherwise exempt from the Act's provisions. Although the magistrate originally found the two Chinese men not guilty because they were exempted, the immigration officials appealed to the High Court, which overturned the decision. The new section became the principal means of deporting deserting seamen, and the dictation test was used more extensively for deporting seamen than it was to prevent entry into the country.[70]

There is perhaps no better illustration of internationalism in action than the story of Chinese seamen and union activism. Their wartime strikes were generated by demands for pay and conditions equal to British sailors, effectively to bring an end to their 'coolie' status and to demonstrate they were not prepared just to be cheap labour. They were assisted by communists both in Britain and in Australia. The China Campaign Committee, which had organised UK support for Chinese resistance to Japan during the 1930s, now worked with the National Union of Seamen to establish a branch of the Chinese Seamen's Union in Liverpool. The Sydney branch of the SUA similarly helped form a Chinese Seamen's Union, which was not registered as an Australian union but remained a branch of the Chinese union.

The help the SUA gave to Chinese seamen caught in Australia was facilitated by federal secretary E.V. Elliott.[71] It fits within the longer, broader international history of unionism among Chinese seafarers. This began in China in 1906 when Chinese leader Sun Yat-sen directed his followers to recruit workers to the cause and agitate for labour unity, prompting union activity to begin in British ports.[72] British radicals and socialists – committed internationalists – approached foreign seafarers as potential allies, working to overcome divisions and differences. With the formation of the Communist Party in 1920, unionists following Comintern directives

[70] Palfreeman, *White Australia Policy*, 83–5.

[71] Records in Seamans Union of Australia E183/3 Minutes Stop Work Meetings, NBAC.

[72] Gregor Benton, *Chinese Migrants and Internationalism: Forgotten Stories, 1917–1945* (London: Routledge, 2007), 52.

to recruit for the communist cause included Chinese seafarers, while British and Australian internationalists identified with the Chinese cause, organised a 'Hands Off China' campaign, and mobilised supporters against Japan in the 1930s.[73] Elliott and the SUA were part of this bigger picture. This was not the first time Chinese seamen came in contact with the SUA, though it was the first formal organisation.

The Australian Chinese Seamen's Union set a precedent for other Australian-based unions established by Indian, Indonesian and Malay seamen. In 1942, the British and Chinese governments reached an agreement for equality of treatment for seafarers, and Elliott negotiated a pay rise and a war risk bonus for those Chinese on the Australian coast. A year later, the arbitration court granted them further increases so that Chinese seafarers were receiving wages and conditions approximating those of Australian seamen.[74] However, there was apparently no attempt made to integrate ships' crews.

By the 1940s, and during the Second World War, the CSU, which was nominally under control from China, was in reality operating more autonomously in Australia and in the UK. This had implications for the shipowners' methods of negotiating, having to deal with union officials rather than call on the Consul General as in the incident at Port Kembla. At war's end, some shipowners attempted to return to pre-war conditions. The Chinese seamen's resistance again took the form of a sit-down, first in the offices of the shipping agent, then at the police station after they were arrested. When their ship sailed without them because they were in gaol, the SUA threatened there could be further industrial action.[75] The ALP government introduced legislation to deport refugees – a large number of Chinese seafarers, who had been allowed to stay for the duration of the war but were now to be treated as illegal immigrants. The Chinese challenged the legislation in the High Court and after the next federal election the incoming government allowed them to stay.[76]

The White Australia policy was a bipartisan policy and there were not many other actions the new government took that were sympathetic to seafarers or the maritime unions. In 1949, the ALP lost government to the Liberal–Country Party coalition led by Prime Minister Menzies, nicknamed 'Pig-iron Bob' since his intervention while Attorney-General in the *Dalfram* dispute. Maritime unions in Australia as they had in the 1920s, once again

[73] Benton, *Chinese Migrants*; Farrell, *International Socialism*, 93–220.

[74] E.V. Elliott, *Merchant Seamen in the War* (Sydney: Seamen's Union of Australia, 1944), 16.

[75] Fitzpatrick and Cahill, *History of the Seamen's Union of Australia*, 182.

[76] Gwenda Tavan, *The Long Slow Death of White Australia* (Melbourne: Scribe, 2005).

faced a hostile legislature, in an international and domestic cold war. That same year, the Chinese Revolution opened a new and very different era of Chinese history and unions.

8.5 Chairman Mao inspects Chinese sailors, 1953
Photograph KEYSTONE-FRANCE/Gamma-Rapho via Getty Images

9

'Standards for All Seamen, Indian, Chinese and European'

Internationalism in the Cold War Asia-Pacific, 1945 to c.1970

The ILO and its Joint Maritime Commission continued to meet during the Second World War. As a member of the UK government, Ernest Bevin was influential in the ILO's success in surviving the war, and also in its becoming part of the new United Nations established after the war. In 1942, he welcomed the meeting of the Emergency Committee of the ILO in London. Still staunchly opposed to communism as threatening to democracy, his support for both the ITF and the ILO as 'practical internationalism' hadn't wavered.[1] Bevin served on the Joint Maritime Commission in the 1930s and his biographer credits him with being 'the leading trade union figure at ILO Conferences where, among other successes, he secured for the seamen's unions the International Charter (1936) on conditions of work for which they had campaigned for sixteen years.'[2] Success, however, was not a single-handed, individual achievement.

The Seafarers' Charter: 'Practical internationalism'

Worker groups at the ILO had to proceed very strategically, with 'tactful handling' to win support from enough government representatives to outvote and overcome the shipowners, while giving little away to those government delegates who were not in agreement with all that workers were demanding.[3] Most of this work was done in committees. 'The question of tactics'

---

[1] Alan Bullock, *The Life and Times of Ernest Bevin*, vol. 2, *Minister of Labour, 1940–1945* (London: Heinemann, 1967), 202, 204.

[2] Bullock, *Ernest Bevin*, vol. 2. See also League of Nations, International Labour Office, *Seamen's Conference, Genoa, June 1920, Report I–IV* (London: Harrison & Sons, 1920).

[3] Details of this process are given by James Tudehope, Report of the Australian Workers Delegate on the 21st and 22nd Sessions (Maritime) of the International Labour Conference, 30 November 1936, to Secretary, SUA, Box E 183, 21/12–21/17, Overseas Organisations, ILO, NBAC.

played a crucial role in the committee discussions, where success in getting substantial concessions could be a disadvantage, subsequently resulting in defeat when the convention came to the general assembly for the vote. The Seafarers' Charter had narrowly missed being passed at the first conference in 1920 and again by one vote in 1929, before it finally succeeded in 1936. Bevin did play a valuable role in advocating for the charter, both during the ILOs wartime meeting in London where he urged the importance of international standards 'for all seamen, Indian, Chinese and European,' and in persuading the UK government to adopt the ILO's Convention. With that achievement in 1940, he then worked to bring Britain's practice into line with the ILO's recommendations on seamen's protection and welfare.[4]

Australian and New Zealand governments also endorsed these measures, although they were initially reluctant signatories to ILO conventions. An Australian, William Caldwell (1892–1984), was employed on the ILO staff from 1921 until he retired in 1953. Caldwell was also responsible for New Zealand and worked to overcome New Zealand's initial reluctance to engage with the ILO by undertaking personal visits there in 1927 and again in 1934–35.[5] Consequently, on the eve of the Second World War, New Zealand had ratified three seafarers' conventions: Seamen's Articles of Agreement Convention, 1926 (No. 22); Placing of Seamen Convention, 1920 (No. 9); and Officers' Competency Certificates Convention, 1936 (No. 53). After the war, in 1946, New Zealand also ratified the Minimum Age (Sea) Convention (Revised), 1936 (No. 58). At that time Australia had only ratified six conventions altogether, including those on seafarers.[6]

Australia and New Zealand had relatively higher labour standards, achieved through the strength of trade union activism and the unique compulsory arbitration system of awards, which had decades earlier incorporated the principle of tripartism on which the ILO was built.[7] This made them

---

[4] Bullock, *Ernest Bevin*, 2:207.

[5] James Cotton, 'Caldwell, William (1892–1984),' People Australia, National Centre of Biography, Australian National University, https://labouraustralia.anu.edu.au/biography/caldwell-william-31016/text38383.

[6] Including placing of seamen (1920); inspection of emigrants (1926); seamen's articles of agreement (1926); minimum wage-fixing machinery (1928); marking of weight (packages transported by vessels) (1929); forced labour (1930). See Joseph Staricoff, 'Australia and the Constitution of the International Labour Organization,' *International Labour Review* 32, no. 5 (1935): 577–609.

[7] C.E. Landau, 'The Influence of ILO Standards on Australian Labour Law and Practice,' *International Labour Review* 126, no. 6 (1987): 669–90. See also Marilyn Lake, 'The ILO, Australia and the Asia-Pacific Region: New Solidarities or Internationalism in the National Interest?' in *The ILO from Geneva to the Pacific Rim: West Meets East*, ed. Nelson Lichtenstein and Jill M. Jensen (Basingstoke: Palgrave Macmillan, 2015), 33–54.

initially dismissive of the value of ILO conventions. Australia had the added issue (shared with other jurisdictions) of being a federal system in which labour law was a state responsibility not a federal power.[8] All six conventions Australia had ratified (i.e., matched with legislation) by 1946 were in areas where the Commonwealth had direct constitutional power or existing legislation. During the Bruce government's term, Australia ratified the 1925 Convention concerning facilities for finding employment for seamen in amendments to the Navigation Act 1912–26, which had only become operational with the foundation of the ILO and the JMC. However, none of the several conventions on wharf labourers was ratified, the government arguing it couldn't do so, 'since the Australian Government has confined "Federal industrial activity to inter-state maritime transport."'[9] Although it passed the draconian Transport Workers Act 1928 directly targeting wharf labourers, none of the ILO dock work conventions of 1929 on protection against accidents was ratified.[10] The failure to activate ILO conventions was tied to other failures.

Australia did not have worker representation on the JMC until 1936, when James Tudehope, secretary of the Marine Cooks, Bakers and Butchers' Association (1913–64) attended the International Labour conference (Maritime Session).[11] Tudehope was founder and secretary since 1933 of the Maritime Transport Council, a loose association of mainly skilled small industry unions located in Sydney. While sailing home a month later, Tudehope reported to the secretary of the SUA that this 1936 conference 'was regarded as the most important, and from the point of view of the workers, the most successful that has so far been held.' He explained this was the first time that seafarers would have an international code, drawn up by the maritime nations themselves, that gave seafarers standards in accordance with those already given to other workers: limited hours, specified overtime

---

[8] K.H. Bailey, 'Australia and the International Labour Conventions,' *International Labour Review* 54, no. 5–6 (1946): 285–308; J.G. Starke, 'Australia and the International Labour Organisation,' in *International Law in Australia*, ed. D.P. O'Connell (Sydney: Law Book Co., 1966), 115–40.

[9] See A981, INT 177, Sea and Seamen, ILO Annual Reports to I.L. Office re Convention concerning facilities for finding employment for Seamen, NAA Canberra; Waterside Employment Regulations, Attorney-General's Paper [correspondence with the ILO]; International Labour Office on the ratification of ILO conventions and legislative limitations on the Commonwealth re industrial matters; and letter, ILO Director, Monsieur Albert Thomas, to Attorney-General, Canberra, series A467, SF16/29, NAA.

[10] Staricoff, Australia and the constitution of the ILO grouped Australia with India in listing the Conventions they had ratified.

[11] Tudehope's documents are mingled with the marine cooks' records at NBAC; MLC records are in E183, NBAC.

and stipulated minimums for crew manning levels. In addition, there were provisions for the shipowners' liability for sickness and injury and insurance provisions for ill and injured seafarers that were previously granted to industrial, commercial and agricultural workers. So, at last, 'after battling with the elements' for 16 years, they had overcome shipowner opposition: 'the hours ship has arrived safely at its destination.'[12]

Tudehope explained the voting process at the 1936 Congress. The first two measures were passed by a substantial majority vote; the third item – promoting seamen's welfare in ports – had passed unanimously. The fourth item required that officers be trained and carry certificates of competency, the fifth gave ordinary seamen holidays with pay. Employer representatives from both Japan and India had opposed the provision of holidays for crew but their arguments were rejected. The measure to raise the age to 15 at which children could start work at sea was approved unanimously. He observed that while the hours and manning provisions did not reach Australian standards, still the workers' delegates found the outcome very satisfactory. The exclusion of officers from the provisions was strange to Australians, members of the Merchant Services Guild, but the Convention would bring benefits to both Australian shipowners and ships' crews. Again, Tudehope pointed out that the holiday leave provision was small by Australian standards, but 'considering the opposition,' having ratings provided even with that much was a starting point, and having a Convention now put seafarers 'in a vastly different position' from previous ILO sessions. He believed the five new conventions would have no difficulty getting passed despite several countries which had voiced opposition to ratification.[13]

The International Seafarers' Charter was distributed in 1944 in 17 languages. It declared that the unequal employment of Asian, African and West Indian seafarers must be brought to an end and that seagoing unions were resolved to working towards achieving that.[14] The JMC met again in London in 1945 and the following year the ILO meeting in Seattle adopted 80 recommendations or conventions affecting the welfare of seafarers. The process of ratification had proceeded under wartime conditions, but shipowner opposition was unchanged from its pre-war position. The International Seafarers' Charter of 1944 covered demands for improved wages, hours and manning. Hours and manning had been dealt with together at the Convention in 1936. Shipowners held that hours and wages also needed to be regulated together and that is what happened when the question was again up for discussion in 1945. This complicated the ratification process

---

12 Tudehope, Report to Secretary, SUA.
13 Tudehope, Report to Secretary, SUA.
14 ITF, *Solidarity*, 103.

meaning there was 'little immediate prospect of wide ratification' and 'an entirely satisfactory international solution for the problem of seafarers' wages, hours and manning arrangements' had yet to be found.[15]

The ILO's engagement with maritime labour was prompted by the actions of big shipping combines which avoided the very competitive nature of international shipping by rate-fixing at ship operator conferences. This resulted in similarities of their operating expenses and revenues and it intensified the shipowners' concern with the other cost factors, namely the outlay for the ships, and of most relevance, the wages and maintenance costs for the crew. This gave a competitive advantage to shipping companies in countries which had lower wages and working conditions.[16]

Protection for international seagoing labour was thus an imperative. Concern for seafarer health and welfare and the collection of information was unanimously agreed to at the JMC's very first meeting. The next conference, in 1921, adopted conventions on the minimum age and a medical examination for people who were seeking employment at sea. In 1924, the ILO joined with the Red Cross, the International Union against Venereal Diseases and the Public Health Office of the Belgian Government to draw up 'the Brussels Agreement,' which was an undertaking to grant treatment, drugs and admittance to hospital, free of charge to seafarers of whatever country who had become infected with venereal disease. This was ratified and implemented 'by a high proportion of the leading maritime countries.'[17] In 1936, the focus was on seamen's welfare in ports, and a comprehensive recommendation was adopted on which government reports were reviewed at its 1942 and 1947 meetings. After discussion at the Copenhagen and Seattle conferences, conventions on medical examination, crew accommodation and food and catering on board ship were adopted.[18] In 1945, the JMC's concern was the International Seafarers' Charter and how the ILO might take action.

Before 1940, Australia also failed to exercise its full voting rights at the ILO sessions by sending only one instead of two government delegates. 'As it is to the obvious interest of Australia to secure the adoption of international labour conventions establishing progressive standards of working conditions,' Tudehope urged it was desirable that the Australian Commonwealth exercised its full voting rights. He intimated that had it done so in 1929, the Seafarers Charter would not have been lost by a solitary vote.[19]

---

[15] 'The Joint Maritime Commission and the Maritime Work of the ILO.'
[16] Goldberg, 'Seamen and the International Labor Organization,' 975.
[17] 'The Joint Maritime Commission and the Maritime Work of the ILO.'
[18] 'The Joint Maritime Commission and the Maritime Work of the ILO.'
[19] Tudehope, Report to Secretary, SUA.

9.1 Delegates to ILO conference which achieved the Seafarers' Charter.
Aftab Ali (bottom right), Seattle, 1946
ILO and Seafarers, pamphlet. MRC

By 1942, Australia had an ALP government, with John Curtin as Prime Minister. Curtin had been Australia's delegate to the ILO in 1924. The ALP remained in power until 1949 and the post-war period saw Australian maritime unionists increase their activism with the ILO.

Dock work and wharf labour was not included in the deliberations of the JMC, which dealt only with the problems of seagoing labour. Port work came within the scope of the loose inland transport section. During the 1950s and 1960s, the ILO held three separate European-hosted inland transport sessions which briefly considered the positions of Asian dockworkers.[20] Jim Healy, WWF secretary, took an active part in one of these commissions in 1957 as an Australian workers' delegate.[21]

The next year, the Prague-based Trade Union International of Transport

[20] International Labour Organization, Inland Transport Committee, Sixth Session, Hamburg, 1957; International Labour Organization, Inland Transport Committee, Seventh Session, Geneva, 1961; International Labour Organization, Inland Transport Committee, Eighth Session, Geneva, 1966.

[21] International Labour Organization, Inland Transport Commission, 1957, MS N147/520,

Port and Fishery Workers wrote to all affiliated unions about 'items of the greatest importance' that 'the most important' of the conventions adopted at the 1946 conference aligning with the Seafarers Charter 'were never ratified and are therefore not valid.' The Trade Union International had approached the ITF to encourage joint action and working together in the best interests of seafarers.[22] Cooperation was, however, not possible in this cold war climate.

SUA secretary Elliott failed to get appointed as Australia's seafarers' delegate. At the very brief 15-minute election for a workers' representative, held by the ACTU on advice from the Department of Labour and National Service, there were three nominees. The experienced James Tudehope polled 31 votes (equal with Elliott), yet an officer, Captain Thomas Martin, from the Merchant Services Guild, with 22 votes, was declared successful.[23] The SUA called a special meeting and sent a letter of protest to the Minister. Consequences for the deliberations of the 1958 ILO Conference (Maritime) followed. In Geneva, Martin sided with the ITF delegates against representatives and workers' delegates from the countries whose trade unions were communist-aligned affiliates.[24] According to the Soviet workers' representative, the ITF objective seemed to be 'to deepen the split in the international trade union movement,' consolidating the shipowners' position as the shipowners 'rudelessly [sic] and tactlessly' pursued their political aims. The ITF-led workers' representatives voted with the shipowners not to reduce the working hours of coastal shipping crews in line with ocean-going ships and opposed the resolution for cultural facilities to be provided on board and also the banning of nuclear testing. Most importantly, they opposed the proposal from the French seamen's representative to make the JMC a tripartite commission by including government delegates in order to prevent the ITF 'plot[ting] with shipowners.'[25]

The major task of the commission remained unchanged: it advised the ILO Governing Body and held special maritime sessions of the ILO to define and adopt seafaring labour standards related to wages, working hours, employment agreements, training requirements, welfare, occupational health and safety

---

NBAC; Tom Sheridan, 'Coastal Shipping and the Menzies Government, 1950–1966,' *Australian Economic History Review* 25 (1995): 3–39.

[22] R. Avila, General Secretary to Affiliated and Friendly Seamen's Organisations, circular no. 20, 3 February 1958, MS E183/21/25, NBAC.

[23] Minutes of Meeting of Trade Unions to Elect a Nominee to Attend the Maritime Committee of the ILO, Trades Hall, Sydney, 5 March 1958, MS E183/21/25, NBAC; SUA, Minutes of Special Meeting of the Sydney Branch, 31 July 1936, MS E183/3/5, 135–6, NBAC.

[24] Correspondence, A. Koetkin, President Central Committee, Maritime and River Workers' Union to E.V. Elliott, 5 August 1958, MS E183/21/25, NBAC.

[25] Koetkin to Elliott, 5 August 1958.

and the transfer of ships to open-registries. The power imbalance remained. The JMC consisted of two Governing Body members, one from workers, another from shipowners, and the equivalent number of regular members and their deputies plus the chairman of the ILO Governing Body. The number of regular members grew over time, from 12 in the late 1940s to 20 in the early 1970s.[26] Nevertheless, unlike other ILO commissions, which were tripartite in structure, the JMC retained its bipartite format from before the war and throughout the cold war period. It excluded governments ostensibly because shipping enterprises often operated outside the boundaries of national legal frameworks. However, this gave the shipowners more power and made it very difficult for the union representatives to bring about change. The ILO could never solve all seafarers' problems, yet it was a forum that shipowners did not underestimate as being one where seafarers could win concessions and exercise power. Cold war antipathies prevented the realisation of that goal.

'[U]nity in action ... in all organisations nationally and internationally'

With the cessation of hostilities in Europe, in May 1945, the ITF once again faced the challenge of reuniting former enemy combatants as members of the organisation. During the war, the ITF and other labour organisations had been exiled to London where they were able to keep working while the Axis powers dominated Europe. Once victory looked assured, individuals often returned to their home bases, but ITF congresses – suspended for the duration – did not resume until the Zurich Congress in 1946. Soon the coming of the cold war undermined the ITF's goal to be inclusive, tolerant of differences and not to force any particular world view on its member unions. Under the new leadership of Jaap Oldenbroek as general secretary, membership – which had previously been made dependent simply on members 'being free of external control' – now became tied to the ideological affiliation of the leadership. Within just a few years, ideological differences had split the international labour movement into two antagonistic camps and created a schism which touched nearly every important decision and facet of the ITF.[27]

As the war was ending, union leaders from many countries shared high hopes of creating a unified overarching body for the global working-class community. They came together in 1945 to form the World Federation of Trade Unions (WFTU), which had broad aims and wide support. Along with the fundamental demands of workers – the right to organise themselves into

---

[26] 'The Joint Maritime Commission and the Maritime Work of the ILO,' 341.

[27] ITF, *Solidarity*, 104–5; Denis McShane, *International Labour and the Origins of the Cold War* (Oxford: Clarendon Press, 1992); Myconos, *Globalizations of Organized Labour.*

unions, the right to work and receive an adequate pay rate – were non-industrial objectives, including the struggle against colonialism and imperialism and the promotion of peace and democratic liberties around the world.[28]

Australian waterside and seafarer union officials welcomed the formation of the WFTU. So did their counterparts in the ILWU that covered virtually all the workforce at west coast ports of the United States and Canada. As an action of working-class solidarity, all three unions not only joined the new organisation but took a leading role in it. Harry Bridges, ILWU president, was elected president of the seamen and dockers' section, while Eliot Elliott, SUA federal secretary, accepted the vice-presidency.[29] Soon their two unions actively lobbied the WFTU to convene a trans-Pacific maritime union conference at which every maritime union in the Pacific region who wanted to attend would have representation.[30]

The initial spirit of collaboration between union leaders across different ideological positions was short lived. Unity collapsed, a 'victim to the mounting pressure of the cold war,' with the announcement of the Marshall Plan in June 1947.[31] While British and US peak labour bodies immediately sought to endorse the plan, their pro-communist colleagues viewed the United States' financial aid to Europe as part of 'a war machine of American imperialists against the liberty and independence of other nations.'[32] Two years later, the British, US and Dutch peak bodies withdrew from the WFTU. Many other Western national trade union centres followed, including those from Australia and New Zealand. By the end of 1949 they had created the alternative International Confederation of Free Trade Unions (ICFTU).[33] The New Zealand Federation of Labour disaffiliated from the WFTU in May 1949 and affiliated to the new organisation in April

[28] World Federation of Trade Unions, Australia, Department of Foreign Affairs and Australia, Department of External Affairs, *Current Notes on International Affairs* 20, no. 3 (1949): 360.

[29] Charles P. Larrowe, *Harry Bridges: The Rise and Fall of Radical Labor in the United States* (New York: L. Hill, 1972), 329; Ahlquist and Levi, *In the Interest of Others*, 192–3. Fitzpatrick and Cahill, *History of the Seamen's Union of Australia*, 187–91, covers the relationship between the WFTU and the SUA.

[30] J. Healy to H. Bridges, 9 June 1947, MS 5/59, ILWU archives.

[31] Anthony Carew, 'A False Dawn: The World Federation of Trade Unions (1945–1949),' in *The International Confederation of Free Trade Unions*, ed. Marcel van der Linden (Berne: Peter Lang, 2000), 174.

[32] *Current Notes on International Affairs*, 361.

[33] Broadcast by A.E. Monk, related to WFTU, MS N21/553, NBAC; ITF, Report on Activities and Financial Report of the ITF for the Years 1948 to 1950, and Proceedings of the International Transport Workers' Congress and the Sectional Conferences held in connection therewith at the Kurhaus, Stuttgart–Bad Cannstatt, Germany, from 21 to 29 July 1950 (London: ITF, 1950), 82–4.

1950; the ACTU followed in September 1951.[34] From then until the end of the cold war the international labour movement was organisationally divided along cold war political lines. While the WFTU was aligned with the Soviet Union, many unions and peak bodies of Western liberal democracies operated under the framework of the ICFTU.[35]

The division created problems for local unions. Numerous stop-work meetings of Australian seamen's union members demanded their leadership retain links with the WFTU. This large-scale grass-roots support sent secretary Elliott to Vienna in 1953 to participate in the WFTU Congress, to the great dissatisfaction of the ACTU.[36] We have also seen how the ACTU prevented Elliott being the delegate to the 1958 ILO Conference. Yet the ACTU also took offence when the ICFTU tried to control international activities by describing union visits to China or Russia as 'acting like a black-leg in the fight for freedom.' ACTU president Albert Monk personally resented the epithet, for himself 'or any other trade unionist ... who has visited China or Russia.' Monk claimed anti-communism was not reducible to simplistic epithets in language that most ACTU affiliated unions would find deprecating. 'Whilst we are affiliated with and recognise that decisions ... of the ICFTU should carry weight with us,' he said, 'we nevertheless reserve the right, as a national body, to determine our policy and actions according to the majority of our affiliated organisations ... particularly ... whether delegates should be sent by us to countries termed as being communist controlled.'[37]

In the following few years, maritime unionists actively lobbied the ACTU to allow them to keep their contacts with the WFTU. The parties eventually arrived at an uneasy compromise: a relationship between Australian unions and the WFTU was acceptable but only in an informal way.[38] Facing no more objections from the national peak body, SUA secretary Elliott and WWF Sydney branch president Jim Young, jointly took part in the WFTU Congress in Leipzig in 1957 as Australian maritime labour representatives

---

[34] E. Baxter, Secretary, New Zealand Federation of Labour, to ICFTU Secretary, J. Oldenbroek, 19 February 1952, MS 292/933/5, MRC.

[35] Anthony Carew, 'Towards a Free Trade Union Centre: The International Confederation of Free Trade Unions,' in van der Linden, *International Confederation of Free Trade Unions*, 195–8.

[36] WFTU Suspended Unions, MS N21/882, NBAC.

[37] Reply by A.E. Monk, President ACTU, to Press Release by ICFTU, relative to visits by Trade Unionists to Iron Curtain countries, 6 October 1959, MS 292/993/9, MRC.

[38] Healy's report to Bucharest Conference, Box 5, Item 5, Waterside Workers' Federation of Australia papers, 1924–1961, with associated papers of James Healy, MS 1049, Mitchell Library, Sydney.

9.2 SUA Federal Secretary Eliot V. Elliott (centre) meeting European
delegates to International Seamen's and Dockers' Conference, Marseilles,
before foundation of World Federation of Trade Unions in Paris, 1949
Tribune, 7 September 1949, 3. SLNSW

and guest speakers.[39] Along with participation in general WFTU forums,
Australian maritime unionists maintained more industry-focused links with
their fellow colleagues from the Trade Union International of Transport,
Port, and Fishery Workers – a department of the WFTU. In 1957, as a
part of his ILO European trip, Jim Healy, WWF federal secretary, went to
Bucharest to attend as an observer an International Conference of Transport
Workers' unions organised by the corresponding WFTU department.
Making sharp remarks about the attacks of 'the right-wing' groups on the
union in the Australian labour movement, Healy gave the audience a lengthy
report about the industrial changes in Australia and the development of new
port technologies.[40]

As the WFTU took the lead in opposing the apartheid regime in South
Africa, Australian dockworkers and seafarers took part in actions that

[39] 'Australians Attend WFTU,' *Maritime Worker* (5 November 1957): 1; 'A Fighting
Record, The World Federation of Trade Unions against Apartheid,' WFTU, [n.d.], MS
N38/1389, NBAC.
[40] Healy's report to Bucharest Conference; 'Healy Exposes False Attacks on I.L.O. Tour,'
Maritime Worker (26 February 1957): 1.

reflected their adoption of a commitment to racial equality and justice.[41] In 1964, a joint meeting of Australian maritime unions delegated Gordon Harris, WWF senior vice-president and Fremantle branch secretary, to attend a WFTU conference in Accra, Ghana, called to mobilise union opposition to apartheid.[42] In addition, in 1965, Norm Docker represented Australian waterside workers at the WFTU Transport Department conference in Sofia, Bulgaria, called to discuss global-scale technological and structural changes influencing stevedoring labour across national borders.[43]

Alongside these direct contacts and informal collaborations with the WFTU, Australian maritime unionists exchanged fraternal reciprocal visits with their counterparts from the USSR and other socialist countries.[44] The coverage of international affairs in the official publications of Australian maritime unions in the 1950s reflected their pro-Soviet alignment. Monk's response illuminates the complexity of internationalism in the global cold war that was dividing the United States and old imperial European powers.

'My experience of Australians is that they are very good fighters,' ITF general secretary Jaap Oldenbroek wrote in 1952.[45] In allusion to the ideological antipathies of the cold war, he said, 'and once they have a grouse against somebody it is well-nigh impossible to bring about a reconciliation.' This judgement was made while outlining the procedure for affiliation of Australian unionists to the ICFTU that Oldenbroek now headed. Indecision over international affiliation because of competing political tendencies, which 'die very hard in any country,' were, he said, especially strong in Australia, 'which was always more or less isolationist because of its geographical position.' In the interwar period, communist organisations wanted to join with the RLIU, the Labor Party preferred affiliation to the International Federation of Trade Unions 'and the non-political elements refused to choose.'[46] In the post-war period, as the choice became more

[41] WWF Biennial Conference Minutes, 27 October 1954, MS N114/140, NBAC.

[42] Ghana Conference, MS N114/480, NBAC; correspondence between N. Docker, WWF Industrial Officer, to WWF Branch Secretaries, regarding Harris's tour, MS N114/480, NBAC; 'Delegation for Africa,' *Maritime Worker* (16 October 1963): 1; 'Solidarity against Apartheid Terror,' *Maritime Worker* (20 May 1964): 3.

[43] 'W.W.F. Delegation Attends Sofia T.U. Conference,' *Maritime Worker* (11 August 1965): 7.

[44] 'Wharf Work in Soviet,' *Maritime Worker* (17 January 1953): 2; 'Soviet Wharfies Now Reaping Fruits of Working Power,' *Maritime Worker* (9 November 1954): 6; 'Jim Healy Sees World Festival,' *Maritime Worker* (20 August 1957): 6.

[45] Jaap Oldenbroek to Vincent Tewson, TUC, 25 March 1952, MS 292/993/5, MRC.

[46] Oldenbroek to Tewson, March 1952.

stark, and more imperative, geography or more accurately regional location, was a factor in how unions conducted their business.

'[F]reeing ... unions from communist domination': The ITF's cold war

The early post-war conflicts in the global labour movement were mirrored in the history of the ITF. At first the organisation was supportive of friendly relations with organised labour from the pro-communist camp and even considered the possibility of formally coming under the organisational framework of the WFTU.[47] In accordance with the principle of working-class unity, the journal allocated a large space for publications of Soviet and Soviet-aligned unionists.[48] Then the ITF made a sharp political turn by taking a rigid anti-communist stance.

In 1946–47, jointly with other international trade secretariats (global union federations), the ITF was engaged in lengthy negotiation with the WFTU over the institutional form of their association. While the pro-Moscow faction of the WFTU insisted on the full incorporation of trade secretariats into their structure in the form of trade departments, the representatives of global union federations – all based in Western countries – demanded substantial organisational and financial autonomy. Their uneasy dialogue was carried on with mutual accusations. The pro-communist press attacked the ITF – the most active of the protesters amongst trade secretaries – blaming it for violating the principles of working-class solidarity.[49] In its turn, the ITF claimed that communist labour forces throughout the world were attempting 'to force it to agree to unconditional dissolution and integration of its membership in the W.F.T.U.'[50] Disagreements eventually resulted in the decision of the 1948 ITF Congress to suspend negotiations and to continue operation as an independent body.[51] As a consequence of these conflicts, in 1947 the French Seamen's Union disaffiliated from the ITF. Other groups of maritime workers, dockers and seafarers followed.[52]

Over the following two years, the conflict between them deepened further. At that time the ITF leadership developed a strong perception

[47] Resolutions adopted by ITF Congress, *ITF Journal* 7, no. 1 (1946): 4.

[48] See several articles on Soviet railways and buses across 1945–46.

[49] ITF, Report on Activities and Financial Report of the ITF for the Years 1946 to 1948, and Proceedings of the ITF Congress, Oslo, Norway, 1948 (London: ITF, 1948) 93–101; Report by Secretary [Monk of the ACTU] relative to WFTU, MS N21/553, NBAC.

[50] ITF, Report ... 1946 to 1948, 101.

[51] ITF, Report ... 1946 to 1948, 248.

[52] ITF, *Solidarity*, 107.

that the WFTU was a political enemy that had nothing in common with free and democratic trade unionism. Jaap Oldenbroek in the position of secretary played a leading role in mounting the opposition of the Western organised labour camp against communist influences in the WFTU. He was the sole representative of international trade secretariats in a preparatory committee of 14 members who drafted a constitution and programme for the 1949 London conference that established the ICFTU.[53] Partially because of support from US union officials, who viewed Oldenbroek as their most loyal ally, and partly because of his organisational abilities, Oldenbroek became the first ICFTU general secretary at that inaugural London conference.

The organisational and ideological division in Europe had immediate implications for Australian and North American maritime unionists who had to break away from the pro-Soviet labour international because of growing external and internal pressure. The ILWU, for instance, was expelled from the US peak body for maintaining its WFTU links. Even more seriously, the leadership of the union was confronted by rank and file opposition. The San Francisco branch, from which Bridges had emerged, even demanded his resignation if he failed to leave. The conflict was resolved in 1950 when the union caucus voted to cease formal relations with the WFTU.[54]

In Australia, the peak organisation, the ACTU, likewise presented the communist minority among its affiliates, including the maritime unions, with an ultimatum of leaving or facing expulsion.[55] With this warning, the WWF Federal Council in 1952 made a collective decision – 'with great reluctance' – to leave. The SUA retained its connection for two more years before also finally yielding to the pressure.[56] Withdrawal from the European body was a pragmatic, deeply rational choice by Australian maritime unionists. The WFTU could hardly provide any practical assistance to them in their domestic industrial conflicts, whereas the ACTU's support, as a subsequent national waterfront dispute in 1954 was clearly to prove, was

---

[53] ITF, Report on Activities and Financial Report of the ITF for the Years 1948 to 1950, 84–5.

[54] Margaret Levi, David Olson, Jon Agnone and Kelly Devin, 'Union Democracy Reexamined,' *Politics & Society* 37, no. 2 (2009): 218–19; Eliot V. Elliott, SUA Secretary to Louis Goldblatt, ILWU Secretary-Treasurer, 24 January 1950, Longshore Foreign Countries Subject File, ILWU; Goldblatt to Elliott, 1 March 1950, ILWU; Paul T. Hartman, *Collective Bargaining and Productivity: The Longshore Mechanization Agreement* (Berkeley: University of California Press, 1969), 22.

[55] Reported by Oldenbroek in letter to Tewson, 25 March 1952.

[56] Letter From SUA to A.E. Monk [ACTU], NBAC; Sheridan, *Australia's Own Cold War*, 83, 114–29; V. Williams, *The Years of Big Jim* (Willagee, WA: Lone Hand Press, 1975), 122.

of crucial importance. They did not, however, find the ITF (or the ICFTU) politically acceptable enough to join.

One dimension of the cold war battle for loyalties was the recruitment of non-aligned parties to join one or other side. As the post-war period saw the ITF resume its anti-colonialism agenda of the pre-war years, its activities resembled something of this larger battle. A concerted initiative to bring former colonies into the organisation began almost immediately and resulted not only in increased numbers of ITF members but also in a greater spread across the globe. Newer countries from the former European colonies in Africa, the Caribbean and Latin America were signed up, and progress was made in parts of Asia, even as most of New Zealand's and Australia's big transport workers' unions remained outside the ITF network.

With Oldenbroek's departure, the 1950 Stuttgart Congress elected Omer Becu as the new ITF general secretary. Similar to his predecessor, Becu had a background of having been a maritime union official and was hostile to communist ideology. With the cold war unfolding and the 1949 split in the global labour movement, the working agenda of the organisation greatly politicised. The Stuttgart Congress declared a fight against 'the endeavours of the Communists' to be a vital priority of their work. In pursuing this objective, the congress adopted a resolution approving the Atlantic Pact and condemning any attempts of dockworkers' unions of Western democracies to ban handling arms and ammunition, 'the purpose of which is to prevent or repel an attack on free people.'[57] Blatantly stating that 'the Soviet intended to use the WFTU as a steppingstone towards world domination,' the congress confirmed a rule that affiliation with it was incompatible with affiliation to the ITF.[58]

This regulation was promptly applied to the New Zealand Waterside Workers' Union. This sole Pacific dockworkers' affiliate was also an official member of the maritime department of 'that agency ... whose hostility towards the ITF is a matter of public notoriety.'[59] The ITF leadership believed that by default this made the New Zealand union an undemocratic 'Communist-controlled organisation' that was trying to provoke frequent disruptive disputes in local ports and conflicts with the New Zealand Labour Government.[60] Along with revoking the union's affiliation, the

[57] 'The Stuttgart Congress,' *ITF Journal* 10, no. 7/10 (1950): 38.

[58] ITF, Report ... for 1948–1950, 4–5.

[59] ITF, Report ... for 1948–1950, 4.

[60] ITF, 'Communist Activities in New Zealand,' Report on Activities of the ITF for the Years 1950 to 1951, and Proceedings of the Stockholm Congress, 1952 (London: ITF, 1952) 64; Relations with Affiliated Organisations, Report ... for 1948 to 1950, 21–2; 'Exclusion of the New Zealand Waterside Workers' Union,' *ITF Journal* 10, no. 7/10 (1950): 54–5.

leadership urged all member organisations to break off their relations with the New Zealand waterside unionists.[61]

The story of the Canadian Seamen's Union similarly demonstrated the divisive character of these post-war policies. In March 1949, that union launched a strike on all Canadian ships to secure a wage increase and to protect the union hiring hall system. The union appealed for solidarity, seeking the help of the ITF and its affiliates. Not only did the ITF deny that help, but it supported the US and Canadian governments during the strike on the grounds that the strike was political by nature – organised by 'Communist elements' and backed by the radical press and by the WFTU.[62] Separately, that same year, the ITF organised in Rotterdam a joint Dockers' and Seafarers' conference which urged trade unions to fight the disruptive activities of the communists and called for the expulsion of the Canadian Union.[63] The 1950 ITF Congress formally enacted this decision.[64]

When the ITF desired to re-establish close connection with regional Asia-Pacific labour immediately after the war, they published several articles on Australia. The five issues of 1945 showed an earlier tolerance for the politically motivated industrial action of Australian maritime unionists. One article by Stan Moran, the WWF treasurer, on the Australian dockworkers' boycott of Dutch shipping in support of Indonesian independence, asked the question, 'What have the struggles of the Indonesians got to do with us?' The article explained that holding up 14 Dutch ships in Australian ports was a part of the WWF political fight 'to liberate all people from Fascism, and what the Dutch are doing in that country is Imperialism, which leads to Fascism if unchecked.'[65] The ITF's new hostile and intolerant attitude to pro-communist sympathies was a tactical error for the goal of building a connection with Asia-Pacific unions.

The 1946 Seattle Maritime Conference brought James Tudehope together with ITF officials and resulted in the subsequent affiliation of the Australian Maritime Transport Council with the ITF. Tudehope proposed, endorsed by both the ITF and the ACTU, to hold a Pacific transport workers' conference in Sydney in 1948. While the wharfies' union received an invitation, it indicated that its assent was dependent on the existence of good relations

[61] ITF, Report ... for 1948–1950, 280.

[62] ITF, *Solidarity*, 111–12.

[63] ITF, Report ... for 1948–1950, 280.

[64] ITF, Report ... for 1948–1950, 279.

[65] Stan Moran, 'Australian Dockers Take Political Action,' *ITF Journal* 6, no. 9/12 (1945): 58–9; 'Nationalisation of Australian Airways,' *ITF Journal* 6, no. 7/8 (1945): 37–9; 'The Rape of the Commonwealth Shipping Line,' *ITF Journal* 6, no. 5/6 (1945): 33–4.

between the WFTU and the ITF. The Australian peak labour body also arranged a meeting of local transport unions, which expressed a view similar to the watersiders.' Unwilling to compromise, the ITF eventually had to cancel the conference.[66] Maritime unions, whose leadership openly avowed their communism, saw little to gain by contact with the ITF when the experiences of the New Zealand and Canadian unions demonstrated, even to non-communist officials and members, that affiliation did not guarantee any degree of outside support.

From Seafarers Charter to Asia-Pacific cold war

During the cold war period, the work of the ILO acquired a new significance and meaning. While fulfilling its main objective of setting up and promoting international labour standards, the ILO machinery also served as the sole direct communication medium for pro-liberal and pro-communist labour bodies after their 1949 split. Despite ideological alignments and conflicts, workers' representatives worked within the ILO framework, and by the nature of their shared responsibilities managed to produce tangible results for the global working class-community by formulating and promoting internationally recognised human and labour rights.[67] In the ILO's efforts to raise maritime labour standards it fostered collaboration and interaction between regional unionists and their fellow European comrades which played an important consolidating role for international labour in the cold war. Apart from bringing together representatives across a wide political spectrum, ranging from the state-controlled USSR unions to the staunchly anti-communist American Federation of Labour, the ILO workers' groups also became more ethically and culturally diverse. The reason for that was increased ILO membership from outside Europe in the post-1945 period. Prior to the Second World War, only six countries from the Asian region were ILO members; this number had tripled by the late 1960s.[68] Correspondence between the Australian High Commissioner and the ILO Governing Body suggests the ILO saw Australia, given its geography, as the gateway to including the South-West Pacific.[69]

---

[66] Problems of Regional Organization, Report ... for 1946–1948, 33–5.

[67] Kari Tapiola, *The Driving Force: Birth and Evolution of Tripartism – The Role of the ILO Workers' Group* (Geneva: International Labour Organization, 2019), 31–7.

[68] Aamir Ali, 'Fifty Years of the ILO and Asia,' *International Labour Review* 99 (1969): 347–62, at 348.

[69] International Organisation in Pacific ILO Social Policy in Dependent Territories, ILO Records, series A1066, P45/148/4, NAA.

The growth in Asian representation on the ILO coupled with the political and economic importance of the region motivated ILO officials to focus more tightly on the problems of local labour. In 1947, the ILO held its first 'preparatory' Asian regional conference in Delhi. The main message of the audience, influenced by Prime Minister Nehru's opening address, was clear. With widespread poverty and misery in many parts of Asia, the ILO had to develop an extensive programme of action and improve local conditions by boosting productivity, social security and occupational health and safety standards. Partially to address these requests, over the following two decades the ILO arranged four more regional conferences concerned with a range of issues, including labour inspection, wages, housing and welfare.[70]

Australia was an integral part of this ILO-led collaboration process. Not only did Australia take part in all Asian conferences but in 1962 it hosted one of these early events in Melbourne. The major rationale for choosing the destination was to enable trade unionists and employers from the region to see Australia's arbitration and trade union machinery and observe its economic, industrial and social conditions.[71] The Melbourne forum became the largest Asian ILO conference to date, with 300 delegates from 21 Asia-Pacific and four European countries – the former imperial powers of Britain, France, the Netherlands and Portugal. The resolutions of the conference emphasised the urgent need to alleviate poverty and hardship suffered by many Asian nations and to raise living standards by implementing polices on employment promotion, vocational training and the improvement of labour–management relations.[72]

Separately to Asian conferences, the Governing Body of the ILO established in 1950 an Asian Advisory Committee, which followed the tripartite structure and consisted of government, employers' and workers' delegates. By the late 1960s, the Committee had run more than a dozen sessions, the overwhelming majority of which were, however, hosted in Geneva. To develop closer and more direct contacts with regional labour, the ILO in 1949 set up an Asian Field Office in India. Along with technical training, the agency provided a channel of communication with regional government and non-government organisations. In 1963, the Field Office was moved to Colombo before merging a few years later with the ILO Liaison Office in Bangkok to form the Regional Office for the ILO in Asia. Concurrently, the ILO established a network of small local representations

---

[70] Ali, 'ILO and Asia,' 351–2; Daniel Roger Maul, 'The ILO, Asia and the Beginnings of Technical Assistance, 1945–60,' in Lichtenstein and Jensen, *The ILO from Geneva to the Pacific Rim*, 118.

[71] ILO Regional Asian Conference, Melbourne 1962, MS N21/1330, NBAC.

[72] ILO Regional Asian Conference.

in Delhi, Tokyo, Karachi and Taipei, all coordinated through the Regional Office.[73]

Asian conferences and regionally based agencies dealt mainly with the fundamental rights of regional workers, such as freedom of association and collective bargaining and equal treatment. The specific industrial problems of Asian maritime labour were included in the agenda of regular ILO sessions. Overall, five Geneva-hosted sessions of the JMC took place between 1950 and 1970, and each session included a few regular members from Asia-Pacific seafarers.[74]

During that period, the Asian region's share of the global shipping tonnage and the seagoing labour market increased roughly sixfold, as many countries embarked on promoting a merchant marine. Japan, traditionally the most developed Asian-region maritime nation, took the lead, followed by India and then Hong Kong. Yet their numbers did not reflect the full extent of the economic importance of shipping to Asian nations, whose workers not only crewed their national flag ships but also the ships of foreign nations. No reliable contemporary statistics were available, but rough estimates suggested that as many as 300,000 Asian residents could earn income by manning merchant vessels in the mid-1960s. That large seagoing labour community was mainly composed of two groups. One included Japanese nationals who were employed on the national flag vessels. Another consisted of Asian seafarers who crewed foreign-registered ships. India was the largest regional supplier of manpower to external markets. Again, no fully reliable statistics were available, but the ILO thought that around 40,000 Indian residents worked aboard foreign-flagged vessels in the mid-1960s.[75]

In seeking to accommodate the specific interests of a growing Asian seafaring community, the ILO developed a broad regional programme of action. The first major step in this direction was an Asian maritime conference organised in Sri Lanka. Along with 14 national delegations, from Australia, Asia and Europe, the audience comprised representatives of international organisations and officials from the principal global labour bodies. The delegates perceived limited employment opportunities, weak trade union organisation and inappropriate recruitment schemes as the most pressing problems of Asian seafarers. As a solution, they called for national governments more adequately to regulate industrial relations in the shipping industry and to improve welfare and medical facilities in ports.

---

[73] Ali, 'ILO and Asia,' 352–3.

[74] 'The Joint Maritime Commission and the Maritime Work of the ILO,' 344.

[75] International Labour Organization, Joint Maritime Commission, Twentieth Session, Geneva, September–October 1967, Conditions of Asian Seafarers, Fourth Item on Agenda (Geneva: International Labour Organization, 1967), 2–3.

The conference further acknowledged the urgent need to develop bona fide Asian shipowners' and seafarers' organisations that would promote effective collective bargaining and consultation. Many also believed that with government support these organisations should regulate the registration and recruitment process and thus control seagoing labour supply.[76]

In 1961, reviewing the working condition of Asian seafarers, a session of the JMC asked the ILO to convene a new Asian maritime conference. With active organisational support from the Japanese government, the conference was held in Tokyo in 1965. Attended by more than one hundred delegates from 15 Asia-Pacific and European countries, the conference adopted several resolutions on labour standards in the global shipping industry. To promote qualification levels of Asian seafarers the conference offered support from the ILO in the form of training facilities and technical knowledge along with assistance in international cooperation.[77] Concerned with poor welfare and medical facilities and recruitment malpractices, the Tokyo conference again called for close collaboration between shipowners' and seafarers' organisations and more active government involvement in rectifying these problems. Overall, the delegates perceived that strong seafarers' unions were a major requisite for a viable maritime industry. As many Asian countries still lacked adequate seagoing labour representation, the conference adopted a separate resolution that asked national governments to give full support to 'properly constituted seafarers' organisations.' The document further recommended closer and more regular contact between governments and shipowners' and seafarers' organisations at both the national and ILO levels.[78]

The ITF in the Asia-Pacific

Ideological antagonism precluding any possibility of effective collaboration in the region pushed the ITF instead to a strategy of establishing a foothold by targeting politically compatible or politically neutral labour bodies. With an inadequately slow growth of membership in the first post-war decade, the 1954 ITF Congress emphasised the need to penetrate into non-European regions and recruit new affiliates. ITF representatives embarked on an extensive programme of visits to Asia. Between 1952 and 1954, general secretary Becu made two official trips to the region to meet local activists, while other officials participated in labour forums in the region organised

---

[76] ILO Asian Maritime Conference, MS N21/766, NBAC.

[77] International Labour Organization, Second Asian Maritime Conference, Tokyo, Japan, 1965, 41–4.

[78] International Labour Organization, Joint Maritime Commission, Twentieth Session, Fourth Item on Agenda, 3–4.

by the ILO and the ICFTU.[79] Becu toured the Middle East, India and Pakistan in 1952. The following year, he went to Karachi to take part in the inaugural conference of the Pakistan Seafarers' Federation. In 1954, the ITF Congress amended the constitution to include opposition to colonialism.[80]

Post-independence India's maritime labour movement was comprised of many regional and industry unions and associations and the ITF was able to play a consolidating role. These meetings in India resulted in the establishment of the short-lived Indian Seafarers' Federation that became an ITF affiliate.[81] More importantly, the ITF was able to recruit two large separate Indian seafarers' unions, one based in Calcutta and another in Bombay, with strong (17,000 and 13,000 respectively) memberships.[82] When the Indian Seafarers' Federation collapsed in 1958, both unions then affiliated directly to the ITF, becoming important regional allies.[83] In early 1959, when Becu made his next visit to India, he helped the affiliated Indian and Pakistani seamen's unions to formulate their claims for national wage improvements. Even though the unions' proposals met strong opposition from shipowners, the Indian National Maritime Board eventually agreed to provide a minor increase in pay rates.[84]

Alongside collaboration with Indian unionists, the ITF re-established the connection with the Japanese labour movement. It took a few letters to local labour activists before the ITF obtained a response from former JSU secretary Mitsusuke Yonekubo, 'a staunch supporter of the I.T.F.,' who still worked as an adviser to the JSU, which was reinstated immediately after the war. Later appointed Minister of Labour, Yonekubo promised to use his influence to prompt the JSU leadership to re-affiliate with the ITF.[85] Meanwhile, the JSU itself sought formal membership to secure international assistance in attaining two important economic objectives. One was the revocation of restrictions imposed on post-war Japan shipping; the other was the extension of international fishing zones for national-flagged vessels.

[79] ITF, Report ... for 1952 and 1953, and Proceedings of London Congress, 16–24 July 1954 (London: ITF, 1954), 22–5.

[80] ITF Reports ... for 1954–1955 and Proceedings of Vienna Congress, 18–26 July 1956 (London: ITF, 1956), 9; ITF, Solidarity, 115.

[81] Arora, Voyage, 13; Indian Seafarers' Federation, Report on Activities of the ITF for the Years 1952 to 1953, 71–2.

[82] ITF, Report ... for 1962, 1963 and 1964, and Proceedings of Copenhagen Congress, 28 July to 6 August 1965 (London: ITF, 1965), 81.

[83] Barnes, Evolution and Scope of Mercantile Marine Laws; Indian Seafarers' Federation, Report on Activities of the ITF for the Years 1952 to 1953, 47; Colaco, History of the Seamen's Union of Bombay, 24–5.

[84] 'Disputes and Industrial Actions,' ITF, Report ... for 1958 to 1959, 42–3.

[85] ITF, Report ... for 1946 to 1948, 17; ITF, Report ... for 1948 to 1950, 14.

Given these pragmatic aims and the successful experience of cooperation pre-war, the JSU's desire to rejoin the labour international was achieved in 1949. The following year, a union delegation attended the ITF Stuttgart Congress at which a JSU representative, T. Nishimaki, was elected to the General Council.[86] The Japanese union took advantage of its new status within the international body, using the congresses to raise questions of concern to Japanese seafarers. These included nuclear tests in the Pacific, a Japanese–Korean dispute over fishing rights and seamen's wage claims.[87]

While forging these links with India's and Japan's organised seafarers, the ITF also sought to establish a permanent presence in the Asia-Pacific region similar to their office which had operated briefly in Japan in the 1930s. This time they set up an Asian Seafarers' secretariat to provide organisational assistance in countries bordering the Indian Ocean as well as the Pacific. The idea arose from the experiences of the British Seamen's Union, which for two years had had its own representative – George Reed – as an adviser to Indian seamen's unions. Several European and US affiliates covered the expenses and, headed by Reed, the Asian office opened in Singapore in 1948. Reed visited a number of Asian port cities, aiding local maritime labour in dealing with shipowners and government, but the office closed in 1949 when his health deteriorated.[88] Over the next few years, a small regional office also functioned in Bombay, managed on behalf of the ITF by the Indian Maritime Union (the local merchant officers' organisation) with the aim of both collecting and disseminating information.[89]

A growing concern that Asia-Pacific labour could be influenced by outside competing political forces and 'would be pulled into whatever orbit exerted the strongest pull' urged the ITF to intensify its regional programme.[90] Consequently, the Executive Board decided to organise an Asian transport workers' conference, and early in 1954 Becu went to Japan to secure the support of local unionists. The conference took place in Tokyo the following year, mostly attracting delegates from the host country. The Japanese government gave official patronage and two Japanese ministers – for transport and labour – took part in the conference deliberations. The delegates adopted several general declarations on the development of regional unionism and positions of regional workers but in practical terms

[86] ITF, Report ... for 1948 to 1950, 9.

[87] ITF, Report ... for 1954 and 1955, 43–5; ITF, Report for 1956 and 1957 and Proceedings of Amsterdam Congress, 23 July to 1 August 1958 (London: ITF, 1958), 55.

[88] ITF, Report ... for 1946 to 1948, 35–6; ITF, Report for 1948 to 1950, 43–5.

[89] ITF, Report ... for 1950 to 1951, 44; 'Bombay Regional Information Office,' Report for 1952 to 1953, 71–2; 'The Story of the Maritime Union of India,' *ITF Journal* 22, no. 11 (1962): 254.

[90] ITF, *Solidarity*, 112.

9.3 Japanese dockworker
at work 1962, ILWU

the most important decision was the institution of an Asian ITF office in
Tokyo.[91] The purpose of this agency involved the coordination of actions
of regional workers, the dissemination of information on ITF activities by
publishing a Japanese-language journal and the recruitment of new affiliates.
Despite its name, the subsequent operation of the Asian office was mainly
restricted to Japan. Only two overseas missions were undertaken by the
office director in 1956–57. One was to Singapore to help local seamen to
set up an employment bureau, another was to Indonesia to encourage the
national Muslim peak labour body to join the ITF.[92] Unsatisfied with the
limited efficiency of the Asian office, the ITF decided in 1959 to relocate it
to Singapore and to leave only a Japanese office in Tokyo.[93]

The following year, the ITF organised a new Asian transport workers'
conference. That was held in Kuala Lumpur, with a larger coverage than

[91] ITF, Report ... for 1954 to 1955, 51–4; Paul Tofahrn, 'The First Asian Transport
Workers' Conference,' *ITF Journal* 15, no. 5 (May 1955): 85–9.

[92] ITF, Report ... for 1956 to 1957, 159–60.

[93] ITF, Report ... for 1958 to 1959, 50–1.

the Tokyo conference – 72 official delegates and observers representing 22 different regional labour organisations The participants were mainly concerned with the weaknesses of an Asian labour movement arising from inner disputes and division and anti-labour legislation in many countries. In seeking solutions to these problems, they called for the intensification of ITF activities in Asia, increasing staff in the ITF Singapore office and setting up an Asian Advisory Committee within the ITF.[94] The subsequent efforts of the ITF to advance in Asia-Pacific produced a mixed result. So far as the recruitment of organised seafarers and dockworkers was concerned, the progress was slow. Only several relatively large maritime unions, from Korea, Malaysia, New Zealand, Singapore and Taiwan, and some smaller maritime unions, had by 1970 been added to the ITF membership list.[95]

The process also occasionally moved in reverse. In 1959, the ITF suspended the affiliation of Australia's Maritime Transport Council on 'the grounds that it would be in the ITF's interest to secure the individual and direct affiliation of Australian maritime organisations.'[96] In this respect, the ITF adopted a proactive position. In 1962, a new ITF secretary – Pieter de Vries – undertook a lengthy tour around Australia and New Zealand to promote the ITF amongst unionists of these countries. However, de Vries showed 'a marked lack of knowledge' of the local labour movement.[97] Adopting cold war rhetoric, he made loud political claims as to 'the urgency of freeing the Australian unions from communist domination' since those were 'now skilfully exploited for the promotion of international communism ... and a swing in this direction would have even graver implications for the survival of trade unionism throughout the world.'[98] Even Charlie Fitzgibbon, the newly elected and actively anti-communist WWF secretary, had reservations about de Vries' visit and avoided having any contacts with him.

---

[94] ITF, Report ... for 1960 to 1961 and Proceedings of Helsinki Congress, 25 July–3 August 1962 (London: ITF, 1962), 50–1; 'The Asian Transport Workers' Conference,' *ITF Journal* 20, no. 12 (1960): 265–71. The ITF Asian office was moved to Kuala Lumpur in 1964, relocated to London in 1979 and to Tokyo in 1995, see ITF, *Solidarity*, 156.

[95] ITF, Report ... for 1968 to 1970 and Proceedings of Vienna Congress, 28 July to 6 August 1971 (London: ITF, 1971), 27–36.

[96] ITF, Report on Activities and Financial Report of the ITF for the Years 1938 to 1946 and Proceedings of the International Transport Workers' Congress held at the Congress House, Zurich, Switzerland, from 6 to 12 May 1946 (London: ITF, 1946), 14; ITF, Report on Activities for the Years 1958 to 1959, 17.

[97] Fitzgibbon, Autobiography (typescript) 159, in Charles Fitzgibbon Papers, MS P102/91, NBAC.

[98] ITF, Report ... for 1962, 1963 and 1964, 43, 74, 80; General Secretary's Visit to Australia, MS N21/1345, NBAC.

9.4 ITF Secretary Charles Blyth attending Asian Seafarers Conference, Singapore, 1973, MRC

Nevertheless, a few small Australian labour transport organisations did join the ITF at that time, only one of which – the Federated Marine Stewards and Pantrymen (in 1958) – was a maritime union. That was added to by the officers' union, the Merchant Services Guild, joining in the mid-1960s.[99] An increase in Australia's representation in the ITF came with a general increase in the number of affiliates, mostly non-maritime unions, from other Asia-Pacific countries. To some extent that was because of the involvement of the ITF in labour disputes on the railways in Malaysia in 1962 and on the docks in the Philippines in 1963, which helped to raise their regional profile.[100] By 1970, 70 regional organisations, which covered all modes of transport – railways, roads, ports and docks, shipping and civil aviation – had become ITF members.[101]

While the list of Asia-Pacific affiliates extended, their interests remained largely under-represented, and the ITF continued to remain a largely Eurocentric institution in the late 1960s. The Executive Board elected at the 1968 Congress reserved 12 places for European unions, yet only two members represented the vast Asian region.[102] The Asian Advisory

---

[99] ITF, Report ... for 1956 to 1957, 29; ITF, Report ... for 1958 to 1959, 18–19; ITF, Report on Activities for the Years 1968 to 1970, 23.

[100] ITF, *Solidarity*, 148.

[101] ITF, Report ... for 1968 to 1970, 27–36.

[102] ITF, Proceedings of the Twenty-Ninth Congress, Wiesbaden, 28 July to 3 August 1968 (London: ITF, 1968), 108.

Committee formed after the 1960 Kuala Lumpur conference was supposed to give more voice to Asian member unions, yet it was only entitled 'to advise or make recommendations to the [ITF] Executive Committee on any matters concerning the ITF's Asian affiliates, either individually or collectively.' Furthermore, the Committee was under the control of the ITF executive, which appointed the six ordinary members from nominations proposed by Asian affiliates. Meetings were also rare. During the first half of the 1960s, the agency summoned meetings only twice: in Tokyo in April 1962 and in Manila in February 1964. Dissatisfied with the minor role Asia-Pacific unions had in the ITF, the regional delegates at the 1965 Congress asked for a meeting with the executive to discuss how to make the Asian Advisory Committee more effective, but their demands brought no practical results.[103]

In part, that institutional inflexibility was a result of inner difficulties experienced by the organisation for most of the 1960s. Deep divisions and conflicts between two European factions within the ITF undermined its ability to respond effectively to new challenges.[104] It was only in 1968, with the election of Charles Blyth, a former British seamen's union official, that the ITF leadership became more consolidated and more focused on problems of new non-European affiliates. Blyth's personality was an important factor in this respect. Unlike his predecessors – Oldenbroek, Becu and de Vries – who were all preoccupied with political issues, Blyth was more labour-oriented. In the words of Harold Lewis, a later ITF secretary, he 'gave a human face to international activities which could otherwise seem remote from daily life,' as he 'preferred to see the ITF in very practical, bread-and-butter terms.'[105] Blyth's election signalled a move away from cold war political polemics. That gradually opened the way to ITF collaboration with those Asia-Pacific unions retaining pro-communist sympathies who had taken their own initiatives.

[103] Harold Lewis, 'International Transport Workers' Federation (ITF), 1945–1965: An Organizational and Political Anatomy' (PhD thesis, Warwick University, 2003), 100–1.
[104] Lewis, 'International Transport Workers' Federation (ITF), 1945–1965,' 67–79.
[105] ITF, *Solidarity*, 146.

10

'Bogeymen of the Pacific'

Trans-Pacific Dockworker Organising, 1940s to the 1960s

In 1942, at the lowest point of the Pacific war, when Australia and the US governments were in a wartime alliance against Japan, Harry Bridges sent Jim Healy a long letter about the ILWU's activities. Healy was elected general secretary of the WWF in 1937 and was now playing a key role in the Australian trade union movement, mobilising support for the war effort. That year he was appointed to the Stevedoring Industry Commission set up by the Curtin Labor government to improve the efficiency of wartime waterfront operations.[1] Australian–American wartime cooperation had begun to change the technology of wharf work with the introduction of forklift tracks and pullets in Australian ports.[2] Pointing out a somewhat slower turnaround of vessels at Australian ports, Bridges offered to 'work out an exchange of ideas and even delegations to better past and present alliances.'[3] Healy responded enthusiastically and welcomed Bridges' 'practical suggestion' of information exchange. What seemed largely aimed at speeding up the movement of military cargo initiated direct contact between the two leaders, who shared an ideological commitment to progressive internationalism.

Harry Bridges had come to represent 'the Australian-accented, indomitable "voice" of the insurgent American worker.'[4] From leading a waterfront strike in 1934, which spread to become a general strike in San Francisco, 'this militant young Australian' was 'the most conspicuous maritime labor leader in the U.S. today,' the subject of a feature article (and on the cover) of

---

[1] Beasley, *Wharfies*, 111–20; Healy to Bridges, 1 February 1943, ILWU.

[2] Malcolm Tull, 'American Technology and the Mechanisation of Australian Ports, 1942–58,' *Journal of Transport History* 79 (1985): 79–90.

[3] Bridges to Healy, 18 August 1942, ILWU.

[4] Janiewski, 'Forging an Australian Working-Class Identity.'

10.1 Jim Healy, general secretary of the WWF, at his desk, [1938]
Photograph Z248-80, NBAC

New York's *Time* magazine (Figure 1.1).[5] In just three years, *Time* noted, Bridges had risen from being a union boss on the San Francisco waterfront to national leadership, and, in the view of anti-labour forces, was 'the bogey man of the Pacific.' He enjoyed great prestige – 'an almost fanatic following' among the rank and file. Bridges had 'spellbinding platform power,' was personally 'incorruptible by cash, favors or flattery' and 'a stickler for union democracy.' To his enemies he was 'an alien agitator, a ruthless doctrinaire, an unscrupulous wrecker with a lust for power,' and efforts by the US authorities to deport him that had begun in 1934 continued for two decades, even (in 1940) leading to special federal legislation to secure it. Bridges finally won his right to stay in the United States in 1955 when the Supreme Court cleared him of allegations that he had lied about his communist party membership when applying for citizenship in 1945. In fact, Bridges consistently maintained that he had learnt his politics in Australia not from Moscow.

Jim Healy (1898–1961) too had a prominent national career. As Bridges was leading the San Francisco strike in 1934, Healy was undertaking a

5 'C.I.O. to Sea.'

study trip to the Soviet Union, sponsored by the union, co-authoring a pamphlet about the experience, which he called *Red Cargo*, and joining the Communist Party of Australia. He remained a staunch CPA member all his life. Healy was originally from Manchester, 'a big and gently spoken man, whose north of England purity of speech was never roughened by Australian experience.'[6] He was born into a labourer's family and raised a Catholic. His father's Irish republicanism exerted a strong influence on Healy's political activities, which began at the age of eight with him assisting electoral canvassers for the British Labour Party. He served in the army during the First World War and arrived in Australia in 1925 with his wife, a Scottish woollen weaver, and three young sons. He found work as a labourer on the Queensland wharves and within a year was elected to the WWF local committee of management and as the union's delegate to the local branch of the Australian Labor Party. The onset of the depression and the Queensland ALP government's failure to relieve the plight of the unemployed fuelled Healy's growing belief in communism as better for workers' interests. He became 'one of the most remarkable of Australian trade union leaders,' making communism 'more palatable to those who were by interest and inclination deeply opposed to it.'[7] Healy and Bridges formed an important trans-Pacific link between waterside workers which they soon extended to New Zealand and Japan.

'[U]nder these changing conditions'

Their connection continued at the end of the war. In an attempt to foster a broader association of cooperation between waterfront unions in the Pacific, Healy joined with Toby Hill, the very militant New Zealand Waterside Workers' Union secretary, to invite Bridges to a New Zealand dockworkers' conference in early 1946. The Scottish-born Hill, like Bridges, had spent some time at sea, and also faced constant charges of being a communist although he was in fact opposed to communism.[8] Bridges, now a US citizen, was free to travel, but a wave of industrial unrest in the United States at the time of the New Zealand conference kept the California delegation at home.[9] Healy sought to promote the proposal of a Pacific maritime labour

   [6] Gollan, *Revolutionaries and Reformists*, 77.

   [7] Gollan, *Revolutionaries and Reformists*, 77.

   [8] Healy and Hill, letter to Bridges, 1 June 1945, ILWU; Tobias McGlinchy Hill, *Dictionary of New Zealand Biography*, https://teara.govt.nz/en/biographies/5h21/hill-tobias-mcglinchy.

   [9] Bridges to Healy, 25 January 1946, ILWU; Bert Roth, *Wharfie 'From Hand Barrows to Straddles': Unionism on the Auckland Waterfront* (Auckland: New Zealand Waterfront Workers' Union, Auckland Branch, 1993), 93–4.

conference in the WFTU, but the European body was reluctant due to financial constraints.[10] The New Zealand union was embroiled in disputes that culminated in a major unsuccessful strike in 1951, the government's deregistration of the union and Toby Hill's resignation. The ILWU retained interest in a closer relationship and Bridges wrote to Healy in 1951 that they were still working on the idea of a pan-Pacific conference and had not given up.[11]

So even though ideas of cooperation between Pacific maritime unionists were in the air in the early post-war years, they did not materialise. Perhaps the most serious obstacle to their execution was the lack of a clear purpose for an alliance, apart from pursuing the general notion of working-class solidarity and unity. The situation changed when the introduction of new technologies on the North American and Australian waterfronts gave a more practical meaning and urgency to their plans. The growing use in the 1950s of a variety of mechanical equipment, ranging from forklift trucks and front end loaders to specialised cranes, made the reduction of waterfront employment a serious concern for waterfront unionists.[12] The technological shift prompted them to seek more permanent channels for information exchange on new developments.

Historically, waterside work was casual due to a very uneven demand. If a lot of cargo waited in port, hands were welcome from all corners, but sometimes no work was available at all. By the 1950s, however, the unions of most developed countries had been able to establish control over the supply of port labour. Through a series of industrial protests, they eventually secured a fairer allocation of available work amongst their membership via government-managed employment agencies or union hiring halls. For the days when work was not available, attendance money had to be provided. The introduction of new technologies undermined this model of labour–management relations, diminishing waterfront employment through greatly improved productivity. New capital-intensive port machinery required well-trained permanent workforces which led to a situation where some workers were regularly employed and highly paid while those engaged through the hiring hall were normally underemployed.[13] Apart from reducing employment prospects on

[10] Healy and Hill to Bridges, 9 June 1947, ILWU.

[11] Bridges to Healy, 11 November 1951, and Healy to Bridges, 3 January 1953, ILWU.

[12] Herb Mills, 'The San Francisco Waterfront: The Social Consequences of Industrial Modernisation,' in *Case Studies on the Labor Process*, ed. Andrew Zimbalist (New York: Monthly Review Press, 1979), 146–8; Australian Stevedoring Industry Authority [ASIA], Report for the year ended 30 June 1963 (Sydney: Australian Stevedoring Industry Authority), 22–3.

[13] P. Turnbull, 'Contesting Globalisation on the Waterfront,' *Politics and Society* 28, no. 3 (2000): 370–1.

the waterfront, new technologies tended to fragment the structure of the waterside labour force and bring dockworkers' unions into demarcation disputes with unionists from other industries.[14] Dockworkers might be substituted by technicians of various kinds who were covered by other unions.[15]

While waterfront unionists had to resolve these new problems within their respective national economic and legal frameworks, their challenges had a common origin. The world-scale technological transformation which developed across national borders from the 1950s to the 1970s influenced stevedoring workforces of different countries in a very similar way and intensified international activities. When Healy was elected to represent Australian transport unions at the ILO Conference in Hamburg in 1957, waterside union officials considered it an opportunity to make closer contact and acquire better information about ports and workers overseas.[16] The union thus allocated funds which allowed Healy to visit 16 countries and conduct an investigation that showed Australia was not far behind 'the modern standard' set for dockworkers worldwide; but Healy reported that still more needed to be done.[17]

Until that time the methods of processing ships' cargoes had been relatively simple, generating a large demand for manual labour.[18] New bulk-loading facilities to manage 'shovelling' commodities – especially grain and coal – had an especially profound implication for dockworkers. The installation of sugar-loading equipment in Australia's Queensland ports made manual handling of bagged sugar almost defunct during the 1950s.[19] As an expression of these new problems, Healy reported to Bridges that, 'Like your own position, the moves here undoubtedly flow from the introduction of mechanised operations and different methods of packaging cargoes,' so that 'the work available to our members constantly decreases.'[20] The shrinkage and erosion of the union membership base threatened to diminish the industrial power

---

[14] Charlie Fitzgibbon, 'The March of Mechanisation,' *Maritime Worker* (15 March 1967): 4; D. Hull, 'Queensland Sugar Ports: Labour and Technological Change,' *Journal of Australian Political Economy* 6 (1979): 60–72.

[15] Stephen Deery, 'The Impact of Technological Change on Union Structure: The Waterside Workers Federation,' *Journal of Industrial Relations* 25, no. 4 (1983): 401–2; Charlie Fitzgibbon, 'Containerisation and Areas of Work,' *Maritime Worker* (26 July 1967): 5.

[16] 'Healy Exposes False Attacks on I.L.O. Tour.'

[17] Sheridan, *Australia's Own Cold War*, 257; [WWF] General Secretary's Report, Seventh All Ports Biennial Conference, September 1958, MS N114/142, NBAC.

[18] Robert B. Oram, *Cargo Handling and the Modern Port* (Oxford: Pergamon Press, 1965), 64–94; Mills, 'The San Francisco Waterfront,' 128–9, 133–9.

[19] ASIA report, 1961, 17; Hull, 'Queensland Sugar Ports.'

[20] Healy to Bridges, 8 May 1958, ILWU.

hard-earned by US and Australian workers in the previous decades. Under these circumstances, the importance of international cooperation increased since it offered a prospect of jointly defined solutions to common problems. Healy also pointed out they could offer assistance to Japan, 'the one country in the Pacific where dockers' conditions are at their lowest' and 'trade union rights are brutally suppressed' while ILO conventions were not ratified.[21]

The US west coast stevedoring industry pioneered the adoption of many technological innovations, and the ILWU accordingly took the initiative in bringing together Pacific maritime labour. In mid-1958, the American union contacted the Australians and proposed a jointly organised conference of Pacific dockworkers to include the Japanese dockworkers' union. The particular purpose of the event was to discuss 'on-the-job' labour problems arising from mechanisation and new methods of cargo handling, and to consider opportunities to reduce work shifts, increase wages and gain other benefits 'under these changing conditions.'[22] Apart from these new industrial issues was a political agenda: the ILWU suggested that the conference should also consider the standing of waterfront labour in developing countries along with the rights of trade unions to participate in solidarity strikes of 'national and international origin.'[23] The response of both Australian and Japanese unions to the ILWU proposal was strongly positive. The Australian union indicated that all Pacific dockworkers' unions, irrespective of their political stance and their country of origin, should be invited to participate in the conference.[24] Tomitaro Kaneda, from the Japanese dockers' union, suggested that the agenda should be broadened to include questions on the enforcement of ILO conventions and opposition to nuclear tests in the Pacific area.[25]

With this strong endorsement, and after some further correspondence, the three unions refined the programme and logistics of the event. The ILWU Executive Board adopted the final resolution in December 1958, with the conference to be held in Tokyo a few months later. Even though invitations to participate had to be forwarded to both WFTU and ICFTU affiliates, the organisers stressed that neither of those bodies would take part in this 'autonomous' conference. The new coalition was to be non-aligned, uniting regional dockworkers' organisations on the basis of their common industrial concerns. The proposed agenda listed a number of practical questions on waterside work covering safety, wages, holidays, hiring, training and trade

[21] General Secretary's Report, September 1958, 99.

[22] Goldblatt to Kaneda, 30 July 1958, and Bridges to Healy, 18 September 1958, ILWU.

[23] Items for All Pacific and Dockworkers' Conference supplied by H. Bridges, MS N114/585, NBAC.

[24] Healy to Bridges, 15 October 1958, ILWU.

[25] Kaneda to Goldblatt, 30 August 1958, ILWU.

union rights. It did not nominate any specific political issues beyond indicating that participating organisations might offer for discussion 'issues of more general trade union and working class importance including such vital matters as the end of nuclear bomb testing, disarmament, etc.'[26]

From the very outset, the conference organisers tried to turn their small coalition into a broader industrial front of Asia-Pacific labour. To this aim and with the secured support of the Madras Harbour Workers' Union and the Indonesian Seamen and Dockworkers' Union, they allocated between themselves the geographical zones of influence to increase conference participation.[27] The ILWU was responsible for recruiting waterfront labour organisations from both Americas. The WWF, correspondingly, was to be accountable for Australia and New Zealand; the JDU for Japan, the USSR and China; the Madras union for India and the surrounding countries, the Indonesian union for its home country, Malaya and the Philippines.[28]

Despite the harmony in interests of these several Asia-Pacific unions, preparation for the conference did not run smoothly. The sheer vastness of the region, coupled with an apparent weakness of unionism in many countries, made it difficult to spread the message of the proposed event. There were political obstacles as well. The conference eventually held in May 1959 was not attended by ILWU secretary-treasurer Louis Goldblatt, since the conservative Japanese government had denied him entry into the country. He was not replaced by another union official.[29] The Indian authorities also prevented Madras unionists from visiting Japan by rejecting their passport applications.[30] However strongly the conference organisers tried to emphasise their political neutrality, they were subjected to bitter criticism by Japanese right-wing labour organisations associated with the ICFTU. Claims were made that the conference was sponsored by 'communistic unions' aligning their actions with a 'communist force of the world.'[31] The ITF also sent a

---

[26] Bridges' letter to organising unions, 3 December 1958, ILWU; Resolution on Pacific Area and Asian Longshore Conference, ILWU Executive Board Meeting, 2 and 3 December 1958, ILWU.

[27] Iyengar (General Secretary of Madras Harbor Workers' Union) to Bridges, 4 November 1958, ILWU; Harsono (Secretary of Indonesian Seamen and Dockworkers' Union) to Bridges, 6 November 1958, ILWU.

[28] ILWU, Proceedings of the Thirteenth Convention, 1959, 338–9.

[29] 'Solidarity beyond Ocean,' Report of the First All Pacific and Asian Dockworkers' Conference, Tokyo, 11–13 May 1959, 12–13.

[30] 'Solidarity beyond Ocean,' 13.

[31] 'Solidarity beyond Ocean,' 10–12; All-Japan Seamen's Union, Dockers, You are watched! The Truth about the International Conference of Dockworkers, February 1959, MS N114/585, NBAC.

10.2 Harry Bridges (left), unidentified interpreter (centre) and
Tomitaro Kaneda (right) at ILWU Conference, 1963, courtesy ILWU

representative to some Asian countries 'for the sole purpose of persuading
dockers' unions not to attend.'[32]

Even so, the Tokyo conference was an apparent success since, for the first
time, maritime labour delegates from different Pacific countries came together
to discuss their contemporary problems. The audience consisted of representatives from the organising unions, the Soviet Sea and River Workers' Union
(SRWU), the Cambodian and Indonesian sea transport unions, along with a
number of Japanese maritime labour organisations in addition to the JDU.[33]
Greetings were also received from New Zealand, India, the Philippines,
Malaysia and China, whose maritime unionists were not able to come to
Tokyo.[34] Apart from the high costs of travelling, diplomatic difficulties could
also get in the way. In the absence of consular ties with Australia, officials
from the Chinese Seamen's Union (which also covered dockers) were unable
to visit Australia when invited to attend because they refused to swear an
affidavit of identity at the British legation in Peking and could only get as far

---

[32] Healy, Report to the First Pacific and Asian Dockworkers' Conference, MS N114/585,
NBAC.

[33] 'Solidarity beyond Ocean,' 18–22.

[34] 'Solidarity beyond Ocean,' 17.

as Hong Kong.[35] The event was also welcomed by left-wing Japanese political and social movements. This was evident by the presence of numerous guest speakers from local socialist and communist parties, the National Union of General Workers (Sohyo) and social organisations such as the Japan Peace Committee and the Asian and African solidarity committee.[36]

The practical work of the conference followed the agenda originally developed by the ILWU. After extensive discussion of different aspects of stevedoring work, delegates adopted several resolutions related to the negative social and economic effects of mechanisation and poor conditions of port labour in developing countries. As far as trans-Pacific labour cooperation was concerned, the most important decision was to set up a Dockworkers' Corresponding Committee (DCC) to maintain contact and 'fraternal relations' between unionised Asian and Pacific dockworkers. Tokyo was designated as the place for the DCC, and Tomitaro Kaneda, the JDU leader, was appointed its secretary.[37]

Tomitaro Kaneda (1910–85) was a long-time militant. Born in Hiroshima to a family of fishermen, on graduating from high school in 1925 he joined the rest of his family in fishing. Two years later, he was in Osaka, a young activist confronting the right-wing leadership of the tramways' union he had joined, and getting arrested often. During the war years he worked for the River Transport Company in Osaka and at the end of the war organised a union for river transport workers with himself as general secretary. Later that year (1945), he established the Osaka port workers' union alliance which in four years had become a national organisation with Kaneda as general secretary. On the unexpected departure of its president in 1952, Kaneda became president, a position he held until his retirement in 1974. That year he was made a life-long member of the Australian union.[38]

The 1959 conference, therefore, produced a loose organisation of Pacific maritime labour in the form of this Corresponding Committee. Just two weeks after the 1959 conference, Kaneda and Jack Hall, Hawaii ILWU regional director, signed a memorandum to specify the purpose and operation of the committee. Following the conference resolution, it was agreed that the new body should work as an Asia-Pacific information centre for regionally organised waterfront labour. In the light of this objective, they decided to publish a monthly bulletin, entitled *DCC News*, that would contain 'basically

---

[35] General Secretary's Report, September 1958, 100.

[36] 'Solidarity beyond Ocean,' 23–38.

[37] Healy, Report to the First Pacific and Asian Dockworkers' Conference.

[38] Biographical details provided by Akinobu Ito, former JDU President, in email to author; Charlie Fitzgibbon to retiring chairman Kaneda, 16 September 1974, WWF All Ports conference MS Z432, Box 40, NBAC.

economic' material on workplace-related problems of dockworkers 'in all Pacific and Asian countries.'[39] There was no formally defined editorial board and it was mainly Kaneda who managed the publication. Over most of the following decade, *DCC News* was circulated around 50 northern and southern American, Asian and Australasian port labour organisations, spreading the message among their membership.[40] Relevant organisational expenses, along with wages for a small administrative team, were jointly met by leading Pacific unions. Half of the money was supplied by the US, Soviet and Australian unions, and the rest by the JDU.[41]

Despite the fact that the Corresponding Committee was supposed to be concerned with practical aspects of watersiders' work, from the very beginning its secretary tried to advance a broader political agenda. The first release of *DCC News* in August 1959 highlighted the participation of maritime unionists in a Hiroshima international peace conference, the prosecution of labour activists in Cambodia, the development of the Matsukawa case (involving accusations of sabotage against Japanese railway workers) and the lodgement of a protest in the national parliament against refusing Louis Goldblatt an entry visa to attend the 1959 conference: these were all somewhat different types of stories from the coverage specified in the Kaneda–Hall memorandum.[42] In subsequent years, *DCC News* continued to circulate a great deal of politically related material on 'the attacks imposed by the capitalist class to emasculate the world movements.'[43]

There were further attempts made to use the Pacific dockworkers' association for attaining specific political aims. In early 1960, Kaneda, as the committee secretary, appealed to the participating unions to boycott Japanese ships for one day in protest against the anti-labour policy of the Japanese government and a new Japan–United States security treaty.[44] The solidarity action of Soviet and Australian unionists was, however, limited to sending messages.[45] The response of the ILWU president was even less supportive. While acknowledging the integrity of Kaneda's call, Bridges stated that

[39] Draft of understanding between Kaneda and Hall, 29 May 1959, ILWU; Healy to Kaneda, 12 June 1959, MS N114/585, NBAC.

[40] List of Unions to which DCC news is sent, ILWU; Tomitaro Kaneda, Report of the Activities of All Pacific and Asian Dockworkers' Corresponding Committee, Second All Pacific and Asian Dockworkers' Conference, Tokyo, June 15–17 1961, 14–15, N114/586 NBAC.

[41] Draft of understanding between Kaneda and Hall, 29 May 1959, ILWU.

[42] Correspondence Committee News, 19 August 1959, ILWU.

[43] Kaneda, Report on the Second All Pacific and Asian Dockworkers' Conference, Tokyo, 1961, 15.

[44] DCC appeal, 25 May 1960, ILWU.

[45] Kaneda, Report on the Second All Pacific and Asian Dockworkers' Conference, 17.

'under present circumstances' union members would not be willing 'to move on anything except to support fundamental trade union issues.'[46] A few months later, Bridges once again criticised Kaneda's intention to encourage Corresponding Committee members to support political opposition in Japan and object to the visit of US President Eisenhower to the country. He stressed that the ILWU had always taken a firm stance on many social and political issues such as disarmament and decolonisation. Yet American dockworkers were only able to support DCC requests if those were related to the 'economic and organisational problems' of Pacific waterside workers and their unions.[47]

The content of many resolutions adopted by ILWU contemporary biennial conventions demonstrates that west coast dockworkers were certainly eager to promote justice and working-class unity on a global scale, but very reluctant to acknowledge openly their support for any political agency outside their home country.[48] Moreover, the timing of organising a large-scale sympathy action, especially on political grounds, was not right. The ILWU leadership was at that time negotiating a new collective bargaining deal, known as the Mechanization and Modernization Agreement, in response to the adoption of new methods of handling cargo. Given the great importance of a successful outcome, the ILWU would not risk disrupting the process by unrelated politically inspired protests.

Forging regional connections

American unionists did not lessen their interest in the DCC scheme or their dedication to the ideas of international working-class unity. In April 1961, the union's convention adopted a resolution proclaiming their support of the work of the Corresponding Committee, their solidarity with 'the longshoremen of Japan in their struggle for decasualisation, for a Port Labor Law, and for the adoption by the Japanese government of the ILO convention on Safety.' The statement further declared 'full support' for a new forthcoming conference of Asia-Pacific dockworkers.[49]

The financial and organisational assistance of the ILWU was, indeed, crucial for holding a new forum of regional maritime unionists. The DCC members initially planned to call their second conference in Indonesia in 1960. Healy wrote to Bridges of his doubts over the Indonesian waterside

---

[46] Bridges to Kaneda, 15 June 1960, ILWU.

[47] Bridges to Kaneda, 27 January 1961, ILWU.

[48] ILWU, Proceedings of Thirteenth Convention, 386–8; ILWU, Proceedings of Fourteenth Convention, 1961, 487–8.

[49] Statement of policy on Asia-Pacific Conference, ILWU, Fourteenth Convention, 1961.

workers' and seamen's union's ability to host the event successfully.[50] With mounting organisational problems, the need for an alternative place became obvious. In these circumstances, Kaneda offered to host the conference in Tokyo once again.[51] The conference, eventually held in June 1961, gathered the usual representatives from the ILWU, the WWF, the Soviet union, several organisations of waterfront labour from Japan, as well as the Indonesian and Chinese maritime unions.[52] This time a WFTU top official, Sattish Chatterjee, attended the conference, on a non-official basis.[53] The organisers adhered to the policy of political neutrality and also sent an invitation to the ITF, whose official attended one session but avoided making any statements.[54]

As at the 1959 conference, much of the discussion centred around the practical aspects of stevedoring work pertaining to employment, mechanisation and safety.[55] As well, the conference considered the question of cooperation between Asia-Pacific dockworkers. In pursuing this objective, the delegates decided to hold an annual International Solidarity Day during which DCC affiliated unions would take coordinated transnational action to promote waterfront labour standards.[56] The dates and demands of such transnational campaigns were to be determined by the DCC in consultation with all participating members.[57]

Organising the first Solidarity Day became the main task of the Committee in the several months following the conference.[58] The programme of action was largely shaped by ILWU suggestions forwarded to Kaneda in October 1961. Developing the trans-Pacific labour partnership into a unity of a wide international participation hinged 'on a broad demonstration of workers in as many of the world's ports as possible over a good economic issue.' As a suitable objective of such solidarity action, the American union offered

---

[50] Healy to Bridges, 22 December 1959, ILWU.

[51] Healy to Kaneda, 9 March 1960, MS 114/585, NBAC; Kaneda's address to participating unions, 20 October 1960 MS 114/585, NBAC; Healy to Kaneda, 17 October 1960, MS 114/585, NBAC.

[52] Report on the Second All Pacific and Asian Dockworkers' Conference, Tokyo, 1961, 8.

[53] Report on the Second All Pacific and Asian Dockworkers' Conference, Tokyo, 1961, 168–9.

[54] ILWU, Report on the Second All Pacific and Asian Dockworkers' Conference, Tokyo, 1961.

[55] Report on the Second All Pacific and Asian Dockworkers' Conference, Tokyo, 36–109.

[56] ILWU, Report on the Second All Pacific and Asian Dockworkers' Conference, Tokyo, 1961.

[57] [WWF] Assistant General Secretary's Report to 1962 Triennial Conference, MS N114/131, NBAC.

[58] Hall to Kaneda, 12 September 1961, and Kaneda to Hall, 8 January 1962, ILWU; Roch to Kaneda, 3 November 1961, MS N114/586, NBAC.

improvements in the standing of port labour in Japan. The proposed international support should take the form of short-term boycotts of Japanese ships, yet the ILWU emphasised especially that the campaign 'should <u>not</u> be tied in with any <u>political</u> objective.'[59]

Early the following year, the Corresponding Committee made an appeal to Asia-Pacific dockworkers to participate in the International Solidarity Action Day on 27 March. The document, signed by all DCC participating unions, declared that Japanese dockworkers were 'still chained by shipping monopolies and their Government to ... semi-feudalistic employment relations with low wages and long hours of work.' As all attempts of local labour to improve the situation brought in only 'terroristic suppression,' the DCC called on members 'to strike a severe blow against Japanese shipping capitalists' on the designated day.[60] In the first days of March, a WWF triennial conference voted to act in support.[61] The ILWU Executive Board also collectively endorsed the proposal, sending around to union branches a circular with a request for a sympathy action.[62]

In responding to this call, the ILWU members in the ports of Ketchikan and Wrangell in Alaska and at Aberdeen, San Francisco, Alameda, Portland and Vancouver on the west coast of the United States and Canada, declared 'extended launch hours' when servicing several Japanese-flag ships on 27 March and sent condemnatory telegrams to Japanese consulates. Other ILWU branches indicated that their members understood the importance of transnational working-class solidarity and would have been willing to act should Japanese ships be presented in their ports.[63]

Australian watersiders in turn expressed their solidarity by holding stop-work meetings in all major local ports on 27 and 28 March.[64] Concurrently, they also organised a nationwide four-hour stoppage in relation to the new domestic industrial award. A leading Australian daily commented that although the union leadership had denied any direct link with the 'Pacific-wide campaign of disruption ... nonetheless, it [was] an unfortunate coincidence to say the least.'[65] Indian dockers of Madras, where the local

---

[59] Hall to Kaneda, 31 October 1961, ILWU [as underlined in the original].

[60] DCC, Call to All the Dockers' Organisations in the Pacific and Asian Region, 8 March 1962, ILWU.

[61] [WWF] Triennial Conference Meetings, 8/3/62, MS N114/131, NBAC.

[62] Bridges' Address to all Longshore, Clerks and Walking Bosses Locals, 9 March 1961, ILWU.

[63] 'ILWU Aids in Japan Dock Fight,' *Dispatcher*, 6 April 1962, 1, 8; 'ILWU in BC Aids Japan Dock Fight,' *Dispatcher*, 4 May 1962, 4.

[64] Historic Asia-Pacific Solidarity Action Day,' *Maritime Worker* (4 April 1962): 5.

[65] 'Pacific-Wide Wharf Hold-up,' *Sydney Morning Herald*, 27 March 1962, 2; '5,000 Wharf Men in Four-Hour Stoppage Today,' *Sydney Morning Herald*, 28 March 1962, 8.

10.3 Tomitaro Kaneda leading Japanese dockers' protest [1962]
Photograph courtesy ILWU

union kept ties with the DCC, also boycotted Japanese vessels for one week in late March along with arranging a 4,000-strong solidarity demonstration. Maritime labour in some Pacific port cites of the USSR, China, North Korea, North Vietnam and Indonesia took part in sympathy rallies held by local unions. The largest protests took place in Japan, where a 24-hour strike at 35 ports paralysed the loading and discharging of 360 ships, including 100 foreign-flagged vessels.[66]

The immediate results of the first Pacific Solidarity Day were summarised by Ted Roach, WWF assistant secretary, as enhancing the prestige of 'our Corresponding Committee ... in the eyes of the workers in the Asian Pacific area [and] that such a Committee can now serve as a rallying point and driving force in the struggle for independent rights of trade unions.'[67] While this may have been an optimistic assessment, given how events unfolded, it was certainly of significance: before the establishment of the DCC, an international campaign on the scale of the 1962 Solidarity Day would not have been possible.

[66] Tomitaro Kaneda, Report of the Activities of All Pacific and Asian Dockworkers' Corresponding Committee, Report and Resolutions of the Third All Pacific and Asian Dockworkers' Conference, Djakarta, 1963, 18–17.
[67] Roach to Kaneda, 3 May 1962, ILWU.

To a great extent, the ILWU's administrative and financial assistance secured the organisation of the third Asia-Pacific dockworkers' conference in Jakarta, Indonesia, in October 1963.[68] As both ILWU and WWF leaders preferred to remain in their home countries, it was Jack Hall, deputy secretary of the ILWU, who headed the delegation of American unionists, and Ted Roach, an active Australian Communist Party member, who was the chief representative of Australian waterside labour. Despite all hopes of the DCC members to expand the representation, the conference was still largely limited to the usual pool of participants. Apart from the ILWU and WWF delegates, the attendance list also included names of officials of the Indonesian maritime union, the Soviet maritime union, the Chinese seamen's union, five Japanese waterfront labour organisations, the North Korean Traffic Workers' Union and a WFTU observer.[69] The newly established Port, Dock and Waterfront Workers' Federation of India also wanted to send 'a strong delegation,' but the Indian government refused to issue exit permits to these unionists on the grounds of Chinese participation in the Jakarta forum at a time of border conflict between China and India.[70]

More broadly, the international hostilities of the cold war made the third Asia-Pacific conference more of a gathering of radical politicians than a conventional meeting of unionists. The years following the first Pacific Solidarity Day were marked by several national and international changes that had a direct impact on the partnership of regional dockworkers' unions. One of those was the deterioration of relations between China and the USSR in the early 1960s. The Sino-Soviet split divided the Chinese and Soviet unionists meeting under the DCC umbrella.

Apart from ILWU delegates intending to discuss economic issues, other participants were much more concerned with general political questions of the day. Kaneda's talk on the operation of the Corresponding Committee included a great deal of criticism of 'American imperialism' and the 'fascist-like' regimes of Japan, South Vietnam and South Korea.[71] Likewise, the official speeches by Chinese and North Korean delegates did not provide much information on the standing of national labour while furnishing a

---

[68] DCC, Call to the Third All Pacific and Asian Dockworkers' Conference, 31 August 1963, MS 114/586, NBAC; Unions to which 'Call' was sent, MS 114/586, NBAC.

[69] Delegates to the Third All Pacific and Asian Dockworkers' Conference, Djakarta, 4–9 October 1963, 2–3, ILWU.

[70] William Ward, James Herman and Jack Hall, ILWU Delegates, Report on the Third All Pacific and Asian Dockworkers' Conference, ILWU; The address by A.S.K. Iyengar, General Secretary of Port, Dock and Waterfront Workers Federation of India to the Third Conference of Asian Dockworkers, 29 September 1963, ILWU.

[71] Kaneda, Report and Resolutions of the Third All Pacific and Asian Dockworkers' Conference, Djakarta, October 4–9 1963, 15–16, ILWU.

vivid description of 'the US imperialists' policies of war and aggression.'[72] The reports from other unions, with the exception of the ILWU, also contained a number of critical remarks on anti-labour actions of local governments and the international political situation.[73]

The character of the conference resolutions reflected the interests of a majority. Just a few out of 17 declarations that were adopted mentioned the work-related problems of dockworkers and the functioning of their occupational organisations, and the rest were devoted to different political and social issues ranging from the condemnation of Malaysia's proclamation to wishing success for the 'Games of the New Emerging Forces,' set up by Indonesia as a counter to the Olympic Games for 'emerging nations.'[74]

On their return home, the ILWU delegates submitted a report to the union Executive Board. Their document provides a more revealing insight into the flow of the conference than the official publication. They described 'time-consuming and aggravating sessions' influenced by the politics of the Sino-Soviet split. The ideological division between the Soviet Union, on one side, and China, North Korea and to some extent Indonesia, on the other, meant that the delegates from these countries failed to compromise on a number of contemporary political issues such as approval of the 1963 Soviet–American–British nuclear test ban treaty and acceptance of the removal of Soviet missiles from Cuba. As a result, the delegates could not mention such controversial topics in the final resolutions 'in the interests of Conference "unity."' The ILWU delegates further claimed that there was 'little need for a regular biennial conference of the All Pacific and Asian Dockworkers as long as they are so narrow in representation as the one just concluded.' Even so, they made a suggestion that the operation of the Corresponding Committee 'should be definitely continued.'[75]

Kaneda attended the 1963 ILWU convention where he delivered a speech on the standing of Japanese dockworkers and the collaboration of unions under the DCC umbrella (Figure 10.2). He pointed out that even though the scale of the second Pacific Solidarity Day held in March 1963 was not as spectacular as the inaugural one, it still demonstrated the ability of

---

[72] Tang Chang, Report of Chinese Delegations [Report and Resolutions of the Third All Pacific and Asian Dockworkers' Conference, Djakarta, 1963], 37–42; Ho Pil Man, Report of Korean Delegation, 64–70; Report and Resolutions of the Third All Pacific and Asian Dockworkers' Conference, ILWU.

[73] Report and Resolutions of the Third All Pacific and Asian Dockworkers' Conference, 29–37, 42–63.

[74] Adopted resolutions, Report and Resolutions of the Third All Pacific and Asian Dockworkers' Conference, 71–87, ILWU.

[75] Ward, Herman and Hall, Report on Third Asian Dockworkers' Conference.

regional labour to mount a collective transnational campaign.[76] The ILWU, indeed, continued to provide financial assistance to the DCC and in May 1965 Kaneda produced an account of the Committee activities since the Jakarta conference. The report did not contain any specific information on the International solidarity days attempted in March 1964 and April 1965, probably because they had such limited impact.[77] Instead, it gave an analysis of the contemporary international situation along with an outline of protest campaigns waged by Japanese, Indonesian, Australian and Canadian waterside workers against the Vietnam War. While sketching the position of unionised waterfront labour in some Pacific countries, it provided no other details on Committee activities apart from stating that it continued publishing the *DCC News* and promoting information exchange at a regional level.[78]

As the practical results of the DCC declined, disagreement among the participating unions mounted. In November 1965, Bridges criticised the transformation of *DCC News* into 'an anti-war bulletin rather than a trade union' publication because of its preoccupation with Vietnam War themes. In line with the views expressed in previous years, he insisted that 'a more strenuous effort should be made to carry detailed information of trade union developments affecting the longshoremen in the countries on the Pacific basin.'[79] A year later, Bridges wanted to know why 'for many months past,' on the pages of *DCC News* there had been no references to the Cultural Revolution in China, where labour organisations were the subject of attack by the Red Guards.[80] Other parts of Bridges' letter condemned publishing unconfirmed stories of atrocities committed by US troops in Vietnam.[81]

The increasing political tension between the USSR and China damaged relations between DCC members. When Kaneda visited Moscow in February 1965, the local union leadership made it clear that they would not contribute to organising the fourth Asia-Pacific dockworkers' conference unless Chinese unionists declined to participate. On his way back to Japan, Kaneda also briefly stayed in China to meet local maritime union officials. They, in turn, expressed their intention to abandon all direct contacts with their Soviet counterparts on the Corresponding Committee. In the light of such a mutual antipathy, Kaneda had to propose that Bridges

[76] ILWU, Proceedings of Fifteenth Convention, 253–63.

[77] DCC appeal for International Solidarity Actions, 1 March 1964, ILWU; DCC Appeal on International Action, February 1965, ILWU.

[78] Report of the Activities of All Pacific and Asian Dockworkers' Corresponding Committee, October 1963–May 1965, ILWU.

[79] Bridges to Kaneda, 15 November 1965, ILWU.

[80] Bridges to Kaneda, 17 January 1967; Kaneda to Bridges, 7 February 1967, ILWU.

[81] Bridges to Kaneda, 10 February 1967; Kaneda to Bridges, 28 February 1967, ILWU.

call off the conference until a later year. Bridges responded that after a detailed discussion his union officials had come to the same conclusion; they were determined to avoid 'another debate between the Soviet and Chinese positions,' as had happened in Jakarta in 1963.[82]

The fourth conference never materialised. In September 1967, the leaders of the Russian and American unions joined their Australian fellow unionists at a WWF triennial conference in Sydney. That meeting provided an opportunity for the parties to discuss the recent working of the DCC. Their exchange of opinions resulted in a decision to disband the Committee. The collective letter they sent to Kaneda explained the reasons for this choice. It claimed that the DCC had ceased to advance dockworkers' solidarity and cooperation in the Asia-Pacific region because of the ideologically biased position of China and North Korea, too great a concern with broad political objectives at the expense of industrial ones, a failure to secure a large representation from regional developing countries and the one-sided character of many articles published in the *DCC News*.[83] Two months later, when the Russian secretary visited Tokyo, he made an attempt to revitalise the DCC concept by suggesting to Kaneda that Chinese unionists be excluded from participation; he received a negative response.[84] This was the final episode in the Corresponding Committee's history. Indeed, Kaneda visited China several times both before 1960 and between 1966 and 1974, when he became secretary of the Japan–China Citizens Friendship Movement Liaison Committee, a position he held for eight years. Items about Australia or from Australia's unions which had appeared occasionally in the JDU publication had ceased by 1977.[85]

Personal ties, common industrial challenges and broad ideological affinities helped at first to nurture exchanges of information, strategy, conferences and even joint industrial action. The bases of such cooperation proved evanescent, however, and the political divisions of the cold war proved too much as differences also emerged in the relationship between 'industrial' and 'political' activism. As the participants from the JDU and communist countries, mainly in Asia, attempted to use the newly formed

[82] Kaneda to Bridges, 23 October 1965 and Bridges to Kaneda, 15 November 1965, ILWU.

[83] Fitzgibbon, Bridges and Shein to Kaneda, 20 September 1967; Bridges to Kaneda, 2 November 1967, ILWU.

[84] Kaneda to Bridges, 11 December 1967, ILWU.

[85] E.g., *Kowan Rodo*, 10 June 1959: 'Australian representative James Healy denied entry visa by Japanese consulate. Australian Waterside Workers' Association took part in three demonstrations/rallies at Japanese consulate, resulting, finally, in the grant of a visa for Mr. Healy'; 'Australia proposed a summit with Japan on containerization,' *Kowan Rodo*, 25 May 1970, Tokyo University Library.

coalition for their political agendas, a conflict grew between them and the Western (and Soviet) representatives whose internationalist objectives were either more pragmatic or differently aligned.

Nevertheless, the establishment and operation of the trans-Pacific partnership of waterside workers, albeit short-lived, was significant and was covered widely in the contemporary press of many local countries. Its impact was even felt in Europe where the ITF was seriously worried over the emergence of this alternative organisation in a region where the ITF had not succeeded in recruiting. There was virtually no representation of regional waterside labour in the ITF in the early 1950s. Accordingly, the WWF journal published no single large article that whole decade on the ITF or the ICFTU in which it was incorporated. Indeed, there seemed to the *Maritime Worker* editorship, and thus to senior union officials, to be no reason to devote much attention to unionists who were labelled by the European communist press as 'fascist beasts,' 'foul hirelings of the warmongers' and 'infamous traitors of the working classes.'[86]

That was to change over the next decade. New leadership took the helm of the WWF, and Bridges' guidance of his union through the difficulties of automation not only won him commendation in the United States as a labour statesman, it also inspired a new direction for the WWF. In 1961, Charlie Fitzgibbon had been a delegate to that year's DCC conference.[87] Two years later, Fitzgibbon attended and spoke at the ILWU convention as the first general secretary in the WWF's history to do so.[88] Unlike Healy, the non-communist Fitzgibbon had no problems obtaining a visa for entry to the United States.

---

[86] ITF, *Solidarity: The First 100 Years of the International Transport Workers' Federation* (Chicago: Pluto Press, 1996), 111.

[87] Fitzgibbon, Autobiography (typescript) 41–2. See also photo of Fitzgibbon, Roach and Hall, in *Kowan Rodo*, 10 July 1961.

[88] Fitzgibbon, Autobiography (typescript) 72; ILWU, Proceedings of Fifteenth Convention, 182–97.

10.4 ILWU and WWF Executives working together, Harry Bridges centre front, Fremantle 1967, ILWU (names of all others are on original photograph)

11

'Giving Us a Voice in World Affairs'
Internationalising Leadership and Activism, 1960 to 1980

Jim Healy's sudden unexpected death in 1961 threw the WWF into an election that is remembered as 'a turning point' in WWF history, 'one of the most historic and significant elections on the wharf in Australia.'[1] This is largely because it is seen in terms of the political allegiances of the leaders and the ideological differences of factions within the union. Charlie Fitzgibbon's election has been taken as a signal that the tide was turning for communist influence in the trade unions and it brought the WWF back to the political centre.

This cold war framing of the leadership change has arguably been overstated. From another perspective, the significance of the change for the union's subsequent history was for bringing the union to international visibility and giving it a prominent role in international activism, most notably in the ITF. The changeover in leadership coincided with massive changes in the shipping industry. New realities, which had begun to impact on the waterfront during Healy's time, accelerated under Fitzgibbon. In subsequent decades, this imperative would drive the union to internationalise. So, while Fitzgibbon's victory was undoubtedly a success for the ALP faction, a longer-term perspective indicates it had even greater significance. Fitzgibbon's task (and achievement) was to steer the WWF through the biggest challenge they had ever faced. For that, he turned to the ITF. Thirty years later, around a dozen port labour organisations from the Asia-Pacific were amongst the members of the ITF.[2]

---

[1] Jim Beggs, *Proud to be a Wharfie* (North Melbourne: Arcadia, 2013), 112.
[2] ITF, Proceedings of Thirty-Fourth Congress, 71.

'[T]he naïve Australian unionist'

Charlie Fitzgibbon (1922–2001), like Jim Healy, came from an Irish Catholic family, one of 14 children. His father was a coal trimmer, a member of the WWF. So were three of his brothers when he started as a junior clerk in the union's office in Newcastle, New South Wales.[3] When that job was made redundant in 1942, the 20-year-old Charlie too became a wharfie and stayed 'on the hook' in the local port for the next 12 years.[4] His career as a union official began with his appointment to the joint position as vigilance officer (or organiser) and president of the Newcastle branch in 1953.[5] From there he became active in politics. He had been a member of the ALP for all the years he had been in the union. He was president of the Newcastle Trades and Labour Council in 1957–59, and then a member of the ALP New South Wales executive, which he continued until 1972.[6] His political connections proved to be valuable when he was running for general secretary against a communist candidate.[7]

He was sceptical about the usefulness of communism and the strategies of class struggle for mobilising workers: yet he 'did not want to be seen or become merely an anti-communist' rather than being committed to 'the long term interest of the members of my union' and doing his best to improve the lives of 'those who employed me.'[8] Ultimately, allegiance to the union was the more powerful and it was that which cemented his hold on power. He became to his admirers 'a giant in the trade union movement,' who 'turned the WWF into a well-disciplined and respected organisation.'[9]

Aiming, in its own words, to help 'rid trade unionism of everything alien, un-Australian and anti-democratic,' the ALP rendered Fitzgibbon considerable support. Party officials and ordinary ALP members actively engaged in printing and distributing election materials, providing advice and raising funds for the campaign.[10] Right-wing labour organisations, especially the Australian Workers' Union, aided him by facilitating his numerous trips

---

[3] Brad Norington, 'Waterfront Union Leader [Fitzgibbon's Obituary],' *Sydney Morning Herald*, 10 March 2001; *Who's Who in Australia* (1983), 306; Fitzgibbon, Autobiography (typescript), 1.

[4] Fitzgibbon, Autobiography (typescript), 5–6.

[5] Fitzgibbon, Autobiography (typescript), 21–2.

[6] *Labor Year Book* (Sydney: Mass Communications Australia, 1973), 244; R.M. Martin, 'The ACTU Congress of 1983,' *Labour History* 45 (1983): 101.

[7] Fitzgibbon, Autobiography (typescript); D. Stephens, 'Unity Tickets and the Victorian Branch of the ALP,' *Labour History* 44 (1983): 70–1.

[8] Fitzgibbon, Autobiography (typescript), 65.

[9] Beggs, *Proud to be a Wharfie*, 118–19.

[10] Fitzgibbon, Autobiography (typescript).

11.1 Charlie Fitzgibbon,
speaking on first visit as
WWF leader to ILWU
conference, 1963
Photograph courtesy
ILWU

around the country to meet the electorate. External assistance, significant though it might have been, was not, however, the decisive factor in Fitzgibbon's victory. ACTU president and later ALP Prime Minister Bob Hawke emphasised Fitzgibbon's ability as 'a vibrant, articulate leader' that made him in the eyes of the union membership the right man for the job.[11] More important, in the view of Tas Bull, another member of the WWF executive and himself a Communist Party member, was the lacklustre opponent the communist faction of the WWF had nominated. Had they chosen the obvious candidate – Norm Docker, a man renowned for his advocacy skills – even Fitzgibbon admitted he would have voted for him. Healy had indeed won a new three-year term in the election held just before he died, so the union had not turned its back on communist leadership. In reflecting on his own success in union elections, Bull concluded that unionists voted for candidates on the basis of their actions, not by ideology, 'on what they do, [not] the labels they wear.'[12]

[11]   R.J. Hawke, *The Hawke Memoirs* (Port Melbourne: William Heinemann, 1994), 52.
[12]   Tasnor Bull, *Life on the Waterfront: An Autobiography* (Sydney: HarperCollins, 1998), 79.

It's true Fitzgibbon wanted to change a deep-rooted public perception of the union as communist-dominated. That idea was actively cultivated to the WWF's disadvantage by political and parliamentary opponents. Fitzgibbon stressed that it 'was overplayed in Australia and was unfair to the great majority of wharfies and Branches.'[13] It created problems in the union's struggles for its members. The Menzies government's industrial relations legislation of the 1950s and 1960s introduced punitive measures designed to curb the unions' militancy and limit their scope for industrial action. Even after Fitzgibbon's election, in 1965, the Liberal–Country Party government made changes to the Stevedoring Industry Act under the pretence that 'Communist leadership of the W.W.F. dishonoured industrial agreements, defied the arbitration system and broke the rules of the trade union movement.'[14] A similar charge was made against the SUA when the government amended the Navigation Act in 1952. The SUA continued to elect communist leaders – Eliot Elliott, who was federal secretary, 1940–78, and Pat Geraghty, who followed him, 1978–92.

Overshadowing their party affiliation differences were the similar challenges the leaders faced. Fitzgibbon too was an internationalist, demonstrated by his vision to join the ITF's campaigns for transport workers worldwide. This was a 'pragmatic internationalism.' Affiliation to a global labour organisation hostile to the Soviet system initially promised to achieve the ALP's and Fitzgibbon's objective of reorienting the pro-communist stance of the wharfies' union. Its consequence was greater as Fitzgibbon led the WWF into a global leadership position of international maritime union activism.

Beginning with Harry Bridges

Connections with the ILWU continued with the Australian union under its new leadership. Within the first year, the ILWU sent a rank and file delegation to visit Australia and New Zealand to compare notes and discuss an exchange of delegates' programme. This was a usual ILWU practice around the region, but they were no doubt also checking out the new leader, gauging the prospects for future cooperation. They reported back to the ILWU conference: 'Aussie dockers are the most militant of all unions' and New Zealand had 'the greatest trade unionist' of all those they had met throughout their trip.[15] This was Edward Isbey, president of the

---

[13] Fitzgibbon, Autobiography (typescript), 163.

[14] Robert Cooksey, 'Political Review,' *Australian Quarterly* 37, no. 4 (1965): 94–105, at 100–1.

[15] Robert Rohatch, Everett Ede and Thomas Trask, 'New Zealand and Australia,' in

North Island WWF. The London-born Isbey (1917–95) was, like many other waterside workers, a former sailor, who served in Britain's merchant navy during the Second World War. He was an unusual wharfie in having completed a diploma in industrial management before becoming a unionist. His political alignment was with the Labour Party, which he joined on his arrival in New Zealand in 1947. A huge unsuccessful strike in 1951 led by Toby Hill had ended with the old union destroyed and two new organisations created, one in the North Island, and the other in the South Island. Isbey started work on the Auckland waterfront three years later, in 1954, and within a very short time was elected to the executive and then the presidency of Auckland WWF. He resigned when he became a NZ MP at the 1969 election. The ILWU delegation clearly saw something distinctive in him as they drew comparisons with their own leader: Isbey 'was to the NZ WWF what Harry Bridges was to the ILWU.'

Both New Zealand waterside unions presidents attended the 1962 WWF All Ports conference where they emphasised their unity and their long tradition of interacting closely with Australia. For their part, the Australian and New Zealand unions welcomed the ILWU as being 'the only union to send a rank and file delegation to meet with other rank and file unionists internationally.'[16] The delegates' report described the problems the Australian and New Zealand unions faced as being: first, compulsory arbitration, which ranked high in both countries as too restrictive of the unions' industrial strength. Next the ACTU was too close to the Australian government, which was hostile to labour: 'The unions are constantly on the watch for vicious anti-labor bills being pushed through parliament by the Menzies government,' and the Prime Minister was not as popular as the US press portrayed him. On the important matter of technological change, the report pointed out that on the waterfront 'mechanization as we in America know it is far behind.' They described 'very antiquated' construction methods across the cities, while 'ships subsidised by the government are now going up to Asian countries to recruit seamen at below Australian standards, while the Aussie seamen are on the beach without a job.' The political orientation of the Australian WWF was also mentioned. The union was 'said to be communist led,' but, contrarily, they said, like Isbey in New Zealand, the Australian general secretary was Labor Party and had guided the union to a more centrist position. The majority (9 out of 12) of Melbourne port's executive were also ALP: only two were CPA and one was Democratic Labor Party (the right-wing alternative to the ALP). Significantly, as an

Second ILWU Overseas Report, to the 15th Biennial Convention of ILWU, San Francisco, April 1963, 7–12, at 9, ILWU.

16 Quoted in Rohatch, Ede and Trask, Report to ILWU.

indication that the ILWU could have confidence for the future, 'rank and file control still prevails' so a union official who did not do a good job would be voted out.[17] By way of adding a lighter, personal, note they spoke of meeting members of Harry Bridges' family – his sister and nephew – living in Melbourne.

Following this 1962 delegation, the ILWU invited Fitzgibbon to attend their conference in San Francisco the next year. This was a simple extension of the pre-existing collaboration between the two organisations. However, the growing internationalisation of the stevedoring industry environment gave such contacts a sharper, more urgent edge. Fitzgibbon thus went to the ILWU conference (Figure 11.1) and then spent nearly three weeks visiting local ports and liaising with labour to learn 'things of value to the Union for the future, in preparing for what must come.'[18] That overseas trip enabled him to perceive clearly the full-scale impact on the waterside workforce brought about by the advanced industry technologies soon to come to Australia. He developed some initial understanding of international organisation as he became fully aware that the WWF would inevitably face massive demarcation conflicts with other unions and a dramatic reduction in membership with a decreased size of the workforce in the very near future.[19]

In the years following his initial trip, Fitzgibbon expanded the geography of his overseas trips by adding numerous destinations around western Europe where the stevedoring industry had also developed extremely rapidly.[20] Many years later, in his unpublished autobiography, he recalled that at each place he was able to increase his learning curve by getting both negative and positive kinds of experience. Visiting Genoa, he discovered the effectiveness of the local financial incentive scheme to promote safe working by stevedoring labour. The Hamburg port overwhelmed him with the high intensification of waterside work and fast ship turnaround. Southampton docks left an unpleasant feeling about the poor system of relations between union officials and the ordinary membership. He was most impressed with the Rotterdam port and the assistance of the local union that helped to develop a thorough knowledge of the local training programme of the workforce and a permanent system of employment.[21] These ideas he brought

17 Rohatch, Ede and Trask, Report to ILWU, 12.

18 Fitzgibbon, Autobiography (typescript), 72–5.

19 Fitzgibbon Autobiography (typescript), 73–5.

20 Charlie Fitzgibbon, C.V., MS P102/26, NBAC; WWF Correspondence with Overseas Unions for 1968, MS N114/111, NBAC.

21 Fitzgibbon, Autobiography (typescript) 87–91, 110, 162; Industry Training Overseas Papers, MS Z432/39, NBAC; WWF correspondence with overseas unions for 1968, MS N114/111, NBAC.

home to help shape his preparation and subsequent approach to leading the WWF into its future. Bridges and the ILWU continued to be an ally.

That the transformation of Australia's stevedoring industry slightly lagged behind some other developed countries gave the WWF leadership time to plan their response and to learn from the experience of others.[22] They did not waste it. Throughout the 1960s, the union was engaged in lengthy and complicated negotiations and enquiries with government and management to frame new policies and rules of industrial relations. Senior union officials regularly asked their fellow overseas unionists to provide specific pieces of evidence on changes in wages, sick leave entitlements and pension schemes, work intensity, working conditions, permanency arrangements and many other interrelated questions to aid the negotiation process.[23]

'[ITF] discuss[es] THE CONTAINER'

The most important innovation in terms of implications for the waterside/ stevedoring workforce came within just a few years with the introduction of container shipping.[24] Containerisation revolutionised wharf labour. Previous efforts to mechanise handling break bulk cargo – that is, 'piece goods' packed individually in bags, boxes, packages – still involved moving a great number of separate cargo items between ship and wharf. This slow process meant merchant vessels had to spend around half of the year in port, and cargo was commonly stored in massive dock warehouses.[25] Placing piece goods in large standardised containers of a convenient shape and volume dramatically reduced the number of individual units loaded on a ship while the unified size of containers considerably eased and accelerated stowage aboard.[26] Not only did containerisation boost stevedoring productivity rates but it further provided an opportunity to move the same container by rail or road without sorting or repackaging its contents in port sheds.[27] These changes

[22] WWF correspondence with overseas unions for 1965, the quote taken from Fitzgibbon's letter to T. O'Leary, then Secretary of the dockers' section of the British Transport and General Workers' Union, MS N114/101, NBAC; 'Overseas Study to Aid Negotiations,' *Maritime Worker* (27 May 1971): 1.

[23] WWF correspondence with overseas unions for 1961–1962, MS N 114/91; for 1965, MS N114/101 and MS N114/112; WWF correspondence with ILWU for 1969–1980, MS Z432/40, NBAC.

[24] 'Union Leaders Discuss the CONTAINER,' *ITF Journal* 30, no. 2 [1970]: 36.

[25] E. Corlett, *The Ship: The Revolution in Merchant Shipping, 1950–1980* (London: HMSO, 1981).

[26] Corlett, *The Ship*.

[27] Frank Broeze, *The Globalisation of the Oceans: Containerisation from the 1950s to the Present* (St. John's, Newfoundland: International Maritime Economic History Association,

completely transformed port infrastructure. As goods were packed in metal boxes that protected their contents from the weather, warehouses were no longer needed. From a very congested and busy place with large storage spaces, wharves became large areas of flat open space – in essence, giant parking lots – places to stack several containers on top of each other and to facilitate all the necessary box movements. Building container terminals on new sites meant many ports were moved from their traditional locations in the hearts of cities to undeveloped areas where a dedicated transport and transfer infrastructure was built.[28]

Containerisation also changed ships. Traditionally, cargo was transported in special holds below the deck. Large metal boxes could hardly fit into these holds. Ships needed to be replaced by large fleets of new, specially designed cellular container vessels where boxes could be lowered directly into 'cells' and stacked one on top of another.[29] Containerisation deprived many seafarers of their jobs. As container shipping followed trends which had already become apparent in the bulk cargo trade, ships grew in size, and the crew to cargo ratio diminished. A calculation made in 1967 suggested that one container ship could replace as many as five or six conventional cargo carriers. To a great extent, this high replacement value reflected the much greater productivity of a container ship, which spent more time at sea moving cargo because of fast turnaround times in port.[30] The number of crew members on an average vessel declined by 40 per cent despite a nearly tripled average deadweight tonnage.[31] Shipowners further downsized ships' crews to reduce operational costs during economic downturns, by increasing automation of shipboard tasks and multiskilling officers and ratings. By the mid-1980s large modern tankers, bulkers and container ships sailing under the major maritime flags had a typical crew of only 23 people. New union–management agreements and statutory regulations set norms for crews of even fewer (18) workers for a number of Japan-, Norway- and German-flagged vessels.[32] Small crew sizes, remote

2002), 9–10; Marc Levinson, *The Box: How the Shipping Container Made the World Smaller and the World Economy Bigger* (Princeton, NJ: Princeton University Press, 2006), 9–11.

[28] Broeze, *Globalisation of the Oceans*, 20–1; Roland, Bolster and Keyssar, *The Way of the Ship*, 353–61; Levinson, *The Box*, 4–6.

[29] Broeze, *Globalisation of the Oceans*, 16–17; Levinson, *The Box*, 19–20; Robert Gardiner, *The Shipping Revolution: The Modern Merchant Ship* (London: Conway Maritime Press, 1992), 46–9.

[30] Broeze, *Globalisation of the Oceans*, 20; Levinson, *The Box*, 248.

[31] 'The Impact of Technologies on Labor in Five Industries,' US Department of Labor, Bureau of Labor Statistics, December 1982, 15–17.

[32] Richard Morris, 'Shipping's New Industrial Relations: The International Context and the Australian Experience,' *Journal of Industrial Relations* (September 1990): 320.

terminals, short turnaround times in port and increased responsibilities increased seafarers' fatigue and stress.[33]

Yet it was the dockside workforce that was arguably the bigger loser. A great increase in productivity brought in with containerisation led to a significant, very large reduction in the need for manpower on the wharves. More general estimates suggested that, ton for ton, handling containerised cargo needed between 5 per cent and 7 per cent of the workforce engaged in processing traditional break bulk cargo.[34] In the light of these looming changes, WWF officials in 1967 anticipated that in the next five years containerisation would have decreased the requirement for manpower in Australian ports by around 70 per cent.[35] Within 20 years, the number of waterside workers indeed dropped from 27,000 to 5,000 and was continuing to decline even further.[36]

But it was not just the technology itself. There was little advantage to containerisation if its geographical coverage was limited to selected nations, ports or routes. Large capital investments had to be made concurrently around the world. Most national carriers were unable to meet the enormous cost, which ultimately pushed them to seek external sources of financing and form joint ventures. This in turn triggered structural shifts in the global shipping industry, breaking down not only traditional company competition but also national borders.[37] Containerisation, therefore, directly encouraged the international consolidation of capital, hence boosting its bargaining power in dealing with maritime unions, typically nation-based institutions. Large transnational consortiums were now entering into the container shipping trade in Australia.[38] With enormous financial and technological power, these new entrants clearly enjoyed a much stronger position against typical nation-based organisations such as the WWF. This imbalance of industrial strength on the national level motivated the WWF and some other Pacific unions to seek

[33] Broeze, *Globalisation of the Oceans*, 233. See Norwegian report, 'The Health of Seafarers,' *ITF Journal* 25, no. 2 (1965): 25–9, 48.

[34] Yrjö Kaukiainen, 'The Advantages of Water Carriage: Scale Economies and Shipping Technology, c.1870–2000,' in *The World's Key Industry: History and Economics of International Shipping*, ed. G. Harlaftis, S. Tenold and J. Valdaliso (London: Palgrave Macmillan, 2012), 64–87, at 71.

[35] Charlie Fitzgibbon, Report on Containerisation and General Shipping Development, MS P102/92, NBAC.

[36] 'Number of Wharfies Down from 27,000 to 5,000; More May Go, Woe the Waterfront,' *Canberra Times*, 14 July 1988, 2; a decade later it was 3,000.

[37] Broeze, *Globalisation of the Oceans*, 29–30, 39–45.

[38] Fitzgibbon, Report on Containerisation.

11.2 Harry Bridges (right), Charlie Fitzgibbon (centre) and Sid Jones (left).
WWF Sydney Branch, 1967
Photographer Douglass Baglin. Courtesy ILWU

approaches to 'the same type of international cooperation around this field of containerisation as the big shipowners [were] doing.'[39]

Reflecting on the complexity of the situation and the tasks facing the union leadership, in 1967, Fitzgibbon said that the massive change the industry was going through was international and on a scale that the union could neither prevent nor slow down. Action was needed, but the choice was stark: to resist change or to take the maximum advantage from change that it was possible to take.[40] Fitzgibbon's approach was to seek maximum advantage. This was the approach also taken by the ILWU. That year, Harry Bridges (and Jim Herman) (Figure 11.2) came to the All Ports conference where he gave the WWF 'a lot of useful advice' about dealing with the pending changes.

---

[39] WWF correspondence with overseas unions for 1969, the quote taken from Fitzgibbon's letter to T. O'Leary, then Secretary of the dockers' section of British Transport and General Workers' Union, MS N114/112, NBAC.

[40] Cited in Stephen Deery, 'The Impact of the National Stevedoring Industry Conference (1965–67) on Industrial Relations on the Australian Waterfront,' *Journal of Industrial Relations* 20, no. 2 (1978): 208.

Bridges also visited the docks and spoke to Sydney's wharfies. It was a very significant event – Bridges' first trip back to Australia in almost 50 years – and also when the WWF and ILWU broke their connection with the DCC, although not with the Japanese dockers. In information labelled 'for members only and [not to] be bandied around,' an SUA member reported the offence Bridges caused by not being available to speak to them also. He was apparently distancing himself from his former union, and still CP-aligned WFTU comrade Elliott, saying: 'there is no affinity, that his union is more closely associated with transport and miscellaneous workers.'[41]

Pursuing their need to develop new strategies, widen the forms of their organisation and amalgamate their forces,[42] the Australian, US and Japanese dockers' unions again agreed to meet, at an international Pacific transport workers' conference (in 1971), to consider the impact of containerisation.[43] The planning meeting scheduled for June 1970, however, was abruptly cancelled by the ILWU at very short notice in order to concentrate on its own issues of a major strike. The ILWU also subsequently failed to attend the 1971 conference.[44] Suddenly the WWF's regional support base was whipped away and its strategy of pursuing regional inter-union affiliation undermined. Fitzgibbon saw an alternative in the idea of affiliation to the ITF, whose performance had impressed him, and he proposed this to the union's Federal Council.[45] As a consequence, he rapidly changed, he said, from being the 'naïve Australian unionist' to becoming the first Australian unionist prominent in the internationally organised labour movement.

[41] Bull, *Life on the Waterfront*, 113–14; 'INTERNATIONAL VISITORS – WWF ALL-PORTS CONFERENCE: (a) Harry Bridges. Federal Secretary Elliott met Harry Bridges at a function organised by the Federal Council of the WWF, when Bridges indicated quite frankly that he was not interested in seamen or the [SUA],' MS N38/208, NBAC.

[42] Fitzgibbon, 'The March of Mechanisation.'

[43] 'Pacific Unions Talks on Container Age Mooted,' *Maritime Worker* (18 August 1969): 7; 'Fitzgibbon on Overseas Tour,' *Maritime Worker* (17 June 1971): 1.

[44] See ILWU Executive Board Minutes, 11 November 1969; memo, William Chester to Harry [Bridges], 12 June 1970; letter, Charlie Fitzgibbon to Harry Bridges, 24 April 1970; letter from Harry Bridges to Australia, New Zealand, Japan, 16 June 1970, draft 1, in ILWU History, Trade Union Relations – Foreign.

[45] Charlie Fitzgibbon, interviewed by Richard Raxworthy, in the Labor Council of New South Wales Oral History Project, 1986 (typescript). ORAL TRC 1948/19, National Library of Australia; also, MS P102/21, NBAC.

From regional to global

By the mid-1960s, the ITF was the oldest and arguably the most prominent labour organisation on the global stage. The organisation had spread its industry coverage to the land and air transport sectors and turned itself into a powerful and influential body uniting well over a hundred national unions, representing the voices of a few million workers.[46] In 1973, strenuous efforts by the ITF to establish principles to safeguard dockworkers facing techno-logical innovation finally resulted in two new conventions being adopted by the ILO – the Dock Work Convention 1973 and the Dock Work Recommendation 1983.[47]

Membership of the ITF promised assistance that offered enhanced power to nationally based unions. It benefited member trade unions through promotion of global solidarity, representation of their interests in intergov-ernmental bodies and provision of information and training facilities. Its two sections – one for dockworkers, one for seafarers – enabled mutual interests to come together. Under the new general secretary, Charlie Blyth (elected in 1968), the ITF took greater interest in areas outside Europe, an encouragement for the WWF to overcome their previous reluctance. Blyth had worked as a seafarer in the 1930s, serving on the Australian coast and in Britain's merchant navy during the war. He had been at sea for 16 years when he came ashore in 1948 to work for the National Union of Seamen and in 1965 was seconded to the ITF to help Hong Kong seamen organise a trade union.[48] Blyth's attention focused less on the cold war and more on the pressing and rapidly increasing problem of open-registry shipping – carriers whose numbers doubled between 1967 and 1972.[49]

The ITF was, nevertheless, still very Eurocentric in its orientation and membership. While from the mid-1950s there was a strong presence of unions from Japan, the Indian unions had more trouble.[50] Unity was difficult given the partition of the country once independence was achieved in 1947. In the years following, there were at times ten different unions organising seafarers and there were conflicts between them.[51] ITF secretary Omar Becu visited India in 1953 to assist with their merger and the formation of the National Union of Seamen of India (NUSI). NUSI joined the ITF in 1954

[46] Lewis, 'International Transport Workers' Federation (ITF), 1945–1965,' 365 (Table 6).

[47] 'A Victory for Dockers at the ILO,' *ITF Journal* 33, no. 3 (1973): 20–2.

[48] 'The New General Secretary,' *ITF Journal* 28, no. 3 (1968): 61.

[49] International Transport Workers' Federation, *Flags of Convenience: The ITF's Campaign* (London: ITF, 1992), 20.

[50] ITF, 23rd Congress, London, 16–24 July 1954, Report ... for 1952 and 1953, 34–5.

[51] Leo Barnes, *Sea of Change* (Mumbai: National Union of Seafarers of India, 1996), 161.

as a single union but with NUSI (Bombay) maintaining a separate identity in the ITF from NUSI (Calcutta), where Bikas Majumdar was general secretary.[52] Born in 1927, Majumdar had come to the labour movement via a youth spent active in the independence movement. His union activism came in response to the cold war when communists gained control of the waterfront and of the Indian Seamen's Union, which had been founded by Aftab Ali.

All was not smooth sailing, however, for Indian unions and the ITF. The new NUSI (Calcutta) boasted an almost complete membership of Calcutta seamen but for many years NUSI (Bombay) could not afford to pay the ITF's affiliation fees.[53] One of the competing unions, The Indian Seafarers' Federation, was expelled from the ITF in 1958 for non-compliance with the ITF constitution, but within a few months had increased its membership threefold, while NUSI's fell to half.[54] Majumdar served on the ITF's Asian Seamen's Committee from the time it was established in 1961 and worked for the ITF in Hong Kong to prevent 'the exploitation of Chinese seamen as cheap labour.'[55] By 1965, the ITF was reporting a decline in Indian seamen's wages; they were falling behind the rising cost of living and parity with real wages in other countries.[56] That year a new leadership was emerging in NUSI (Bombay), which carried out its first strike to protest against the shipowners' refusal to negotiate over wages. The shipowners were forced to the bargaining table and NUSI followed up with more successful strikes in the early 1970s.[57]

Australian and New Zealand unions continued to be under-represented in the ITF for more than a decade after the Indian unions joined.[58] From its foundation in 1902, the WWF had, as had the SUA (and the ILWU), consistently refused all requests to join the ITF. While 'political incompatibilities' may have become the major cause of WWF 'indifference' to ITF existence since 1950, this does not quite explain the prior reluctance in the Edo Fimmen era.[59] Concentrating on ideological differences also ignores the question of practical necessity.[60] Australian wharf labourers chose not

[52] Arora, *Voyage*, 15; 'Profile,' *ITF Journal* 28, no. 4 (1966): 73.

[53] Barnes, *Sea of Change*, 161.

[54] Arora, *Voyage*, 16.

[55] 'Profile,' *ITF Journal* 28, no. 4 (1966): 73.

[56] Peter de Vries, 'Are Indian Seamen Getting a Fair Deal?' *ITF Journal* 25, no. 5 (1965): 97–9.

[57] Barnes, *Sea of Change*, 160.

[58] Lewis, 'International Transport Workers' Federation (ITF), 1945–1965,' 178.

[59] Lewis, 'International Transport Workers' Federation (ITF), 1945–1965,' does not explore the earlier period, 178–9.

[60] Bull, *Life on the Waterfront*, 131.

to commit their energies and resources to an organisation whose interest in the Asia-Pacific was limited or non-existent and whose political agenda was unsympathetic to theirs. There were, in short, more pronounced *regional* obstacles in the way that gave the WWF little reason to join, while the Eurocentric nature of the ITF made it of little relevance to Australian shore-based maritime workers. This changed as the WWF's industrial power weakened. Joining the large international community of organised labour represented by the ITF, and actively contributing to it, promised additional, global rather than regional, support in any local industrial disputes. Fitzgibbon put the suggestion to the 1970 WWF conference on grounds that affiliation 'would give the Federation a voice in world affairs and it is desirable to widen our international contacts.'[61] This had been a long time coming and was a significant reversal of policy. Yet members of the ITF Executive Board promptly agreed to accept the WWF into membership so that Fitzgibbon was able to attend the ITF Congress in Vienna in July 1971 as an official delegate, which finalised the process of formal engagement.[62]

The decision opened a new chapter in both organisations' histories. The timing of the WWF affiliation coincided with the ITF decision to resume activism against open-registry vessels. The ITF hoped that its newest affiliate would contribute much to this global-scale campaign.[63] The following decades thus brought new meaning to the Australian union's regional identity. Other countries of the Asia-Pacific region actively supplied the cheap workforce for the growing flag of convenience (FOC) shipping fleets. As the sector grew rapidly, so did the demand for seafarers from developing Asian countries. This put the local maritime unionists in those countries – concerned with defending their access to crewing opportunities – at odds with the west European countries wanting to protect the standard of seafarers' wage rates, set by national negotiations or the ILO and pursued by the ITF. The strategy of removing cheaper competition and protecting Asian seafarers from exploitation was not easy for the ITF to implement. 'At times,' NUSI general secretary Leo Barnes said, 'the ITF Secretariat does not show enough understanding of the situation in Asia.'[64]

---

[61] Minutes of 21st All Ports Conference, 2 October 1970, MS Z432, Box 19, NBAC; 'Overseas Study to Aid Negotiations,' *Maritime Worker* (27 May 1971): 1.

[62] Fitzgibbon, Autobiography (typescript), 163, 166.

[63] Fitzgibbon, Autobiography (typescript), 163, 174.

[64] Barnes, *Sea of Change*, 163.

'We Asians have differing opinions compared to our Western colleagues'

The 1971 Vienna Congress, which Fitzgibbon attended as the new Australian affiliate, was also the first ITF Congress attended by NUSI's new general secretary Leo Barnes (1932–2001). He was highly qualified, a former seafarer, born in Bombay, the fifth child in his family, who had first gone to sea in 1954 following the lead of an uncle and brother-in-law who worked on passenger ships. After a brief apprenticeship in the engine room of a training ship, his first job, as a coal trimmer, on a British ship, gave him valuable experience of the conditions of Indian crews. The officers were British, the crew were Indian and Barnes recalled the difficulty of speaking up for themselves in the face of injustices.[65] At the urging of a fellow crew member, and his brother in the printmakers union, he joined NUSI in 1960, which he recalled was at that time a weak organisation, with low membership and leaders that were distrusted by the rank and file. He was sent for leadership training at the ICFTU Asian Trade Union College in Calcutta, returning to be appointed organiser for NUSI a year later (Figure 11.3). From organiser he rose in just four years to the position of secretary (in 1965) and general secretary in 1968.[66]

Barnes was recognised for his 'indomitable spirit and ambition,' being a regular churchgoer, well-liked by shipowners, always polite and freely available to journalists, and stoic in the face of severe health problems.[67] He had diabetes, kidney disease, and in his later years had both legs amputated, yet still turned up for work each day. He had left school as an 11 year old, when his father died of TB, and spent ten years taking odd jobs to help support the family. He nevertheless had continued with his education, completing secondary school while going to sea, and graduating BA (Economics) from Bombay University in 1967. He said he wanted to study economics 'to be able to understand the shipping industry better. I wanted to improve my work for the trade union by educating myself further,' so he went on to study law, receiving a Master of Laws degree (LLM) in 1974. He then 'conducted research on the conditions for Indian seafarers,' for which he received a PhD in 1980. All this study was undertaken while working for the union.[68] He held a Harvard University Trade Union Fellowship in 1973.

---

[65] Barnes, *Sea of Change*, 158.

[66] Arora, *Voyage*, 17.

[67] 'Shippie Ahoy,' *Times of India*, 20 August 2001, 4.

[68] Barnes, *Sea of Change*, 161. The thesis was published in 1983. In recognition of his services to shipping, the Indian government made him a Justice of the Peace in 1969 and Special Executive Magistrate in 1975. See Arora, *Voyage*, 16, 18; Blanche Barnes, *Leo Barnes: The Lion of the Seas. Selected Biographical Notes* (Mumbai: Leo Barnes Foundation, 2008).

11.3 Newly appointed organiser Leo Barnes,
making his first speech at NUSI meeting, 1961
Photograph courtesy of Barnes Family and Leo Barnes Foundation, Mumbai

The ITF had first raised the matter of FOC shipping and its implications for seafarers at the ILO Joint Maritime Commission in 1933. Their concern then was that flags were transferred to the flag of another country on ships they were working on. The International Mercantile Marine Officers' Association sought an investigation into flag transfers 'where conditions of employment are on a lower level than in the country of origin.' But, 'after a prolonged exchange of views,' the JMC decided it would be too difficult to distinguish genuine transfers from those 'made primarily in order to take advantage of lower wages and working conditions.' The ITF raised the issue again in 1947. And again, they failed to get the shipowners to agree. This time, 'the shipowners felt that the evidence available was not sufficient,' while agreeing that 'where transfers were deliberately made for the purpose of lowering the standards ... they were to be condemned.'[69]

[69] 'The Joint Maritime Commission and the Maritime Work of the ILO.'

Without sanctions from the JMC, after the Second World War, shipowners gradually increased transferring the registration of their fleets to less developed, open-registry countries that offered lax regulatory and tax regimes. Sailing under a FOC made it possible to recruit any nationals to crew the ship. Not surprisingly, FOC shipowners minimised crewing costs by paying much lower rates and cutting on-board accommodation and safety expenses. This was the old problem of hiring cheap labour (previously called 'coolie competition') on terms and labour standards that had motivated activism by maritime organisations since the nineteenth century. Now it was no longer being described, and opposed, as 'coloured' or 'Asiatic' labour, but the power of the shipowners to exploit vulnerable, especially unorganised, labourers was stronger than ever. Maritime unions in developed countries very soon began to perceive 'flagging out' as a dangerous practice of undermining established national labour standards by replacing their members with non-unionised seafarers from less economically developed regions.[70]

The ITF appealed in 1958 to organised labour all around the world to implement a week-long international boycott of FOC vessels. Even though Australian maritime unionists were politically hostile to the ITF, they responded to the call by delaying at Fremantle a Costa Rican steamer – the only FOC ship that happened to be visiting Australia.[71] Several years later, they once again demonstrated their willingness to cooperate with the ITF. In 1963, in collaboration with the ACTU, the SUA initiated a domestic campaign against the attempts by local companies to use foreign-registered and foreign-manned ships to transport coastal cargo.[72] Although aiming to enforce national manning levels and employment conditions on coastal shipping, Australian unionists acknowledged that it was practical to bring their localised protests in line with the ITF international crusade against FOC vessels 'to force all ships back to the flags of countries in which genuine control lies.'[73] This cooperation stalled in the

---

[70] 'Flag of Convenience I.T.F. Policy,' *Seamen's Journal* (March 1963): 57; 'SUA Attitude to Runway Flag and Permit Coastal Ships,' *Seamen's Journal* (May 1963): 98; S. Koch-Baumgarten, 'Trade Union Regime Formation under the Conditions of Globalization in the Transport Sector: Attempts at Transnational Trade Union Regulation of Flag-of-Convenience Shipping,' *International Review of Social History* 43 (1998): 397–8; Lillie, *A Global Union for Global Workers*; Lennart Johansson, *Funny Flags: ITF's Campaign, Past, Present, Future* (Stockholm: Utbildningsförlaget Brevskolan, 1996).

[71] ACTU Circular to Secretaries of All Waterfront Unions, 29 November 1959, MS N38/287; J. Healy, WWF Secretary to H. Souter, ACTU General Secretary, Flags of Convenience, 5 January 1959, MS N38/287, NBAC.

[72] SUA Federal Office Report, 25 October 1963, MS N38/287; 24 September 1963, SUA Victorian Branch stop-work meeting resolution, MS N38/287, NBAC.

[73] 'Flag of Convenience I.T.F. Policy,' *Seamen's Journal*; 'SUA Attitude to Runway Flag

1960s when the ITF did not implement actions against open-registry carriers and only resumed when the FOC campaign was reignited with the WWF's affiliation to the ITF.

Having become an ITF affiliate, the WWF quickly became an important player in this campaign, which the ITF's Fair Practices Committee (FPC) was responsible for coordinating and managing.[74] In late 1971, Fitzgibbon was appointed to this Committee, a small body of around 20 representatives of predominantly western European unions.[75] The unions from countries supplying the labour did not participate in formulating this policy.[76]

Soon the local press was reporting that Australia's maritime unions were 'about to put a shot across the bows of ships which are sailing disreputably.'[77] These were either under 'flags of convenience' or manned with 'crews of convenience,' which were ships, which, irrespective of their country of registration, engaged cheap-wage crews. They now made up about one-fifth of the world's shipping tonnage and included even some registered under the Australian flag in Pacific Island nations like Papua New Guinea. Australian exporters and importers were chartering 'flag of convenience' ships and crews to carry their cargoes. The WWF joined with seven maritime unions at a meeting in Sydney in 1972 to reveal their actions. When a ship identifiably sailing under a 'flag of convenience' or using a 'crew of convenience' entered any port on the Australian coast, the unions would now refuse to provide labour or services until they had ensured trade union requirements were met and that the ship was covered by an ITF agreement on wages and conditions of safety, repatriation and other workers' rights. These protections were set at the standards applying in Britain while the ITF drew up terms for an improved agreement. The campaign received endorsement from the ACTU and the NSW Labor Council; it had the potential of providing work for Australian crews on Australian ships.[78]

Within the first couple of months, they had won ITF contracts for crews of South Koreans, Filipinos, Ghanaians, Indians, Chinese, Argentinians and Thais on 11 ships calling into Australian ports. Among them was a Swedish-owned ship carrying a Hong Kong crew being paid low wages. Another was a ship jointly owned by Dutch and South African interests whose African crew had their wages trebled, to a minimum of about

and Permit Coastal Ships,' *Seamen's Journal*.

74 ITF, 31st Congress, Stockholm, 7–15 August 1974, Report on Activities for the Years 1971 to 1973, and Proceedings ... (London: ITF, 1974), 105.

75 ITF, 31st Congress, Stockholm, 7–15 August 1974, Report, 105.

76 Koch-Baumgarten, 'Trade Union Regime Formation.'

77 'Warning Shot to Convenience Ships,' *Tribune* (Sydney), 27 March 1972, 4.

78 'Warning Shot to Convenience Ships.'

11.4 WWF officials (left to right): J. Andrews, T. Roach, L. Quelch;
SU official D. Dan; SPDU official Paddy Troy; Shipwrights' Union C. James,
at ACTU Conference, Perth, 1965
Daily News, 22 November 1965 © West Australian Newspapers Ltd

AU$220 a month. ITF general secretary Charlie Blyth wrote to the WWF congratulating them and pointing out that this was a tangible expression of the abhorrence of apartheid. 'Nothing,' he said, 'has caused so much consternation among the shipowning fraternity for the last ten years than your participation in this campaign.'[79]

Two years later, the unions and the ITF were taking credit for assisting 600,000 seafarers from the Indian subcontinent to raise their wages between 100 per cent and 200 per cent. This was the difference between what they were being paid and the standard wage set by the ILO of a minimum monthly

---

[79] 'Maritime Men Thanked,' *Tribune* (Sydney), 15 August 1972, 12.

wage of AU$80 a month. While it was 'poor by Australian standards,' it was a massive increase on what Indian, Pakistani and Bangladeshi seafarers were then receiving. In just 18 months, Australia's maritime unions were instrumental in securing AU$300,000 back pay for Asian seafarers crewing foreign-flag ships and in getting shipowners to pay into the fund the ITF had set up to help Asian unions. They signed ITF wage agreements rather than face industrial disputes when they visited Australian ports.[80]

'Maritime men thanked'?

It was not, however, quite as welcome as it seemed. The Indian organisations didn't differentiate between Indian-flagged or foreign-flagged ships: all paid much the same rates and provided the same conditions on board. So, with the ITF's reinvigorated campaign in 1972 they started having problems. A ship crewed by Indian nationals which was boycotted in Australia by the WWF and had an ITF Agreement signed, had not received their ITF wages when the crew arrived back in India and signed off. Barnes' attendance at his first ITF Congress meant he almost immediately ran up against the impact of the WWF's activism. He pointed out there were flaws in the ITF's strategy. 'No shipowner would be willing to pay 35 Indians' the ITF rate. Barnes alluded to the difficulty of recruiting Westerners (as pointed out in a Norwegian study), when he said: 'People in the west don't want to go to work at sea anymore, they aren't interested in being seafarers.' Also, in some Asian countries – Singapore, Korea, Taiwan and Japan – workers could earn double a seafarer's wage by working on shore. That 'leaves only a group of Asians willing to do seafaring work – [from the] Philippines, India, Pakistan, Bangladesh, Sri Lanka and Indonesia' – and there were more of them seeking work than there was work that could be provided by their own national flags, 'so they must go to FoC.'[81] To Asian trade unions, flags of convenience were in actuality 'flags of need.' Barnes saw the ITF strategy as therefore 'dominated too much by the European affiliates of the ITF, who push through decisions which are not realistic, and whose effect does more harm than good.' When many workers in India earned no more than US$10 a month, even US$100 was a ten-fold increase. The ITF agreement was US$1,000 per month and the Asian affiliates opposed it being increased even further because it was totally unrealistic for the region. The standards

[80] '600,000 Asian Seamen Gain from I.T.F. Campaign,' *Tribune* (Sydney), 16 July 1974, 4.

[81] Barnes, *Sea of Change*, 162, 164. He was referring to the Norwegian study, 'The Health of Seafarers,' *ITF Journal* 25, no. 2 (1965).

being pushed for by the ILO and the ITF were not necessarily transferable across all circumstances.[82]

With the success (from the ITF's view) of WWF action against flagged-out vessels, the 1974 ITF Stockholm Congress elected Fitzgibbon to the ITF General Council. Along with that, the delegates appointed him the chairman of the dockers' section committee. As the chairman of this committee Fitzgibbon also assumed two other leadership roles – the joint chairman of the seafarers' and dockworkers' section and joint chairman of the ITF's Fair Practice Committee.[83] He was the first Australian to reach this level.

The Committee's new plan of action in 1974 involved using the industrial and organisational power of affiliated maritime unions from developed countries. The Committee proposed that unions check the safety and employment conditions on board open-registry vessels when they called in to ports. If the conditions were inadequate, the unions were expected to force shipowners to accept a standard ITF agreement on seafarers' wages and contract terms and to subscribe them to the ITF Welfare Fund by using a threat of industrial action. To coordinate the efforts of affiliates on a global scale, the ITF appointed several regional inspectors, one of whom was permanently based in Sydney.[84] But a deep conflict developed between the ITF and Asian seamen's unions of developing countries, most notably India. Barnes attended the ITF's 1974 Congress in Stockholm where he criticised it for what he claimed was licensing FOCs instead of sending them back to national ownership. He said: 'We Asians need to be better integrated into the campaign in order to improve its effectiveness' and, he pointed out, 'We Asians have differing opinions compared to our western colleagues.'[85]

In 1976, Fitzgibbon thus led a delegation of two other ITF officials to India to meet with NUSI officials to negotiate an agreement. NUSI proposed that shipowners should be required to use the difference between the ITF wage rate and the low wages that were currently being paid to crew to employ more seamen and to have it paid into a welfare fund. This was the total crew cost (TCC) concept. The ITF's committee rejected the idea and wanted direct payment made to the crew, in order, the Indians thought, 'to save western jobs.' Indian seamen preferred to have the job, not risk it

[82] 'Flags of need' is Koch-Baumgarten's phrase. See Barnes, *Sea of Change*, 166, 164.

[83] In June 1973, he was Australian adviser to the ILO and by 1979 was appointed to a Committee of Experts to revise the ILO Code of Safety and Health in Dock Work, MS N114/948, NBAC.

[84] ITF, 31st Congress, Stockholm, 7–15 August 1974, Report on Activities for the Years 1971–1972–1973, 106; Report of Fitzgibbon to Special Council Meeting, WWF, 27 January 1972, on ITF Fair Practice Committee, MS N114/951, NBAC.

[85] Barnes, *Sea of Change*, 163.

with the higher wages being demanded. They were already better off than many of their fellows by getting a seagoing job: he 'gets a job only once in a lifetime and would not like to lose it in lure of ITF wages.'[86] Two years later, a clash occurred when a ship was detained in Scotland but the Indian and Greek crew refused the ITF wages. NUSI supported their resistance and accused the ITF of reducing the employment prospects of Asian seamen. The risk was that if a shipowner was forced to pay the higher rate in one port, they could just unload the crew and hire a cheaper crew in the next. The ITF responded by suspending the Indian union from the ITF in 1978.[87] Asian maritime unions organised their own conference in Singapore. Barnes remembered later, 'I was further critical of the fact that our region was represented on the ITF Executive Board by delegates from Australia and Japan, two highly developed countries both quite unaware of poverty, need and mass-unemployment that are typical of most other countries in Asia.' There was 'no whole-hearted, all-inclusive participation in the campaign by all affiliates' of the ITF, according to Barnes. 'The Asian reality does not look like that in the West.'[88]

In 1979, the ITF Congress proposed that payment should be determined on an all-crew basis, the TCC concept, not paid individually to crew members, thus satisfying the Indian and other Asian affiliates concerns.[89] This was a remarkable achievement. 'Despite their primarily national and self-interested orientation, competing ... and conflicting material interests (between trade unions in capital-exporting countries and labour-exporting countries),' the unions had created a system within the ITF that '"translates" the instruments of national interest politics (organisation, minimum standards through collective contracts and legal enactment) to the international level.' The ITF had managed, in 'this hitherto unique example of transnational cooperation,' to achieve a regime that 'regulates the rights of trade union organisation and representations on ships, [and] sets collective international minimum standards, procedures for their implementation and control and for the regulation of conflicts, and institutionalizes decision-making.'[90] NUSI was reinstated to ITF affiliation and by the 1980s the labour-supplying countries were represented by Asians serving on the ITF.

Fitzgibbon's work had paved the way for a broader participation of Asia-Pacific labour in the ITF – had even succeeded in getting the ITF for the first time to hold their Executive Board meeting in Sydney in 1982. But

---

[86] Arora, *Voyage*, 22, 23.
[87] Arora, *Voyage*, 24. See also Koch-Baumgarten, 'Trade Union Regime Formation.'
[88] Barnes, *Sea of Change*, 163, 166, 164.
[89] Barnes, *Sea of Change*.
[90] Koch-Baumgarten, 'Trade Union Regime Formation,' 373–4.

11.5 Leo Barnes speaking at ITF meeting [1970s] Leo Barnes Foundation

joining the ITF and pursuing its policies against open-registry shipping had also positioned Australian unionists as part of Western Europe rather than with its Asia-Pacific neighbours. 'We in Asia' did not include Australia. That may have been inevitable once the British Empire was dismantled and neither Australia nor India was any more a colony. Or perhaps it was inevitable because their economic development dramatically diverged, and organisation of the ITF fell along economic lines: those countries exporting capital against those supplying labour. Australia fell in with the richer Western countries which were not supplying labour. Europe has had greatest influence on decision-making. The power of trade unions in the capital-exporting countries has been able to be directed against Asian countries, closing the labour market to them.[91]

Between 1964 and 1980, the global FOC tonnage increased fivefold and the absolute number of vessels fourfold; the percentage of shipping going from 4.5 per cent in 1950, to 18 per cent in 1970 and by the 1990s to 41 per cent.[92] Large-scale deregulation had devastated ITF-affiliated dockers' unions, making them dependent on seafarers to retain their union strength and causing many more to become involved in the FOC campaign.[93] The SUA's position on joining the ITF nevertheless remained ambivalent.

---

[91] Koch-Baumgarten, 'Trade Union Regime Formation.'

[92] Flag of Convenience and 40/40/20 concept by Patrick Geraghty, SUA Federal Secretary, MS Z129/21, NBAC. Statistics are from Koch-Baumgarten, 'Trade Union Regime Formation,' 377.

[93] ITF, 'Transport Workers: Beyond 2000,' Progress Report.

The SUA stood out among Asia-Pacific seagoing unions as the only large and well-established national organisation which did not join the ITF. The ideological differences between the ITF and the SUA remained while the SUA was aligned to the WFTU. In addition, the character of the Australian shipping industry encouraged the SUA to keep a tighter focus on domestic rather than global developments. The economic importance of coastal trade started declining. Between 1972 and 1982, the Australian interstate fleet shrank from 100 to 72 vessels, depriving many domestic seafarers of jobs.[94] Paradoxically, in the mid-1970s, the SUA was able to secure reduced hours, redundancy payments and compensation for lost jobs. The average Australian ships' crew also consisted of 37 people, which compared well with the British (33) and the Scandinavian (28).[95] It was only in the mid-1980s that government, shipowner and trade union representatives reached a deal to optimise staffing arrangements in line with new shipping technologies.[96]

In early recognition of the importance of Australian unionists in the flagged-out registries campaign, ITF general secretary Blyth made an official visit to Australia in 1973. As well as meeting WWF officials, Blyth visited the SUA headquarters, met members of its committee of management and gave a detailed interview to the union journal, emphasising that organised labour with different political ideologies should work together for mutual benefit.[97] The SUA still did not establish formal connections but actively supported the organisation's anti-flag of convenience campaign. In collaboration with their waterside comrades, Australian seafarers inspected vessels and imposed short-term boycotts in line with ITF recommendations.[98] The efforts of the two Australian unions produced a substantial result. Every year in the decade following 1972 the operators of somewhere between 30 and 50 flagged-out ships visiting Australia signed ITF-recognised bargaining agreements with their crews.[99]

By the early 1980s, when Fitzgibbon retired from the position of union secretary and also left the international body, virtually all major Asia-Pacific

---

[94] *Seamen's Journal* 37, no. 7 (1982): 186.

[95] John W. Spiers, *Default to Decline: The Transformation of Australian Shipping Post WWII* (Saarbrücken: VDM Verlag, 2009).

[96] Morris, 'Shipping's New Industrial Relations.'

[97] 'Interview with I.T.F. General Secretary … No Cheap Labour "Bolt-Hole" for Shipowners,' *Seamen's Journal* (September 1973): 224–5.

[98] 'Wages and employment conditions of ships' crews signed up to ITF agreements,' N38/290, NBAC; 'Wages and employment conditions of ships' crews signed up to ITF agreements,' MS N38/291; 'Actions taken against FOC vessels,' MS N38/291, NBAC.

[99] Vessels covered by ITF/ITF-approved agreements, Annual Reports, MS Z432, Box 42, NBAC.

maritime nations had representation in the ITF seafarers' section.[100] The ITF also commenced arranging regional forums for Asia-Pacific dockworkers. The Asia-Pacific Regional Dockworkers' conference was summoned in Kuala Lumpur in 1983.[101] Three years later, representatives of the Australian, US, Japanese and New Zealand dockworkers' unions met in Tokyo for a Pacific Area Dockworkers' Seminar.[102] Finally, the dockworkers' unions of the United States and Japan also joined the ITF.

Tas Bull attended the ILWU conference in 1983, and 'as respectfully as possible,' urged them to consider the benefits to themselves and to the ITF of joining, 'because of the kind of solidarity support that we can give to working people,' which he said was an 'investment in our own future and our own security.'[103] Emeritus president Harry Bridges encouraged looking into it, but the old loyalties resurfaced. He also pointed out that the WFTU was a more powerful body and should also be considered. Another delegate spoke from personal experience of having seen the organisation at work on the New Zealand coast: 'It is a marvellous organization for human rights.' The motion to investigate was carried unanimously. Accordingly, in 1985, the union Executive Board formally decided to join the ITF, specifying 'the need for greater coordination and consultation between maritime unions ... given the rapid spread of new technology.' The following year, Jim Herman, the president, attended the ITF for the first time.[104] Finally, in 1996, the Japanese union also joined.

On Fitzgibbon's retirement, the Australian union elected as its new general secretary Norm Docker, who might have been nominated as the communist faction's candidate back in 1961. His term was brief as ill health forced his early retirement, and in 1984 Tas Bull (1932–2003) took over (Figure 11.5). He came from a long line of Norwegian seafarers – both his father and grandfather had inspired a love of seafaring – and he spent his early years crewing out of Tasmania where they had settled and where he was born. He explained his unusual name (Tasnor) came from this joining of Tasmania and Norway. Bull had joined the CPA because of influences

---

[100] ITF, 35th Congress, Luxembourg, 31 July–8 August 1986, Report on Activities for the Years 1983–1984–1985, i–xvii.

[101] Asia/Pacific Regional Dockworkers' Conference, Kuala Lumpur, 1983, http://mrc-catalogue.warwick.ac.uk/records/ITF/DK/1/2/2.

[102] See 1986 Pacific Area Dockworkers' Seminar, Tokyo, http://mrccatalogue.warwick.ac.uk/records/ITF/DK/2/3/20/2.

[103] Tasnor Bull, 'Remarks to Longshore, Clerk and Walking Boss Caucus of the International Longshoremen's and Warehousemen's Union,' 21 April 1983, 5, 14–18, and discussion following, 26–8, ILWU.

[104] 'ILWU Builds Bridges at International Transport Congress,' *Dispatcher*, 14 November 1986, 5; materials on ILWU, http://mrc-catalogue.warwick.ac.uk/records/ITF/DK/2/3/17/2.

from members of the SUA he sailed with.[105] He started work on the Hobart wharves in the mid-1950s, and this experience meant he brought the two sections of the ITF together in a timely conjunction. Bull took up the programme of internationalising the WWF with characteristic gusto. He urged other unions to become affiliates. He became assistant chair of the ITF dockworkers' section and member of the Executive Committee.

At the end of the twentieth century, the Asia–Pacific was the region contributing most to the growth in the ITF. Yet some things had not changed. Tas Bull remarked when writing his memoirs (1998) that the ITF still had only met in the Southern Hemisphere three times. Western Europe was still the largest grouping of affiliates. The Executive Board's decision to hold its 1998 ordinary congress in New Delhi, India, was only the second time it had been held outside Europe and the first ever in a developing country.[106] Two years earlier, NUSI celebrated its centenary, laying claim to a tradition of organising almost as old as the ITF itself by tracing its origins to the Christian Goa Club founded in Bombay. There were 34,000 members of NUSI, and they worked on both Indian-flagged ships as well as FOCs, prompting – indeed enabling – Leo Barnes to claim India ought to be seen as more than a labour-supplying country. In 1987, he became the first Asian seafarer member of the ILO's Joint Maritime Commission.

The ITF's understanding of 'regional activities' had increasingly grown to mean helping unions in developing countries, but a very old problem lingered. As the organisation approached the new millennium and planned its own centenary, it noted 'little concrete progress had so far been made on the measures to combat ... racism and xenophobia,' though discussions were being held about 'including non-discrimination clauses in ITF-approved agreements for seafarers.'[107] In the end, the ITF's most important role was the co-ordination of international solidarity. 'Everything it does is aimed at making it better at delivering that solidarity when it is needed.'[108] Having played such an important activist role in delivering that internationalism, soon the Australian union too was glad of support.

---

[105] Bull, *Life on the Waterfront*, 13–46.
[106] ITF, *Solidarity*, 160–1.
[107] ITF, 'Transport Workers: Beyond 2000,' Progress Report, 26, para. 108.
[108] ITF, 'Transport Workers: Beyond 2000,' Progress Report, 47, para. 223.

11.6 Tasnor Bull in front of portrait of Jim Healy, 1990s
Photographer Patrick Hamilton
© Newspix

12

'Protect[ing] Workers against Shoddy Foreign Companies'

International Labourers and National Unionists,
1960s to 2000

In the mid-1960s, the SUA recognised that 'more and more we in Australia are becoming part of Asia' as Australia's future was tied to Asian economic investment in 'the development of our hemisphere.'[1] Great industrial changes were taking place in shipping, and the union was alerting members to the relationship between their industry and the development of Australia's natural resources, 'our harbours and rivers' and the ports used to ship its resources overseas. Extensive port development was taking place in Western Australia to facilitate the export of iron ore to Japan. A dredge, 'one of the most powerful in the world,' was deepening the approach channel and harbour at Port Hedland so that large bulk carriers could use the port. When it was finished, the tonnage of ships able to use the port would be almost doubled.[2] The union proposed to demand that a percentage of this vast mineral wealth should be carried in Australian ships, with Australian crews, and they embarked on a campaign for an extension of the national shipping line.[3] They simultaneously sought closer ties to unions in the region.

Elliott accordingly reached out to the Japan Seamen's Union, which was ideologically affiliated with the anti-communist ICFTU and the ITF. He had his first meeting with the Japanese union's president while returning from a visit to North Korea in 1967. For these union officials, connection across cold war divides was not easy. It took 'a number of contacts (both in the Japanese and Australian language[s])' before the officials of the JSU agreed to meeting with the SUA secretary.[4]

[1] 'En Route to Korea for May 1 Celebrations,' 110.

[2] J.E. Fitzgerald, Queensland branch secretary, 'Major Role of Shipping in Australia's Development,' *Australian Seamen's Journal* 21, no. 5 (1966): 98–9.

[3] Fitzgerald, 'Major Role of Shipping.'

[4] 'Homeward Bound through Hong Kong and Japan,' *Australian Seamen's Journal* 22, no. 6 (1967): 150.

The Japanese union was larger by comparison (140,000 members), included fishermen, and covered everyone on board except the master, yet ironically the president and the assistant secretary of its International Department were captains, not deck crew as in Australia. Elliott remarked on the use of a limousine, and the modern high-rise building, the president – 'Fortyish, heavy set, hard' – and a conversation that was more of an interrogation: 'how and why I came to Japan, who I knew and who I met.' Elliott encouraged 'the need for closer contact, international relations and assistance etc.' He felt the results of the meeting were 'very superficial' but might in the future prove of value, while a long and informative talk with the dock workers' president Tomitaro Kaneda was 'most enlightening.'[5] In Kaneda's view, 'the All Japan Seamen's Union represents the right wing of [the] Japanese labor movement and is a second self of the Government.'[6] Nevertheless, in a spirit of internationalism transcending ideological divisions, Elliott followed up with the JSU, sending fraternal greetings to the annual convention a few months later. On that initial visit, Elliott also met with other Japanese workers: rank and file seafarers and dockers' union representatives, and talked with them of 'our common problems, of the need for greater understanding and peace.'[7] Six years later, the JSU president visited the SUA headquarters in Sydney (Figure 12.1).

Elliott's overtures towards the JSU were made at the height of a dispute that had erupted in Port Hedland involving members of the JSU who had been brought in to help with the dredging. At the same time, the Australian National Line (ANL) was extending its services beyond the coast, with two Australian-flagged ships on the Australia–Japan route.[8] The unions had actively promoted the idea that ANL should expand internationally to challenge the monopoly of foreign-flag ships in moving cargo between Australia and other countries.[9] Their leaders and members were confident that ANL could effectively provide the basis of a national overseas merchant fleet. That would generate greater employment for an on-shore and seagoing workforce and reduce the exorbitant amounts paid to overseas shipping companies for transporting Australian cargo.[10] The government (and general public) came to develop similar perceptions of ANL's business potential.

---

[5] 'Homeward Bound through HK and Japan.'

[6] Tomitaro Kaneda, President, JDU to Patrick Troy, Secretary, MUA of WA, 24 February 1969, SLWA, Battye Library, MN 862, Records of the Maritime Workers' Union of Western Australia, ACC 3012A-3016A, 5665A.

[7] 'Our Greetings to Japanese Seamen,' *Australian Seamen's Journal* 22, no. 10 (1967): 254; 'Homeward Bound through HK and Japan.'

[8] 'ANL on Overseas Trade Routes,' *Maritime Worker* (9 December 1968): 3.

[9] 'Peace, Socialism, Unity. Triennial Conference,' *Maritime Worker* (21 March 1962): 6.

[10] 'O'seas National Shipping Line – Opponents Have No Argument,' *Seamen's Journal* (1963): 30; 'Forward – An Overseas Line,' *Seamen's Journal* (July 1964): 141–2.

12.1 Crew of *Iron Parkgate* welcome Kogi Murakami, president of All Japan
Seamen's Union, to the SUA, September 1973
Photograph NBAC N38/1064

However, closer business ties to Japan in the Port Hedland development
reignited some older deep-seated concerns in the Australian maritime
unions' struggle for rights. Bringing in contracted labour from Asia raised
the old spectre of indentured labour when the press in early 1965 reported
that 'Japanese experts' were to be allowed in to help with the dredging of
Port Hedland harbour.

'Japanese cheap labour threat'

In the mid-1960s, the White Australia policy was in decline, but restrictions
were still in effect and Asians officially needed to meet strict government
requirements to enter the country. Taking jobs that Australians could do
was not one of those. Only experts – specialists, executives, technicians
needed to operate plants and that were otherwise unobtainable in Australia
– were permitted. Japanese business investors 'considering joint ventures
or independent enterprises' were encountering 'the formidable barrier of
restrictions on the permanent or long-term entry of Japanese ... employees.'[11]
The government therefore made changes to the law to accommodate them
and facilitate the entry of Japanese workers. The Minister for Immigration

[11] 'Trade with Japan May Soon Be More Lopsided,' *Canberra Times*, 5 June 1965, 14.

in the Menzies Liberal–Country Party government gave authority for the entry of Japanese 'technicians' for a limited period and subject to temporary residence status. They were permitted to work under contract on dredging Port Hedland harbour for the Californian Utah Construction Company, requiring only that their employment was to be on the same conditions as Australians.

In federal parliament, the Labor Party wanted the government to ensure that only Australian workers would be employed in the dredging. The government was reassuring that 'if permits were given … they would be subject to Australian award conditions and they would be expected to become members of the relevant Australian trade unions.'[12] Soon the government was defending its decision to allow a limited number of foreign workers on the Port Hedland project: instead of having an all-Japanese crew working under US supervision, 'a suitable ratio for the employees to be used was 20 American, 27 Australians and 20 Japanese.' The press reported that 'The trade union involved had agreed.'[13] This was the Australian Workers' Union. To other unions, who had not been informed, bringing in the Japanese crew 'violate[d] every labour condition tediously established over a hundred years of struggle in Australia.' They objected to imported indentured Japanese labour being used when Australian workers were not being given the opportunity even to apply.[14] Furthermore, the government amended section 102 of the Navigation Act to allow the Japanese to operate tugs, although local tug masters' tickets only enabled them to operate tugs in Western Australia, not in other jurisdictions and certainly not in foreign ports.[15]

Enacting these changes was a strategy for the rapid development of Western Australia's mineral resources that local unionists saw as consistent with the Liberal government's anti-unionism. 'They suspend Australian law so as to make it possible for foreign monopolies to keep out Australian unionism,' WA maritime unionist Paddy Troy said. '[T]hey create situations … [with] no thought for the welfare of the Australian people but only for the profits.'[16] Troy was secretary of the Ship Painters and Dockers (later the Seamen and Dockers), the WA branch of the SUA. He attacked the employment 'of so-called Japanese "specialists"' for being 'a violation of Australian

---

[12] 'Japanese to Help WA Dredging Project,' *Canberra Times*, 21 May 1965, 4.

[13] 'Why We Let in 20 Japanese,' *Canberra Times*, 22 May 1965, 9.

[14] This is elaborated in Murray Shaw, *Bamboo Curtain over Port Hedland: The Anatomy of a Political and Industrial Dispute* (Canning Vale, WA: self-published, 2013).

[15] Letter from Murray Shaw to Trades & Labor Council (WA Section), 14 October 1967, 2, Japanese Indentured Labour, 1960s, ACC3012A-144, SLWA, Perth.

[16] Paddy Troy, reported in 'Jap. Crewmen Take Place of Local Labour,' *Tribune* (Sydney), 2 August 1967, 12.

conditions.'[17] They were in fact 'deck hands, firemen, and a bulldozer driver. All the work performed could be done by workmen already domiciled and unemployed in Australia.' He said a similar Dutch dredge was working in Fremantle, presenting no problems to Australian workers. And the possible shortage of Australian labour willing to do the Port Hedland work had not been shown. Another, the *Western Eagle*, had done a major dredging job at Dampier, manned by locally recruited and otherwise inexperienced labour. However, imported Japanese labour was more attractive to the employers 'because of their indentures': labour turnover on the two-year dredging contract showed the difference. Among the American crew members, it was 100 per cent. Among the Australians, 'because of the poor conditions,' it was 700 per cent. Among the Japanese, the turnover was nil. They had no choice. 'No wonder the indentured workers, unable to protest, were preferred by the employers!'[18] The companies were ensuring a stable workforce, 'no matter how bad the conditions,' by bringing workers 'thousands of miles from home with no opportunity of returning, except through company channels.'[19] Since the early nineteenth century, 'being able to leave the employment' was a crucial component of the legal definition of 'free labour.'[20]

Motions carried by the WA Trades and Labor Council condemned the state and federal governments for collaborating in bringing in overseas workers to replace locals. The *Tribune* reported that the argument that local skilled workers were unavailable was false. Employers and state governments feared a labour market that was favourable to Australian workers would push up wages to compensate for the isolation and difficult conditions.[21] Their goal was to keep a cap on union activity for wage demands.

A prominent Japanese industrialist, Eiichi Ogawa, head of the Japanese company which 'lent' the technicians to work the dredge, visited Australia a few months after the work commenced. He 'dropped a clanger' at a press conference 'that was echoing days after he had gone.' He suggested that 'to counter any labour shortage on iron-ore development projects' and accompanied 'with an equalisation of wages to avoid disturbing Australian labour,' that 'educated Japanese workers should be allowed into WA.' The press reported that Ogawa was 'a trifle peeved' at the slow progress on the dredging job and thought he 'could well have been having a dig at Australian workers and their methods.' Although some of the locals had been surprised with what had been accomplished, the company had expected

---

[17] 'Jap. Crewmen Take Place of Local Labour.'
[18] 'Japanese Cheap Labour Threat in North-West,' *Tribune*, 23 August 1967, 1.
[19] '"Confer" Pledge won on Foreign Labour,' *Tribune*, 30 August 1967, 12.
[20] Quinlan, 'Regulating Labour,' 303–24.
[21] See Shaw, *Bamboo Curtain*, 8.

twice as much. Ogawa said: 'his company could not take on any other dredging jobs on the north-west coast unless it was able to operate under its own conditions.'[22] Pointedly, he drew attention to the significance of the proportion – only one-third – of the 60-man crew working on the *Alameda* dredge who were Japanese. The clanger that reverberated afterwards was his suggestion that as the Japanese were the only market for the iron ore they should be allowed to provide the labour needed: that the mines, ports and railways being developed were effectively 'owned' as theirs.[23]

Two years later, 'feeling was running high in Port Hedland.'[24] as the original workers went home to Japan at the end of their contracts and it became clear that even more were now coming on a new dredge (*Kokuei Maru*, no. 1). The non-Japanese workers on the original dredge now went on strike in protest at this news of an all-Japan crew and the expansion of numbers of Japanese labourers to 60 or more.[25] The strikers claimed that this was 'not a racial question but is opposition to indentured labour being introduced into Australia.'[26] The unions were making it clear that their opposition was 'to cheap labour, not to Japanese workers as such,' and they called for the Japanese workers to be repatriated and compensated.[27] The previous year, rank and file SUA members in Darwin had been joined by Japanese seamen marching on May Day, after which they had adjourned to drink together in the Workers' Club. The crew of the *Baralga* and *B P Endeavour* then wrote, as SUA members, to the JSU members crewing the MS *Nagashima Maru*, optimistic of better understanding, 'regardless of nationality.' In a veiled reference to the 1942 bombing of Darwin, and what historians have described as 'the long shadow cast by Japan's brutality to Australian POWs,' they spoke of war that was driven by 'narrow-minded national prejudices' as they instead extended 'the hand of working-class friendship and mutual co-operation' to their 'working-class compatriots.'[28]

The strike now engulfing them began with dredge men, members of the AWU, and several Merchant Services Guild tug masters, while 'support and practical help' came from the SUA WA branch and particular crews on the *Iron Warrior*, *Koojarra* and *Yarrunga*.[29] They were joined by members of the

[22] 'In WA this Week Mr O. Drops a Brick,' *Canberra Times*, 25 September 1965, 2.

[23] *West Australian*, 18 September 1965, quoted in Shaw, *Bamboo Curtain*, 22, which also quotes the responses.

[24] '"Confer" Pledge won on Foreign Labour.'

[25] 'Port Strike,' *Canberra Times*, 23 September 1967, 3.

[26] '"Confer" Pledge won on Foreign Labour.'

[27] 'Japanese Cheap Labour Threat in North-West.'

[28] 'Message to Japanese Seamen in Darwin Again Makes History,' *Australian Seamen's Journal* 21, no. 5 (1966): 99; Walker and Sobocinska, *Australia's Asia*, 3.

[29] 'Port Hedland Dispute: Guild Thanks Seamen,' *Australian Seamen's Journal* 22, no. 12

Boilermakers' Union, the Amalgamated Engineering Union, the Australian Workers' Union and the Electrical Trades Union, although workers at the Mount Newman dredging project voted to continue working with the Japanese labourers.[30] It became an 'on-again off-again struggle' spanning several years, involving the WA Trades and Labor Council and the state and Commonwealth governments.

The CPA paper *Tribune* stirred matters by using language referencing the war, calling the arrival of the second dredge 'a second Japanese invasion of Australia,' and describing it as 'the establishment of a beach-head of indentured labour.'[31] The crux of the strikers' argument was that there was no need for overseas labour. 'If we don't make a stand now, what is to stop them from coming in to work the mines and so on?'[32] It 'could lead to the use of many more Japanese contract workers at other development projects financed by foreign capital.'[33] The mainstream Perth press concurred: '[I]t is wrong to import foreign workers – whether they are Japanese, American or European – under contract or indenture to do jobs that Australians could do.' Important principles were being ignored. Utah Dredging Company's refusal to be questioned by the press indicated its main interests seemed to be to get 'a captive labour force ... and to defer to its Japanese partner which owns the dredge.' The Commonwealth government 'appears only to have thought of immigration technicalities' and the state government was apathetic and failing to take a stand.[34]

The WA Trades and Labor Council secretary Jim Coleman 'feared the introduction of Japanese labour at Port Hedland was a test case' that could set a precedent. The Japanese contractors had been enabled 'to abrogate Australian law, wages, conditions and trade union practice.' A letter from the Department of Labour and National Service revealed that the initial six months' entry permits were renewable for periods of four months, thus enabling continuing extensions 'to the detriment of Australians ... on Australian wages and conditions.'[35] Furthermore, while the new Japanese vessel was to be fully manned by a Japanese crew, the previous dredge was to be docked and overhauled in Singapore – also 'a job which could and

---

(1967): 323; letter to TLC (WA) signed by 20 crew on the *Alameda*, members of AWU and five members of MSG, 26 August 1967, copy sent to P. Troy. ACC3012A-144, SLWA, Perth.

[30] '350 Strike over Japanese,' *Canberra Times*, 30 September 1967, 1.

[31] 'Japanese Cheap Labour Threat in North-West.'

[32] 'Japanese Cheap Labour Threat in North-West'; letter to *West Australian*.

[33] 'Boos, Jeers at Japanese Dredge Workers,' *Canberra Times*, 29 September 1967, 7.

[34] 'Principles Ignored,' *West Australian* (Perth), 24 August 1967; Murray Shaw wrote, congratulating him, 'it captured our sentiments exactly.' Murray Shaw to G. Richards, editor, *West Australian* (Perth), 5 September 1967, ACC3012A-144, SLWA, Perth.

[35] 'Japanese Cheap Labour Threat in North-West.'

should be done at Fremantle.'[36] Importing overseas labour 'should not have been envisaged before consultation and agreement with the trade union movement.'[37]

The erosion of Australian labour conditions was demonstrated in the lack of credentials being required of the imported labourers. Australian tug skippers had completed three years' 'sea time,' had passed exams, and were required to 'have local knowledge of any port in which they are employed.' These skilled and trained personnel were to be replaced by imported labour which did not have to meet these requirements. 'Americans and Japanese have and still do operate tugs without any qualifications. They are not members of the local union, require no local knowledge and disregard the safety practices which are 50 per cent of the examinations for Harbour and Lights qualifications.'[38] Consequently, the WA Trades and Labor Council decided by an overwhelming majority 'to condemn State and Commonwealth governments for collaborating in the use of indentured Japanese labor at Port Hedland.' They demanded that WA projects use Australian labour; that the Japanese workers on the dredges be repatriated, compensated adequately and paid an additional 13 weeks' wages at current Australian rates.[39]

The strikers' stand brought the Utah company president from the United States to seek a settlement.[40] Finally, union pressure forced the American–Japanese combine Utah–Jild [Japanese International Land Development] to guarantee that Japanese workers would only be employed if Australians were not available.[41] Dredge men and tug masters went back to work, claiming 'a 100 p.c. win in their stand for the employment of Australians.' The terms agreed to included the repatriation of the Japanese, the training of Australians to replace them and no victimisation of the strikers.[42] However, the leader of the strike, tug master Murray Shaw, was squeezed out of the industry. Troy subsequently paid tribute to the striking dredge men but particularly Shaw, who had never given up and 'without doubt [had made] the most inspiring contribution' of all.[43]

---

[36] Paddy Troy, quoted in 'Jap. Crewmen Take Place of Local Labour.'

[37] 'Jap. Crewmen Take Place of Local Labour.'

[38] 'Japanese Cheap Labour Threat in North-West.' They were nominally, at least, members of the AWU, not the maritime unions, the MSG, the SUA or the Seamen and Dockers Union led by Paddy Troy. When he tried to sign them up, the Industrial Commission ruled against it. Shaw, *Bamboo Curtain*, 145.

[39] 'Japanese Cheap Labour Threat in North-West.'

[40] 'Americans in Dredge Clash,' *Canberra Times*, 28 September 1967, 1.

[41] 'Guarantee Won on Japanese Labor,' *Tribune* (Sydney), 4 October 1967, 12.

[42] 'Win All the Way at Port Hedland,' *Tribune* (Sydney), 24 April 1968, 1.

[43] Letter, P. Troy to K. Hull, 23 April 1968, Japanese Indentured Labour, 1960s, ACC3012A-144, SLWA, Perth.

12.2 Japanese workers (JSU members) walking through Australian
union picket line, Port Hedland, 1967
Photograph © West Australian Newspapers Ltd

In writing his account of the events decades later, Shaw emphasised the
deception, secrecy and collusion he had discovered between the companies,
employer association and government departments that had converted
him into a strike leader. His union, the Merchant Services Guild, later
Maritime Officers' Union, was not previously known for its militancy. The
unions that were – the SUA and the WWF – played only an auxiliary role,
attending meetings and donating to strike funds, although the Fremantle-
based Ship Painters and Dockers under Paddy Troy's leadership played a
significant part.

The Japanese dredge men, however, were also unionists, members of the JSU, who in Australia joined the AWU (Figure 12.2). The JSU officials in Japan kept a watch on events unfolding, visited their members in Australia and wrote directly to the WA Trades and Labor Council secretary Coleman to confirm their understanding of the issues. Their letter expressed a wish that the Trades and Labor Council might help their members find a way to work in peace in Western Australia. It concluded with a reminder that their organisations were brothers under the banner of the ICFTU, and also with the AWU.[44] Subsequently, the JSU invited Coleman to visit Japan and discuss the issues. His report presented to the Trades and Labor Council painted a more favourable impression than Elliott's had done to the SUA the year before. Coleman concentrated on his conversations with Japanese union officials, who said they 'fully accepted the Australian unions' position and policies,' and had never intended 'to disturb our interests and rights in any way.' They were, however, confused by the change from the AWU's original approval of Japanese labour being used.[45]

Coleman's observations on other Japanese workplaces, comparing their labour standards with Australia's, was published in the *West Australian*.[46] Paddy Troy promptly wrote to the Japanese Dockworkers' Union president, Kaneda, asking him to comment, so that facts 'are properly known to the people of Australia': 'Certainly it is a very different picture to that which I gained through reading' *DCC News* (which Kaneda edited).[47] In reply, Kaneda confirmed that the story about Japanese working conditions was biased by the political leanings of the JSU: 'the information given by this union ... is not necessarily correct.'[48]

This dispute illustrated how complex region and race were as shaping factors in maritime union activism in the second half of the twentieth century. The conflict was not with the workers, who were also unionists, or the fact they were Japanese, and when the strike was over they all shared a jug of

[44] Ryo Kamisawa, International Affairs Dept., JSU, to J.W. Coleman, TLC, 15 November 1967, ACC3012A-144, SLWA, Perth.

[45] J.S. Coleman, Report to the TLC, Executive Members, Circular No. 2/1969, 24 January 1969, ACC3012A-144, SLWA, Perth. See also correspondence from JSU to AWU, 1st July 1968, ACC3012A-144, SLWA, Perth.

[46] 'Working Conditions in Japan Praised,' *West Australian*, December 1968. A full account of his visit was presented to the TLC, Executive Members, Circular No. 2/1969, 24 January 1969, ACC3012A-144, SLWA, Perth.

[47] Paddy Troy to Tomitaro Kaneda, Report of All Pacific and Asian Dockworkers' Corresponding Committee, 8 January 1969, SLWA, Battye Library, MN 862, Records of the Maritime Workers' Union of Western Australia, ACC 3012A-3016A, 5665A.

[48] Tomitaro Kaneda, President JDU, to Patrick Troy, Secretary, MUA of WA, 24 February 1969, Battye Library, MN 1327, Papers of Patrick (Paddy) Troy, ACC 4154A, 4779A, 8339A.

beer.[49] But the dispute had brought the trade unions' long opposition to the introduction of indentured labour once again into view with all its echoes of past references to cheap Asian labourers.[50] Government policies were helping a continuing 'relentless push to import cheap foreign labour ... for the benefit of Australian businesses at the expense of Australian workers.'[51] It actually exposed how 'shoddy foreign companies' like the Utah–Jild partnership treated organised workers and were changing the landscape for Australian labour. Sometimes, as in the case of ANL, Australian businesses too were disadvantaged in the new world of multinational globalised capital.

National merchant fleet v. flag of convenience shipping

The ANL's penetration into international shipping markets coincided with the dramatic rise of flag of convenience shipping. The WWF and the SUA action in the ITF-orchestrated battle against FOCs was pursued in their own interests but also benefited Australian national shipping, in particular the ANL. Some users of shipping services preferred to chart Australian-flag vessels on Australian sea routes due to the possible delays in local ports caused by union boycotts if they used flagged-out vessels. Furthermore, higher crew wages on ships gained by the ITF benefited Australian shipowners by reducing foreign competitiveness.[52]

In 1974, the SUA and the WWF joined with their New Zealand counterparts to impose partial protective measures for the national shipping of both countries. The unions' officials signed an accord to keep the trans-Tasman trade for Australian- and New Zealand-crewed ships only.[53] That agreement effectively prevented foreign flag vessels from penetrating into Australia–New Zealand sea routes. Even though the governments of both countries were critical, the unions' accord helped to increase demand for Australian vessels, including those of the ANL,[54] whose market share in the trans-Tasman trade increased more than fivefold in the years 1980 to 1986.[55]

The SUA also placed a total ban on the employment of FOC vessels in the coal trade in New South Wales in 1981 when virtually no Australian-

[49] Shaw, *Bamboo Curtain*, 128. Efforts were made to recruit them to the SUA.

[50] 'Guarantee Won on Japanese Labor,' *Tribune* (Sydney), 4 October 1967, 12.

[51] Shaw, *Bamboo Curtain*.

[52] Laffer, 'Australian Maritime Unions and the International Transport Workers Federation,' 127.

[53] 'Australian and N.Z. Unions Agree on Trans-Tasman Trade,' *Seamen's Journal* 28, no. 2 (February 1974): 29–30.

[54] Spiers, *Default to Decline*, 200.

[55] Australian Bureau of Transport Economics, *Review of Trans-Tasman Shipping* (Canberra: AGPS Press, 1987): 171.

flag vessels were engaged in exporting coal. The union boycott continued for seven years during which time all New South Wales coal was exported only in non-FOC vessels, which included ANL bulk carriers.[56] Many stop-work meetings of waterside workers called on the union's Federal Council to fully support the SUA in the struggle to maintain an Australian shipping industry and the ANL.[57] Some WWF branches also took direct action in support of the seafarers.[58]

With pragmatic acknowledgement of the economic importance of the ANL, not only for the union membership but for the whole national economy, the SUA and the WWF were consistent in ensuring that the ANL operated as a profitable shipping enterprise. The degree of union assistance grew over time in response to the mounting difficulties of the ANL. The unions' support became an important factor in the company's financial survival. The SUA summarised these efforts thus:

> [Being] protected from industrial disputes, the Union has fought overseas shipowners to assist the entry and maintenance of ANL in overseas trade; our members have given hundreds of thousands of dollars and willingly given their free time and energy ... we have applied political pressure to protect and develop the Australian National Line.[59]

The campaign was not without cost to the Australian unions. By 1979, the L-NP coalition government, this time under Prime Minister Malcolm Fraser, was once again amending the law – both the Navigation Act and the Arbitration Act – to constrain union militancy further. Seafarers were then describing the Navigation Act as 'one of the most vicious pieces of legislation to be drawn up against a group of Australian workers.' The Navigation Act 1912 had been amended several times over the decades, always by conservative governments, and each time in conjunction with penal sanctions and more limitations being imposed on trade unions in the arbitration court. The 1970s amendments gave even more power to the employers. 'Sections of the Act are unjust and one-sided and should have been removed years ago,' an SUA member wrote. Most disturbingly, penalties made seamen's rights of defence very limited or non-existent when

[56] Australian Seagoing Unions' Press Release, MS Z129/21, NBAC; Clifford B. Donn and G. Phelan, 'Australian Maritime Unions and Flag of Convenience Vessels,' *Journal of Industrial Relations*, 33, no. 3 (1991): 336; Australian Shipping Commission, Australian National Line, Annual Report (1982), 7; (1983), 11.

[57] WWF Federal Council Meeting, September 1983, Resolutions of stop-work meeting submitted for consideration of Council, MUA Library (Sydney).

[58] WWF Federal Council Meeting, September 1984, Officers' reports, MUA Library (Sydney).

[59] 'C.O.M. Minutes,' *Seamen's Journal* 39, no. 4 (April 1984): 93.

they were fined and logged by the master. 'We have not got the right to refuse to pay a fine if we think we were dealt with unjustly … [fines] can be deducted from your wages,' without consent.[60]

Other provisions of anti-union legislation introduced by the Fraser government were amendments to the Trade Practices Act, introduced by Minister for Industrial Relations, John Howard. This Act, notably under section 45, was to be an effective tool in curbing solidarity protest actions by imposing a financial penalty on unions striking when they were not directly parties to a dispute. Provisions under this legislation were also used against the maritime unions engaging in FOC actions.

In 1985, the Australian Federal Court ordered the WWF's funds to be frozen. The court was hearing a suit that had been brought against the union by Green Island Cement Ltd, a company registered in the Panama Republic and managed from Hong Kong. The company was operating the ship *Sea Prosperity* with crew from Third World countries recruited by a Philippines manning agent. The actual owner of the FOC was unknown.[61] The legal action was, however, national. It was precipitated in the Australian court because the WWF and the SUA, for the ITF, had negotiated and retrieved back pay of the equivalent of AU$312,500 when the *Sea Prosperity* was docked in the Queensland port of Townsville. They had sent these funds through to the ITF headquarters in London for distribution to present and previous crew members. The suit for damages was brought against all of them: the WWF, the SUA, the ITF and two individuals, the ITF inspector and an SUA port delegate. The company could do so under section 82 of the Trade Practices Act 1974, which allowed that loss or damage incurred by another person acting in contravention of the Act could be recovered. This legislation had been amended several years previously, specifically to incorporate measures that would inhibit union activism.

The SUA's assistant federal secretary, Patrick 'Taffy' Sweetensen, declared it was wrong: 'when we are trying to protect workers against shoddy foreign companies … [and] those vessels trading in Australian ports operate under absolutely atrocious conditions' that shipowners had the power of 'a shaky Australian law' to use against them. The maritime unions threatened militant action, the Australian Chamber of Shipping warned that stoppages would cause 'costly delays to vital export shipments.'[62]

In essential respects, these were the customary battle lines that had been drawn for much of the twentieth century. The strong determination

---

[60] H. Leonard, 'Navigation Act Vicious, Biased,' *Seamen's Journal* 34, no. 8 (1979): 247.

[61] 'Waterside Workers' Funds Frozen. Unions Impose Shipping Bans,' *Canberra Times*, 4 January 1985, 3.

[62] 'Waterside Workers' Funds Frozen.'

12.3 Mike Fleming (AMOU), Paddy Crumlin and John Coombs (MUA) and
Dave Morgan (NZSU), at ITF Asia-Pacific conference, Manila [1990]
Courtesy MUA

of organised seafarers and dockworkers to claim and defend minimum
labour standards and their rights with militant action was being met
with opposition from shipowning businesses and business organisations.
They were often helped along by laws passed by anti-labour governments
committed to the removal of labour protections and refusing to acknowledge
workers' collective rights. The previous two decades had seen significant new
developments that shaped this struggle and the complex internationalism
of the shipowning enterprise shows what the unions were up against when
protecting labour standards. By the 1980s new business structures were
complicated and obscure, generated by technological and structural shifts in
the maritime sector that made the focus of struggle both more difficult and
necessarily internationalised.

What they could not do was run the shipping industry. Even though
the decision to make ANL an international carrier was logical in principle,
implementation was poor and managerial execution 'politically and commer-
cially mishandled.'[63] The SUA could not save the national carrier when it

---

[63] Interview with David Looker, ANL Marketing Manager, 4 April 2018. The demise
of ANL and its ultimate sale is told in Dmytro Ostapenko, '"Communists They May Have
Been": Australian Maritime Unionists and the National Shipping Line, c.1950–90,' *Labour
History* 116 (2019): 57–81.

fell victim to neo-liberal government policies and a final sell-off by the incoming (in 1996) L-NP government under John Howard, architect of the Trade Practices Act amendments. This was a hard-right government with an anti-union workplace reform agenda. Howard had the maritime unions, especially the wharf labourers, firmly in view in his determination to smash unions, what former WWF organiser Greg Combet called 'an ideological preoccupation with deep roots' in Australia's political history 'dressed up as an issue of workplace productivity on the docks.'[64] Soon, the international progressive press was announcing 'class war has engulfed Australian ports' as a 'battle on the docks' was taking place in Australia.[65]

Supporting the wharfies in every worker's fight

Union-bashing was not new and had worked politically for the previous L-NP governments of Robert Menzies (1949–66) and Malcolm Fraser (1975–83), and before them Stanley Bruce (1923–29). Now in this post-cold war era, long after communist leadership could be a disruptive force, the Howard government's 'clandestine machinations' in league with the private employer (Patrick Stevedores) echoed the 'secrecy, deception and collusion' that had prompted the Port Hedland strike of the late 1960s. As the government set out to destroy trade unionism and shift the balance of power irrevocably from labour to capital, they had the waterfront directly in their sights. 'Ports have become a universal testing ground for trashing guarantees of job security, slashing wages and eliminating unions,' United States-based journalist David Bacon wrote, and it was now happening in Australia.[66]

The April 1998 waterfront dispute – which began just on 30 years after the Port Hedland dispute ended – stands out as an emblematic confrontation. This was 'the strike that changed Australia,' that became 'a massive battle' so important that today 'few Australians will have forgotten.'[67] Its significance was more far-reaching than the Australian waterfront. A US reporter recognised 'the battle on the docks' was 'being fought on behalf of millions of workers to whom this global vision seems like a nightmare.' He said, 'Not only in Australia but across the world the docks are the arena where neoliberalism meets resistance from below.' From Liverpool to New Zealand, to Mexico and Japan, dockers were fighting against 'the inequality of power in a world in which giant conglomerates dictate economic direction

---

[64] Combet, *The Fights of My Life*, 75.
[65] David Bacon, in *The Nation* (New York), 18 May 1998, 6.
[66] Bacon, in *The Nation*, 18 May 1998, 6.
[67] Max Ogden, *A Long View from the Left* (Melbourne: Bad Apple Press, 2020).

to country after country.'[68] A Port Workers' Charter had been adopted at the ITF Congress in Rotterdam in 1990 in response to 'clear evidence of a general attack by certain European governments and port employers on the working conditions and job security of port workers' by adoption of 'unregulated casualization and exploitation.'[69] In 1995, New Zealand waterside workers were still in a five-year battle when they called on ITF support in their fight against another orchestrated move to de-unionise the workforce by a coalition of government, business and primary producers' organisations.[70]

These events in Australia revealed what happened when capital concentration, technological modernisation and structural shifts in the global maritime sectors in the late twentieth century tended to undermine the historically strong bargaining power of Western maritime unions. Erland Linst, a Swedish trade union leader, reportedly warned striking Sydney waterside workers 'If you lose this fight ... the [tactics] will move to other countries in Europe and the United States.' The implication was 'If longshoremen, historically among the most militant and best-organised workers, can be forced to accept this, every union is vulnerable.'[71]

A rich seam of academic and popular writing recounts in detail how the dispute evolved as a secret conspiracy of the government and was shaped by various economic and political actors.[72] Had the MUA lost the struggle the result would have ultimately empowered the government and disadvantaged

[68] Bacon, in *The Nation*, 18 May 1998, 6.

[69] ITF, European Port Workers Charter, 1990, MS 648/DK/2/3/20/2, MRC.

[70] 'Casualization and Non-Union Labour in New Zealand Ports,' ITF Circular No. 175/S.70/SS.29/D.41/1995, 6 July 1995, MS 648/DK/2/3/2/3, MRC.

[71] Bacon, in *The Nation*, 18 May 1998, 6.

[72] Graeme Orr, 'Conspiracy on the Waterfront,' *Australian Journal of Labour Law*, 11 (1998): 159–85; John Wiseman, 'Here to Stay? The 1997–1998 Australian Waterfront Dispute and Its Implications,' *Labour & Industry: A Journal of the Social and Economic Relations of Work* 9, no. 1 (1998): 1–16; Braham Dabscheck, 'The Waterfront Dispute: Of Vendetta and the Australian Way,' *Economic and Labour Relations Review* 9, no. 2 (1998): 155–87; B. Dabscheck, 'The Australian Waterfront Dispute and Theories of the State,' *Journal of Industrial Relations* 42, no. 2 (2000): 407–516; Richard Morris, 'A Watershed on the Australian Waterfront? The 1998 Stevedoring Dispute,' *Maritime Policy & Management* 27, no. 2 (2000): 107–20; Stuart Macintyre, 'The Third Time as Rodomontade,' *Overland* 150 (1998): 5–10; C. Sheil, 'Trade Unions, Individual Contracts and the MUA's Doppelganger,' *Journal of Australian Political Economy* 59 (2007): 95–117; C. Sheil, 'The Productivity Commission and the Waterfront Dispute: A Cautionary Tale,' *Journal of Australian Political Economy* 79 (2017): 39–64; Helen Trinca and Ann Davies, *Waterfront: The Battle That Changed Australia* (Sydney: Doubleday, 2000); Caroline Smith, 'Internationalising Industrial Disputes: The Case of the Maritime Union of Australia,' *Employee Relations* 32, no. 6 (2010): 557–73. See also Rowan Cahill, 'Maritime Internationalism,' *The Guardian* (CPA), 12 March 1999, www.academia.edu/9121812/Maritime_Internationalism.

12.4 MUA official addresses newly arrived supporters, fellow unionists from
the Building Workers' Union, MUA waterfront dispute, April 1998
Photographer Francis Reiss. National Library of Australia

other Australian unions. Collective interest led others to act in support of
the MUA. Nationally, non-maritime unionists and community activists
from all corners provided a vital source of support.

> A thousand protesters in Fremantle met police, attack dogs and
> club-wielding guards who tried to escort scab trucks out of the terminals.
> In Brisbane twenty strikers chained themselves to railroad tracks to
> stop the cargo. More than 2,500 dockers and supporters in Melbourne
> marched on [Minister] Reith's office. Workers from other unions, and
> even other countries, defied bans on solidarity pickets and stepped into
> the places of M.U.A. strikers constrained by injunctions.[73]

Their active involvement in the dispute – which was leaving 'more than
11,000 containers, holding 30,000 tons of cargo, [to] sit stranded on the
Melbourne and Sydney docks' – helped to transform the industrial conflict
into a mass-scale public protest. The government's hardline ideology did not
accord with the public's. Among members of the business community who

---

[73] Bacon, in *The Nation*, 18 May 1998, 6.

were appalled at the government's actions was P&O, a competitor on the waterfront who was not prepared to use the same tactics and to do so at the behest of the government.[74]

This great willingness of domestic non-maritime organised labour to back up the MUA in 1998 reflected the central historical role the WWF and the SUA had taken in the national and international labour movement. Maritime unionists had continually held executive positions in the ACTU. They had engaged in various actions of working-class solidarity and had a long history of participation in many social campaigns for disarmament, Aboriginal land rights and environmental protection, which consequently provided the opportunity to forge strong links with associated social and community groups. They had acted decisively to combat a negative perception created by decades of L-NP legislative agendas and the conservative media's portrayals of unionists as obstructionist, self-centred and communist. Before their amalgamation, the WWF and SUA in the 1980s had actively cooperated with the then Labor government to advance a national shipping economic agenda. They strategically ran large-scale public campaigns to increase public awareness of the importance of Australia's shipping enterprise, thereby positioning themselves as socially conscious organisations whose members worked for the benefits of the nation.

The MUA was also able to call on a wide pool of international support to mount a broad and powerful opposition in a very short time. This too was based on strategic alliances and actions taken by the preceding generations of Australian maritime unionists. The ILWU had a long and close association with the WWF and got involved instantly, within hours of Patricks firing their workforce. Seven ILWU leaders, including the president Bruce McWilliams, were arrested as dozens of people picketed outside the Australian consulate in San Francisco.[75] The ILWU took other actions, holding up ships coming from Australia, or forcing them to bypass west coast US ports, and inviting Australian unionist Max Ogden, who was travelling in the United States at the time, to speak about the dispute to the ILWU annual conference.[76]

Help also came from the ITF with its global association of transport workers' unions. As Tas Bull had told the ILWU in 1983, the ITF was 'an international which acts in solidarity and organizes action in support of affiliates who are in difficulty ... a genuine international prepared to stand up.'[77] The WWF's long collaboration and continuing important role in the

[74] Combet, *The Fights of My Life*, 94.
[75] Bacon, in *The Nation*, 18 May 1998, 6.
[76] Ogden, *Long View from the Left*.
[77] Bull, Remarks to Longshore, Clerk and Walking Boss Caucus of the International

ITF structure was now called on. The ITF had used its muscle in Dubai the previous year so that United Arab Emirates authorities cancelled the visas of those ex-military personnel Patricks was training there to replace the unionised waterfront workforce in Australia. The scheme collapsed. With its hundreds of affiliates all around the world, the ITF threatened to launch a global industrial action in defence of the MUA. The National Farmers' Federation thought the ITF was a 'paper tiger,' but it was a threat to be taken seriously given the great power of international labour and the long history of the ITF's transnational industrial campaigns. Stevedores in overseas ports refused to unload cargo that had been loaded by non-union labour. Ships were returned to ports; some containers returned to shippers who had been able to sell the contents to other buyers; the contents of some other containers were destroyed.[78]

This was a full-scale and brutal attack on unionised dockworkers, 'men not inclined towards a backward step when it comes to defending their industrial conditions.'[79] The MUA mobilised a powerful resistance with careful strategies. They had good leadership in John Coombs, 'mildly spoken ... humble in his aspirations ... but a strong and courageous leader in the tough and demanding unionism of the waterfront,' who had taken on the role of general secretary in 1993.[80] Strong support came from Jenny George and Bill Kelty of the ACTU and its resources. Greg Combet recalls the three elements that were keys to their success. 'We knew our cause was right ... we displayed solidarity ... [there was] planning and execution ... At the centre of that, the legal strategy was critical.' Summing it up, Combet writes: 'a sense of purpose and collective discipline ... The labour movement is at its best when it displays these characteristics.'[81] Combet gives full credit to the great legal team because ultimately the MUA won their case in the Federal Court, which also found there was the probability of a conspiracy.

The MUA – 'the backbone of the labour movement' – survived the government-orchestrated attack in 1998, preventing a loss that would impact on other unions and socially progressive movements nationally. The rousing mantra, 'MUA! Here to Stay!' was born. As Tom Walsh had said back in 1925, 'We got what we have here because we were prepared to fight.' The

---

Longshoremen's and Warehousemen's Union, 21 April 1983, 5, ILWU.

78 Steve O'Neill, Australia, Department of the Parliamentary Library, Information and Research Services (1998), 'The Waterfront Dispute: From High Court to Settlement, Summary and Comment, Canberra: Department of the Parliamentary Library (unpag.).

79 Combet, *The Fights of My Life*, 72.

80 Paddy Crumlin, 'Vale John Coombs,' 1 September 2021; Combet, *The Fights of My Life*, 80.

81 Combet, *The Fights of My Life*, 93.

12.5 Public rally of supporters listening to Leigh Hubbard, secretary, Trades Hall
Council, Melbourne, April 1998
Photographer Jessie Marlow. H99.23/11 SLV

fight to defend minimum standards and rights to union organisation would
be carried into the twenty-first century.

By the time of the 1998 strike the older waterfront precincts were
redeveloped and transformed into tourist precincts or high-rise housing
estates. Technology had transformed much of the maritime workplace
and removed most of the workforce, which brought new challenges to the
members of ships' crews and port gangs. While they suffered the shrinkage
and fragmentation of their membership base and, as an inevitable result, the
reduction of their traditionally strong industrial power, the maritime unions
nevertheless retained their determination as 'true-blue internationalists' to
combat global capitalism's power and impact on workers' lives. In 2016, the
MUA amalgamated with the Construction Forestry Mining and Electrical
Union in a move to preserve their hard-won union power.

13

Conclusion

In the 1990s, prominent Indian unionist Leo Barnes was claiming, 'The seamen's lot is not yet an enviable one.'[1] The vast majority of Asian seafarers were employed on foreign-flagged ships given the numbers looking for work and the shortage of national ships. Stories of shipowners going bankrupt and crew members being abandoned in foreign ports without pay were becoming more common. Many major problems remained to be tackled and seafarers faced anomalies, difficulties and complexities in the bewildering plethora of laws that applied to them. Implementing a single seafarers' code for simplified and easily enforceable laws was 'the most important need of the hour,' still to be achieved. Barnes' comments were reminiscent of the 'economic helplessness' and 'unfreedom' of seafarers that US and Australian observers had noted of their own conditions at the start of the twentieth century. Their efforts to establish international safeguards for their international industry were, however, paying off.

That seafarers had rights was finally encoded in the ILO Maritime Labour Convention (MLC) 2006 (No. 186). It was a century since Australia's Hughes' Royal Commission (1906) exposed unacceptable conditions on British ships and insisted on Australian standards that would influence the UK Merchant Shipping Act 1906. The ILO's 65th maritime convention laid down minimum requirements regarding employment (wages and age of recruitment), standards on board (accommodation and recreational facilities) and health (medical care) and welfare (social security).[2] It represented a major breakthrough in comparison with previous international labour standards. MLC 2006 was comprehensive in its design to protect the world's

---

[1] Barnes, *Sea of Change*, 97–8.

[2] Patrick Bolle, 'The ILO's New Convention on Maritime Labour: An Innovation Instrument,' *International Labour Review* 145, no. 1–2 (2006): 135–42.

more than 1.2 million seafarers, and its format, content and procedures were highly innovative.[3]

MLC 2006 was the culmination of the decades of activism by the ITF and its affiliated maritime organisations, the end point of the trajectory that had moved from enacting labour protections in an imperial frame to enshrining rights in a global forum that has been the theme of this book. A lack of rights increased a Master's capacity to discipline and punish seagoing labour. The unions' push to redress this power imbalance at sea, with a system of enforceable regulations, was the achievement of Australia's and New Zealand's earlier initiatives and was now captured in the ILO's latest convention. MLC 2006 consolidated the many previous ILO conventions, but recognised the close correlation between social, safety, working and living conditions on board ship, and explicitly identified improvements.

While it laid down important protections for seafarers, Article IV for the first time used the language of rights – to a safe and secure workplace; fair terms of employment; decent living and working conditions; and various forms of health and social protections. This was a major achievement for seafarers. In the negotiations leading up to the new convention the shipowners wanted the word 'rights' removed. According to the shipowners' representative, 'this convention is not a Bill of Rights for seafarers, but rather a consolidation of minimum maritime labor standards and the term "rights" should not be used.' The seafarers' group's position was the opposite – that the 'term "rights" should be used.' They wanted serious breaches of 'seafarer rights,' as set out in the convention, to be grounds to detain a vessel from sailing.[4] After one occasion when shipowners were being recalcitrant, the seafarers' group stood up as a block and walked out of the meeting. They got their way.

In 2006, another milestone was reached when MUA national secretary Paddy Crumlin became chair of the ITF dockers' section, co-chair of the pivotal Fair Practices Committee regulating labour standards in agreements on over 10,000 ships, and in 2010 was elected international president. The ITF, with offices in Delhi, Sydney and Tokyo, now represents over one million transport workers, covers 39 countries, and has the largest transport union membership outside of Europe. The first of its listed objectives is to increase union membership.[5]

---

[3] Bolle, ILO's New Convention. For a more critical appraisal, see Paul Bauer, 'The Maritime Labour Convention: An Adequate Guarantee of Seafarer Rights, or an Impediment to True Reforms?' *Chicago Journal of International Law* 8, no. 2 (2008): 643–59.

[4] Quoted in Lillie, *A Global Union for Global Workers*, 114 (Table 6.2).

[5] ITF Asia-Pacific, 'Solidarity with Transport Unions in Asia-Pacific,' www.itfglobal.org/en/region/itf-asia-pacific.

This study has shown how regional distribution of seafarers crewing the world fleets changed over the course of the twentieth century. OECD countries have declined in importance as labour suppliers, and open-registries, with their multinational crews, have increased. Shipowning companies able to employ foreign crews at their local rather than OECD wage rates reduced labour costs, avoided or minimised their taxes, and diminished the recruitment of highly qualified officers from traditional maritime countries.[6] Region and race have been critical factors in shaping this history of maritime unions navigating the globalising shipping industry. The locus of seafarer recruitment shifted to the Asia-Pacific and Australia's regional position gave its maritime unions a unique perspective from which to bring influence internationally.

Organisations of maritime labourers under the ITF umbrella have always identified as *international* workers while they sought to retain protections to *national* shipping and national labour standards, simultaneously building a movement of global solidarity that was able to meet the challenges they faced locally. Applying national minimum labour standards to all, 'regardless of race or country,' was a means of protection for both local and international labour. Protests had begun on the Australian coast in the late nineteenth century with racialised categories of workers which were hard to reconcile with their commitment to the norms of an egalitarian, democratic labour movement – international brotherhood, tolerance of diversity and adoption of common goals. Over the course of the twentieth century, unionists struggled with their differences. The language of racialisation altered but the problem of shipowners cheapening labour costs through recruitment of unprotected labour, usually from poorer regions of the world, continued to undermine the working conditions of maritime workforces across the lines of colour. The question posed by the *Westralian Worker* back in 1925 – 'Is a coolie standard inevitable?' – remained alive to be fought whenever governments and business interests sought to drive down labour's wages and conditions.

A major theme of this book has been the maritime industry's unique employment conditions, a factor built into the deliberations of the ILO. The ILO's first major congress in 1920 was on maritime labour, and subsequently the ILO has given more attention to seafarers and wharf labourers than any other group of workers. Its Joint Maritime Commission was designed to deal with the unsuitability of laws for land-based labour in dealing with a config-

---

[6] David Glen, 'What Do We Know about the Labour Market for Seafarers? A View from the UK,' *Marine Policy* 32 (2008): 845–55; H.R. Northrup and R.I. Rowan, *The International Transport Workers Federation and Flag of Convenience Shipping* (Philadelphia: University of Pennsylvania Press, 1983).

13.1 MUA rally to commemorate 1938 *Dalfram* dispute, Port Kembla,
NSW, 2006. NBAC

uration of multinational and transnational crews, owners and operators. It
set about establishing an International Seafarers' Code and, as open-registry
shipping increased and even accelerated, recruiting labour from among the
poorest nations and people, the ILO developed new international labour
standards. While they have not prevented the expansion of open-registry
shipping, they have had success in ensuring crews are given minimum labour
standards when ships operate on the coast and land in the ports of nations
which are signatories to the ILO conventions, the most significant of which
was MLC 2006.

The passage of MLC 2006 was hailed as a watershed moment in the
ILO's long history.[7] It gave the maritime industry the distinction of being
the only industry to maintain an internationally set minimum wage. It was
held up as an example of successful labour regulation — indeed, a model
for other rapidly globalising sectors – in achieving an international labour
regulatory framework. It incorporated the principle of Port State Control,
which empowered local authorities to inspect foreign ships coming into their
ports and identify problems according to an internationally agreed regime

---

[7] Bolle, 'The ILO's New Convention on Maritime Labour: An Innovation Instrument.'

of protocols. To some analysts, Port State Control was more important and effective in ensuring safety at sea than having flag states.[8] The process generated data that could enable authorities to point to further health and safety protections where there were deficiencies. Stipulating the measures to be taken by a port state gave it extra clout.[9]

The MLC came into effect in 2013. It was very soon ratified by Australia and by most major maritime nations, including (from the Asia-Pacific region) Japan (in 2013), India (in 2015) and New Zealand (2017). Under Prime Minister Jacinda Ardern, New Zealand changed the funding of facilities and welfare services for crews coming ashore by imposing a maritime levy which came into force on 1 July 2021.[10] China – the country with the largest number of seafarers – had not ratified although the MLC did still impact significantly on Chinese policy and regulation 'as well as in the attitude and behaviour of the key stakeholders.'[11] Japan, as a major shipowning power, believed its ratification of the Convention would be significant in improving labour conditions while also ensuring fair competition for shipowners – 'strengthening competitiveness' for the national shipping industry.[12] India, reflecting its history as a labour-supply country, described it as a 'bill of rights' for seafarers, providing them not only with 'fundamental rights as workers,' but also with what were stipulated minimums in international standards for living and working conditions. India implemented the provisions of MLC 2006 by amending its Merchant Shipping (Maritime Labour) Rules 2016.[13]

Under the federal labor government led by Prime Minister Julia Gillard, Australia gave effect to MLC 2006 when it repealed and rewrote the century-old Navigation Act 1912. This was the first time an ALP government had undertaken major amendment to the Navigation Act, and it promised to reinvigorate Australian coastal shipping. The move was welcomed by the Maritime Union, optimistic it would lead to more jobs and a secure future

---

[8] Marina Liselotte Fotteler, Despena Bygvraa and Olaf Jensen, 'The Impact of the Maritime Labor Convention on Seafarers' Working and Living Conditions: An Analysis of Port State Control Statistics,' *BMC Public Health* 20 (2020): 1–9.

[9] Ministry of Foreign Affairs, Japan, Press Release, 2013.

[10] Editor, 'New Zealand Amends Legislation to Provide Seafarer Welfare Funding,' 19 July 2021, Maritime Fairtrade, *Shining a Light*, https://maritimefairtrade.org/new-zealand-amends-legislation-to-provide-seafarer-welfare-funding/.

[11] Pengfei Zhang and Minghua Zhao, 'Maritime Labour Convention 2006 and the Chinese Seafarers: How Far is China to Ratification?' *Marine Policy* 61 (2015): 54–65.

[12] Ministry of Foreign Affairs, Japan, Press Release, 2013, reiterating the ILO's claims.

[13] India, Directorate General of Shipping, Ministry of Ports, Shipping and Waterways, Mumbai, Maritime Labour Convention, www.dgshipping.gov.in/Content/MaritimeLabourConvention.aspx.

for Australian shipping.[14] Their optimism was dashed when the ALP lost government and managing the process was left to the incoming L-NP – opponents of the new Act and promising to bring in anti-union legislation. The new government predictably amended the Navigation Act 2012 and associated delegated legislation.

In Australia, non-compliance with the Navigation Act 2012 involves a detention (the ship not being allowed to depart) or a ban from Australian ports. The first report of MLC 2006 in action by the Australian Maritime Safety Authority (AMSA) noted that AMSA had conducted 3,222 PSC inspections, resulting in 163 detentions in 2019, and a ban had been imposed on nine vessels in the four years preceding.[15] AMSA also collected data on companies subjecting seafarers to 'unethical crewing practices, unfair contracts, the delay or non-payment of wages, the denial of shore leave and the refusal of repatriation.' They noted that serious breaches of the MLC were happening on board and undertook to ensure that when visiting Australian ports seafarers would be 'afforded the requirements they deserve.'[16] The report concluded that MLC 2006 had been successful both in providing fair and decent conditions and in enhancing shipping services, and it had improved the reporting culture: the number of complaints from seafarers had increased, as the existence of a strong relationship between AMSA and ITF inspired a growing confidence among seafarers that Australia's regulatory authorities would take their complaints seriously. Australian unionists played a significant role in that work.

When in 2020 the COVID-19 pandemic struck, 96 countries covering 90 per cent of the world's shipping fleet had ratified MLC 2006.[17] The pandemic illuminated the vulnerability of a precarious workforce and 'the historical imbalances in labour conditions at sea.'[18] At first, attention focused on the international cruise ships' industry when alighting passengers placed domestic populations at risk. Soon, with national borders and ports closed around the world, the crews were the centre of a humanitarian crisis unfolding.[19]

---

[14] 'Gillard Government Ends Year on Political High,' *Maritime Workers' Journal* (spring/summer 2012): 5.

[15] Australia Maritime Safety Authority (AMSA), Maritime Labour Convention Annual Report (2019).

[16] AMSA, Maritime Labour Convention Annual Report (2019). For an international report, see Fotteler, Bygvraa and Jensen, 'The Impact of the Maritime Labor Convention on Seafarers' Working and Living Conditions.'

[17] Reported in Fotteler, Bygvraa and Jensen, 'The Impact of the Maritime Labor Convention on Seafarers' Working and Living Conditions.'

[18] Christiaan De Beukelaer, 'COVID-19 Border Closures Cause Humanitarian Crew Change Crisis at Sea,' *Marine Policy* 132 (2021).

[19] Jim McIlroy, 'Unions Slam Mistreatment of Ruby Princess Crew,' *Green Left* 1261

13.2 Cruise ship *Ruby Princess*, Sydney Harbour, March 2020. Before it returned to its home port in the Philippines, locals in Wollongong organised care packages for the grateful crew Photographer Dean Lewins. AAP Photos

As many as 400,000 seafarers were at times trapped on board, kept at sea, unable to change over with alternative crews, take shore leave or be repatriated to their homes, in contravention of guarantees provided by MLC 2006.

This was a situation potentially eroding the value of MLC 2006 and the working conditions of all seafarers well into the future.[20] 'Unfortunate and innocent seafarers' who relied on port authorities to ensure their rights rather than risk being blacklisted as troublemakers by employing agents were now stranded, forced to remain on board for safety reasons, virtually imprisoned and unpaid for months. Ships were being permitted to sail without first ensuring that 'adequate funding was available to repatriate ALL crew members in the event of financial or other abandonment.'[21] It showed why ratification of MLC 2006 was necessary.

Unions continue to play an important political role in the development of policies to squeeze out substandard shipping. Where once this focused on the physical standards of the ship, it has increasingly turned to labour standards for the crews. Particularly worrisome is the fishing industry, which is the least regulated, and has become the focus of campaigns against modern slavery. Out there, in the transnational space of the oceans, 'where no one is watching,' the consequences can be shocking: 60 per cent of seafarers in the fishing industry reported seeing another seafarer murdered at sea.[22] But safety has worsened in other parts of the industry too. In 2012, the Sydney office of the ITF was calling for an investigation into three deaths on board a Panamanian-registered Japanese bulk carrier then in port in Newcastle, a number of fatalities which ITF Coordinator Dean Summers had never encountered in all his years of experience at sea.[23]

Studies have shown that national origin remains an important part of the identity of shipowners despite the rise of open-registries and diverse nationalities of crews. Ultimately, the system is still controlled by nation-states,

---

(15 April 2020), www.greenleft.org.au/content/unions-slam-mistreatment-ruby-princess-crew. 'As the Virus Rages on Shore, Merchant Seamen Are Stranded on Board … Trapped in Floating Prisons,' *The Economist*, 18 June 2020; 'Cargo-Ship Crews Are Stuck at Sea,' *The Economist*; Philip Teoh, 'The Impact of the Covid-19 Pandemic on Shipping,' *Maritime Executive*, 4 July 2020, www.maritime-executive.com/editorials/the-impact-of-the-covid-19-pandemic-on-shipping.

[20] De Beukelaer, 'COVID-19 Border Closures.'

[21] [Master Mariner US Coast Guard] William Doherty, 'Opinion: It's about Time the U.S. Ratifies MLC, 2006,' Editorial, *gCaptain*, 21 February 2020, https://gcaptain.com/opinion-bouchard-ordeal-shows-need-for-mlc-2006-ratification-by-u-s/.

[22] See reports by the *New York Times* investigative journalist Ian Urbina, *The Unlawful Ocean* (New York: Vintage, 2019).

[23] 'Gillard Government Ends Year on Political High,' 4.

and worker strategies for leverage depend on cooperation between those at sea and those handling cargoes on shore as well as between unions in labour-supplying countries and in countries where ships are owned.[24] This book has traced a history of unions making those connections and developing those strategies. International networks formed by maritime unionists in the preceding century – their internationalism in action for fair standards of labour conditions – has demonstrated the practical importance of unity and solidarity beyond the immediate local, national workplace.

Internationalism was a hard path to follow. These maritime men knew the value of collective action and never lost sight of the importance of unions. Harry Bridges had learnt his politics in Australia. The founders of the ITF spent formative years there. The history of Australian maritime unions shows how the struggle for rights has been long and sustained. Organisational power has brought some much-needed protections. That story of endurance has relevance for workers today. As the ITF looked to the twenty-first century and its own second century as an organisation, it urged the political necessity of unions remaining relevant to the changing workforce, 'by highlighting the international dimension of their work.'[25] In a world of increasing challenges, declining union membership and power, it is well to remember this story of a 'true-blue' internationalism for labour's rights.

[24] J. French and K. Wintersteen, 'Crafting an International Legal Regime for Worker Rights,' *International Labor and Working Class History* 75 (2009): 145–68.
[25] ITF, 'Transport Workers: Beyond 2000,' Progress Report, 46, para. 220.

Select Bibliography

Published primary sources

Albrecht, Arthur, 'International Seamen's Union of America: A Study of its History and Problems,' *Bulletin of the United States Bureau of Labor Statistics* no. 342 (Washington, DC: U.S. Bureau of Labor, 1923).

Arora A.K., *Voyage: Chronology of Seafarers' Movement in India* (Mumbai: National Union of Seafarers of India, 1996).

'As the Virus Rages on Shore, Merchant Seamen Are Stranded on Board ... Trapped in Floating Prisons,' *The Economist*, 18 June 2020.

Australia, Department of Foreign Affairs and Australia, Department of External Affairs, *Current Notes on International Affairs* 20, no. 3 (1949): 361.

Australia Maritime Safety Authority, Maritime Labour Convention Annual Report 2019.

Australian National Maritime Association, *Australian Shipping: Structure, History and Future* (Melbourne: Australian National Maritime Association, 1989).

Barnes, Leo, *Sea of Change* (Mumbai: National Union of Seafarers of India, 1996).

Beggs, Jim, *Proud to be a Wharfie* (North Melbourne: Arcadia, 2013).

Brown, W. Jethro, 'The Strike of the Australian Waterside Worker: A Review,' *Economic Record* 5, no. 1 (1929): 22–33.

Bull, Tasnor, *Life on the Waterfront: An Autobiography* (Sydney: HarperCollins, 1998).

Butler, Harold, 'Problems of Industry in the East with Special Reference to India, French India, Ceylon, Malaysia and the Netherlands Indies,' ILO Studies and Reports 29 (Geneva: International Labour Organization, 1938).

'Cargo-Ship Crews Are Stuck at Sea,' *The Economist*, 20 June 2020.

Combet, Greg, *The Fights of My Life* (Melbourne: Melbourne University Press, 2014).

Desai, Dinkar D., *Maritime Labour in India* (Bombay: Servants of India Society, 1940).

Doherty, William (Master Mariner US Coast Guard), 'Opinion: It's About Time the U.S. Ratifies MLC, 2006,' Editorial, *gCaptain*, 21 February 2020, https://gcaptain.com/opinion-bouchard-ordeal-shows-need-for-mlc-2006-ratification-by-u-s/.

Elliott, E.V., *Merchant Seamen in the War* (Sydney: Seamen's Union of Australia, 1944).

Gay, A.E., *England's Duty to Her Merchant Seamen* (Adelaide: Sands & McDougall, 1906).

Goldberg, Joseph P., 'Seamen and the International Labor Organization,' *Monthly Labor Review* 81, no. 9 (1958): 974–81.

Hall, Benjamin T., *Socialism and Sailors*, Fabian Society Tract 46 (London: Fabian Society, 1893).

Hawke, R.J., *The Hawke Memoirs* (Melbourne: William Heinemann Australia, 1994).

'The Impact of Technologies on Labor in Five Industries,' U.S. Department of Labor, Bureau of Labor Statistics, December 1982, 15–17.

India, Directorate General of Shipping, Ministry of Ports, Shipping and Waterways, Mumbai, Maritime Labour Convention, www.dgshipping.gov. in/Content/MaritimeLabourConvention.aspx.

International Transport Federation, Report on Activities and Financial Report of the ITF for the Years 1938 to 1973, and Proceedings … (London: ITF, 1946–1974).

——. *Solidarity: The First 100 Years of the International Transport Workers' Federation* (Chicago: Pluto Press, 1996).

McIlroy, Jim, 'Unions Slam Mistreatment of Ruby Princess Crew,' *Green Left* 1261 (15 April 2020), www.greenleft.org.au/content/unions-slam-mistreatment-ruby-princess-crew.

Mann, Tom, 'Conditions of Labour in New Zealand,' *The Nineteenth Century and After: A Monthly Review* 52, no. 307 (1902): 393–9.

——. 'The Industrial and Social Outlook in Australia,' *Social-Democrat* 13, no. 8 (1909): 337–43.

——. 'The Political and Industrial Situation in Australia,' *The Nineteenth Century and After: A Monthly Review* 56, no. 331 (1904): 475–91.

——. *The Position of Dockers and Sailors in 1897 and the International Federation of Ship, Dock, and River Workers* (London: Clarion Newspaper Co., 1897).

——. *Tom Mann's Memoirs* (London: Labour Publishing Co., 1923).

Mazarello, Theodore G., *Maritime Labour in India* (Bombay: Maritime Union of India, 1961).

Mogi, Sobei, *Japanese Shipping and the Seamen's Trade Union Movement* (Amsterdam: International Transport Workers' Federation, 1931).

Ogden, Max, *A Long View from the Left* (Sydney: Bad Apple Press, 2020).

Pulsford, Edward, *The British Empire and the Relations of Asia and Australasia: Immigration Restrictions in Australasia* (Sydney: W. Brooks & Co, 1905).

Roth, Bert, *Wharfie 'From Hand Barrows To Straddles': Unionism on the Auckland Waterfront* (Auckland: New Zealand Waterfront Workers' Union, Auckland Branch, 1993).

Shaw, Murray, *Bamboo Curtain over Port Hedland: The Anatomy of a Political and Industrial Dispute* (Canning Vale, WA: self-published, 2013).

Tapiola, Kari, *The Driving Force: Birth and Evolution of Tripartism – The Role of the ILO Workers' Group* (Geneva: International Labour Organization, 2019).

Whitlow, Jon, 'Maritime Concerns of the International Transport Workers' Federation,' in *Current Maritime Issues and the International Maritime Organization*, ed. Myron H. Norquist and John Norton Moore (The Hague: Martinus Nijhoff, 1999), 177–89.

Secondary sources

Adams, Caroline, *Across Seven Seas and Thirteen Rivers: Life Stories of Pioneer Sylhetti Settlers in Britain* (London: THAP Books, 1987).

Ahlquist, John S., and Margaret Levi, *In the Interest of Others: Organisations and Social Activism* (Princeton, NJ: Princeton University Press, 2013).

Ahuja, Ravi, 'Mobility and Containment: The Voyages of South Asian Seamen, c.1900–1960,' *International Review of Social History* 51 (2006): 111–41.

———. 'Networks of Subordination – Networks of the Subordinated: The Ordered Spaces of South Asian Maritime Labour in the Age of Imperialism (c.1890–1947),' in *The Limits of British Control in South Asia: Spaces of Disorder in the Indian Ocean Region*, ed. Ashwini Tambe and Harald Fisher (London: Routledge, 2009), 13–48.

Alderton, Tony, *The Global Seafarer: Living and Working Conditions in a Globalized Industry* (Geneva: International Labour Office, 2004).

Ali, Aamir, 'Fifty Years of the ILO and Asia,' *International Labour Review* 99 (1969): 347–62.

Andrews E.M., *Australia and China: The Ambiguous Relationship* (Melbourne: Melbourne University Press, 1985).

Arnesen Eric, *Waterfront Workers of New Orleans: Race, Class and Politics, 1863–1923* (New York: Oxford University Press, 1991).

Bailey, K.H., 'Australia and the International Labour Conventions,' *International Labour Review* 54, no. 5–6 (1946): 285–308.

Balachandran, G., 'Circulation through Seafaring: Indian Seamen, 1890–1945,' in *Society and Circulation: Mobile People and Itinerant Cultures in South Asia, 1750–1950*, ed. Claude Markovits, Jacques Pouchepadass and Sanjay Subrahmanyam (Delhi: Permanent Black, 2003), 89–130.

———. 'Conflicts in the International Maritime Labour Market: British and Indian Seamen, Employers, and the State, 1890–1939,' *Indian Economic and Social History Review* 39, no. 1 (2002): 71–100.

———. 'Cultures of Protest in Transnational Contexts: Indian Seamen Abroad, 1886–1945,' *Transforming Cultures Ejournal* 3, no. 2 (2008): 45–75.

———. *Globalizing Labour: Indian Seafarers and World Shipping, c.1870–1945* (New Delhi: Oxford University Press, 2012).

———. 'Making Coolies, (Un)making Workers: "Globalizing" Labour in the Late 19th and Early 20th Centuries,' *Journal of Historical Sociology* 24, no. 3 (2011): 266–96.

———. 'Recruitment and Control of Indian Seamen, Calcutta, 1880–1935,' *International Journal of Maritime History* 9, no. 1 (1997): 1–18.

———. 'Searching for the *Sardar*: The State, Pre-capitalist Institutions and Human Agency in the Maritime Labour Market, Calcutta, 1850–1935,' in *Institutions and Economic Change in South Asia*, ed. Burton Stein and Sanjay Subrahmanyam (Delhi: Oxford University Press, 1996), 206–36.

———. 'South Asian Seafarers and their Worlds *c.*1870–1930s,' in *Seascapes: Maritime Histories, Local Cultures and Transoceanic Exchanges*, ed. Jerry Bentley, Renate Bridenthal and Kären Wigen (Honolulu: University of Hawaii Press, 2007), 186–202.

Banivanua-Mar, Tracey, *Violence and Colonial Dialogue: The Australian–Pacific Indentured Labor Trade* (Honolulu: University of Hawaii Press, 2007).

Barnes, Blanche, *Leo Barnes: The Lion of the Seas. Selected Biographical Notes* (Mumbai: Leo Barnes Foundation, 2008).

Barnes, Leo, *Evolution and Scope of Mercantile Marine Laws Relating to Seamen in India* (Bombay: Maritime Law Association of India, 1983).

Barrie, F.B., *The Conscription Plebiscites in Australia, 1916–1917* (Melbourne: North Melbourne Historical Association, 1974).

Bauer, Paul, 'The Maritime Labour Convention: An Adequate Guarantee of Seafarer Rights, or an Impediment to True Reforms?' *Chicago Journal of International Law* 8, no. 2 (2008): 643–59.

Beasley, Margo, *Wharfies: A History of the Waterside Workers Federation of Australia* (Rushcutters Bay, NSW: Halstead Press, 1996).

Bennett, James, 'The New Zealand Labour Movement and International Communism, 1921–38,' in *Lenin's Legacy Down Under: New Zealand's Cold War*, ed. Alexander Trapeznik and Aaron Fox (Dunedin: University of Otago Press, 2004), 73–93.

Bentley, P., 'Communist Trade Union Leadership and Strike Incidence – With Specific Reference to the Waterside Workers' Federation,' *Journal of Industrial Relations* 12, no. 1 (1970): 88–97.

Benton, Gregor, *Chinese Migrants and Internationalism: Forgotten Stories, 1917–1945* (London: Routledge, 2007).

Benton, Gregor, and Edmund Terence Gomez, *The Chinese in Britain, 1800–Present: Economy, Transnationalism, Identity* (London: Palgrave Macmillan, 2008).

Bhagavan, Manu Belur, *India and the Cold War* (Chapel Hill: University of North Carolina Press, 2019).

Bollard, Robert, *In the Shadow of Gallipoli: The Hidden Story of Australia in World War I* (Sydney: NewSouth Publishing, 2013).

Bollé, Patrick, 'The ILO's New Convention on Maritime Labour: An Innovative Instrument,' *International Labour Review* 145, no. 1 (2006): 135–42.

Bollinger, Conrad, *Against the Wind: The Story of the New Zealand Seamen's Union* (Wellington: New Zealand Seamen's Union, 1968).

Brett, Judith, *The Enigmatic Mr. Deakin* (Melbourne: Australia Text Publishing Co., 2017).

———. 'Stanley Melbourne Bruce,' in *Australian Prime Ministers*, ed. Michelle Grattan (Sydney: New Holland Publishers, 2000), 126–38.

Brody, David, 'American Labour Law as a Model for Australia? Or, Can You Get Here From There?' *Labour History* 97 (2009): 189–98.

Broeze, F[rank], *The Globalisation of the Oceans: Containerisation from the 1950s to the Present* (St. John's, Newfoundland: International Maritime Economic History Association, 2002).

———. 'Militancy and Pragmatism: An International Perspective on Maritime Labour, 1870–1914,' *International Review of Social History* 36, no. 2 (1991): 165–200.

———. 'The Muscles of Empire: Indian Seamen and the Raj,' *Indian Economic and Social History Review* 18, no. 1 (1981): 43–67.

Broomham, Rosemary, *Steady Revolutions: The Australian Institute of Marine and Power Engineers, 1881–1990* (Sydney: UNSW Press, 1991).

Buchanan, Tom, *East Wind: China and the British Left, 1925–1976* (Oxford: Oxford University Press, 2012).

Bullock, Alan, *The Life and Times of Ernest Bevin*, vol. 1, *Trade Union Leader, 1881–1940* (London: Heinemann, 1960).

———. *The Life and Times of Ernest Bevin*, vol. 2, *Minister of Labour, 1940–1945* (London: Heinemann, 1967).

———. *The Life and Times of Ernest Bevin*, vol. 3, *Foreign Secretary, 1945–1951* (London: Heinemann, 1983).

Burgmann, Verity, *Revolutionary Industrial Unionism: The Industrial Workers of the World in Australia* (Cambridge: Cambridge University Press, 1995).

Burton, Valerie, '"Whoring Drinking Sailors": Reflections on Masculinity from the Labour History of Nineteenth-Century British Shipping,' in *Working Out Gender: Perspectives from Labour History*, ed. Margaret Walsh (Aldershot: Ashgate, 1999), 84–101.

Cabanes, Bruno, *The Great War and the Origins of Humanitarianism, 1918–1924* (Cambridge: Cambridge University Press, 2014).

Cable, Boyd, *A Hundred Year History of the P&O Peninsular and Oriental Steam Navigation Company, 1837–1937* (London: Ivor Nicholson & Watson, 1937).

Cahill, Rowan, 'Maritime Internationalism,' *The Guardian* (CPA), 12 March 1999, www.academia.edu/9121812/Maritime_Internationalism.

Cain, Frank, *The Origins of Political Surveillance in Australia* (Sydney: Angus & Robertson, 1983).

Carew, Anthony, 'A False Dawn: The World Federation of Trade Unions (1945–1949),' in *The International Confederation of Free Trade Unions*, ed. Marcel van der Linden (Berne: Peter Lang, 2000), 167–84.

———. 'Towards a Free Trade Union Centre: The International Confederation of Free Trade Unions,' in *The International Confederation of Free Trade Unions*, ed. Marcel van der Linden (Berne: Peter Lang, 2000), 195–8.

Carment, David, 'Sir Littleton Groom and the Deportation Crisis of 1925: A Study of Non-Labor Response to Trade Union Militancy,' *Labour History* 32 (1977): 46–54.

Chan, Wai Kwan, *The Making of Hong Kong Society: Three Studies of Class Formation in Early Hong Kong* (Oxford: Clarendon Press, 1991).

Cherny, Robert, 'The Making of a Labor Radical: Harry Bridges, 1901–1934,' *Pacific Historical Review* 64, no. 3 (1995): 363–88.

Colaco, A, *A History of the Seamen's Union of Bombay* (Bombay: Pascoal Vaz, 1955).

Coleman, Verna, *Adela Pankhurst: The Wayward Suffragette, 1885–1961* (Melbourne: Melbourne University Press, 1996).

Cooksey, Robert, 'Political Review,' *Australian Quarterly* 37, no. 4 (1965): 94–105.

Corlett, E., *The Ship: The Revolution in Merchant Shipping, 1950–1980* (London: HMSO, 1981).

Couper, Alastair, *Sailors and Traders: A Maritime History of the Pacific Peoples* (Honolulu: University of Hawaii Press, 2005).

Cowen, Zelman, *Isaac Isaacs* (Melbourne: Oxford University Press, 1967).

Creighton, M., 'Fraternity in the American Forecastle, 1830–1870,' *New England Quarterly* 63, no. 4 (1990): 531–57.

Curthoys, Ann, 'Conflict and Consensus: The Seamen's Strike of 1878,' in *Who Are Our Enemies? Racism and the Australian Working Class*, ed. Ann Curthoys and Andrew Markus (Sydney: Hale & Iremonger, 1978), 48–65.

Dabscheck, Braham, 'The Australian Waterfront Dispute and Theories of the State,' *Journal of Industrial Relations* 42, no. 2 (2000): 407–516.

———. 'The Waterfront Dispute: Of Vendetta and the Australian Way,' *Economic and Labour Relations Review* 9, no. 2 (1998): 155–87.

Darnell, Maxine, 'Responses and Reactions to the Importation of Indentured Chinese Labourers,' University of New England, School of Economic Studies, Working Paper Series in Economic History no. 99-2 (November 1999), www.une.edu.au/__data/assets/pdf_file/0011/13340/ehwp99-2.pdf.

Day, David, *Contraband and Controversy: The Customs History of Australia from 1901* (Canberra: AGPS, 1996).

De Beukelaer, Christiaan, 'COVID-19 Border Closures Cause Humanitarian Crew Change Crisis at Sea,' *Marine Policy* 132 (2021): 1–5.

Deery, S., 'The Impact of the National Stevedoring Industry Conference (1965–67) on Industrial Relations on the Australian Waterfront,' *Journal of Industrial Relations* 20, no. 2 (1978): 202–22.

——. 'The Impact of Technological Change on Union Structure: The Waterside Workers Federation,' *Journal of Industrial Relations* 25, no. 4 (1983): 399–414.

Dixon, Conrad, 'Lascars: The Forgotten Seamen,' in *Working Men Who Got Wet*, ed. Rosemary Ommer and Gerald Panting (St. John's, Newfoundland: Memorial University of Newfoundland, 1980), 265–81.

Donn, Clifford B., and G. Phelan, 'Australian Maritime Unions and Flag of Convenience Vessels,' *Journal of Industrial Relations* 33, no. 3 (1991): 329–39.

Donovan, P.F., 'Australia and the Great London Dock Strike: 1889,' *Labour History* 23 (1972): 17–26.

Ellmoos, Laila, 'The Deep Sea and the Shallow Water: Masculinity, Mateship and Work Practices on Sydney's Waterfront in the 1950s,' in *Playing the Man: New Approaches to Masculinity*, ed. Katherine Biber, Tom Sear and Dave Trudinger (Annandale: Pluto Press, 1999), 186–99.

Farrell, Frank, *International Socialism and Australian Labour: The Left in Australia, 1919–1939* (Sydney: Hale & Iremonger, 1981).

Fink, Leon, *Sweatshops at Sea: Merchant Seamen in the World's First Globalized Industry* (Chapel Hill: University of North Carolina Press, 2011).

Fisher, Michael H., 'Working across the Seas: Indian Maritime Labourers in India, Britain, and in between, 1600–1857,' *International Review of Social History* 51 (supplement 2006): 21–45.

Fitzhardinge, L.F., 'W.M. Hughes and the Waterside Workers,' *Australian Journal of Political History* 2, no. 2 (1957): 169–80.

——. *William Morris Hughes: A Political Biography*, vol. 1 (Sydney: Angus & Robertson, 1964).

Fitzpatrick, Brian, and Rowan Cahill, *A History of the Seamen's Union of Australia* (Sydney: Seamen's Union of Australia, 1981).

Fitzpatrick, D., and M. Anderson, *Seafarers' Rights* (Oxford: Oxford University Press, 2005).

Foster, Leonie, 'Shipwrecks and the White Australia Policy,' *Great Circle* 36, no. 2 (2014): 68–84.

Fotteler, Marina Liselotte, Despena Bygvraa and Olaf Jensen, 'The Impact of the Maritime Labor Convention on Seafarers' Working and Living Conditions: An Analysis of Port State Control Statistics,' *BMC Public Health* 20, no. 1 (2020): 1–9.

Fowler, Josephine, 'From East to West and West to East: Ties of Solidarity in the Pan-Pacific Revolutionary Trade Union Movement, 1923–1934,' *International Labor and Working-Class History* 66 (2004): 99–117.

———. *Japanese and Chinese Immigrant Activists: Organizing in American and International Communist Movements, 1919–33* (New Brunswick, NJ: Rutgers University Press, 2007).

French, J., and K. Wintersteen, 'Crafting an International Legal Regime for Worker Rights,' *International Labor and Working Class History* 75 (2009): 145–68.

Gajewska, K., 'Varieties of Regional Economic Integration and Labor Internationalism: The Case of Japanese Trade Unions in Comparison,' *Economic and Industrial Democracy* 34, no. 2 (2013): 247–68.

Gardiner, Robert, *The Shipping Revolution: The Modern Merchant Ship* (London: Conway Maritime Press, 1992).

Glen, David, 'What Do We Know about The Labour Market for Seafarers? A View from the UK,' *Marine Policy* 32 (2008): 845–55.

Gollan, Robin, *Revolutionaries and Reformists: Communism and the Australian Labour Movement, 1920–1955* (Canberra: ANU Press, 1975).

Grant, David, *Jagged Seas: The New Zealand Seamen's Union, 1879–2003* (Christchurch: Canterbury University Press, 2012).

Green, Anna, *British Capital, Antipodean Labour: Working the New Zealand Waterfront, 1915–1951* (Dunedin: University of Otago Press, 2001).

Harford, Shelley, 'A Trans-Tasman Union Community: Growing Global Solidarity,' *Labour History* 95 (2008): 133–49.

Hartman, Paul T., *Collective Bargaining and Productivity: The Longshore Mechanization Agreement* (Berkeley: University of California Press, 1969).

Helmore, Basil A., 'Validity of State Navigation Acts,' *Australian Law Journal* 27 (21 May 1953): 16–19.

Hirson, Baruch, and Lorraine Vivian, *Strike across the Empire: The Seamen's Strike of 1925 in Britain, South Africa and Australasia* (London: Clio Publications, 1992).

Hirst, John, 'Labor and the Great War,' in *The Australian Century: Political Struggle in the Building of a Nation*, ed. Robert Manne (Melbourne: Australia Text Publishing Co., 1999), 47–65.

Horne, Gerald, *Red Seas: Ferdinand Smith and Radical Black Sailors in the United States and Jamaica* (New York: New York University Press, 2005).

Hossain, Ashfaque, 'The World of the Sylheti Seamen in the Age of Empire, from the Late Eighteenth Century to 1947,' *Journal of Global History* 9, no. 3 (2014): 425–46.

Hughes, Steve, and Nigel Haworth, 'A Distant Detachment: New Zealand and the ILO, 1919–1945.' n.d., www.ilo.org/public/english/anniversary/90th/download/events/newzealand/hughes2.pdf (no longer available).

Hull, D., 'Queensland Sugar Ports: Labour and Technological Change,' *Journal of Australian Political Economy* 6 (1979): 60–72.

Hyslop, Jonathan, 'British Steamship Workers, c.1875–1945: Precarious before Precarity,' *Labour History* 116 (2019): 5–28.

———. 'Steamship Empire: Asian, African and British Sailors in the Merchant Marine *c.*1880–1945,' *Journal of Asian and African Studies* 44, no. 1 (2009): 49–67.

Janiewski, Dolores, 'Forging an Australian Working-Class Identity through Myth, Story-Telling and Maritime Mateship: Becoming Harry Bridges,' *Labour History* 116 (2019): 113–43.

Jenkinson, Jacqueline, 'Black Sailors on Red Clydeside: Rioting, Reactionary Trade Unionism and Conflicting Notions of "Britishness" following the First World War,' *Twentieth Century British History* 19, no. 1 (2008): 29–60.

Johansson, Lennart, *Funny Flags: ITF's Campaign – Past, Present, Future* (Stockholm: Utbildningsförlaget Brevskolan, 1996).

'The Joint Maritime Commission and the Maritime Work of the ILO,' *International Labor Review* 62, no. 5 (1950): 337–63.

Jones, Nicolette, *The Plimsoll Sensation: The Great Campaign to Save Lives at Sea* (London: Abacus, 2007).

Kanuk, L., 'The UNCTAD Code of Conduct for Liner Conferences: Trade Milestone or Millstone –Time Will Soon Tell,' *Northwestern Journal of International Law & Business* 6, no. 2 (1984): 357–72.

Kaukiainen, Yrjö, 'The Advantages of Water Carriage: Scale Economies and Shipping Technology, *c.*1870–2000,' in *The World's Key Industry: History and Economics of International Shipping*, ed. Gelina Harlaftis, Stig Tenold and Jesús M. Valdaliso (Basingstoke: Palgrave Macmillan, 2012) 64–87.

Khan, Yasmin, *India at War: The Subcontinent and the Second World* War (New York: Oxford University Press, 2015).

Kirk, Neville, *Transnational Radicalism and the Connected Lives of Tom Mann and Robert Samuel Ross* (Liverpool: Liverpool University Press, 2017).

Kirkaldy, Adam, *British Shipping: Its History, Organisation and Importance* (Newton Abbot: David & Charles, 1970 [1914]).

Kirkby, Diane, 'Maritime Labour, Men of Power and the Dynamics of Activism,' Keynote Address to Labour History Conference, Perth, 2019.

———. *Voices from the Ships: Australia's Seafarers and Their Union* (Sydney: UNSW Press, 2008).

Kirkby, Diane, and Lee-Ann Monk, 'Indian Seamen and Australian Unions Fighting for Labour Rights: "The Real Facts of the Lascars' Case" of 1939,' *Labour History* 113 (2017): 209–39.

Kirkby, Diane, and Dmytro Ostapenko, 'Pursuing Trade Union Internationalism: Australia's Waterside Workers and the International Transport Workers Federation, *c.*1950–1970,' *Labour History* 110 (2016): 57–75.

———. '"Second to none in the international fight": Australian Seafarers Internationalism and Maritime Unions Against Apartheid,' *Journal of Contemporary History* 54, no. 2 (2019): 442–64.

Kitchen, J.G., *The Employment of Merchant Seamen* (London: Croom Helm, 1980).

Koch-Baumgarten, Sigrid, 'Edo Fimmen: An Iron Fist in a Silken Glove: A Biographical Sketch,' in *The International Transportworkers Federation, 1914–1945: The Edo Fimmen Era*, ed. Bob Reinalda (Amsterdam: Stichting beheer IISG, 1997), 52–68.

——. 'Trade Union Regime Formation under the Conditions of Globalization in the Transport Sector: Attempts at Transnational Trade Union Regulation of Flag-of-Convenience Shipping,' *International Review of Social History* 43 (1998): 369–402.

Laffer, K., 'Australian Maritime Unions and the International Transport Workers Federation,' *Journal of Industrial Relations* 19 (1977): 113–32.

Lahiri, Shompa, 'Patterns of Resistance: Indian Seamen in Imperial Britain,' in *Language, Labour and Migration*, ed. A.J. Kershen (Aldershot: Ashgate, 2000), 155–78.

Lake, Marilyn, 'The ILO, Australia and the Asia-Pacific Region: New Solidarities or Internationalism in the National Interest?' in *The ILO from Geneva to the Pacific Rim: West Meets East*, ed. Nelson Lichtenstein and Jill M. Jensen (Basingstoke: Palgrave Macmillan, 2015), 33–54.

Lake, Marilyn, and Henry Reynolds, *Drawing the Global Colour Line: White Men's Countries and the International Challenge of Racial Equality* (New York: Cambridge University Press, 2008).

Landau, C.E., 'The Influence of ILO Standards on Australian Labour Law and Practice,' *International Labour Review* 126, no. 6 (1987): 669–90.

Lane, Tony, *The Merchant Seamen's War* (Manchester: Manchester University Press, 1990).

Larrowe, Charles P., *Harry Bridges: The Rise and Fall of Radical Labor in the United States* (New York: Laurence Hill, 1972).

Lee, David, *Stanley Melbourne Bruce: Australian Internationalist* (London: Continuum, 2010).

Levi, Margaret, David Olson, Jon Agnone and Kelly Devin, 'Union Democracy Reexamined,' *Politics & Society* 37, no. 2 (2009): 203–28.

Levinson, Marc, *The Box: How the Shipping Container Made the World Smaller and the World Economy Bigger* (Princeton, NJ: Princeton University Press 2006).

Lichtenstein, Nelson, and Jill M. Jensen, *The ILO from Geneva to the Pacific Rim: West Meets East* (Basingstoke: Palgrave Macmillan, 2015).

Lillie, Nathan, *A Global Union for Global Workers: Collective Bargaining and Regulatory Politics in Maritime Shipping* (New York: Routledge, 2006).

Lockwood, Rupert, *War on the Waterfront: Menzies, Japan and the Pig-Iron Dispute* (Sydney: Hale & Iremonger, 1987).

Louis, L.J., 'Recovery from the Depression and the Seamen's Strike, 1935–6,' *Labour History* 41 (1981): 74–86.

Macintyre, Stuart, *The Reds* (Sydney: Allen & Unwin, 1998).

——. 'The Third Time as Rodomontade,' *Overland* 150 (1998): 5–10.

McLean, Kama, *British India, White Australia: Overseas Indians, Intercolonial Relations and the Empire* (Sydney: NewSouth Publishing, 2020).

McShane, Denis, *International Labour and the Origins of the Cold War* (Oxford: Clarendon Press, 1992).

Manjrekar, Naina, '"Violent and Not Quite Modern"? Lascars and Everyday Resistance across the Sail–Steam Divide,' *Labour History* 116 (2019): 29–55.

Marsh, Arthur, and Victoria Ryan, *The Seamen: A History of the National Union of Seamen, 1887–1987* (Oxford: Malthouse Press, 1989).

Martin, R.M., 'The ACTU Congress of 1983,' *Labour History* 45 (1983): 101–12.

Martínez, Julia, '"Coolies" to Comrades: Internationalism between Australian and Asian Seamen,' in *Labour and Community: Historical Essays*, ed. Ray Markey (Wollongong: University of Wollongong Press, 2001), 295–312.

——. 'Questioning "White Australia": Unionism and "Coloured" Labour, 1911–37,' *Labour History* 76 (1999): 1–19.

Matsumura, Takao, 'Anglo-Japanese Trade Union Relations between the Wars,' in *The History of Anglo-Japanese Relations 1600–2000*, vol. 5, *Social and Cultural Perspectives*, ed. Gordon Daniels and Chushichi Tsuzuki (London: Palgrave Macmillan, 2002), 265–80.

Maul, Daniel Roger, 'The ILO, Asia and the Beginnings of Technical Assistance, 1945–60,' in *The ILO from Geneva to the Pacific Rim: West Meets East*, ed. Nelson Lichtenstein and Jill M. Jensen (Basingstoke: Palgrave Macmillan, 2015), 110–33.

Meaney, Neville, *The Search for Security in the Pacific, 1901–14* (Sydney: Sydney University Press, 1976).

Merrett, John, *The Making of the AWU* (Melbourne: Oxford University Press, 1986).

Millar, Ann, ed., *The Biographical Dictionary of the Australian Senate*, vol. 1 (Melbourne: Melbourne University Press, 2000).

Mills, Herb, 'The San Francisco Waterfront: The Social Consequences of Industrial Modernisation,' in *Case Studies on the Labor Process*, ed. Andrew Zimbalist (New York: Monthly Review Press, 1979), 127–55.

Morris, Richard, 'Australian Stevedoring and Shipping Labour Under the Transport Workers Act, 1928–47,' *Great Circle* 11, no. 2 (1989): 17–31.

——. 'Mr. Justice Higgins Scuppered: The 1919 Seamen's Strike,' *Labour History* 37 (1979): 52–62.

——. 'Shipping's New Industrial Relations: The International Context and the Australian Experience,' *Journal of Industrial Relations* 32, no. 3 (1990): 317–33.

——. 'Shipping's New Industrial Relations: A Reply to Byrne and Hess,' *Journal of Industrial Relations* 34, no. 4 (1992): 589–92.

——. 'A Watershed on the Australian Waterfront? The 1998 Stevedoring Dispute,' *Maritime Policy & Management* 27, no. 2 (2000): 107–20.

Muir, Kathie, "'Thugs and Bullies": The Deployment of Rogue Masculinity in the Campaign for Workers' Rights on Site,' *Australian Feminist Studies* 28, no. 75 (2013): 30–49.

Myconos, George, *The Globalizations of Organized Labour, 1945–2004* (Basingstoke: Palgrave Macmillan, 2005).

Nelson, Bruce, *Divided We Stand: American Workers and the Struggle for Black Equality* (Princeton, NJ: Princeton University Press, 2001).

——. 'The "Lords of the Docks" Reconsidered: Race Relations among West Coast Longshoremen, 1933–1961,' in *Waterfront Workers: New Perspectives on Race and Class*, ed. Calvin Winslow (Urbana: University of Illinois Press, 1998), 155–92.

——. *Workers on the Waterfront: Seamen, Longshoremen, and Unionism in the 1930s* (Urbana: University of Illinois Press, 1988).

Northrup, H.R., and R.I. Rowan, *The International Transport Workers Federation and Flag of Convenience Shipping* (Philadelphia: University of Pennsylvania Press, 1983).

O'Connor, P.S., 'Keeping New Zealand White, 1908–1920,' *New Zealand Journal of History* 2, no. 1 (1968): 41–65.

Olssen, Erik, 'The Seamen's Union and Industrial Militancy, 1908–13,' *New Zealand Journal of History* 19, no. 1 (1985): 14–37.

Oram, Robert B., *Cargo Handling and the Modern Port* (Oxford: Pergamon Press, 1965).

Orr, Graeme, 'Conspiracy on the Waterfront,' *Australian Journal of Labour Law* 11 (1998): 159–85.

Ostapenko, Dmytro, "'Communists They May Have Been": Australian Maritime Unionists and the National Shipping Line, c.1950–90,' *Labour History* 116 (2019): 57–81.

Ostapenko, Dmytro, and Diane Kirkby, "'Australian Sailors Wanted": Labour Supply and Australian Shipping, c.1870–c.1914,' *Australian Economic History Review* (2021), http://doi.org/10.1111/aehr.12232.

Palfreeman, A.C., *The Administration of the White Australia Policy* (Melbourne: Melbourne University Press, 1967).

Park, M., 'Trade Liberalization and Organized Labour in the Asia-Pacific Region: Barriers to Labour Internationalism,' *Globalizations* 11, no. 1 (2014): 71–81.

Pearce, Robert, in 'Ernest Bevin: Robert Pearce Examines the Career of the Man Who Was Successively Trade Union Leader, Minister of Labour and Foreign Secretary,' *History Review* (December 2002). www.gale.com.

Pettit, Phyllis N., *The Wellington Watersiders: The Story of Their Industrial Organisation* (Wellington: New Zealand Waterside Workers' Union, 1948).

Pirio, G. Alonso, 'A Note: Minorities' Responses to Racism in the British Seamen's Union,' *Comparative Studies of South Asia, Africa and the Middle East* 4, no. 2 (1984): 56–8.

Quinlan, Michael, 'Industrial Relations before Unions: New South Wales Seamen, 1810–1852,' *Journal of Industrial Relations* 38, no. 2 (1996): 269–93.

——. 'The Low Rumble of Informal Dissent: Shipboard Protests over Health and Safety in Australian Waters, 1790–1900,' *Labour History* 102 (2012): 131–55.

——. 'Precarious and Hazardous Work: The Health and Safety of Merchant Seamen, 1815–1935,' *Social History* 38, no. 3 (2013): 281–307.

——. 'Regulating Labour in a Colonial Context: Maritime Labour Legislation in the Australian Colonies, 1788–1850,' *Australian Historical Studies* 29, no. 111 (1998): 303–24.

Quinlan, Michael, and Constance Lever-Tracy, 'From Labour Market Exclusion to Industrial Solidarity: Australian Trade Union Responses to Asian Workers, 1830–1988,' *Cambridge Journal of Economics* 14, no. 2 (1990): 159–81.

Radi, Heather, '1920–29,' in *A New History of Australia*, ed. Frank Crowley (Melbourne: Heinemann, 1974), 357–414.

Rediker, Marcus, *Between the Devil and the Deep Blue Sea* (New York: Cambridge University Press, 1987).

Reinalda, Bob, ed., *The International Transportworkers Federation, 1914–1945: The Edo Fimmen Era* (Amsterdam: Stichting beheer IISG, 1997).

Richardson, Len, 'Dole Queue Patriots,' in *Strikes: Studies in Twentieth Century Australian Social History*, ed. John Iremonger, John Merritt and Graeme Osborne (Sydney: A&R and ASSLH, 1973), 143–58.

Rickard, John, *H.B. Higgins: The Rebel as Judge* (Sydney: Allen &Unwin, 1984).

Rowley, Chris, and John Benson, eds, *Globalization and Labour in the Asia Pacific Region* (London: Frank Cass, 2000).

Rübner, Hartmut, 'The International Seamen's Organisations after the First World War: Professional and National Interests in Conflict,' in *The International Transportworkers Federation, 1914–1945: The Edo Fimmen Era*, ed. Bob Reinalda (Amsterdam: Stichting beheer IISG, 1997), 77–88.

Ryan, K.J., 'Beatrice Webb, Sydney Webb, Ben Tillett and the Australian Socialist League's Rivalry with the New South Wales Labor Party,' *Journal of Australian Studies* 16, no. 33 (1992): 63–75.

Saville, John, 'Britain, Internationalism and the Labour Movement between the Wars,' in *Internationalism in the Labour Movement, 1830–1940*, ed. Frits van Holthoon and Marcel ven der Linden (Leiden: Brill, 1988), 565–82.

Sheil, C., 'The Productivity Commission and the Waterfront Dispute: A Cautionary Tale,' *Journal of Australian Political Economy* 79 (2017): 39–64.

——. 'Trade Unions, Individual Contracts and the MUA's Doppelganger,' *Journal of Australian Political Economy* 59 (2007): 95–117.

——. *The War on the Wharves: A Cartoon History* (Sydney: Pluto Press, 1998).

Sheridan, Tom, *Australia's Own Cold War: The Waterfront under Menzies* (Melbourne: Melbourne University Press, 2006).

——. 'Coastal Shipping and the Menzies Government, 1950–1966,' *Australian Economic History Review* 25 (1995): 3–39.

Sherwood, Marika, 'The Comintern, the CPGB, Colonies and Black Britons, 1920–1938,' *Science & Society* 60, no. 2 (1996): 137–63.

——. 'Race, Nationality and Employment among Lascar Seamen, 1660–1945,' *New Community* 17, no. 2 (1991): 229–44.

Shompa, Lahiri, 'Patterns of Resistance: Indian Seamen in Imperial Britain,' in *Language, Labour and Migration*, ed. A.J. Kershen (Aldershot: Ashgate, 2000), 155–78.

Simpson, Ian, 'Cultural Encounters in a Colonial Port: The 1806 Sydney Muharram,' *Australian Historical Studies* 43, no. 3 (2012): 381–95.

Smith, C., 'Internationalising Industrial Disputes: The Case of the Maritime Union of Australia,' *Employee Relations* 32, no. 6 (2010): 557–73.

Spiers, John W., *Default to Decline: The Transformation of Australian Shipping Post WWII* (Saarbrücken: VDM Verlag, 2009).

Stanziani, Alessandro, *Bondage: Labor and Rights in Eurasia from the Sixteenth to the Early Twentieth Century* (New York: Berghahn Books, 2014).

Staricoff, Joseph, 'Australia and the Constitution of the International Labour Organization,' *International Labour Review* 32, no. 5 (1935): 577–609.

Starke, J.G., 'Australia and the International Labour Organisation,' in *International Law in Australia*, ed. D.P. O'Connell (Sydney: Law Book Co., 1966), 115–40.

Stephens, David, 'Unity Tickets and the Victorian Branch of the ALP,' *Labour History* 44 (1983): 55–74.

Stubbs, Peter, *Australia and the Maritime Industries* (Melbourne: AIDA Research Centre, 1983).

Tabili, Laura, 'The Construction of Racial Difference in Twentieth-Century Britain: The Special Restriction (Coloured Alien Seamen) Order, 1925,' *Journal of British Studies* 33, no. 1 (1994): 54–98.

——. 'Race is a Relationship, and Not a Thing,' *Journal of Social History* 37, no. 1 (special issue, 2003): 125–30.

——. *'We Ask for British Justice': Workers and Racial Difference in Late Imperial Britain* (Ithaca, NY: Cornell University Press, 1994).

Tavan, Gwenda, *The Long Slow Death of White Australia* (Melbourne: Scribe, 2005).

Taylor, Paul, *The Sailors' Union of the Pacific* (New York: Ronald Press, 1923).

Teoh, Philip, 'The Impact of the Covid-19 Pandemic on Shipping,' *Maritime Executive* 4 (July 2020), www.maritime-executive.com/editorials/the-impact-of-the-covid-19-pandemic-on-shipping.

Thornton, R.H., *British Shipping* (Cambridge: Cambridge University Press, 1939).

Trinca, Helen, and Ann Davies, *Waterfront: The Battle That Changed Australia* (Sydney: Doubleday, 2000).

Tsuzuki, Chushichi, *Tom Mann, 1856–1941: The Challenges of Labour* (Oxford: Clarendon Press, 1991).

Tull, Malcolm, 'American Technology and the Mechanisation of Australian Ports, 1942–58,' *Journal of Transport History* 79 (1985): 79–90.

Turnbull, P., 'Contesting Globalisation on the Waterfront,' *Politics and Society* 28, no. 3 (2000): 367–91.

Urbina, Ian, *The Unlawful Ocean* (New York: Vintage, 2019).

Vassiley, Alexis, '"There's No Flies at Noonkanbah but the Scabs Are on the Way": Trade Union Support for Aboriginal Rights during the Noonkanbah Dispute, 1979–80,' *Labour History* 110 (2016): 77–95.

Visram, Rozina, *Asians in Britain: 400 Years of History* (London: Pluto Press, 2002).

Walker, David, *Anxious Nation* (Brisbane: University of Queensland Press, 1999).

Walker, David, and Agnieszkia Sobocinska, eds, *Australia's Asia: From Yellow Peril to Asian Century* (Perth: UWA Press, 2012).

Walker, R.B., 'Media and Money: The London Dock Strike of 1889 and the Australian Maritime Strike of 1890,' *Labour History* 41 (1981): 49–56.

Wemyss, Georgie, 'Littoral Struggles, Liminal Lives: Indian Merchant Seafarers' Resistances,' in *South Asian Resistances in Britain, 1858–1947*, ed. Rehana Ahemed and Sumita Mukherjee (London: Continuum, 2012), 58–74.

Wheeler, Fiona, 'Sir John Latham's Extra-Judicial Advising,' *Melbourne University Law Review* 35, no. 2 (2011): 651–76.

White, Jon, 'The Port Kembla Pig Iron Strike of 1938,' *Labour History* 37 (1979): 63–77.

White, Joseph, *Tom Mann* (Manchester: Manchester University Press, 1991).

Willard, Myra, *History of the White Australia Policy to 1920*, 2nd. ed. (Melbourne: Melbourne University Press, 1967).

Williams, V., *The Years of Big Jim* (Perth: Lone Hand Press, 1975).

Winter, Jay, *Socialism and the Challenge of War: Ideas and Politics in Britain, 1911–18* (Abingdon: Routledge, 1974).

Wiseman, John, 'Here to Stay? The 1997–1998 Australian Waterfront Dispute and Its Implications,' *Labour & Industry: A Journal of the Social and Economic Relations of Work* 9, no. 1 (1998): 1–16.

Yarwood, A.T., *Asian Migration to Australia: The Background to Exclusion, 1896–1923* (Melbourne: Melbourne University Press, 1964).

Zhang, Pengfei, and Minghua Zhao, 'Maritime Labour Convention 2006 and the Chinese Seafarers: How Far is China to Ratification?' *Marine Policy* 61 (2015): 54–65.

Index

Printed and bound by CPI Group (UK) Ltd, Croydon, CR0 4YY

09/09/2024

14553066-0002